BEYOND
BORDERS

Elizabeth G. Ferris

BEYOND BORDERS

REFUGEES, MIGRANTS AND HUMAN RIGHTS IN THE POST-COLD WAR ERA

WCC Publications, Geneva

Cover design and photo: Rob Lucas

ISBN 2-8254-1095-0

© 1993 WCC Publications, World Council of Churches,
150 route de Ferney, 1211 Geneva 2, Switzerland

Printed in Switzerland

Table of Contents

Foreword

At this point in time, as key players in the international community strive to respond to the daunting political demands and immense humanitarian needs of our global post-cold war environment, Elizabeth Ferris has made a deliberate and successful effort in this book to step back and gain perspective.

By placing humanitarian principles and action in a broad historical context, and by exploring the link between the specific roles of non-governmental organizations (NGOs) and worldwide political, economic and social issues, she has gained insights and formulated concrete recommendations which can be useful to governments, the United Nations system, regional intergovernmental bodies and private voluntary agencies alike. In studying the total picture, she has actually succeeded in focusing on regional and thematic avenues for integrated action by the international community as a whole.

The reasons and consequences of coerced displacements of people are the backdrop of her book. Cross-border and internal population movements have assumed dimensions beyond the response capacity of any single governmental or international body. While 1-1.5 million refugees returned home in 1992, another 3 million were forced to flee their countries, bringing to 18 million the world refugee population. An estimated 24 million persons are displaced within their own countries, having fled conflict, persecution, drought, famine, environmental and economic decline and even total anarchy. A transitory population of nearly 40 million, not recognized as refugees, are being compelled by these same factors to cross borders and may have little or no access to protection or humanitarian assistance.

For the United Nations, particularly the UN High Commissioner for Refugees, these statistics are a daily reality of human suffering. Three groups of persons are of concern to UNHCR: those defined as refugees under the statute annexed to the General Assembly resolutions of 1950 setting up the Office of the High Commissioner; those defined as returnees in accordance with a General Assembly resolution passed in 1985; and displaced persons whom UNHCR is called upon to assist pursuant to requests from the Secretary General or resolutions adopted by the General Assembly.

Moreover, the massive scale and complex nature of human displacement in the world today have challenged the United Nations system and the entire international community to take diversified but concerted action which includes: (1) prevention through pre-emptive assistance and protection in countries of origin; (2) emergency response through life-sustaining assistance and protection monitoring of displaced persons; and (3) solutions through the promotion of political, economic, social and environmental conditions for enduring return to places of origin in safety and dignity, for local integration or for resettlement.

These humanitarian actions can only be designed and carried out through collaboration among partners of a distinct but inter-related and complementary nature: national governments, international institutions and, the emphasis of this book, non-governmental organizations, including church groups. Indeed, as Dr Ferris describes in this book, churches and church-related agencies among NGOs have frequently been called upon to play vital roles in protecting and assisting uprooted people.

Over forty years of collaboration with NGOs has been a rewarding educational process for UNHCR. Keeping abreast and responding adequately to the evolution within the NGO community is a continuous challenge at both institutional and personal levels. The limited traditional concept of NGOs as mere "implementing agencies" has long been replaced by the wider concept of interdependent and mutually supportive "operational partners". The scope of collaboration has widened as NGOs have assumed greater and, in some countries, pivotal roles in advocacy, fund-raising, information exchange, public awareness, technical development and environmental preservation.

The development of effective partnership among UN agencies, NGOs, governments and other entities serves as a useful blueprint for action in today's international humanitarian environment. This partnership framework is almost prophetic in announcing the future international climate portrayed in this book.

Elizabeth Ferris presents numerous recommendations towards NGOs. She raises basic global challenges posed by uprooted people today: conflict resolution, the peace processes and the international response system to the political, economic, environmental and social causes and consequences of displacement. In doing so, she has made of this book required reading for all persons concerned about human displacement today and tomorrow, including government analysts and policy-makers, legislators, UN officials, academics, and those in NGOs and churches.

In presenting the major players of the international theatre earlier, I deliberately reserved reference to the common human denominator without whom governments, UN institutions, regional intergovernmental bodies and NGOs could accomplish nothing: the individual human beings who, in the face of human suffering, react beyond the borders of indifference, despair and acquiescence.

It gives me pleasure to commend this book because it will help its readers to understand the imperative link between humanitarian work and global human development, and because it is an act of solidarity in the pursuit of human ideals.

March 1993   Sören Jessen Petersen
                           Director, Executive Office and External Relations
                           United Nations High Commissioner for Refugees

Introduction

The war in the former Yugoslavian republics creates the largest refugee movement in Europe since the second world war. Italy forcibly deports thousands of Albanians back to Albania, explaining that they're not refugees. Half of Liberia's population is displaced as a result of the ongoing violence in the country. Four years after Soviet troops are withdrawn from Afghanistan close to 6 million refugees remain in camps in Pakistan and Iran. In Germany, neo-Nazi groups seize a Sri Lankan Tamil and tie him to railroad tracks where he loses a leg.

The budget of the United Nations High Commissioner for Refugees jumps from $500 to $900 million in one year. But it's still not enough.

In the 1985 Ethiopian famine, a woman carries her two children for days until she has to choose which one she leaves by the side of the road. In Mozambique, children stare with unseeing eyes — eyes that have seen too much violence, too many atrocities — while relief workers wonder whether they will ever be normal. The break-up of the Soviet Union raises the spectre of the migration of millions of people as ethnic tensions and economic difficulties increase. Where will they go? Will anyone take them in? Can they be kept out? What will it mean for their countries — if they leave? And if they are forced to stay?

Once again, there is growing talk of compassion fatigue as the scale of human need increases. Particular situations of war and violence and the uprooted people they produce are on the front pages of daily newspapers for a few days and then move to the back pages — or completely out of sight. But the problems go on.

Discussion of refugees inevitably brings up the question of definitions. Who is a refugee? Who is entitled to a privileged claim on the

*world's resources? The old definitions seem irrelevant in a world
where people are uprooted on every continent for a complex interplay
of reasons. Migrants travel from rural areas to cities, from cities in
their home countries to cities further away in search of work, in search
of survival. Organized syndicates smuggle people into Northern countries; thousands of women and children in Asia are sold to work as
prostitutes in other countries.*

*Governments of the North treat the economic migrants as crimi-
nals. Governments of the South deplore the brain drain. Almost 75
percent of doctors trained in Zaire and the Philippines work outside
their country.*

*But people continue to cross national borders, to leave their
countries, in search of a better life, in search of safety.*

This book is about the movement of people — the forced migration
of human beings which is taking place on every continent. People leave
their homes for many reasons — because they can't support themselves
or their families at home, because the crops have failed, because the
environment will no longer sustain them, because of war or persecution,
because they want a better life for their children. They will continue to
leave their homes in the future. In fact, virtually all of the international
political and economic trends seem to point to an increase in the forced
migration of people in the years ahead, not a lessening of it. The
pressures of population, economic scarcity and environmental degradation will all become even more compelling reasons for people to leave
their communities. Moreover, these pressures will undoubtedly result in
political and social conflicts as resources become scarcer in relation to
population. Those conflicts, unless the world learns to handle conflicts
non-violently and to confront problems more quickly and successfully,
will produce further displacements of people. Migration itself will
become — is becoming — a hot political issue on every continent,
provoking angry reactions from host populations and posing a challenge
to governments.

The presence of so many refugees and migrants is a sign of a troubled
world. It is impossible to look at refugees and the way the international
community responds to them without realizing that their presence is an
indication that something is terribly wrong in the international system.
The question of refugees and migrants is a *justice* issue. People are
uprooted because of economic and social injustice; people are too often
forced to flee their homes when they struggle for justice or confront the
powers and principalities of this world.

The question of refugees and migrants is also a *peace* issue. People are uprooted by wars; their fate depends on a resolution of the conflict which led to their displacement and to reconstruction of their war-torn communities. But refugees are often a part of the peace process as well. In Central America and Cambodia, for example, questions about repatriation of refugees were a catalyst for peace negotiations. Governments and insurgent forces alike could delay agreements on ceasefires and the composition of new military forces for a long time, but the question of the refugees — "what do we do about the returnees?" "how do we ensure that they can live in safety?" — were an immediate pressure pushing the negotiations forward.

Beyond borders: the book

The objectives of this book are threefold:

— to analyze the current developments of the movement of people in a broad political and economic context;

— to analyze specific regional situations in which the pressures of the movement of people have led to changes in the international system for responding to uprooted people; and

— to look beyond the current debate to suggest some alternative ways in which the international system can respond to growing need and to suggest a plan of action for NGOs and churches.

These three objectives reflect my assessment of the current state of research and analyses available on this subject. First, a global context is needed to understand what is happening on the international level. Too often, NGOs and churches are so involved in a particular issue or a particular situation that they don't see the larger picture. Secondly, this global analysis must be rooted in concrete experiences. Too often, academics talk in the abstract without relating these abstract concepts to specific situations which are always more complex than general theories suggest. The second section of the book also seeks to provide some insights into what makes for effective action by NGOs and churches and to identify some characteristics of effective advocacy. Finally, the concluding chapter on alternative visions stems from the realization that it is usually easier for academics, churches and NGOs alike to criticize current governmental practices than to advocate concrete and realistic alternatives. But if NGOs and churches are to play a role in the construction of a new system, they must have a vision of what it is they are working towards. This book seeks to identify the components of such a vision which can serve as a basis for advocacy.

Before engaging in these issues, however, it is necessary to "set the stage" by looking at some of the global forces which shape the way forced migration is perceived and responded to.

A world moving beyond borders

The world is moving beyond borders on many fronts. The movement of people is one of many transnational forces pushing the world, for better or worse, into a global community. To give a few well-known examples:

• Transnational corporations plan and market their products on a global basis. They often take advantage of differences in national settings and add a few accent marks here and there in the marketing process. But they see the world as a global shopping mall.

• Beyond the interests of the capitalist corporations, there are global economic forces, enshrined in institutions such as the World Bank and the International Monetary Fund, which affect all countries of the world. Issues of international debt and daily quotations of gold futures link the remotest villages with the centres of global economic power. These economic interests transcend the narrow interests of particular governments or specific corporations. But taken together they are a powerful illustration of the transnational character of world economic transactions.

• Communications are becoming globalized. Videos, television, radio, printed matter extend into the farthest corners of the globe. Cable Network News (CNN) brought the Gulf war into the living rooms, pubs and villages in many parts the world. The concentration of control of the media in the hands of a few is troubling in many ways, but the fact is that the world's people are increasingly seeing and hearing the same news and advertisements for the same products.

• Transportation links are making it possible for more people to travel to more places than ever before. Airplane travel is extensive and new routes are constantly being added. New airports are built, and new roads through remote jungles (often in search of export products), with the result that it is much easier to travel to another country than ever before. The revolutionary potential of this transformation of transportation and communication links is often taken for granted. But it is a revolution with implications we are only beginning to understand.

• In the aftermath of the cold war and the Gulf war, there is renewed interest in the United Nations — and beyond the United Nations — in new ways of working together. And there seems to be a growing realization that there is a chance to shape effective instruments of international co-operation to replace the squandering of political energy on ideological conflicts.

• In Europe and elsewhere, governments are moving "beyond borders" in seeking new forms of economic and political co-operation with one another. The European Community is exploring new ways of regional co-operation in political, economic, social and cultural fields. Although the process is uneven and unpredictable, Europe will certainly be different in the future. As governments in various regions begin to grasp the implications of living in a unipolar world (or at least a militarily unipolar world), and as they see the example of the European Community, pressures will undoubtedly increase for the development of new forms of international co-operation, perhaps on a regional level at first, followed by negotiations between regions.

• We've been told for years that the consequences of environmental neglect are beyond the scope of a particular country; there is some evidence that that message is now beginning to sink in. Clearly there is a growing awareness about our interconnectedness and the fragility of the physical environment in which we live. We are still far from a consensus on how to balance concern for the environment with the compelling pressures of poverty and injustice. But just as Chernobyl's effects went beyond borders, so too people in every region are asking what will happen to their land, their water and their air if present trends are not reversed and countries do not co-operate to protect the environment.

• One of the most dramatic consequences of these pressures to move beyond borders is the development of transnational elites, of a class of people who share certain capitalist values and interests beyond borders. The elites of Brazil and Malaysia, for example, have more in common with each other and with Swiss industrialists than with peasants in their own countries. The very concepts of North and South are becoming increasingly superficial. While church meetings have persistently mouthed the words that there are poor in the North and rich in the South, the development and growth of a transnational elite — an elite which operates beyond borders — must change the way we think about the world.

• This transnationalization of the elites is, fortunately, accompanied by growing global ties between many other groups. For example, it is possible today to speak of a worldwide indigenous movement where indigenous groups are beginning to see that they have more in common with indigenous peoples in very different parts of the world than with their own governments. We see an incredibly rich and complex web of relationships between non-governmental organizations, now numbering in the tens of thousands. Professional groups, peace groups, humanitarian agencies, church groups — the list goes on and on of people who are anxious to be in contact with people in different countries on particular issues. Citizen exchanges, letters, faxes, trips, tours, are all binding the world ever closer in a clearer awareness of human interdependence than ever before.

Of course, these changes are not all positive. There are many negative consequences of living in a globalized world, including the disappearance of languages, of ethnic cultures — the pain within families as teenagers reject their traditions and embrace the consumer culture. The planes that bring travellers from far-away places may also bring AIDS. Tourism distorts and corrupts local cultures even as it offers some possibility of developing trans-cultural awareness. As wealth and information become increasingly concentrated in the hands of a few, people perceive that they are losing control of their own lives, that decisions made in far-away places have a greater effect on family and community life than decisions made by families and communities. A globalized world may not be a better, more meaningful world, for its people. But it is a fact that we live, if not in a globalized world, in a globalizing one.

But still borders remain

While the pressures for the world to move beyond borders are substantial and growing, there are counter-tendencies as well. Issues of ethnic identity are becoming more important and leading to more conflicts and to more nation-states. Even as the world becomes a global shopping centre and CNN is received by television sets around the world, there are *more*, not fewer, national borders. The consequences of the break-up of the Soviet Union are hard to foresee, but it is clear that there are real and powerful forces pushing for the establishment of new national states. In the Horn of Africa, Eritrea has become a de facto independent state, Somaliland has declared its independence from Somalia and there is growing talk about a separatist solution in southern Sudan. In Yugoslavia, Scotland and Quebec, the drive for independence is changing the political landscape of those countries — and the world.

So, even as the world is becoming globalized, there are more national borders, and within those borders, more emphasis on ethnic, regional and national values. Perhaps this is a reaction to the negative consequences of globalization, an attempt by groups and individuals to assert their own identity in a world where the pressures to conform to a global norm are increasing. Often these pressures are translated into anti-foreign or "anti-different people", into expressions of racism or ethnic rivalry. Instead of confronting global advertising or rebelling against unseen banks operating in distant lands, the tendency is to express this fear by lashing out at those people, those foreigners who are most visible — at strangers living in a strange land.

Within the countries of the North, the backlash against immigration and foreigners has acquired a new ferocity. Riots in Germany, attacks on hostels for asylum-seekers in Switzerland, and campaigns for "English-only" in the US are current examples, but there are many more. In both the South and the North, ethnic conflicts, often accompanied by demands for political autonomy, have killed and maimed and displaced millions of people. And these ethnic conflicts have often been exploited and intensified by colonial powers or by super-powers jockeying for superiority. While the world has changed, the legacy of this intervention continues and is played out in the high civilian casualties from mines laid in wars past and by arms which continue to be exported in great quantities.

The world is far from being a single global village.

Beyond borders: some academic issues

The forced migration of people — though certainly not a new phenomenon in human history — has acquired increased political significance in today's interdependent international system. Contemporary refugee migrations involve millions of people on all continents and affect political processes in diverse regimes. Governments of industrialized and developing countries alike struggle to formulate coherent policies towards refugees, migrants and displaced people. Both democratic and authoritarian regimes seek to contain the political fall-out resulting from the arrival of masses of displaced people. Refugees have become both a symbol of social change and a human reminder of the political violence which pervades the contemporary world.

Political scientists have traditionally paid little attention to refugees and displaced people, largely interpreting such migrations as marginal to the central processes of international politics. In the great debates over the causes of war and the conditions for peace, refugees are usually seen as the tragic but politically irrelevant by-products of conflict. This study begins with a different premise: refugees and other uprooted people have a significant political impact in many ways, and the study of forced migration is essential to a broad understanding of the complexity of international and national political phenomena.

Scholars have approached the study of refugees and uprooted people in different ways; the particular approach used determines in large measure the questions which are asked and the solutions which are recommended. Although most scholars use a variety of explanatory factors, five principal theoretical approaches can be identified. They tell us a lot about the issues which have been seen as important, about different perspectives and the particular sets of values which have influenced academic studies of uprooted people.

Uprooted people as a humanitarian/emergency issue

This has been the dominant paradigm for understanding uprooted people for many years. Uprooted people are the victims of wars or authoritarian governments, earthquakes or volcanoes. The principal issue is how to ensure that they get the assistance and security they need. The focus in this approach is on the individual victim forced to flee his or her home and on devising the appropriate response strategies. So, the appropriate response to refugees fleeing communist regimes was resettlement in Western countries. The appropriate response for a refugee emergency in the Horn of Africa is more rapid deployment of material assistance. In the longer term, this approach points to the need for early warning of refugee flows, for natural disaster preparedness, and for the political will to make sure that the needed assistance is available. This approach depends on the good will of governments, the astuteness of multilateral agencies, and the support of non-governmental organizations. By seeing uprooted people in humanitarian terms, as victims of disasters (either man-made or so-called natural disasters), this approach has been able to generate political support from governments of varying ideologies, to create a certain amount of humanitarian "space" for action, and to help a large number of individuals begin a new life.

By focusing on the human beings involved, this approach has been able to build political support for refugee/emergency issues. Media campaigns have focused on needy victims with the unspoken message that the individual's suffering is not the result of his or her actions. Resettlement work for refugees in the US, Canada, Australia and New Zealand has involved millions of Christians and community groups through sponsorship programmes, mobilized billions of dollars, and had a dramatic impact on the development of multi-cultural societies. Moreover, through contact with individual refugees, by hearing their stories and understanding a little of their situations, millions of people in these resettlement countries have had the opportunity to understand something of what is happening in another part of the world.

But those seeing uprooted people only in the context of humanitarian need and emergency response have been less able to see the *patterns* of the movement of people. The uprooting of people is rather seen as a sporadic, temporary emergency situation. There is less emphasis on the causes of the uprooting or on taking preventive measures.

This way of looking at uprooted people was the dominant approach to refugee issues from the early days of the League of Nations when the initial attempts were made to develop an international response — and an international responsibility — to people uprooted by forces beyond their control. While it remains the dominant way of thinking within the United Nations High Commissioner for Refugees (UNHCR) and NGOs working with refugees, it is being increasingly challenged as the number of refugees continues to increase, as people are uprooted for longer periods of time — sometimes for generations — and as the reasons for uprooting become more complex. People leave not only because they are caught in the crossfire of a civil war or because of a knock on the door in the middle of the night. They also leave because of economic and political pressures that act in more complicated ways — through a series of intervening variables, to use social science language — and which don't qualify as "emergencies", at least not as that term is generally understood.

Increasingly too this perspective is being challenged by a call that more should be done to address the *causes* which force people to flee. But addressing the causes is usually a political act — e.g. confronting a dictator or mediating in a civil war — which challenges the very notion of refugees and displaced people as a humanitarian, non-partisan issue requiring a humanitarian, non-partisan response.

Refugees and migrants as a foreign policy/security issue

During the 1970s and 1980s scholars began to adopt a more analytical response (and began to ask why different refugee groups were treated differently). It became more commonplace to analyze the situation of uprooted people from the perspective of national foreign policy and/or national immigration policy. Today, this approach has taken a new form in focusing on refugees and migrants as a security issue, perhaps as a result of changing definitions of what security means in a post-cold-war world.

This paradigm explains the ways in which governments respond to a specific situation of forced displacement in terms of the government's foreign-policy objectives. The approach is based on the realization that while there exists a substantial body of international law and norms, national governments must in the end decide whom to admit into their territories. Control of national borders remains the essence of national sovereignty and national sovereignty remains the linchpin of the international political system.

While a government may abuse, repress and even slaughter its own citizens with relative impunity, the flood of refugees which results from such actions quickly becomes the "business" of other nations. The way in which a government responds to refugees from a neighbouring, or even a distant, nation will be affected by relations between the governments, and will in turn greatly influence future relations between those countries. At the same time, policies towards refugees of another nation reflect the domestic, economic and political tensions of the host country. Thus, Malaysia's reactions to Vietnamese asylum-seekers has less to do with Malaysian-Vietnamese relations than with Malaysian political concerns over upsetting a delicate national ethnic balance. Or as Loescher and Scanlan persuasively demonstrate, US policy towards refugees was determined largely by US foreign policy. Over 95 percent of refugees admitted to the US between 1950 and 1985 came from countries with communist or leftist governments.[1] As they (and many others) argue, this meant that refugee policy was not a simple humanitarian response to people in need. The statistics in the mid-1980s for US treatment of Central American asylum-seekers make this clear: although the violence in El Salvador and Guatemala resulted in widespread suffering and high civilian casualties, less than 3 percent of asylum claims from Salvadorans and Guatemalans received a positive response from the US government, while 80 percent of Nicaraguan asylum claims were approved. Similarly, the Honduran government adopted very different policies towards the Nicaraguan and Salvadoran refugees on its territory — differences which can be explained by looking at Honduran foreign policies and the external and domestic influences which shaped them.

Today, as the cold war gives way to a more ambiguous understanding of security, more scholars (as well as politicians) are looking at refugee issues as security concerns. Thus the prestigious International Institute of Strategic Studies in London has embarked on a project to look at the security issues involved in the displacement of people. As Loescher argues, there is growing awareness that mass migrations are the result of breakdown of national security and that they pose fundamental challenges to the security of nations.[2] But while the approach has changed, the fundamental assumption remains: the possible movement of massive numbers of people from South to North is a threat to the security and well-being of the North and must be dealt with as a foreign-policy priority.

This approach adds a clear political dimension to the analysis of the impact and the causes of forced displacement of people and, as such, it represents a move towards a more sophisticated understanding of refugee movements. It is rooted in the national level of analysis — which is certainly appropriate, given the central role which the nation-state plays in determining how refugees and migrants are treated. It has been less politically astute, however, at drawing the connections between a nation's refugee policy and its foreign policy in terms of responsibility for the violence itself. Thus US foreign policy towards Central America certainly played a role not only in the way in which refugees were treated by the US government, but in the extent and the conduct of the wars themselves. A focus on security is also much more applicable to governments of the North than to those of the South. While there is clearly a security dimension in Hong Kong's policy towards Vietnamese asylum-seekers, the foreign-policy and security concerns are less evident in Africa where refugees from a variety of regimes have generally been welcomed by countries with few resources to care for them.

Uprooted people as a human-rights issue

The issue of forced migration is a fundamental issue of basic human rights on several levels. The Universal Declaration of Human Rights states that individuals have a fundamental right to live free of governmental persecution and to leave their country of origin. It is not, however, accepted as a basic human right that such individuals be *accepted* by the governments of other nations. The right to grant asylum is a right reserved to governments, not to individuals, no matter how persecuted. Although there have been some efforts in recent years to move towards recognition of individual rights to apply for asylum, such a right is far from being recognized by the international community. Academics and activists using a human-rights approach study the ways in which refugees and asylum-seekers are treated by host governments in terms of human-rights criteria. Increasingly too they are looking at human-rights issues in analyzing the treatment of migrants, especially now that the new International Convention on the Rights of Migrants has been passed and is open for ratification. On another level, refugees are often produced precisely because basic human rights are being violated by their governments. In spite of international norms upholding individual rights, violation of such norms is unfortunately common among the world's governments. Thus, victims of one government's violence are at the mercy of other governments for protection and security. The delicate process of balancing state rights against individual rights is an unresolved issue which is brought to the fore by an analysis of uprooted people.

With a human-rights approach, researchers and activists look beyond the United Nations High Commissioner for Refugees in arguing that uprooted people have needs which are greater than UNHCR is able to meet. Rather, agencies such as the UN Commission on Human Rights must become involved in examining the human-rights components of displaced people and in assuring protection in situations where UNHCR has no such mandate. One particular issue which human rights advocates are addressing is the situation of internally displaced people — that is, people who are uprooted from their communities because of violence but who remain within their national borders. These individuals, as will be seen later, are particularly vulnerable to violence but they are not recognized as refugees. Through the international human-rights machinery, however, advocates hope that their needs can be addressed.

Uprooted people and development

Unlike those who see the displacement of people as a humanitarian/ emergency situation, growing numbers of scholars and activists are looking at the underlying causes and consequences of forced migrations as development issues. Until two years ago, when substantial movements from (former) Eastern Europe began, most of the world's refugees came from third-world countries and sought refuge in neighbouring third-world nations. The pressures they placed on host governments and the reasons they fled lead, perhaps inexorably, to the issue of development. What is the relationship between underdevelopment and emigration? While this question has been explored with respect to economic migration (e.g. people who leave their countries because of poverty and aspirations for a better life), such connections have not been adequately analyzed with reference to refugees. The relationship between economic underdevelopment and repressive political institutions is a close (albeit poorly understood) one, but it cannot be ignored in trying to understand the causes of forced migration of people.

Development issues must also be addressed in analyzing the policies of third-world governments towards refugees and migrants from other countries. Developing countries face overwhelming economic and political difficulties in providing for their own populations; the presence of large numbers of refugees — particularly when international assistance is insufficient — exacerbates such difficulties. A developmental approach is particularly necessary in light of the fact that refugees increasingly stay for long periods of time. They remain as refugees or internally displaced people for years; emergency assistance is not a long-term solution. Thus the ICARA I and II process in Africa (International Conference on Assistance to Refugees in Africa) brought together governments, the UN and NGOs to analyze ways in which refugee assistance could be undertaken in light of developmental needs and priorities in African states. Similarly, the relationship between economic development and environmental issues is becoming more clearly understood and is increasingly a factor in the way in which refugees and migrants are treated.

Uprooted people as an international systemic issue

Another group of scholars look at the issue of displaced people and migration in terms of its impact on the international system's functioning and ability to respond to common challenges. In terms of the causes of displacement, more work has been done on labour migration than on politically-motivated migration. For example, Wallerstein's world-systems approach conceived of the world as a global system in which national boundaries are not the principal determinants of transnational resource flows.[3] Responding to the needs of international capitalism, the world-system can be conceptualized in terms of an international division of labour with peripheral, semi-peripheral and centre nations, according to the type of labour performed by each. Similarly, international labour migration responds to the differential living standards and labour needs of certain areas of the globe.

A global approach to refugee migrations would look for parallel causes in politically-induced migrations. As Zolberg states, "[m]uch as the international migrations reflect the economic structure and concomitant processes of the international system that produces them, so the flows of refugees largely reflect the political structure of that same system".[4] Changes in the role of the state and the processes of state-building, and emerging patterns of conflict resulting from the rise of bureaucratic-authoritarian regimes seeking to direct processes of economic development, thus reflect generalized changes in the international system.

The concept of "undercasting immigration" utilized by Hoffman-Nowotny to study labour migration may be useful in understanding systemic determinants of politically-induced refugee flows. Thus he maintains that emigration is caused by an increase in structural tensions within a given society — tensions that are transferred to other societies through a process he calls "undercasting immigration". [5] On a global level then, to extend Hoffman-Nowotny's ideas, structural political tensions in turbulent societies are transferred to other, less troubled areas as a systemic means of coping with distress. In a systemic framework, the international system is thus moving towards equilibrium through functional means of tension reduction by forcing people to leave more troubled areas for safer places — in essence, by spreading the trouble and the tension around.

Some of those using a systemic approach to analyze the situation of uprooted people focus on the ways in which the international system has responded to the challenge of dealing with mass migrations. Thus, Loescher has used international regime analysis as a way of understanding how the international system sought to respond to refugees in the aftermath of the first world war and the Russian revolution and the way in which that international regime has changed and adapted to new circumstances. [6] He identifies the elements of the regime — defined as the set of conventions, rules and norms guiding international action — as including the following components:

— the definition of refugees as enshrined in the 1951 UN Convention and the 1967 Protocol;
— the establishment of the United Nations High Commissioner for Refugees in 1951 and the steady enlargement of its mandate;
— the constellation of principles and accepted ways of behaviour as incorporated in national legislation and practice.

He finds a number of changes in the regime — changes brought about in the decade of the 1980s as the number of refugees, migrants and asylum-seekers threatened to overwhelm the international system. But while there is growing consensus that the present international system has fallen apart, the outline of a new international regime is not yet clear.

* * *

I have briefly outlined five of the major approaches used to interpret what is happening with the forcible uprooting of people — humanitarian/emergency approaches, foreign policy/security, human rights, development, and an international systems approach. Each of these approaches grew out of a particular set of circumstances. Beginning with a humanitarian/emergency approach in the 1920s, the tentative outlines of both national and international responses to uprooted people were developed.

A consensus grew up that it was the responsibility of the international system — and not just of the governments of the countries to which they happened to flee — to provide for their well-being. Later analysts began to question just how "humanitarian" this response was, particularly of the governments which were the major players in the "refugee game". By looking at foreign-policy issues, and later at security concerns, they showed that factors other than altruism were behind these national policies towards refugees and displaced people. As people were uprooted for longer periods of time and as they came to place very heavy burdens on host governments, there was growing concern about the developmental consequences of the presence of such large numbers of people. This was a time when people were beginning to question the Western capitalist models of economic growth as unilinear and inevitable, and also a time when the realization was growing that refugees were going to remain on the scene for a long time. As awareness grew in the 1970s about human rights and as NGOs, governments and international agencies focused on human-rights violations, it was perhaps logical that a human-rights approach should be used to understand both the causes and the treatment of displaced people. Finally, incorporating both the developmental and the human-rights perspective, those adopting a systemic approach began to search for the global patterns in these large-scale migrations of people and the national and international responses to them.

All five of these theoretical approaches are still in use; all ask valid questions about why people flee and what can be done. But each theoretical approach asks a different set of questions leading to a different set of policy recommendations. Thus, an analyst with a developmental approach will be much more concerned with whether a particular group of refugees or displaced people is becoming self-sufficient than with the nature of the human-rights violations that produced the displacement. Or an analyst concerned with foreign-policy-making will look at the domestic, political and economic factors that determine a particular government's response. A systemic analyst will study the response of the international system as a whole, while the foreign-policy analyst will be more likely to see the international system's response in terms of the interaction of national policies.

All five theories were developed at particular points in time (and thus reflect the dominant concerns of those times). The present global situation is raising new questions which affect all of them. One example was the decision by US President George Bush and other governments allied against President Saddam Hussein in the Gulf war to provide assistance to

Iraqi Kurds in Iraq over the objections of the Iraqi government. This action has the potential to alter fundamentally the whole international system for dealing with displaced people. The decision was certainly made for foreign-policy reasons related to the war effort. At the same time, an equally large number of displaced Liberians in desperate circumstances were being largely ignored by the international community. From a human-rights viewpoint, it would seem that the interests of protecting victims of human-rights violations overcame, for a moment at least, the imperative of national sovereignty — raising all kinds of questions about under what conditions international and unsolicited intervention is justified. Certainly a human-rights perspective would raise the issue of the applicability of such actions in other situations. A developmental perspective would look at the impact of the refugee movements on the government of Iran which for a time was spending $10 million per day to care for the refugees while international assistance poured into neighbouring Turkey. And the developmental analyst would ask what is going to happen to those people in the long term. What are the consequences, for Iraq, Turkey, Iran and the whole Middle East, of the massive population displacement that occurred as a result of the invasion of Kuwait and the Gulf war? The humanitarian/emergency perspective would similarly raise questions about the consequences of the action on the widening of humanitarian space for action in other situations. Does this mean that a precedent has been set that could justify such intervention in the future? And from a systemic perspective, does this weaken or strengthen the capacity of the international system to respond to internally displaced people? Is a new norm or justification being created?

This study uses elements of all five theories in analyzing the nature and consequences of population displacement. In the final chapter an effort will be made to draw together different theoretical approaches in analyzing forced uprooting as a global justice issue and in suggesting future reactions to present trends.

Beyond borders: some theological issues

For Christians and other people of faith, the question of uprooted people raises a different set of issues. What is the appropriate response to a person forced to flee his or her community? What is the theological significance of exile in this day and time? How should religious traditions work with governments and intergovernmental agencies to minister to the needs of uprooted people? How can they ensure that they're not being co-opted or used by those governments?

The Bible is full of stories of people in exile. The theme of exodus, of a people wandering in the wilderness, is central to both the Jewish and Christian faiths. Christ's own homelessness and his universal message create a Christian imperative for responding to refugees and exiles. Throughout the Bible, people are called to offer hospitality to strangers and exiles. Moreover, the refugees bring messages for those who choose to hear and have much to teach those who respond to their voices. In today's world as well, those wandering in the wilderness challenge us to understand the reasons behind their exile and to respond to their suffering.

Christians working with refugees have long sought guidance from the Bible. In recent years, a number of theological studies have been prepared which reflect on specific aspects of biblical teachings about refugees and exiles. These studies can be organized around three themes: the experience of exile for the refugees themselves, biblical teachings on responding to refugees, and the messages which refugees bring in challenging Christians today.

The experience of exile

> Weeping, we sat beside the rivers of Babylon thinking of Jerusalem. We have put up our lyres, hanging them upon the branches of the willow trees; for how can we sing the Lord's song in a foreign land? (Ps. 137:1-4)

For the refugee forced to leave his or her land, the experience of exile is a painful one. Over and over again, the children of Israel call out to God in the pain of their exile. Over and over again, God hears their voices in the wilderness. The image of God hearing the cries of those suffering in a strange land and bringing them out of Egypt into the land of milk and honey is a powerful expression of God's love.

For the Christian, exile has had a deeper meaning. Christ himself was a refugee, suffering persecution for his religious belief. In a poignant message he underlined the pain of the uprooted: "Foxes have holes. Birds in the air have nests. But the Son of Man has nowhere to lay his head" (Matt. 8:20). Moreover, we are told that Jesus will come again and ask who helped him when he was a stranger. From the earliest times, Christians have seen themselves as strangers in this world, as persons without full civil rights. "For us our homeland is in heaven and from heaven comes the Saviour we are waiting for" (Phil. 3:20). As Leuninger says, Christians "in the last analysis belong everywhere and yet are at home nowhere".[7] In the early Christian tradition, sojourning Christians travelled outside the institutionalized church channels, bringing their messages of hope to the oppressed. In fact, some of the earliest missionaries were refugees — individuals forced to leave their homelands because of their Christian beliefs.

Strangers were the first to come to worship the Christ child. In Acts 8 we read that the first missionaries who brought the gospel beyond Jerusalem were refugees who had to leave the city. A turning point came in 313 AD with the conversion of Emperor Constantine: Christians who had been outcasts without civil rights now began to think of themselves as full citizens, trying to live as citizens of "our two kingdoms, that of heaven and of this world". [8]

In the Old Testament, it is in exile that Israel discovers the wider and universal aspects of its faith. The years spent wandering in the wilderness deepen the people's faith in God and bring the children of Israel into closer relationship with one another. It is in exile and as a result of persecution that Christians discover the meaning of practising their faith in a strange land. The theme of pilgrimage occupies a central place throughout the Bible — of individuals called to leave their homes to seek God and to do his will. But those who have been forced to leave their homes for other reasons may also become pilgrims in the sense that their faith sustains them in exile and deepens as a result of their experiences.

In Costa Rica, Guillermo Chaves worked with Salvadoran refugees in developing a theology of exile. Beginning with the testimonies of the refugees themselves, the exiles explored what it means for their faith to live in exile. The conditions under which they leave, their religious commitment in their communities of origin, and the experiences of exile are discussed and examined in a dynamic theological process. The refugees themselves, many with experience in progressive base communities, come to see their exile as an opportunity to deepen their faith and to witness in a strange land. They see their experience as refugees as preparation for ministry back home and as creating an opportunity for theological reflection. The Salvadoran refugees in Costa Rica are poor and frequently alienated from the local population. Yet as they begin the process of theological reflection based on their own concrete experiences, they are creating a church of exile and a theology of exile which may well have implications far beyond their small communities.

In some cases when people are forced to flee their communities because of escalating violence, pastors and church leaders accompany them into exile. Thus in Liberia at the height of the violence, 80 percent of Liberian pastors left the country and the Liberian Council of Churches set up temporary headquarters in Sierra Leone. When many of the refugees returned to Liberia, the pastors returned as well, seeking to bring an end to the violence and to begin the more difficult task of reconciliation. In a few cases, such as the Russian Orthodox Church Outside of Russia, new church structures are created by exile communities. When conditions change in the country of origin, tension may develop between these church structures created in exile and those in the homeland.

Responding to the refugees

> When a stranger sojourns with you in your land, you shall not do him wrong. The stranger who sojourns with you shall be to you as the native among you and you shall love him as yourself, for you were strangers in the land of Egypt. I am the Lord your God. (Lev. 19:33-34)

As Danesi explains, there are two words for stranger in the Old Testament: *Nolchrt* (2 Sam. 15:19-20), the passing stranger or wanderer whom it was impossible to assimilate, and the *ger* or resident stranger.[9] While the passing strangers have the right to hospitality, they are not allowed to enter the temple or to offer sacrifices. The word *ger* carries with it the conception of a people under attack who have been driven out of their land by famine or war. The concept of strangers seeking refuge, not a hostile people, carries with it a different set of expectations for the host community. In Israel the *ger* could be accepted completely (although they had to be circumcised), not by a process of absorption, but rather by sharing in the fullness of life. This process was a communal experience in which the strangers were accepted and recognized on their own terms, and not with the goal of making them into Israelites.[10] Under Judaism, the mandate of hospitality for foreigners, *Hakhnsasat orehim* (bringing in guests), became a true moral force.

The theme of hospitality and the role of the stranger is further developed in the New Testament with emphasis on brotherhood, equality, and the theme of loving one's enemy. The ability to respond to the poor and suffering becomes the mark of the individual's essential love for God. Christ's message that "whatsoever you do for the least of my brothers, you do for me" (Matt. 25:31-45) makes it clear that by welcoming the stranger, the Christian is fulfilling Christ's teaching. The universality of Christ's teaching is evident in that the distinction between brother and stranger is drawn in the New Testament, only to be rejected. The Christian is called to witness in the oikoumene, the whole inhabited earth.

Danesi notes that a semantic transformation occurs in the New Testament in which the word for *stranger* becomes equivalent to the word for *guest*. [11] Welcome and hospitality become the essential expressions of love for one's neighbour (John 4:19, 3:17-18). The parable of the Good Samaritan uses a stranger to develop the theme of the need for charity towards foreigners. Christ associates himself, at least in part, with the Old Testament figure of the *ger* rejected by fellow countrymen and hunted by Herod (Luke 13:31-33).

Marshall notes that there are three ways of expressing compassion towards the refugee in the Bible: (1) charity, (2) restoring people to useful and productive life, and (3) ensuring that the systems make it possible for the individual to have a life of dignity and of self-realization. [12] This theme of the Christian responsibility to work for justice as a response to the needs of exiles runs throughout the Bible. In the Old Testament, there is a constant emphasis on justice in terms of rectifying the situation of the poor, the marginalized and the alien. The Old Testament tradition of gleaning was thus not an act of charity, but rather the law of the land. In working towards justice, people of faith are responding to the greater human needs of the exile. They are not only listening to the voice of the refugee, but they are living in accord with God's teachings.

This biblical concern with justice has led churches to see themselves as first and foremost on the side of the weak.The expression of church solidarity must thus go beyond church boundaries. The church has an imperative to serve as the voice of the voiceless. Refugees have no voice in the governments of their countries of exile. Thus the church has a special and unique role to play in ensuring that refugee voices are heard.

In the Old Testament, the claiming of sanctuary has a long tradition. Adonijaha and later Juab sought protection from Solomon by laying hold of the horns of the altar. David refers to his seeking protection in a place of worship. "For God will hide me in shelter in the day of trouble and conceal me under cover of the Lord's tent, setting me high upon a rock" (Ps. 27:4-6).

Cities of refuge are mentioned on several occasions in the Old Testament (Ex. 21:13; Num. 35:6-28; Deut. 4:41-43, 19:4-13), apparently reflecting the historical fact that the right of asylum was commonplace at the local altars of Yahweh. Residents of the cities of refuge were charged with the task of protection "lest innocent blood be spilt" (Deut. 19:10). Asylum in the cities of refuge was specifically for those accused of manslaughter and fleeing the rigid code of vengeance. At the gates of the six cities of refuge, the killing stopped.

In the early years of Christianity, the concept of the church as a refuge became extended to those fleeing persecution of many types. In the early

church, the clergy sought to prevent bloodshed by acting as inter-
mediaries between criminals and those desiring vengeance, using the
weapon of excommunication to keep at a distance the lords thirsting for
revenge. During the medieval period in Europe, when an accepted code
of justice had not yet emerged, the churches proclaimed their right to
grant asylum to refugees. It was in medieval England, however, where
the greatest exercise of sanctuary occurred. For several centuries, at any
given time more than a thousand people were under the protection of the
church. The extension of sanctuary included a provision by which an
individual in church sanctuary could foreswear all rights to protection
under the king's law and be allowed to leave the kingdom. As Kellerman
says, "it was as though every church door stood at the boundary of the
nation-state".[13] The theological basis of the sanctuary and the church's
early tradition as a place of refuge have been used by US churches in the
anti-slavery movement of the nineteenth century as well as in the
protection of Central American refugees in the sanctuary movement.

The themes of hospitality, acceptance, sanctuary and the struggle for
justice are all part of biblical teachings on Christian responses to refugees.
But theological reflections on refugees and exiles go beyond exhortations
to aid individuals forced to flee their homes. They include the theme of
the refugee as messenger, as teacher for those with whom they come into
contact.

Messages from exile

> In Christ there is no Jew nor Greek, slave nor free, male nor female, for
> you are all one in Christ Jesus. (Gal. 3:28)
> Continue to love each other like brothers, and remember always to
> welcome strangers, for by doing this, some people have entertained angels
> without knowing it. (Heb. 13:1-2)

Christ knew himself to be an outcast from his own country (Matt.
13:54-55, John 4:44). He knew his task wasn't limited to one fold (John
10:16). For believers in Christ, there is only one true kingdom, the one to
come, where there will be no strangers, where all will be one in the
kingdom of heaven. This universal family of Christ changes the whole
meaning of national and tribal boundaries as depicted in the Old Testament. As Danesi says: "The brothers [and sisters], who qualified as such
in the Old Testament by being members of the chosen people, are
succeeded in the New Testament by the brothers who feel themselves to
be such as children of the same Father."[14]

This theme of universalism, of seeking to live in accord with the values of the kingdom while still inhabiting this earth, is a recurrent one throughout the New Testament. The message from Jesus Christ is clear: the strangers, the refugees, the outcasts are to be treated as brothers and sisters. In seeking to live in accord with God's teachings, conflicts with state authorities are at times perhaps inevitable. Governments which limit benefits to one particular group or refuse protection to those fleeing for their lives are not acting in accord with the values of the kingdom. In many different national contexts, Christians have felt called upon, because of their faith, to oppose their governments.

But the messages which refugees bring us go beyond the often serious conflicts between church and state. As Van Eek explains, the account of the dispersion of the Jews in AD 70 is a model for refugees and for ourselves. Like those Jews, we can no longer put our security in a physical place. We may be forced to scatter if we "seek first the kingdom of God" and identify ourselves as people of God. In a sense, refugees are "marked" people, marked by suffering.[15] The refugees challenge us to share liberation or exodus or dispersion, to have our priorities right, and to accept the suffering that may be the price for working for God's kingdom. Refugees challenge us to make a pilgrimage with them.

Leuninger develops this theme, viewing the church as a communion of exiles, of exiles who are at the same time free men and women. Going back to the Old Testament, he notes that between the Exodus from Egypt and the eschatological reconciliation of all peoples is the churches' task with respect to exiles. Through communion with the refugees, through recognition of the church as a community of exiles, Christians are called to deepen their faith. On many continents, the church too is in physical flight and "she too suffers in her own body the fate of the refugees".[16] By recognizing that communion, by becoming aware of that shared fate, the Christian is challenged to do much more than respond to the expressed needs of the refugee. The Christian must engage in a much more difficult task: that of changing his or her life. "In this sense, the refugee has become a sign of the underlying exile and homelessness of the Christian. He becomes for the church an exhortation to convert from being all too established and conformed in an unjust world."[17]

The church as a community of exiles has taken on concrete form in the work of Chaves with Salvadoran refugees in Costa Rica. There the refugees work with Costa Rican Christians to define a church of exile. Together they are learning of the opportunities which exile creates — the opportunity not only to deepen their faith, but to challenge Christians in their country of exile as well as Christians back home. Through analysis and prayer, they struggle to understand their experiences and, in doing so, they are transforming a community of believers.

* * *

In today's world, Christians are challenged by the gospel to respond to the needs of uprooted people, to extend hospitality and to work for justice and reconciliation. In seeking to put their faith into practice, they are often led to confront difficult questions.

The challenge of living in accord with Christian beliefs in the values of the kingdom often conflicts with the pressures of living in a world of nation-states based on a different set of values. Christians are not outside those national values; in fact, in many countries religious values are an essential component of national or ethnic identity. And in many situations, churches play a role in legitimizing their governments — even governments which abuse human rights and limit the freedoms of churches. This tension between church and state has long been recognized as a dilemma for Christians. But with reference to the emerging theology of exile, a different set of questions is raised. What is the responsibility of the individual Christian and the church when a government deports asylum-seekers back to war-ravaged countries where their lives are at stake? What does it mean to live by the values of the kingdom — "in Christ there is no Jew nor Greek" — when the world is structured into more than 170 different nation-states and where the country in which you are born determines your chances to live? In today's world, should Christians be working for the abolition of national borders — when it is clear that the existence of those borders serves to keep needy people out? It is difficult to imagine a world "beyond borders" where people could move and work freely without impediment by national governments. Economic disparities between North and South would probably disappear as a result of free migration and an open global labour market. The standard of living of those in the North would perhaps plummet in the face of widespread migration from the South. Conflicts would not disappear in a world without borders; ethnic, political, economic and religious differences would undoubtedly continue to lead to violence and suffering. But a world without nation-states would have to provide for other means of conflict-resolution than the present system based on promotion of national security and interests. These are far-reaching and perhaps utopian issues and they challenge Christians seeking to understand what it means to live in today's world of nation-states by the universal values of the kingdom.

Christian witness towards refugees and exiles is also challenged by the fact that most of today's refugees and displaced people are not Christians. While most Christians respond to the needs of uprooted people as human beings, respecting their own religious beliefs, the interfaith dimension of refugee work can lead to greater understanding of other faith dimensions. In recent years, there have been initiatives to strengthen interfaith co-operation on service to refugees and migrants; as will be discussed later, these are important initiatives which are necessary to respond to the needs of uprooted people. But there is another component of such co-operation which relates to theological understanding. By seeking to understand the way in which the different faith traditions view refugees and strangers, the theological self-understanding of Christians can be deepened and the basis laid for more comprehensive co-operation between faith communities in working with uprooted groups. There are many common roots between the Jewish and Christian faiths — but also some important differences which need to be explored and recognized.

Given the large number of Muslim refugees and migrants and the large number of Christian agencies working with them, it seems particularly important to understand Islamic traditions of asylum and reception of refugees. Elmadmad is one of several scholars who have looked more closely at the development of Islamic beliefs in this area. For example, he notes that traditions of Arab hospitality in the pre-Islamic era dictated respect for and protection of the guest who should not be handed over to an adversary, regardless of the cost to the host. Under Islam, persecuted persons should not stay in the place of their persecution, but have the responsibility to flee elsewhere. The Muslim "should provide protection to asylum-seekers as it is a way of disseminating Islamic faith and its humanitarian principles... Moreover, asylum is the duty of the political leader of the Muslim community, who cannot oppose any asylum granted by any individual under his authority."[18] No protected person can be attacked after asylum is granted and his or her life, property, honour and freedom of consciousness should be safeguarded and protected. A person who has been granted asylum is not obligated to become a Muslim, but this protection is not extended to criminals and is also temporary, normally given for a period of one year. After that the refugee is expected to leave — either to go to another safe place or return home — or to live permanently within the Islamic community and adopt Islam.[19]

Islamic, Jewish and Christian understandings of responsibilities towards refugees share certain characteristics and diverge in important ways. By studying the similarities and differences, we may be able not only to understand each other better, but also to deepen our understanding of our own faith-based response to the strangers in our midst. Thus exploring the roots of other faith communities' response to refugees is a way of both increasing interfaith understanding and discovering common themes which could serve as a basis for a more effective faith-based response.

Theological reflection is an essential step for Christians working with uprooted people. Their response to refugees and migrants is not only a humanitarian act of reaching out to people in need, but also a reflection of their desire to translate the gospel message into concrete service to refugees. But in order to develop effective advocacy on behalf of uprooted people, Christians today also need to understand the system created by governments to respond to uprooted people.

NOTES

[1] Gil Loescher and John Scanlan, *Calculated Kindness: Refugees and America's Half-Open Door, 1945 to the Present*, New York, Free Press, 1986.

[2] Gil Loescher, "Mass Migration as a Global Security Problem", in *World Refugee Survey 1991*, Washington, DC, US Committee for Refugees, 1991, pp.7-14.

[3] Immanuel Wallerstein, *The Modern World System*, New York, Academic, 1974. Also by the same author, *The Capitalist World Economy*, New York, Cambridge University Press, 1979.

[4] Aristide R. Zolberg, "International Migrations in Political Perspective", in *Global Trends in Migration: Theory and Research on International Population Movements*, eds Mary M. Kritz, Charles B. Keely and Silvano M. Tomasi, New York, Center for Migration Studies, 1981, p.19.

[5] Hans-Joachim Hoffman-Nowotny, "Sociological Approaches toward a General Theory of Migration", in *ibid.*, pp.74-76.

[6] Gil Loescher, "The European Community and Refugees", in *International Affairs*, vol. 65, no. 4, 1989, pp.617-636.

[7] Herbert Leuninger, "The Theological Basis for the Churches' Work with Refugees", paper prepared for the ecumenical consultation on asylum-seekers in Europe, Rheinfelden, Germany, October 1985, p.4.

[8] *Ibid.*, p.5.

[9] P. Giacomo Danesi, "Towards a Theology of Migration", in *Church and Migration: A Selection of Documents for Study and Action*, prepared by WCC Migration Secretariat for the WCC's fifth assembly, dossier 13, December 1981.

[10] A. Lacocque, "The Strangers in the Old Testament", *in ibid.*

[11] Danesi, *op. cit.*

[12] Robert Marshall, "Theological Reflections", prepared for Canada-US church consultation on refugee protection and safe haven, Washington, DC, New York, Church World Service, April 1985.

[13] Bill Kellerman, "The Hospitality of God", in *Sojourners*, April 1983, p.28.

[14] Danesi, *op. cit.*

[15] Arie Van Eek, "Theological Reflections", in *Building Bridges: Report on Recommendations of the Canada-US Church Consultation on Refugee Protection and Safe Haven*, Washington DC, April 1985. For further reflection on the concept of refugees as "marked" people, see Frans Bouwen, "An Ecumenical Concern: The Participation of Refugees", study paper for WCC-CICARWS Refugee Desk, Geneva, 1980, and thesis for faculty of theology, Leiden, Netherlands.

[16] Leuninger, *op. cit.*

[17] *Ibid.*

[18] Khadija Elmadmad, "An Arab Convention on Forced Migration: Desirability and Possibilities", in *International Journal of Refugee Law*, vol. 3, no. 3, July 1991, p.472.

[19] *Ibid.*

1. Understanding the Rules of the Game

People are on the move. On every continent, individuals, families and communities are forced to abandon their homes and villages. But uprooted people are not all the same. They don't leave for the same reasons, they certainly aren't treated by governments in the same way, they face very different fates. How they are treated depends on why they leave and where they go, and even when they arrive. The rules of the game — the structure of the international system for dealing with uprooted people — is not an academic issue. They determine the fate of individual human beings and have a profound impact on the societies to which they flee. Understanding these rules is an essential first step to action to address the human needs.

A Vietnamese arriving in Hong Kong on 14 June 1988 was automatically placed in the queue for resettlement. He or she might have to wait a few years, but eventually would board a plane for the US, Canada, Australia, or another developed country. The Vietnamese was assumed to be a refugee and entered the refugee system, which at that time and place meant resettlement for all but a handful of difficult cases (e.g., people with prison records). But a Vietnamese arriving in Hong Kong on 15 June 1988 found a different situation. The rules had changed. Instead of a ticket to a Western country, Vietnamese arriving after the cut-off date found themselves in closed camps, detention centres, prisons where they were to wait until either they were determined by legal authorities to be refugees or they could be sent back to Vietnam. An international conference in Geneva, attended by representatives of 88 countries, had come up with a plan, called the Comprehensive Plan of Action, which fundamentally altered the rules for treatment of

Vietnamese. No longer would they automatically be considered as refugees and become eligible for resettlement. Like asylum-seekers in other parts of the world, their cases would be reviewed by legal authorities, and if they could show evidence of persecution according to accepted international definitions, they would be treated as refugees and be eligible for resettlement. If not, they would be sent back to Vietnam. As expected, 90 percent of the Vietnamese were found not to be "genuine refugees" and were placed in the closed camps. The hope was that they would return voluntarily and not have to be forced back to Vietnam (a sensitive point, particularly to the United States). To make sure that those whose asylum claims had been rejected would choose to return to Vietnam, conditions in the camps were made as uncomfortable as possible. Surrounded by high fences topped with razor-sharp barbed wire, the camps consist of rows of barracks separated from each other by concrete passageways. Former prisons, the detention centres are dismal and bleak — without a single blade of grass or tree, and nowhere for children to play. They are over-crowded with families assigned to a single bunk which are stacked three-high. These are places without privacy, without dignity, where barrels of lukewarm food are hauled in twice a day. They are violent places where armed gangs control the camp, where rape is common. They are terrible places.

The international system for refugees and migrants

The international system, the rules of the game for responding to the needs of uprooted people, consists of three essential component parts. First there are the definitions, which identify the people of concern to the international community. These definitions are important because the way people are defined or labelled is related to the way in which the actors — governments, international agencies, NGOs, churches — see their responsibility for them. A second component of the international system is a body of law — international conventions, national legislation, norms and expectations — which spell out the responsibility of the international community for those who fall within the definition. The third component is made up of implementing actors, including both national governments and the international and regional mechanisms established to make sure that the international laws and norms are implemented.

These three components of the international system for dealing with uprooted people — definitions, laws and implementing actors — interact with one another. The UNHCR, for example, can shape the definition of refugees by gradually expanding its mandate to assist and protect uprooted people who don't formally fall into the definition of refugees. Moreover, the system is a dynamic one that has evolved over the last seventy years in response to changing political and economic realities and to new power configurations.

The rules are all based on the recognition that it is national governments that are the basic actors in the international system. Indeed, if there were no nation-state system, if we lived in a world without borders, there would be no refugees, no migrants, and no reason to develop laws or procedures for dealing with them. While often couched in humanitarian — even moral — rhetoric, decisions about how to deal with refugees and migrants are fundamentally decisions based on national interests. Thus, the whole international system for dealing with the movement of people is based on the explicit recognition that it is the responsibility of states, and states alone, to determine who can enter their territory. Indeed the principle of national sovereignty itself is based on the premise that governments control access to territory. This is the most basic underpinning of national sovereignty. If governments had no control over who could enter their countries, the nation-state system would collapse. Thus, on the very first day of its independence, the government of Latvia began issuing visas for travel to its territory. It would no longer be the government of the Soviet Union that would determine who could enter Latvia. The government of Latvia recognized, as have many other governments over the years, the fundamental importance of not only physically controlling its borders but sending a symbolic message that it was now a truly independent country. While international laws can prescribe that certain defined groups of people should be allowed to enter the territory of other states, and while the United Nations agencies can monitor, advise, and sometimes plead with governments on behalf of particular groups of people, it is the national government that makes decisions about who will be allowed to enter and to stay. In fact, of course, national governments often have difficulties in implementing this border control, but international law recognizes their right to do so.

The central role of national sovereignty is also evident in the way in which the international community has responded to the movement of people. Governments with more power have had more say in shaping all three components of the international system. When powerful countries feel threatened by the movement of people into their territories, they take actions not only to close the doors to their borders but to restrict the international rules of the game. This is precisely what is happening in the

international system today — as will be explored in chapter 5. The rules
are changing. In order to understand the importance of these changes it is
necessary to look at how the rules themselves have evolved over the past
seven decades. The sections that follow describe the three components of
the international system for dealing with the movement of people.

A little history...

Long before international attempts to respond to the needs of people
uprooted by war and persecution, individuals, churches and other private
groups provided immediate assistance to those forced out of their homes.
With the emergence of organized voluntary associations (the precursors
of the non-governmental organizations or NGOs) in the middle of the
nineteenth century, organizational capabilities were in place, capabilities
that were channelled into relief activities in the early decades of the
twentieth century.

The scale of human tragedy in the aftermath of the Russian revolution, the Armenian genocide of 1915, and war in the Balkan states,
brought refugee issues to public attention and led to a clamour for
humanitarian response. In the absence of an international governmental
forum, churches and voluntary agencies took the lead in responding to the
needs of refugees and other war victims. Even from today's vantage point
where humanitarian relief has become a major undertaking, the scale of
the assistance offered by NGOs in these early years is amazing. For
example, a consortium of agencies organized the Armenian Committee
for Relief in the Near East, known as Near East Relief, which raised $20
million, sent relief teams into affected areas, fed an average of over
300,000 people a day, established and administered all hospital services
for Armenia and took charge of over 75,000 orphans. [1]

The importance of these private organizations goes beyond the provision of humanitarian relief. As Marrus explains, between the end of the
first world war and the establishment of the League of Nations High
Commissioner for Refugees in 1921, hundreds of thousands of refugees
were kept alive by NGOs and "by keeping so many alive, the private
organizations helped to maintain the pressure of the refugee crisis. In the
long run, this activity helped to elicit a response from governments and
from the international agencies set in place after the first world war." [2]

Specifically, the League of Nations took action in 1921 by naming
Fridjhof Nansen as the League of Nations High Commissioner for
Refugees. Nansen, a Norwegian statesman and well-known explorer, was
an energetic worker for the rights of displaced people. For twelve years he

worked on behalf of specific refugee groups, which were named by the League of Nations as in need of assistance. The main emphasis of Nansen's office was in providing legal protection to uprooted people and he persuaded governments to register refugees who couldn't be returned to their homelands and to provide them with valid legal documents for additional travel or residence in a country. These Nansen documents enabled refugees to begin a new life. With virtually no funds and little administrative capacity, his office managed to act in many cases to assist the uprooted victims of war. But the functions of the League's High Commissioner were limited. While such travel documents were issued as a result of international agreements, the actual administration — and all material assistance — was carried out by governments. League functionaries "were able only to observe the application of the international agreements by governments, to persuade more governments to adhere to the agreements and to propose alterations, improvements and extensions. Thus, the international machinery had primarily political and technical functions but very restricted executive tasks."[3]

Nansen died in 1930 and was succeeded in 1933 by an American, James G. McDonald, who immediately ran into problems as he desperately sought a solution for the growing number of Jewish refugees in a context of increasing anti-Semitism in Europe and the rise of Hitler. Frustrated, he resigned in 1936 because he believed that an effective multinational response to a large-scale human tragedy had reached a dead-end. The international community was unable to respond to the needs of this large group of vulnerable people or even to surrender sovereignty to an international body. Louise Holborn, who has written the definitive history of UNHCR, notes that the more binding and comprehensive the nature of the agreements relating to refugees, the fewer tended to be the number of states which ratified them. In 1922 for example, an agreement providing documents for Russian refugees was adhered to by 56 governments. A convention on the status of refugees coming from Germany, proposed in 1938, obtained only three ratifications.[4]

In 1938, a meeting at Evian-les-Bains, France, created an Intergovernmental Committee on Refugees (IGCR) to deal with the flight of political and Jewish refugees. The conference, known for the refusal of Western governments to admit more Jewish refugees into their territories, in spite of growing evidence of the scale of persecution in Germany, is evidence of the fact that the international community was unable to respond. The IGCR worked with NGOs to smuggle Jews out of Germany, but during its years of existence it was able to move only 4,000 Jews to safety.

While governments were unwilling to deal with the question of Jewish refugees, American Jews, through various NGOs, worked to provide some assistance. This followed a tradition whereby US Jewish organizations were deeply involved in promoting immigration of Jews, first to the US and later to Palestine. By mid-1917, for example, a million Jewish refugees in Russia were being helped by American Jewish organizations. In Palestine in 1916, a British report at the time notes that only 18,000 of the 82,000 Jews in the country were self-supporting; the rest depended on financial support from the American Jewish community.[5]

During the second world war, the results of the international community's unwillingness to find humanitarian solutions for Jewish refugees in the 1930s, when solutions were still possible, came back to haunt world leaders. Out of the shame and the guilt came a recognition that this must never be repeated, that the international community has a responsibility to enable people to find refuge outside their countries when they have no protection from their governments.

Thirty million Europeans were uprooted as a result of the second world war. The UN Relief and Reconstruction Agency (UNRRA) was established in 1943 in the context of intergovernmental planning exercises and emergency relief programmes for liberated states. The mandate of UNRRA was to assist in the repatriation of people displaced by war. Only incidentally did it assist victims of political persecution. Together with NGOs, UNRRA shared management of camps and assembly centres; at one point in time, it managed several hundred such camps. It was in existence only for four years, but during that time it helped some 7 million displaced people return to their countries.

Politically, UNRRA faced difficulties with the onset of the cold war. Several of its repatriation exercises were criticized for their involuntary nature, particularly the deportation of displaced people back to the Soviet Union where some were killed. While UNRRA took the position that no one should be forced to return to their country of origin, it did not emphasize legal protection of refugees. Initially some 100,000 people, mainly Eastern European or Soviet nationals, declined offers of repatriation. Then their numbers began to swell. By the beginning of 1946, about 2 million people who sought refuge, not repatriation, were in camps and other temporary quarters.[6] UNRRA came under growing criticism as the USSR refused to allow it to operate in its German zone and sought the forced repatriation of some of its nationals. US President Harry Truman decided to let the agency die and it stopped operations in 1947. The feeling seemed to be that it would be easier to create a new organization than to resolve the existing problems with UNRRA.

In 1948, the UN General Assembly set up the International Refugee Organization (IRO) with only 18 members. The IRO was also conceived as a temporary agency, with only a three-year mandate (later extended by 18 months). Unlike UNRRA, the IRO was intended to help find permanent solutions, principally resettlement, for the 1.5 million remaining refugees. Like UNRRA, the IRO's operations were hampered by the deepening cold war. For example, IRO could not operate in the Soviet-occupied zone of Germany. It was also frustrated by the lack of any comprehensive set of legal arrangements with regard to refugees.

Finally, in 1951, the United Nations General Assembly created another temporary agency, the United Nations High Commissioner for Refugees (UNHCR) with a three-year mandate and a budget of $300,000 — at a time when 1.25 million refugees fell under its mandate. The mandate of UNHCR has since been renewed — at first every three years, later every five. The UNHCR was to be the international community's implementing agency for the assistance and protection of refugees.

But equally important, perhaps more important, was the agreement in 1951 to sign a convention which defined who is a refugee and established minimum standards of treatment for refugees. The signing of a convention on refugees and the creation of UNHCR went hand in hand. This convention and this definition form the bedrock of the international community's response — not just to refugees, but to the whole group of people forced to leave their homes.

However, one important group of uprooted people, the Palestinians, were largely excluded from this emerging international refugee system. Following the Israeli-Arab war of 1947-48, some 600-760,000 Palestinian Arabs fled their country. At the same time that efforts were being made to find a political solution to the crisis, in 1948, the UN General Assembly established the UN Relief for Palestine Refugees (UNRPR) to take care of the immediate needs of the refugees. In 1949, the General Assembly established the United Nations Relief and Works Agency for Palestine Refugees in the Near East (UNRWA) to respond to the needs of the Palestinians. UNRWA began its operations in 1950, as a temporary agency with a temporary mandate. Like UNHCR, this mandate has been renewed repeatedly by the UN General Assembly. But unlike UNHCR, UNRWA's mandate extended only to the provision of assistance to the refugees and not to protection. As will be discussed below, this more limited mandate has had far-reaching consequences for the treatment of refugees under UNRWA's mandate. Not only was a separate UN agency established for the Palestinian refugees, but in 1951, when the Convention on refugees was drafted, it was decided to exclude Palestinian refugees who were assisted by UNRWA from the Convention. The issue of Palestine was considered too political by the powerful governments of the time to be included in the new Convention and new UN refugee agency. Thus a separate system emerged for the international community's response to Palestinians, a system which is examined in greater detail in chapter 9.

Before looking at the elements of the present international system for refugees and migrants, it is useful to draw a few lessons from those important formative early years when the international community was grappling with a way to respond to the needs of uprooted people.

First, from 1921 when the League set up its office of the High Commissioner for Refugees until 1951 when the UN Convention on refugees was signed, refugee groups to be protected were specifically named groups (Greeks, Turks, Russians, Armenians, etc.). There was no "definition" of refugees. In effect by naming specific national groupings, a mass determination procedure was carried out which included victims of war as well as victims of individualized persecution. [7]

Secondly, the international system which emerged grew out of the *European* experience. The definition, norms and institutions were created to meet the needs of uprooted people in post-war Europe. This wasn't because all of the world's refugees at the time were in Europe. In 1947 India was partitioned, creating religious minorities in both India and Pakistan. The ensuing violence left about 500,000 dead and led to the uprooting of about 15 million people fleeing what were now international borders to what they considered their homeland. As Zolberg et al. point out, these were extremely poor populations whose problems were much greater than those of the Europeans for whom the new international instruments were created. [8] But the international instruments were not applied to those uprooted on the Indian subcontinent. In the decades following the establishment of UNHCR, there have been increasing efforts to reshape the definition and to reorient the work of UNHCR and other actors towards non-European situations. While these have been somewhat successful, the fact remains that the efforts took place within a Euro-centric model which was developed and designed to meet specific Western needs in Europe during the immediate post-war era.

Thirdly, in negotiations leading to the formation of UNHCR and the signing of the UN Convention, "Western governments were not interested in creating a substantial and independent new refugee agency, but rather in limiting their financial and legal obligations to refugees".[9] In other words, the system which emerged was designed to respond to a specific problem because the absence of such a system would have meant heavy burdens on particular countries — precisely those countries which had political power in shaping the new post-war world order.

A fourth characteristic of these formative years was the fact that the United States was the principal world power and controlled the political environment in which the negotiations on refugees took place. The US considered refugees in the same framework as national security and, as the cold war developed, saw some political benefit from the continued influx of refugees from communism. The international actors which developed during this period — the UNHCR, UN Relief and Works Agency for Palestine Refugees in the Near East (UNRWA), the Inter-governmental Committee for European Migration (ICEM), and later the UN Korean Reconstruction Agency (UNKRA) were all supported and used by the US government in pursuit of its own foreign-policy objectives. For example, the creation of ICEM, which was to be a technical agency concerned with facilitating the migration of Europeans, primarily Eastern Europeans, out of the region, was beyond the reach of the UN — and the USSR. This meant that the USSR would have no voice in matters of migration from Western Europe. It also meant that migration issues would be treated separately from refugee issues — a separation that is becoming increasingly hard to sustain.

Finally, the role of NGOs and, within the NGOs, the religious communities was crucial in the early years of the emergence of an international refugee system. The NGOs and the churches were the main agencies which tried to respond to the human needs of people displaced by the Russian revolution and the Armenian genocide. The Jewish aid organizations had played the leading role in advocating an international response to Jews seeking to leave their countries during the 1930s and, when that failed, in mobilizing for their assistance. And it was NGOs which pushed hard for the creation of a United Nations system in which governments would assume the principal responsibilities for assisting and protecting uprooted people. Not only did they press governments in this direction, they also served to raise public awareness about the needs of uprooted people and other victims of war which provided some popular support for the new system.

So, the international system in operation today is the product of these historical experiences. In order to understand how the system works, we look now at the first component of the international system — the definition of who is to benefit from the system.

Definitions

1. Refugees and migrants

Present estimates are that there are about 17 million refugees (and asylum-seekers) in the world, 20 million internally displaced people, 30 million "regular" migrants and another 30 million migrants who are in another country in an "irregular status". These 100 million or so people fall into different categories, categories based on the reasons the person has left his or her country, on the degree of coercion, and on the extent to which protection of the host government is available. The most basic distinction is made in terms of their motivation for leaving their countries or communities. Those who go to another country for primarily economic or personal reasons are considered migrants. This includes those who are transferred by their companies, students studying abroad, temporary guest workers, people moving to live with relatives in another country, and diplomats, as well as those who overstay their visas to work on the black market and those who bypass normal immigration channels to enter a country. Although their situation varies enormously, they share the common motivation that they left their country, temporarily or permanently, because of their work situation. Within that work situation, there is a world of difference between a diplomat or multinational company transfer and the family that leaves because it can no longer survive at home or the woman or man who works abroad in order to support a family back home.

The basic distinction in the international system between refugees and migrants is based not only on economic versus political motivation for flight but also includes a tacit assumption that refugees are those who are *forced* to leave their countries while migrants have some degree of *choice* in the decision to leave. But that distinction is no longer valid in many cases. The patterns of South-North migration make it clear that most people leave their countries not because they want a *better* job, but because they simply cannot survive at home. To what extent can one talk about *choice* in the case of Filipina maids working in Europe to support children living back home or Ethiopians who walked for hundreds of miles because their land was parched and their animals had died?

The legal system makes a different distinction between refugees and migrants. Refugees are considered to be those who no longer enjoy the protection of their government. While migrants may be in a terrible economic situation, if they are sent back they do not have to fear for their lives. They still enjoy the protection of their governments — even if they cannot survive economically back home.

We will return to the question of the distinction between economic and political motivations for migration; in fact, the blurring of these distinctions is presently the single greatest threat to the whole international system of responding to movements of people. Leaving aside for a moment the continuing debate over the relationship between economic and political motivations for flight, there are also serious shortcomings within the definition of a refugee.

2. Who is a refugee?

Refugees have been defined in different ways at different points in human history. For most of recorded history, the expectation was that people living in conquered territory would come under the rule of the victor. While there have always been individuals fleeing political persecution, the growing importance of national boundaries greatly increased the political significance of such movements. As Dirks argues, "sovereignty and nationalism are essential precursors of the modern refugee phenomenon. Thus, until recently, refugees could be found primarily in the older nation-states and occasionally in Latin America. As the colonial areas of Africa and Asia acquired independence in the 1950s and 1960s, the refugee phenomenon quickly arose there."[10] Of course, it may be that such migrations were identified as refugee movements only when national boundaries were drawn. The establishment of national borders — particularly when existing cultural and ethnic settlement patterns were not taken into account — has created monumental political problems leading to mass refugee movements. These refugee movements are very different from those of earlier eras.

Since the second world war, the principal legal definition of refugees has been that incorporated into the 1951 UN Convention Relating to the Status of Refugees and its 1967 Protocol which extended the Convention's provisions to current refugees. This definition of refugees was designed to meet the needs of individuals fleeing persecution in the post-war era. Although conditions have changed since this definition was developed, the UN definition remains the single most widely used formulation for determining refugee status today. The convention defines a refugee as:

> any person who, owing to a well-founded fear of being persecuted for reasons of race, religion, nationality, membership of a particular social group or political opinion, is outside the country of his nationality and is unable or, owing to such fear, unwilling to avail himself of the protection of that country, or who, not having a nationality and being outside the country of his former habitual residence, is unable or, owing to such fear, is unwilling to return to it.

Furthermore, the UN Convention provides a set of rights for refugees, including the right of *non-refoulement* — that is, the right not to be forcibly repatriated to the country of origin.

Today 106 countries have ratified either the 1951 Convention or the 1967 Protocol and the UN definition of refugee has been incorporated into many nations' laws. Yet the definition has serious shortcomings.

Refugees as individual victims of persecution

The definition excludes those individuals who are displaced by violence or warfare and who have not been singled out for individual persecution. The UNHCR *Handbook on Procedures and Criteria for Determining Refugee Status* states that "an applicant must normally show he individually fears persecution". Most of the world's wars (and most of the world's refugees) are found in the third world where counter-insurgency campaigns displace whole communities and where casualties among non-combatants are high. But these displaced individuals are not considered refugees under the UN definition. While the UN procedures don't require that the concerned persons are persecuted because of their individual activities (rather than as members of a persecuted group), they must be able to show reasons why, as individuals, they have a well-founded fear of persecution. Where they cannot show that they have been individually singled out for persecution, their claims of refugee status are not upheld. The US government, for example, has consistently refused to grant refugee or asylum status to Salvadorans and Guatemalans fleeing the violence of their countries, arguing that generalized conditions of war are insufficient grounds for granting refugee status. As Elliott Abrams, then US Assistant Secretary for Human Rights and Humanitarian Affairs, stated: "The key to the concept of asylum is targeting. It's not sufficient to note that the country [an applicant comes from] is repressive, violent or poor. You must show something about you as an individual that would make you a target of persecution — your religion, your race, or something."[11]

In practice, this emphasis on individual persecution leaves considerable discretion to the governments which apply the definition to individual asylum-seekers. For example, Kälin notes that using a restrictive interpretation, "German courts have repeatedly decided that torture of members of militant organizations in Turkey or Sri Lanka does not constitute political persecution because such persons are not ill-treated by the authorities because of their political opinions, but out of a desire to protect the integrity of the state".[12] However, using a more liberal interpretation, the German federal constitutional court decided in 1989 that actions directed against Tamil militants and against Tamil civilian populations might, under certain circumstances, constitute political persecution.[13]

Internally displaced people

A second group of people excluded from the UN definition of refugees consists of those individuals who have been displaced or persecuted because of the violence, but who, for one reason or another, have not left their country of origin. Thus, during the violence in El Salvador since 1979, over one million Salvadorans (out of a population of 4.5 million) left their home communities, but approximately half of them remained within El Salvador. In most cases, internally displaced people leave their home communities for the same reasons as refugees: generalized violence, widespread violation of human rights, fear. Sometimes they remain within their own countries because of distance from a border or because the violence makes long-distance travel dangerous. Although systematic data are lacking, it is reasonable to assume that the more mobile sectors of the population are more likely to make it to an international border. Mothers of small children, the elderly and the physically disabled are likely to remain closer to their homes as internally displaced people.

The internally displaced, because they are closer to the conflict, are more vulnerable to ongoing violence and harassment. Thus in Sri Lanka, internally displaced people are subjected to bombings and the ongoing conflicts between insurgent groups and the government. Young people are also particularly subject to forced recruitment by the two sides in the conflict. But these internally displaced individuals are not entitled to either the legal guarantees or to the material assistance offered under the auspices of UNHCR. In fact, provision of relief is made more difficult by the violence; roads may be impassable, relief convoys may be subject to attack, and warring parties may view such activities with suspicion. Thus, the difficulties of providing both protection and assistance for the internally displaced in the Sudan, Liberia and Mozambique are far greater than for refugees from those same countries living in neighbouring countries. Another serious problem is the fact that governments may view the displaced people as "subversives" who are supporting the insurgent forces. Thus in the Philippines and Guatemala, displaced people may be reluctant to identify themselves, even when churches and other groups make such assistance available. To do so may raise suspicion from governmental authorities and the police. Moreover, the activities of relief officials working with displaced people in conflict zones are often viewed with suspicion by both governments and rebel forces. Thus churches and NGOs working with Salvadoran displaced people have been viewed as supporting the insurgent forces and have faced harassment and intimidation by military forces.

In such situations where human need is great and where provision of relief assistance is difficult, internally displaced people have no recourse to the body of refugee law which provides certain minimum standards of assistance. In these situations, international humanitarian law and the work of the International Committee of the Red Cross (ICRC) are vitally important but often insufficient to meet the needs of the people.

Humanitarian law

Humanitarian law is concerned with the status and protection of civilian non-combatants, some of whom may be displaced persons or refugees. The Geneva Conventions of 1949, and particularly article 3 common to the four conventions, have been ratified by all but two states, making it a well-accepted rule of current international law. This article is binding on all parties in the conflict, whether they have ratified the Convention or not and whether the conflict is a war between states or an internal conflict. The over-riding right accorded to all "persons taking no active part in the hostilities" including displaced persons is to "be treated humanely" in all circumstances. Certain acts are categorically prohibited under this article, including violence to life and/or person, outrages on personal dignity, and the carrying out of executions without previous judgment pronounced by a regularly constituted court. Furthermore, each party to the conflict is under a duty to provide all sick and wounded, including displaced persons, with adequate medical care.

Protocol II Additional to the Geneva Conventions relating to the Protection of Victims of Non-International Armed Conflicts creates a number of other significant rights. This Protocol actually prohibits the parties to an internal conflict from displacing civilian non-combatants except for their own safety. "Where such displacements are unavoidable, article 17 operates to guarantee displaced persons adequate conditions of health, hygiene, shelter, nutrition and safety." Children receive additional guarantees. "They are to be provided with the aid and care that they require, and, in particular, an education, the possibility of reunion with their family, protection from military recruitment up to the age of fifteen years, and the possibility of evacuation to safer areas." But Protocol II is of limited effectiveness as many governments tend to view it as infringing upon their national sovereignty and thus it was agreed that its provisions would only apply in specific situations — where "dissident armed forces or other organized armed groups, under responsible command, exercise such control over a part of its territory as to enable them to carry out sustained and concerted military operations and to implement this Protocol".

According to the International Committee of the Red Cross, the most important measures to be noted in terms of civilian protection for refugees are the prohibition of recourse to starvation as a weapon of war, the protection of objects indispensable to survival (drinking water installations and supplies, harvests, etc.) and the obligation of the parties to the conflict to allow free passage to relief for civilian groups. [14]

Under the provisions of these conventions and their protocols, the ICRC is mandated to protect and assist displaced persons and refugees who are victims of armed conflict. The main components of this mandate are:

— representations to governments and armed movements to promote understanding and acceptance of the law of war and certain humanitarian principles;
— active protection through the deployment of delegates in sensitive areas, access to refugee camps and visits to places of detention;
— medical, food and material assistance;
— setting up of reception facilities and construction of camps; and
— tracing and family reunification. [15]

Unlike UNHCR, the ICRC does not base its activities on the 1951 Convention or the 1967 Protocol, but rather on international humanitarian law. "It is the outbreak of an armed conflict, whether international or otherwise, that gives rise to the application of international humanitarian law, i.e., the Geneva Conventions of 1949 and their Additional Protocols of 1977... it is of no importance whether the refugees to be protected have crossed an international border because of well-founded fears of persecution or by reason of armed conflict, or whether they have moved from one part of their own country to another."[16]

But, of course, in situations of war, conflicting parties typically ignore international humanitarian law. In some cases ICRC is able to provide assistance to internally displaced people as in Somalia. In other cases, such as Bosnia-Herzegovina, because of ongoing violence the ICRC has had to periodically withdraw its staff.

A United Nations report

In February 1992, the United Nations Secretary-General issued a report on internally displaced persons, prepared in response to a March 1991 request by the United Nations Commission on Human Rights which had in turn been urged to take up this issue by several non-governmental organizations — primarily the World Council of Churches and the Friends World Committee on Consultation.[17] Although various UN statements and documents had urged that the issue of the internally displaced be given more visibility, this was the first time that the UN system had prepared such an analytical report. It provides important information about who the displaced are and indicates the shortcomings in the present international refugee system.

In looking at the international system of refugee assistance and protection, the exclusion of internally displaced people seems inhumane. It must be understood in the context of national sovereignty. States are presumed to be responsible for citizens within their territory which precludes international action without the support of the concerned government. In fact, of course, churches, NGOs and some UN bodies have been involved in a number of initiatives to provide assistance and sometimes protection to such groups as evidenced by cross-border operations into Ethiopia, Sudan and Pakistan. But these ad-hoc initiatives point to the need for an international regime for internally displaced people. Internally displaced people are often perceived as destabilizing forces for the governments involved who prefer to deal with the problem without an international presence — or witness. But other governments, particularly of neighbouring countries, may also be concerned that the internally displaced — and the violence which provoked their flight — may spill over into their countries.[18] As recognition grows that the internally displaced are part of the same phenomenon as refugees, various intergovernmental and NGO initiatives have been launched to address those needs — needs which are unmet by the international system for refugees.

Regional instruments

As we have seen, the international definition of refugees has serious shortcomings. But the 1951 Convention and 1967 Protocol are supplemented by a growing body of regional laws dealing with refugees. While the Asia/Pacific region has not developed such legal instruments, in both Africa and Latin America important initiatives have been undertaken.

In contrast to the narrow definition of refugee status of the 1951 UN Convention, in 1969 the Organization of African Unity (OAU) developed a Convention Governing the Specific Aspects of Refugee Problems in Africa which expanded the UN definition to include those individuals displaced by generalized conditions of violence. The OAU definition of refugee thus includes

> every person who, owing to external aggression, occupation, foreign domination, or events seriously disturbing public order in either part or the whole of his country of origin or nationality, is compelled to leave his place of habitual residence in order to seek refuge in another place outside his country of origin or nationality.

The OAU Convention reflects the reality of the African refugee situation and 42 African governments are party to it.

While expanding the definition of refugee from that of the 1951 Convention, the OAU definition also excludes internally displaced people and those uprooted by economic disasters. Moreover, as Oloka-Onyango has shown, the OAU Convention sought to balance refugee protection and the prevention of subversive activities committed by refugees against their home states. [19]

In 1984, representatives of ten Latin American governments adopted the Declaration of Cartagena which incorporated a broader definition of refugee than that of the 1951 UN Convention. Specifically, the Declaration defined as a refugee those who met the UN criteria, but also those "who have fled their country because their lives, safety or freedom have been threatened by generalized violence, foreign aggression, internal conflicts, massive violation of human rights or other circumstances which have seriously disturbed public order". [20] This was a far-reaching definition, which went beyond even the OAU definition and "despite the 1984 Cartagena Declaration's non-binding nature, Central American nations accept it as a document confirming the legal rules of asylum for the region". [21]

Beyond official definitions

While the UN definition seeks to provide a universal definition of refugee status to be applied by all governments at all times, in fact, most definitions are political. As Suhrke points out, politicized definitions have the advantage that governments can regulate the number of refugees quite easily with little pretence of an equitable refugee policy. [22] While most states have acceded to the UN Convention, there is substantial variation in the way in which the definition is applied in specific situations.

Governments subscribing to the UN definition use political persecution as the principal criterion for granting refugee status. Individuals leaving their homelands for economic reasons, no matter how pressing, are not considered refugees. As many have pointed out, the victims of economic hardship and starvation may be as needy as those fleeing political persecution. In fact, Keely notes that political dissidents may have more control over the timing of their move out of the country than economically motivated migrants. He explicitly sees refugees as the product of underdevelopment. [23]

As governments increasingly use economic oppression as a tool of warfare, the distinction between political and economic motivations for flight breaks down. In fact, ten years ago a World Council of Churches meeting included those who are "victims of systematic economic deprivation" in their working definition of refugees. Where armies burn fields and destroy warehouses as they seek out opposition forces — whether in Cambodia, Afghanistan or Guatemala — there is a mixture of economic and political repression at work. Most refugees probably leave their home countries for a mixture of political and economic reasons.

In addition to economic and political motivations for flight, there is growing recognition of the environmental causes of migratory movements. This includes such factors as nuclear or chemical disasters (e.g. Chernobyl), desertification, deforestation, global warming and drought-induced famine. Certainly many are forced to flee their countries for these reasons. Jodi Jacobsen of the Worldwatch Institute places the number of environmentally-motivated migrants worldwide at 10 million people and estimates that the figure could rise to 60 million by the end of the decade. [24]

At the same time that many scholars, churches and activists talk of the need to expand the definition of refugee to include other categories of migrants — who may be equally as needy as those fleeing political persecution — others resist the trend towards broadening the term to include environmentally and economically-motivated refugees out of concern that the word "refugee" will become meaningless if it is stretched too far. As Feen notes, if everyone is a refugee, then no one is a refugee and the term loses meaning. [25] The argument is that nations, particularly first-world nations, cannot accept all of the world's needy people; by lumping the economically deprived with the politically persecuted, there is a risk that governments will close the doors to all. This is a theme to which we shall return later in this book.

Even when political persecution is the sole criterion for refugee status determination, there is wide variation in the way the term is used. Governmental retribution because of refusal to perform military service is sometimes considered political persecution and thus reason for granting refugee status while at other times it is not. The UNHCR handbook states that when the military service refused is condemned by the international community, then it can be considered grounds for refugee status. Yet, clearly, this injects a further political element into the question of refugee status determination. Should Serbs or Croats be considered as refugees when they leave their country to avoid serving in the military forces?

The existence of what Stein calls "anticipatory refugees" (those who sense the danger early and leave) in contrast to "acute refugees" (those who leave with little time for preparation) further impedes consistent application of the UN definition. [26] Yet anticipatory refugees, even though they may not have clear proof of direct persecution, may be as needy as acute refugees. There are other problems with defining refugees in terms of their political persecution. Many cases exist where refugees leave their homelands for a variety of reasons, including primarily economic motivations, but where they will face political retribution if they return home. Thus, many of the Cubans who left Cuba in the 1980 Mariel exodus did so for economic and personal reasons (e.g. family reunification). And yet their fears of political reprisals if they should return home were probably well-founded.

In addition to problems of defining refugees, very serious difficulties arise when the definitions are actually implemented. As Jaeger explains, governments are adept at overcoming the UN criteria for refugee status in seeking to limit mass refugee flows. [27] Physical prevention of refugees from arriving, such as interdiction at sea of vessels carrying asylum-seekers, has been used by the US government to prevent Haitians from arriving in the country. Detention of foreigners after arrival, when used as a conscious policy to deter or to intimidate individuals from applying for refugee status, is another common means of limiting refugee arrivals in practice. The procedures by which refugee status is determined frequently serve to further restrict the granting of refugee status, regardless of the way in which refugees are defined in law.

The question of defining refugee status at times appears to be an exercise in semantics, considering the urgency of the need of those seeking protection. As Keely argues, the question of who is a refugee is the wrong question. "The starting point should be how to deal with people displaced by war, government policy, a legacy of underdevelopment, and a struggle for independence, not efforts to stretch and trim a definition from another context."[28] Yet the way in which refugees are defined is an incredibly important issue — for the safety of the refugees themselves, for the receiving nation and for the country of origin.

The difficult moral questions raised by the dilemma of whom to accept as refugees brings up questions about the nature of the society, the responsibility of individuals for other human beings, and whether a rank ordering of need or persecution can be developed. Is a political dissident more deserving of refuge than a starving child? Do individuals singled out for persecution warrant protection more urgently than masses of people displaced by war in their village? The decision of whom to include and whom to exclude as refugees thus has consequences far beyond the immediate question of "who gets in". The danger, of course, is that by broadening the concept of refugee to include people in other kinds of need — even equally urgent need — public support for generous admission policies towards refugees may decline.

Churches and NGOs are not bound by the internationally accepted UN definition of refugees. In some cases, such as the World Council of Churches and the World Alliance of YMCAs, churches and ecumenical groups have formulated their own definitions of refugees which broaden the UN definition. And, in practice, churches and NGOs have shown much greater flexibility in working with uprooted people, including internally displaced people, than either governments or intergovernmental organizations. These broader definitions are important because they enable churches and NGOs to respond to people in need — whether or not they meet the formal criteria of international conventions. But as more and more needy people are falling outside these international definitions, at least as applied by governments, NGOs and churches find themselves under increasing strain.

At the same time that churches and NGOs have applied a broad definition of refugee in their own work, they have also consistently urged governments to respect the UN Convention and to apply the internationally-accepted definition in a broad and humane manner. This advocacy work must go hand in hand with efforts to provide assistance to uprooted people. Thus, CIMADE in France has pressed the French government to consider Sri Lankan Tamil asylum-seekers as refugees under the convention — even as they provide assistance to those asylum-seekers whose claims are rejected by the government. The South African Council of Churches provides food and other relief items to unrecognized Mozambican refugees in their country at the same time that they use international forums to press for their recognition — as refugees — by the South African government.

Sometimes in their desire to protect asylum-seekers, churches have made mistakes; embarrassing incidents have occurred as when it was discovered that the asylum-seekers passionately defended by a church organization turned out to be drug traffickers. These cases weaken church credibility. But churches and NGOs argue that it is better occasionally to make mistakes on the side of being too inclusive than to make mistakes in the other direction — and deport people whose lives may be in danger.

As the debate about definitions intensifies, churches and NGOs are challenged to think more deeply about the definitions which they use in their own work. The difficult moral questions of setting priorities of needs among uprooted people apply to churches and NGOs as well as to governments. Should churches extend the same efforts to migrants forced to leave their countries to survive, as to refugees fleeing warfare? Should churches do more for refugees than for the often impoverished host countries in which they live? Is there a theological as well as a humanitarian distinction to be made between groups of needy people?

The movement within the churches to exercise a "preferential option for the poor" and to work with the "neediest of the needy" may mean in practice that churches are challenged to work with the difficult cases of refugees who are criminals or displaced people who have committed atrocities during war. It is always easier to work with groups whose needs are widely recognized — victims of famine or torture, for example — rather than with those refugees who are angry, demanding and sometimes violent. But many organizations are able and willing to assist the victims of famine and torture; perhaps the churches and NGOs are challenged to work with other groups whose needs are not so widely recognized. By engaging in the reflection on definitions — on who has a privileged claim on the churches' resources and energies — churches can deepen their commitment and their effectiveness in working with uprooted people. The issue of definitions goes far beyond discussion of legal instruments; it goes to the heart of church and NGO service to refugees and migrants.

NOTES

[1] Bruce Nichols, *The Uneasy Alliance: Religion, Refugee Work and US Foreign Policy*, New York and Oxford, Oxford University Press, 1988, pp.32-33. Michael R. Marrus, *The Unwanted: European Refugees in the Twentieth Century*, New York, Oxford University Press, 1985, pp.83-84.

[2] Marrus, *ibid.*, p.83.

[3] Leon Gordenker, *Refugees in International Politics*, London, Croom Helm, 1987, p.21.

[4] Louise Holborn, *Refugees, A Problem of Our Time: The Work of the United Nations High Commissioner for Refugees* (2 vols), Metuchen, NJ, Scarecrow Press, 1975, p.16.

[5] Nichols, *op. cit.*, p.34.

[6] Gordenker, *op. cit.*, pp.24-25.

[7] Charles P. Keely, "Filling a Critical Gap in the Refugee Protection Regime", in *World Refugee Survey 1991*, Washington, DC, US Committee for Refugees, 1991, p.23.

[8] Aristide R. Zolberg, Astri Suhrke and Sergio Aguayo, *Escape from Violence: Conflict and Refugee Crises in the Developing World*, Oxford, Oxford University Press, 1989, p.2.

[9] Loescher, "The International Refugee Regime", paper presented at annual meeting of the International Studies Association, London, UK, 1989, p.15.

[10] Gerald Dirks, *Canada's Refugee Policy: Indifference or Opportunism?*, Montreal, McGill-Queens University Press, 1977, p.2.

[11] *Washington Post*, 22 April 1983, p.A13.

[12] Walter Kälin, "Refugees and Civil Wars: Only a Matter of Interpretation?", in *International Journal of Refugee Law*, vol. 3, no. 3, p.439.

[13] *Ibid.*, p.440.

[14] Lawyers Committee for Human Rights, *The Human Rights of Refugees and Displaced Persons: Protections Afforded Refugees, Asylum-Seekers and Displaced Persons under International Human Rights, Humanitarian and Refugee Law*, New York, Lawyers Committee for Human Rights, May 1991, pp.10-12.

[15] International Committee of the Red Cross, *ICRC Activities for Refugees and Displaced Persons*, no. 280, 1991, pp.14-15.

[16] League of Red Cross and Red Crescent Societies and International Committee of the Red Cross, *The Movement and Refugees*, Geneva, 1991, p.6.

[17] *Analytical Report of the Secretary-General on Internally Displaced Persons, prepared for the UN Commission on Human Rights,* E/CN.4/1992/23, 14 February 1992.

[18] Keely, *op. cit.*, p.1991.

[19] Joe Oloka-Onyango, "Human Rights, the OAU Convention and the Refugee Crisis in Africa: Forty Years After Geneva", in *International Journal of Refugee Law*, vol. 3, no. 3, July 1991, p.458.

[20] Cartagena Declaration, section III.3.

21 Eduardo Arboleda, "Refugee Definition in Africa and Latin America", in *International Journal of Refugee Law*, vol. 3, no. 2, 1991, p.187.

22 Astri Suhrke, "Global Refugee Movements and Strategies of Response", in *US Immigration and Refugee Policy*, ed. Mary M. Kritz, Lexington, MA, Lexington Books, 1983, p.161.

23 Charles P. Keely, *Global Refugee Policy: The Case for a Development-Oriented Strategy*, New York, Population Council, 1981.

24 Jodi Jacobsen, "Environmental Refugees: A Yardstick of Habitability", *Worldwatch Paper*, no. 86, Washington DC, Worldwatch Institute, 1988. For further information on environmental issues and refugees, see Essam El-Hinnawi, *Environmental Refugees*, Nairobi, United Nations Environment Programme, 1985; also *Environmental Refugees — A Discussion Paper*, prepared by the World Foundation for Environment and Development in co-operation with the Norwegian Refugee Council, Oslo, 1992.

25 Richard Feen, "Our Brother's Keeper? Theories of Obligation in US Refugee Policy", in *World Refugee Survey 1983*, Washington, DC, US Committee for Refugees, 1983, p.47.

26 Barry N. Stein, "The Refugee Experience: Defining the Parameters of a Field of Study", in *International Migration Review*, vol. 15, 1981, pp.320-330.

27 Gilbert Jaeger, "The Definition of 'Refugee': Restrictive vs Expanding Trends", in *World Refugee Survey 1983, op. cit.*, pp.5-9.

28 Keely, *Global Refugee Policy, op. cit.*, p.25.

2. Actors in the International Refugee System
Governments and Intergovernmental Organizations

The main actors in the international refugee game are the governments. Governments, intentionally or not, help to create refugees by their policies. Governments of receiving countries decide how they will be treated. Governments, acting through the UN General Assembly, the UNHCR executive committee and various regional bodies draft international laws, agree on the enhancement or limits of previously-agreed mandates and call on other international bodies to act. Governments of receiving countries may deal with refugees within their immigration, development, justice, foreign affairs or security ministries. In determining their policies towards arrivals of refugees, governments often use a mixture of humanitarian, political, economic and socio-cultural factors in deciding how to respond to the new arrivals. These policies are affected by the scale of the influx, by legal and cultural traditions, by outside pressures, and by the political needs of the country's leaders. Policies towards one group of refugees may or may not influence policies towards other groups of refugees. Thus, the Hungarian government responded generously to the arrival of Hungarian-speaking refugees fleeing persecution in Romania while refusing to recognize asylum-seekers from third-world governments. The US government has accepted most Cubans fleeing the Castro regime while deporting thousands of Haitians fleeing violence in their country.

Thus governments are the primary actors in the international refugee system. They act directly in providing bilateral assistance to refugees and in receiving refugees for settlement or resettlement. They act indirectly through multilateral institutions, particularly the UN High Commissioner for Refugees, UNRWA and the International Organization for Migration, but increasingly through regional instruments as well. Their efforts are supplemented — and sometimes challenged — by a host of non-governmental actors. The following sections provide an overview of some of these actors.

The United Nations High Commissioner for Refugees

The UNHCR was created by a General Assembly Resolution on 14 December 1950 with a three-year mandate. The early years of UNHCR's existence were difficult ones. With a budget of only $300,000 and only 33 staff, all at headquarters in Geneva, UNHCR was expected to respond to the needs of over a million refugees in Europe. It was prevented from raising funds on its own and had no mandate to assist refugees, but rather had to work through NGOs. An even greater problem was the fact that it did not have the needed political support from member governments, particularly from the United States. These were the years of the cold war, where once those uprooted because of the second world war were settled, the remaining refugees were those fleeing communist regimes in Eastern Europe. For the US, refugees from communism were a political issue, an issue of national security, an issue far too important to entrust to a multilateral institution — even one in which the US exercised disproportionate influence. The existence of other organizations — notably ICEM and the US Escape Programme — meant that UNHCR was bypassed on the important issues of the day. As Gallagher says: "The 'cold-war refugee' problem was, by and large, being addressed through alternate arrangements that did not involve the UN system. Had it not been for a $3 million grant from the Ford Foundation, it is doubtful that the agency would have been able to continue to function."[1]

From 1956 — when the Hungarian exodus began — the mandate of UNHCR has been expanded by successive UN requests. This expansion of activities enabled it to respond flexibly to situations of human need. It was made possible in part because Western governments, the linchpin of the international refugee system, found such actions useful to respond to particular situations and because they were not threatened with the demands of mass influxes. The flows from Eastern Europe could be dealt with by resettlement in North America — which met certain foreign policy and domestic political needs — or by integration in Western Europe which was facilitated by the cultural similarities between East and West. The UNHCR was needed to assist refugees in other parts of the world.

The renewal of the cold war in the late 1970s meant an increase in the number of refugees and asylum-seekers worldwide. In 1979, the exodus of hundreds of thousands of Vietnamese boat people, the flight of hundreds of thousands (later to become millions) of Afghans following the country's invasion by the Soviet Union, and the exodus of large numbers of Central Americans, all placed huge new demands on the international refugee system. Between 1965 and 1980, UNHCR's expenditures rose from $5.52 million to $500 million.[2] With greater responsibilities and an expanded mandate, UNHCR had become a major actor on the international scene. Although the number of asylum-seekers in Western countries was relatively small, "this was the era when the UNHCR came to be perceived as the champion of asylum-seekers, and a critic of governments".[3] But in spite of the rapid growth, there were signs of underlying tensions. Bureaucratic and financial expansion did not keep up with its increased responsibilities. By the mid-1980s, the organization was under serious challenge from the very governments which had supported its expansion in earlier decades. Moreover, cracks began to appear in the international consensus which underlay the whole international system of refugee protection and assistance. Since the second world war, the system has been based on the common understanding that it is the responsibility of the international community to respond to needs of refugees — wherever they appear in the world. Perhaps the most telling example of that international commitment was in the case of South-east Asia.

Around 1985, the tensions surrounding UNHCR's role and more broadly the breakdown of the international consensus began to be evident. For the next five years, UNHCR was to undergo a financial, administrative and political crisis which is, as yet, unresolved. As Guest notes, "by 1985, UNHCR was under formidable pressure. The administrative structure set up in 1950 was too fragile to sustain the huge expansion of responsibilities, and the UNHCR alienated several major donors by its forceful stand."[4]

In 1986 Jean-Pierre Hocké was elected High Commissioner by the General Assembly. As former director of operations for the ICRC, he was widely acknowledged to be a strong and efficient administrator. Hocké reorganized the administrative structure of UNHCR: the ensuing confusion led to serious morale problems among staff. More fundamentally, the funds needed to sustain UNHCR's expanding programme were not available from donors who were losing confidence in its ability to manage its resources. In spite of Hocké's stated plan to reduce expenditure and staff, the staff grew from 1,716 when he took office to 2,297 when he left. The UNHCR's budget in the same period increased from \$458 million to \$574 million.[5]

Hocké argued that the budget increase was necessary because of the growth of the world's refugee population by 1.5 million and said that he was just responding to governments' request that he implement repatriation on a large scale. In fact, as Roger Winter noted, between 1985 and 1990, UNHCR's per capita expenditure on refugees dropped from \$46 to \$38 — a decline that would be even more significant if inflation were taken into account.[6]

The funding mechanisms for UNHCR's activities were, and continue to be, inadequate to enable the agency to respond to the needs of refugees. Unlike most UN agencies, UNHCR receives over 90 percent of its funds by direct solicitation of governments. While Western governments have traditionally responded generously to politically popular groups of refugees, they are far less generous with development-related programmes for African refugees. Western governments provide the funds for UNHCR and have the power to shape its policies. The top 17 contributors in 1989 provided 97 percent of the agency's resources.[7] This means that UNHCR is completely dependent on a small group of Western donors who not only earmark their contributions to specific refugee groups, but who often fail to deliver their pledges on time.[8] This financial structure not only creates uncertainty for UNHCR planning, but also makes UNHCR vulnerable to political pressure.

In 1989, for the first time ever, the UNHCR executive committee refused to approve the budget of the High Commissioner and instead created a governmental working group to review every aspect of UNHCR's administration and financial management. Hocké resigned in October 1989, beset by administrative and personal difficulties. Thus, at the time of its fortieth anniversary, UNHCR found itself grappling with a 15 percent reduction in staff and funds and "buffeted by the aftermath of one of the most extraordinary governmental assaults ever on an international agency. The hiatus in leadership, the loss of staff morale, the critical, almost contemptuous attitude of governments: all this diverted the UNHCR, deprived it of vital resources, and weakened the agency's ability to stamp its authority on the evolving global refugee crisis."[9]

After making their pledges in October, governments rarely deliver the money on time. In October 1988 the donors accepted Hocké's budget but refused to put up all the money promised. Hocké cut programmes by \$70 million, but found that he was still \$40 million short. The working group established to review all of UNHCR's work finally reported in May 1990, recommending a combined budget of $550 million, some $150 million less than needed for the programme of the new High Commissioner, Thorvald Stoltenberg.

> The working group did immense damage. As well as acting in an aggressive and hostile manner towards demoralized UNHCR officials, diplomats from donor governments made it clear that their sole aim was to save money, instead of defining the UNHCR's role in the world and then allocating the needed resources. In the process, they destroyed part of the UNHCR edifice created by generous Western funds over the past forty years. Camp assistance, including food, was reduced, threatening the nutrition of some 200,000 refugee children. Protection seminars were cancelled. Eighteen branch offices were closed. Hopes of establishing a strong UNHCR presence in Eastern Europe were dashed. Camps in Hong Kong remained desperately underfunded, adding to the pressure on detained Vietnamese. Worst of all, the UNHCR lost 15 percent of its dedicated, committed staff. [10]

Throughout the crisis, UNHCR insisted that while the budget cuts were affecting assistance to refugees, its protection function remained a priority. With the election of Sadako Ogata as UN High Commissioner for Refugees in 1991, the immediate financial difficulties eased a bit. Donor governments seemed willing to give the new High Commissioner a chance to enact her programme and prospects of increased Japanese financial assistance provided a breathing space for UNHCR. Perhaps even more important, the massive relief programmes developed in the aftermath of the Gulf war and the high visibility (and cost) of repatriation in Cambodia increased UNHCR's credibility in the international arena. Western governments were, once again, reminded that they needed a strong UNHCR in these circumstances and that it was in their best interests to provide the financial means for UNHCR to act effectively.

But the easing of the immediate financial crisis is probably a temporary phenomenon. The structural difficulties in financing the organization's work remain. While the Cambodian peace plan and displaced Kurds were politically important issues to the West, in a dozen other situations — of less political importance to the West — UNHCR budgets were still being cut.

The crisis at UNHCR emerged in 1985 on several different levels. On one level it was an asylum crisis. As European countries began to receive far higher numbers of asylum-seekers, UNHCR was perceived as the enemy of European governments for exercising its protection role. European governments were critical of UNHCR's policies of intervening in their internal asylum policies. It was one thing for UNHCR to be critical of Southern governments for not protecting refugees, it was quite another matter when UNHCR began to challenge their own policies. At a more fundamental level, the crisis at UNHCR reflected the underlying structural problems of the international system — problems of the growing disparity between North and South, of the increasing inter-relationship between economic and political decisions, of the difficulties of creating environmentally sustainable development policies. On yet another level, the crisis wasn't a crisis of UNHCR at all: it was a governmental crisis as Western governments, which had largely been responsible for creating the international refugee system, now sought to place limits on their responsibility to it.

The International Organization for Migration (IOM)

The Intergovernmental Committee for European Migration (ICEM) was founded in 1951 and began operations in early 1952 in order to help deal with the problem of displaced persons and refugees in Europe and to facilitate the orderly migration of nationals from Europe. In comparison with UNHCR, ICEM was to have a "technical-operational mandate" which would furnish special migration services to ensure orderly migratory movements and the settlement of the migrants in their countries of adoption, would promote the co-operation of governments and international organizations in the field of migration, and would make all necessary arrangements for the transfer of migrants and refugees to countries of immigration and resettlement.

Like UNHCR, ICEM was created as a temporary organization in response to migration issues stemming from the aftermath of the second world war. Its operations too have been gradually expanded to acquire a global orientation. But while UNHCR was established as a UN agency with a clear mandate to provide protection to refugees, ICEM was set up independently of the UN framework and was intended to provide technical services to facilitate migration. Presently the organization has 39 member states and 25 states with observer status.

Throughout the 1950s ICEM assisted migrants seeking to leave Western Europe, mainly for Australia and Canada. In the aftermath of the Hungarian refugee movement in 1956, ICEM resettled 180,000 Hungarians from Austria and Yugoslavia. Throughout the 1960s the organization worked with a number of situations in which people who weren't traditional refugees needed assistance to migrate elsewhere, e.g. people obliged to leave former colonial territories, Belgians from the Congo,

minority groups from Egypt, European nationals from the newly independent countries of Tunisia and Morocco, Armenians entering Lebanon
from Bulgaria, Romania and Egypt. In 1973, ICEM helped Chileans
detained or sentenced for political crimes to go into exile, assisting a total
of some 29,000 persons over a period of five years. ICEM expanded its
work in the 1980s with the initiation of a Return of Talent Programme to
Latin American nationals living in the US, followed by programmes for
returning professionals to Africa and migration for development activities
in Asia. After the Iraqi invasion of Kuwait, almost 200,000 foreigners
were repatriated under the auspices of the organization.

In recognition of the changing nature of its work, the organization was
renamed the International Organization for Migration (IOM) in
November 1989. Following a change in its constitution in 1989, the
objective of IOM is "to ensure, throughout the world, the orderly
migration of persons who are in need of international migration services".
Unlike UNHCR, IOM works with all kinds of migrants — permanent
immigrants, economic migrants, refugees, people returning to their home
countries, etc. In the mid-1980s the IOM's council agreed to emphasize
the link between migration and development and to take into account the
needs of developing countries. Presently, IOM carries out four functions:

— the handling of orderly and planned migration of nationals who desire
  to migrate to other countries for purposes of employment;
— the transfer of qualified human resources who will be in a position to
  contribute to the development of the receiving countries;
— the organized transfer of refugees, displaced persons and other individuals in need of international migration services; and
— the provision of a forum to governments, intergovernmental organizations and non-governmental organizations to exchange experiences
  and promote co-operation and co-ordination of efforts on international
  migration issues.

In terms of its involvement with refugees, IOM has played an
important role in facilitating resettlement to third countries. In fact, of the
4 million migrants assisted by IOM since its inception, two-thirds have
been refugees. IOM's particular area of expertise lies in the technical side
of movements, such as working out the financial aspects of the transfer,
making transportation arrangements (chartering flights, for example),
medical screening, ensuring reception upon arrival and assisting with
travel to final destinations. IOM also works closely with UNHCR in
arranging transportation for mandate refugees who seek to return voluntarily to their countries of origin. Moreover, IOM works with exiles who

had to leave their countries for reasons similar to those of recognized refugees but who never formally applied for refugee status and thus don't qualify for UNHCR-assisted return. For example, IOM has carried out these kinds of programmes at the request of the governments of Argentina and Uruguay.

In comparison with UNHCR, IOM has played a relatively minor role in shaping the international system for response to uprooted people. Its mandate and expertise are acknowledged to be in the technical field, rather than in the area of international law. But in the last few years, IOM has shown both a capacity for rapid response to emergency situations (as in the repatriation of foreign nationals from the Gulf) and a commitment to addressing some of the larger issues of migration. As the distinctions between economic migrants and political refugees become less distinct, many expect IOM to play a more assertive role in the future.

The United Nations Relief and Works Agency for Palestine Refugees in the Near East (UNRWA)

Following the partition of Palestine in 1948 and the first Arab-Israeli war, the Palestinian refugees lived in difficult conditions for the first two years. Assistance was provided to them by Palestinian voluntary groups including women's groups in the West Bank and by the Red Cross and other international voluntary organizations. In 1950, with no international agreement permitting the refugees to return to their homes, the United Nations set up an agency with the cumbersome name of the United Nations Relief and Works Agency for Palestinian Refugees in the Near East (UNRWA). Like UNHCR, the organization was intended to be a temporary one as the Palestinian refugee situation was seen as a short-term phenomenon. However, unlike UNHCR, UNRWA's mandate was limited to providing assistance — and not protection — to Palestinian refugees.

In practice, this has led to some confusing applications. Palestinians outside the Middle East fall under UNHCR's mandate and are subject to its protection function, while Palestinians living in the Middle East come under UNRWA's mandate which does not have a protection function.

The UNRWA has undergone a steady growth in its capacity and the scope of its activities. In 1950 the agency assisted 900,000 Palestinians with a budget of $10.8 million and 5,800 staff. In 1985, it worked with 2 million registered refugees with a budget of $200 million and 17,000 employees. [11] The UNRWA works with registered refugees, both within and outside camps in Lebanon, Syria, Jordan, the West Bank and the

Gaza Strip. Its contributions in the field of education have been particularly important over the years as thousands of Palestinians have been educated in UNRWA-operated schools. Paradoxically, this education has enabled many Palestinians to find jobs in other countries, particularly in the Gulf states, as employment opportunities in the region have not kept pace with the output of UNRWA's educational facilities. As will be seen in chapter 9, UNRWA has faced particular difficulties in working with the Israeli authorities in administering its programmes in the occupied territories.

Like UNHCR, UNRWA has no fixed funding allocations from the United Nations and depends on UN members to allocate funds on an annual basis. In practice, UNRWA has suffered serious financial shortages over the years.

The broader UN family of agencies

In addition to these three intergovernmental organizations — UNHCR, IOM and UNRWA — other UN agencies become involved in specific refugee situations, including the UN Disaster Response Organization (UNDRO), the World Food Programme (WFP), the Food and Agriculture Organization (FAO), the UN Children's Fund (UNICEF), the International Labour Organization (ILO), and the World Health Organization (WHO). In recent years, as the long-term consequences of large refugee influxes have become more apparent, the UN Development Programme (UNDP) has become increasingly involved in working with governments trying to carry out development programmes in countries dramatically affected by mass influxes of refugees and migrants.

All of these organizations were set up to respond to humanitarian need and to implement the goals set out in the first article of the UN Charter: "to achieve international co-operation in solving international problems of an economic, social, cultural or humanitarian character, and in promoting and encouraging respect for human rights and for fundamental freedoms for all without distinction *as to* race, sex, language or religion" (emphasis mine).

Presently two-thirds of the UN's annual $4-5 billion budget is related to development and humanitarian assistance. The UN's social and economic role is generally considered to be more effective than its work in peace and security issues, and few could deny some of the tremendous advances made in the fields of health and disaster response. But the UN has become an unwieldy bureaucracy. Its decision-making structures are cumbersome (to put it mildly) and confusing. The Nordic UN Project and the Stockholm Initiative both focused on the lack of mechanisms for priority-setting.[12] The Nordic UN Project found that while the UN is important as a forum for raising issues, it may not necessarily be the most appropriate body for acting on them. And yet the trend is clearly for the UN to become more operational. Presently about half of the UN's employees are operational — that is, carrying out development or other projects.

The growth of the UN's operational role has been at least partially conditioned by the patterns of financing. The funding base of the specialized agencies is changing from "regular budget" to "extra-budget". In other words, UN agencies have to go out and raise funds for particular projects. This means that programmes and priorities are developed in response to where the funding is. Extra-budgetary contributions rarely cover full costs of a project, with the consequence that there are fewer resources for the normative work that no one but the UN can do. Presently, for example, 58 percent of FAO's budget and 32 percent of UNESCO's come from extra-budgetary sources.

In practice, the work of these intergovernmental agencies is shaped by their financial needs as well as by their governing bodies. These financial and institutional interests also shape their relationships with each other.

The dynamics of relationships between UN agencies is often competitive as they seek support from the same donors. They compete for "turf", that is, visibility on the big issues. To be visible in such cases is perceived as generating public and political support and financial resources. A premium is placed on independent action rather than on a co-ordinated UN response. The lack of co-ordination between UN agencies has become legendary. This is apparent on the everyday field operational level, but becomes particularly acute in situations of emergency response where many UN agencies and often hundreds of NGOs are involved. There seems to be general agreement that the UN system has succeeded best in some of its ad-hoc operations. The Office for Emergency Operations in Africa (OEOA) has been particularly successful because of strong leadership in co-ordinating groups at headquarters and field levels, as well as for its consolidated appeals, well-conducted public relations and a secretariat of seasoned relief practitioners. A more general pattern has been late and conflicting information reaching governments from different UN agencies, with the needs and channels of assistance often only vaguely specified. The lead agency concept, in which one UN agency is given a co-ordinating role for the others, has not often been successful. As the Nordic UN Project says, "the lesson we have learnt from our study is that co-ordination cannot be forced upon sovereign organizations". Unless agencies perceive such co-ordination to be in the best interests of their institutions, it will be difficult to sustain.

In this chapter we have seen that governments, acting through the United Nations and other intergovernmental forums, have established a number of agencies, each of which has a specific mandate and a specific acknowledged area of expertise. In practice, these mandates and areas of expertise overlap. Refugee children, for example, might receive protection from UNHCR, food from the World Food Programme, and medical care through UNICEF or WHO. When there is good co-ordination between the UN structures, the children may benefit from the multitude of channels of assistance. But when co-ordination is lacking, when agencies jockey for position and visibility with each other, they may suffer.

The UNHCR, as the principal UN body working with refugees, must thus respond to the wishes of governments which created it and which provide the financial and political support necessary for its operations. But UNHCR also works in an environment of other competing UN agencies and a world in which hundreds, perhaps thousands, of NGOs raise issues and make demands. Balancing these competing demands and interests with those of refugee needs is a difficult and confusing task.

NOTES

[1] Dennis Gallagher, "The Evolution of the International Refugee System", in *International Migration Review*, vol. 23, no. 3, p.582.

[2] Lawyers Committee for Human Rights, *The UNHCR at 40: Refugee Protection at the Crossroads*, New York, Lawyers Committee, 1991, p.42.

[3] Iain Guest, "The United Nations, the UNHCR, and Refugee Protection: A Non-Specialist Analysis", in *International Journal of Refugee Law*, vol. 3, no. 3, July 1991, pp.585-605.

[4] *Ibid.*, p.591.

[5] Lawyers Committee, *op. cit.*, p.85.

[6] Cited by Lawyers Committee, *ibid.*, p.88.

[7] Nicholas Morris, "Refugees: Facing Crisis in the 1990s — A Personal View from within UNHCR", in *International Journal of Refugee Law*, special issue, September 1990, p.52.

[8] See Guest, *op. cit.* p.594 for more detailed discussion of the budgetary process in UNHCR.

[9] *Ibid.*, pp.588-589.

[10] *Ibid.*, pp.593-594.

[11] Independent Commission on International Humanitarian Affairs, *Refugees: Dynamics of Displacement*, London, Zed Books, 1986, p.22.

[12] See for example *The United Nations: Issues and Options: Five Studies on the Role of the UN in the Economic and Social Fields*, studies commissioned by the Nordic United Nations Project, Stockholm, 1991.

3. Non-Governmental Actors in the International Refugee System
Churches and NGOs

In this talk I have spoken from the perspective available to the non-governmental organizations. We clearly do not see the whole picture. But it should be noted that we are seeing more and more of the picture. I refer to the fact that governments and international organizations are being excluded from an increasing range of fields that formerly they saw were theirs to "co-ordinate". The international organizations cannot work at the Thai-Burma border, they are restricted in their work in Cambodia, they do little in Vietnam. They cannot enter Tigray or Eritrea. But in these areas the private agencies carry the burden. Moreover in some places where the international organizations can act, the NGOs do the bulk of the work. They are more flexible, more lightly structured, less costly. But they do need support. They sometimes lack experience, infrastructure and sound judgment. [1]

While we have seen that governments largely determine the rules of the "international refugee game" — both directly through national policies and indirectly through the creation of intergovernmental mechanisms — non-governmental organizations have emerged as major actors in the international refugee system. As Raper notes, in some cases NGOs operate in areas where governments cannot act. Even in cases where the international machinery is in place, NGOs perform valuable functions in implementing policies and assistance programmes, in raising public awareness about particular situations and in advocating political changes.

There are major differences between the ways in which governments and NGOs operate. NGOs tend to be more loosely organized; while this gives them greater flexibility, it also means that much of their operations lie outside public view. Governments and intergovernmental organizations must account, to varying degrees, for their policies and budgets.

While NGOs are accountable to their constituents, in practice the degree of accountability varies enormously.

The role of NGOs in the international refugee system is poorly understood; most scholars treat NGOs only in passing and the information provided by churches and NGOs themselves is usually designed to mobilize support for their programmes rather than to provide impartial analyses. This chapter looks at the emergence of NGOs as actors in the contemporary refugee system, considers some of the differences among NGOs and their internal structures, and identifies some of the challenges and shortcomings they face in responding to the needs of uprooted people.

A little more history...

Non-governmental organizations have a long history, one with roots in the early missionary societies, the labour movement and the emergence of political parties. As we have seen, in the years before the second world war, private groups were central in providing relief to victims of war and disasters — in part because the international community did not have structures for governmental response. Throughout the inter-war years, for example, it was NGOs which mounted large-scale relief activities — activities which were, for the most part, made possible by private contributions. For example, between 1914 and 1924 the Armenian Relief Administration, together with the European Children's Fund and the European Relief Council, was responsible for delivering over $5 billion worth of relief to people in Europe. [2] During the formative period of the League of Nations and later the United Nations, NGOs played important roles in both providing relief to needy people and in pressing governments to develop intergovernmental mechanisms for responding to these needs. Many Western NGOs emerged in the period immediately after the second world war to respond to the needs of displacement and reconstruction in Europe. Between 1945 and 1949, almost two hundred NGOs sprang up to help the victims of the war, mainly focused on Europe. [3] But as the immediate post-war needs were met, many of these NGOs faced the question of what their role should be in the future. Oxfam, for example, entered into long debates in 1948 about whether they should continue operations now that European recovery seemed assured. Oxfam, like many NGOs, decided to broaden its focus to include development work outside Europe. [4]

The nature of relationships between NGOs and the international organization charged with caring and protecting refugees changed with the creation of UNHCR in 1951. UNHCR was to be the spokesperson for refugees and to provide legal rights while leaving care and assistance to voluntary agencies. In other words, UNHCR was not intended to be operational, but rather to work through NGOs. The budgets of many NGOs in the early years were considerably larger than UNHCR's operational budget. The NGO-UNHCR relationship was a symbiotic one. While NGOs needed a strong UNHCR to provide protection for refugees, UNHCR was dependent on NGOs for provision of assistance. In the 1950s, contracts were worked out between UNHCR and the voluntary agencies, and in some countries special committees of agency representatives and UNHCR were formed. [5]

During the 1950s and 1960s NGOs, particularly religious agencies, continued to provide substantial relief and were essential to the functioning of the refugee regime. One 1953 analysis found that fully 90 percent of post-war relief was provided by the religious agencies. [6] But churches and NGOs also took the lead in lobbying for resettlement opportunities and in providing the resources needed for resettlement of the hundreds of thousands of Hungarian refugees. The Year of the Refugee, 1959-60, marked the high water point in co-operation between private and public agencies.

While NGOs were consolidating their structures and expanding their operations, individual churches in all parts of the world tried to help refugees arriving in their communities by providing food, shelter and moral support. Although overshadowed by the emergence of large church-related aid agencies and by international NGOs, these individual expressions of local diakonia continue to provide important services to uprooted people. Some of these small church-based initiatives grew into specialized church agencies — with the same range of strengths and weaknesses as the NGOs described here. Others remained as tiny temporary activities carried out on a voluntary basis by church members who had other full-time jobs but who wanted to do something to help refugees arriving in their countries. The emergence of large church-related Northern church agencies and their secular counterparts had a definite impact on the expression of local diakonia. On the one hand, the large agencies were able to develop expertise in working in an increasingly specialized arena. They were able to mobilize greater resources and to distribute those resources more efficiently than the voluntary efforts of individual congregations. The agencies developed close working relationships with UNHCR, governments, and the dozens of other NGOs emerging to work in the same field. In the best of cases, the large church agencies were able to mobilize congregational support and to assist individual churches and ecumenical groups in their diaconal work with refugees. But over the years, the growth of these agencies — in all parts of the world — may have led to a partial abdication of responsibility by local congregations. Instead of asking themselves "what can we do to help these Chilean or Sudanese or Vietnamese refugees?", the tendency was to refer them to a church agency or another NGO. However, in emergency situations local congregations still play an important role in meeting the immediate needs of refugees and often in alerting the agencies and, through them, the international community, to the needs of the foreigners.

While individual church congregations continued to work on the local level, the international NGOs continued to expand their activities and their ways of working together. In 1962, ICVA (International Council of Voluntary Agencies) was formed, almost twenty years after the founding of the American Council of Voluntary Agencies. By 1963 the agencies recognized that ICVA needed to consider development issues in working with refugees and a Committee on Relief and Development was established as a way of avoiding refugee dependency.

From the early 1960s until the early 1980s, NGOs grew in size and scope of activities. Between 1960 and 1970, almost three hundred major new NGOs were created, mostly on development issues[7] but some were involved in refugee assistance as well. However, in spite of this growth, their expansion did not keep up with the growth in intergovernmental organizations, particularly with UNHCR. The steady expansion of its mandate meant that UNHCR could now act in situations from which it had previously been excluded. The growing number of refugees in Africa and other third-world regions increased the cost of relief. Governments devoted more resources to bilateral refugee aid, often channelled through NGOs, which meant that NGOs became increasingly dependent on government funding. More government funds meant greater organizational capacity for NGOs but also a weakening of their independence.

The whole issue of government funding was a highly politicized one in the United States, particularly as the consensus between NGOs and the US government began to break down during the Vietnam war. Shortly thereafter, the dramatic departure of thousands of Indochinese in the aftermath of the Vietnam war tested the international refugee regime and led paradoxically both to an expansion of NGO activity and to their increasing subordination to governmental purposes. US NGOs became dependent not just on the US government for funds to resettle refugees —

but also on continued flows of refugee cases for their institutional survival.

The US-based NGOs were the largest and most powerful, and differed from their European counterparts in several important ways. While many European NGOs were — and are — dependent on government funding (and increasingly on funding through European Community institutions), until the early 1980s, almost all of their efforts were undertaken in third-world countries. Resettlement was generally handled by governments with small NGOs providing specific services to facilitate refugee integration. But the primary emphasis was on refugee relief and development elsewhere. In contrast, in the United States, many NGOs provided assistance to refugees abroad but there were also "refugee" agencies focused on resettlement. NGOs which were involved in both resettlement and overseas refugee assistance generally kept the two functions separate; given the impact of US government funding patterns, the resettlement agencies or arms of agencies generally had more resources than those providing assistance abroad. In some cases, such as Church World Service, government contracts for resettlement enabled the rapid expansion of its resettlement operations and strengthened other CWS programmes.

But these patterns changed, both in Europe and in the United States, in the 1980s. The proliferation of NGOs, the growth of indigenous NGOs in third-world countries, and changing understandings of development meant that Northern NGOs came under increasing pressure to decrease their direct involvement in provision of service abroad and to support the development of local institutions. Institution-building and empowerment replaced concepts of community organizing, which had largely been carried out by expatriate staff in the 1960s and 1970s. The impact of dependency theorists and the extrapolation that foreign aid agencies were perpetuating dependency in another, albeit "altruistic", form meant that agencies began to change their mode of operation. Moreover, as refugee situations dragged on and a consensus emerged that these situations were no longer short-term disasters but rather long-term phenomena, the costs of refugee assistance dramatically increased. At least in the short term, it is much more expensive — and certainly requires much more expertise — to enable refugees to become self-sufficient than to provide them with the requisite number of calories per day. The economic crises experienced in most third-world countries in the 1970s and 1980s further increased the pressure on the international system not only to respond to individuals in need but also to do so in a manner that did not provoke resentment from nationals of the asylum country. At the same time, the expansion in the quantities of aid available increased the stakes of the "refugee industry", as some writers began to refer to it.

Another impetus for change in the activities of Northern NGOs working with refugees came from the increasing numbers of asylum-seekers arriving at the borders of Western countries. In the United States, the Mariel situation, followed by the awareness of the large number of Central American asylum-seekers, challenged NGOs which had previously been involved with refugees through resettlement. These NGOs had worked closely with the US government, providing services to resettled refugees in return for substantial sums of money. But with the rise of Central American solidarity organizations and the arrival of large numbers of Central Americans, churches and NGOs were challenged to act in new ways; relationships with the government underwent considerable change. From negotiating contracts and administering projects in close co-operation with the US State Department, the agencies found themselves embroiled over protection issues with both INS (Immigration and Naturalization Service) and the State Department whose advisory opinions were crucial in asylum determination proceedings.

Although this process was most obvious in the United States, it also occurred in varying degrees in most Western countries. Although not as closely involved with resettlement, most European NGOs working with refugees had enjoyed close relationships with their governments in administering their overseas refugee assistance programmes. The major national refugee councils (Norwegian Refugee Council, Danish Refugee Council, etc.) had been involved in either small-scale refugee integration projects at home or in major refugee assistance projects abroad (or both) when the number of asylum-seekers increased dramatically in their own countries. In some of the countries, the NGOs took the lead in opposing their governments' restrictive policies over new arrivals. In other countries, new NGOs emerged as the large established refugee NGOs either reacted timidly or could not act. For example, the Norwegian Refugee Council's mandate prohibits it from acting on behalf of refugees in Norway. In Canada, relations between the Canadian Council for Refugees (formerly known as the Standing Conference of Canadian NGOs working with Refugees) and the Canadian government deteriorated sharply in the late 1980s as the government introduced much more restrictive asylum legislation. The Inter-Church Committee for Refugees of the Canadian Council of Churches, to take another example, had previously lobbied the government for higher admission quotas for refugee resettlement and had developed services which complemented those provided by the government. But by 1989 the churches were involved in a major court challenge to take the government to the supreme court.

These were major challenges and changes in the way NGOs understood their roles in society and their relationships with the refugees. The context of refugee work on the domestic and foreign levels had changed dramatically in the space of a decade. The proliferation of agencies, the rise of evangelical and conservative political groups and the politicization of refugee issues has meant that NGOs are assuming new roles. In particular, refugee agencies have become increasingly involved in the *protection* of refugees as UNHCR's ability to do so has diminished. Similarly, as UNHCR has become more involved in assistance and in the logistical side of refugee relief, the impact of NGO funding in shaping assistance patterns has decreased.

The present NGO scene

Hundreds, perhaps thousands, of NGOs are involved in some way with refugee work. In 1986 the UN High Commissioner for Refugees, Jean-Pierre Hocké, noted that UNHCR at that time had operational agreements with some 250 NGOs and warned of the rapid proliferation of other NGOs. NGOs vary immensely — from small churches and solidarity groups providing food and shelter to refugees to large international NGOs with multi-million dollar budgets. NGOs differ also in their geographic concentration, expertise, political and religious affiliation, relationships with governments, experience, etc. These enormous differences make generalizations about NGOs almost impossible. They also explain in part the difficulties which NGOs have had in co-ordinating their efforts.

Taken together, NGOs bring enormous resources to the field of refugee relief and development; but even so, these resources are overshadowed by governmental contributions. Including development work, in 1968, the total overseas aid of NGOs (the bulk of which was administered by the hundred or so largest) was $510.2 million. By 1974 this had doubled to $1.22 billion, and by 1980 had doubled again to $2.4 billion. While NGOs were increasing their levels of assistance, so were governments. In the mid-1980s, the governments provided six dollars in assistance for every one distributed by NGOs. Moreover, much of the funds administered by NGOs actually come from governments. [8] Unfortunately, because of different organizational and reporting procedures information is not available about specific funding for refugee assistance provided by NGOs.

North versus South in the NGO world

While most NGOs which work with refugees are active in third-world countries (as that is where most of the world's refugees are), there are major differences between so-called "indigenous NGOs", those which are based in and supported by countries in which refugees are found, and those which are based in Northern countries and carry out operations, including support for indigenous organizations, in Southern countries. While both groups are clearly NGOs, the Northern-based NGOs are more international in focus and generally command far greater resources than their counterparts in the South. While Northern NGOs, often referred to as international NGOs, frequently seek to work with and to strengthen the voluntary sector in third-world countries, in practice this support is quite difficult. Bolling and Smith refer to a number of ways in which US-based NGOs can support their indigenous counterparts, including establishment of local offices, hiring of local staff and turning over of the office to their local counterparts once they have the necessary experience.[9] While there are certainly such cases — notably the large Lutheran World Federation refugee programme in Tanzania — this kind of turnover is relatively rare. In fact, the tendency seems to be in the opposite direction as large Northern agencies, including church-related agencies, are increasing their physical presence in third-world regions in order better to monitor and control the implementation of projects. Even as the rhetoric of solidarity and empowerment has grown among Northern NGOs, the North-South divide among NGOs working with refugees seems to be growing.

This North-South split seems less apparent in ecumenical refugee circles than in the secular NGO world, perhaps because many Northern church agencies work directly with church bodies in the South and because of the existence of forums where differences in orientation can be more openly debated. But even within church circles, the North-South split is often evident. Northern church agencies often feel that their primary responsibility is to the poor and to the refugees — rather than to their church partners in the South. When they judge that other Southern NGOs are more effective providers of assistance to refugees, they may decide to channel their funds to those secular groups, bypassing the churches. The refugee service of the World Council of Churches has persistently stressed the importance of working through local church structures and strengthening their capacity where necessary, rather than diverting resources to other groups. But sometimes the issues are not so clear-cut for churches and church-related agencies seeking to assist refugees and displaced people. In some countries, church refugee work is inefficient and lacks accountability. Funds intended for refugees are sometimes diverted to meet other church priorities. In other cases, churches may be reluctant to take actions on behalf of refugees which might get them into trouble with political authorities. Or they may not be interested at all in working with refugees in their country or may share the biases of their societies in viewing the refugees as troublemakers or rebels. In those situations, the only way for Northern church agencies to support refugee work is to work through other NGOs. But such decisions inevitably raise problems in ecumenical relationships.

Some of the North-South differences in both the secular and church world are the result of different structures and resource bases. While Northern NGOs are often specialized, with different departments, for example, dealing with refugees, emergencies, human rights and development, Southern NGOs seem to have more integrated tasks and have a more holistic vision of the interconnectedness of the problems they face. Organizations such as Diaconía working with returning refugees in El Salvador, for example, usually work with development issues and human rights as well as with returnees and displaced people. Sometimes this causes confusion as Salvadoran NGOs can't understand the complexity and compartmentalization of Northern NGO structures where one person can't respond to requests for assistance in several different areas. There is also some resentment at the differences in resources available to Southern NGOs, who are in the "front line" of refugee assistance, and to Northern NGOs who command greater resources while working at headquarters far removed from the needs, the pressures, and sometimes the dangers of Southern organizations.

Religious versus secular

While religious NGOs share many characteristics with their secular counterparts, there are also important differences — related to differences in their constituencies and self-perceptions. For Christian organizations, the presence of local churches and other Christian groups provides a ready-made constituency that is not parallelled by other NGOs. For Jewish agencies, there is a similar constituency among the synagogues and Jewish organizations among the diaspora. Historically, Jewish agencies have been primarily concerned with providing assistance to Jewish refugees; in the aftermath of the Holocaust they worked on the political level to make it possible for Jews to leave countries where they felt persecution. They also provided substantial assistance to individual refugees to enable them to resettle and adapt to new countries. In their efforts to protect Jewish refugees, the Jewish agencies have played extremely important roles in shaping national and international policies towards refugees in general. Islamic NGOs have only recently emerged and their activities are primarily limited to areas where there are large numbers of Muslim refugees.

Unlike Muslim and Jewish NGOs, church-based NGOs have major operations in countries where there are few Christian refugees but see their mission as global in nature. Lanphier found that "the specifically religious or confessional value structure of NGOs may be attractive to refugees, even though it differs from their own traditions". [10] He goes on to explain that "the symbolic status of an established Western church signals a service organization which is universal and widely accepted in the third world. The emphasis falls more upon the distinctiveness of the religious from the political than upon the nature of the authoritative ecclesiastical structure. However tenuous they may appear, religious auspices confer a certain trustworthiness and credibility upon the NGO personnel." [11] This trustworthiness and credibility is often transferred into the political sphere as well where both governments and refugees see a certain legitimacy in the lobbying role played by church-based NGOs.

It is important to emphasize that there are enormous differences within the Christian NGO community. Evangelical groups have been accused of proselytism and there are many stories floating around NGO circles of cases where assistance was conditioned on participation in religious services. (This of course is not limited to Christian groups as more and more reports in early 1992 spoke of Islamic relief agencies in Sudan requiring conversion to Islam as a condition for assistance.) In other cases, the line between mission and service becomes quite fuzzy as in some camps in Thailand where birth control information is provided in Christian education classes. At the other extreme is the statement by a Roman Catholic priest working with refugees in Malawi who said "given the vulnerability of many of the refugees I work with, sometimes it seems more Christian for me *not* to say mass in the refugee camps than to do so".

In some cases, such as Guatemala, fundamentalist religious groups serve political ends; they are perceived as offering a personal "salvationist" response to political problems. Among some church-based NGOs, there is close collaboration with local bishops and ecclesiastical structures — which sometimes puts limits on how far the NGO can go in lobbying and challenging structures. Other Christian NGOs, such as the World Alliance of YMCAs, include affiliates which are moving to address root causes, and others which are more concerned with providing recreational opportunities to urban refugees.

It is perhaps for these reasons that Kent found through many interviews that there was a conceptual divide, if not distrust, between secular and religious NGOs. [12]

In terms of the changing orientation of NGOs from charity to advocacy (discussed in greater detail below), for church-related NGOs, the challenge is often not only to make the conceptual move within their agency's staff, "but more importantly may require diffusing this awareness among officials in the NGO's parent (church-ecclesiastical) structure". [13] In the long term, this process can have far-reaching results, given the spread of Christian churches throughout many societies, but in the short term it can be quite frustrating for agency staff confronted with hierarchical church structures.

Flexibility and innovation as NGO strengths?

It is generally (and often uncritically) accepted that the smaller size of NGOs (in comparison with governments and intergovernmental organizations) gives them greater flexibility in responding to refugee needs. Moreover, the fact that NGOs often mobilize volunteer labour enables them to keep costs down. Gorman notes that rarely does an NGO spend anywhere near the average 20-30 percent in overheads that government agencies and international organizations do. [14] Smith finds that NGO administrative and management costs are usually only 5-6 percent of total costs. He cites the case of a water programme in Latin America sponsored by CARE which was implemented at a cost of $6 per household; the same programme would have cost the Canadian International Development Agency (CIDA) $60 per family and the International Development Bank (IDB) $160. But he also found a lack of NGO accountability for the expenditure of these funds. [15] In the case of US-based NGOs, Wright maintains that if the government were to take over the functions provided by NGOs, the costs would increase four times. [16]

The greater flexibility of NGOs is usually cited as their principal advantage in comparison with other actors in the international refugee system. Because they generally have smaller bureaucracies and less cumbersome decision-making procedures, they can respond more quickly to emergency situations. They are freer to experiment with small-scale innovative projects which can serve as a basis for future projects. In many cases, for example, NGOs and churches can provide assistance to individuals displaced by violence who do not meet the formal governmentally-applied or UNHCR definitions of refugee. Because of this flexibility, their efforts often complement those of UNHCR. In Argentina and Greece, to cite only two examples, there have been many instances where the UNHCR office would refer cases to churches because their own procedures prevented them from assisting particular groups of people in need. In other cases, NGOs were able to be more flexible in granting assistance, such as support for education, to individual refugees who were in particularly difficult circumstances — circumstances which didn't fall within the official criteria for government-sponsored programmes.

While it is generally acknowledged that their flexibility and innovation is an NGO strength, the lack of systematic evaluation makes generalizations difficult. The few studies which exist are based largely on the experiences of US-based NGOs. [17] Certainly NGOs exhibit a marked lack of concern with programme evaluation — or making such evaluations public — which makes it difficult to draw conclusions. NGO representatives maintain that the lack of time for evaluation and the need to protect confidentiality of sources are the main reasons for this. But without a process of evaluation it is difficult for NGOs and outsiders alike to know how successful a particular approach has been.

The voluntary labour and the in-kind contributions of their constituencies are rarely included in descriptions of the resources which NGOs bring to refugee work. The congregational involvement of US, Canadian, Australian and New Zealand churches in refugee resettlement, for example, has amounted to billions of dollars since the second world war. Similarly, at the height of the Ethiopian famine, media attention focused on the hundreds of thousands of metric tons of grain contributed by Western donors. But the volunteer efforts of the various liberation movements and the large soup-kitchen operations of the churches in Ethiopia represented a substantial and often invisible contribution to the relief operations.

Although in comparison with other actors, NGOs on their own are able to provide only "a small fraction of the financing required to cope with a large-scale influx of migrants requiring emergency care", [18] their role is indispensable in the provision and implementation of refugee assistance. Even their harshest critics would not want to see the disappearance of NGOs and the assumption of their roles by governments and large intergovernmental organizations.

A glance inside the NGO world

NGOs and churches are important actors in the international refugee scene, but there is little research on how they actually operate: how they set priorities, how they implement programmes, how they make decisions. In some refugee situations, dozens of NGOs compete with one another in offering services to refugees. In other situations, where the need is equally urgent, there are few NGOs present. While most, perhaps all, NGOs talk about the need to address root causes of refugee movements, few actually make this a priority. Some international NGOs devote resources to education and advocacy in Northern countries, but most see their main purpose as assisting refugees in third-world countries. Some Southern NGOs include public education or awareness-raising in their programmes with varying degrees of success.

The refugee department of the All Africa Conference of Churches has emphasized awareness-raising among its constituency for the past decade. Recognizing that the churches' natural strength is their large and varied constituencies, AACC has sought through various initiatives to raise awareness about refugees and about the root causes which displace them. By providing materials and promoting the African Refugee Sunday (20 June), AACC encourages local congregations to remember refugees — at least on one Sunday during the year. In 1987, AACC and WCC organized a seminar for both church-related and secular journalists who brainstormed together about ways that they could use existing communication channels to raise awareness about refugees in their countries. Three years later, AACC organized another meeting — this time for church leaders — to inform them about the plight of refugees. At that meeting, perhaps more effective than the presentations and background papers were the visits to camps of Mozambican refugees in Malawi. Church leaders from countries with few refugees were moved by the conditions of the refugees and also by the work of the Malawian churches. Given the structure of most churches, raising the awareness of the bishops and other church leaders has the potential of contributing to public education of a large number of church members.

Constituency pressures

From the little research available, it appears that NGO actions are determined by several factors: pressure from their constituencies, the

need to secure funds, and the desire to promote their agency's values —
even in the absence of significant constituency pressure and even when
funds are not readily available. There also seems to be a fair amount of
inertia; once a programme has been started, the tendency is to continue to
support the programme, even when the refugee situation has changed and
needs have decreased. This is due in part to familiarity with a particular
situation, to the importance of maintaining relationships, and to the fact
that it is simply easier to continue supporting a programme than to go
through the additional work of stopping an ongoing programme and
starting a new one.

As we have seen, NGOs have different constituencies — constituencies which are often related to sources of agency financial support. Rädda
Barnen, the Swedish Save the Children, has several constituencies: the
children it is trying to assist and the families and communities in which
they live; the Swedish public on whom it depends for financial and moral
support; the Swedish government which provides most of the agency's
funds. The Christian Council of Tanzania similarly has several constituencies whom it seeks to please through its work with refugees: the
refugees themselves, the Tanzanian churches, the Tanzanian government
and UNHCR, the All Africa Conference of Churches and the World
Council of Churches on whom it depends for financial support. Sometimes there are conflicts between the demands from these constituencies.
The churches may be interested in providing charitable assistance to
needy people while the refugees may want a different kind of programme
and funding agencies may be primarily concerned about financial
accountability.

Church-related refugee organizations are most fundamentally responsible to the churches which make up their membership — whether the
Christian Council of Tanzania, the Jesuit Refugee Service, or the World
Council of Churches. Sometimes this pressure is directly expressed as
when a church demands assistance for a particular refugee situation.
Sometimes the lack of constituency pressure or church interest is interpreted as support for the agency's actions. Many church members may be
generally supportive of their churches' refugee programmes, but not have
the time or interest to follow the programmes closely.

Membership-based NGOs, such as Amnesty International or Save the
Children, face a different set of pressures. They need to provide more
information to the constituency to demonstrate the effectiveness of the
agency's actions — and to sustain the support. In comparison with the
churches' constituency, members in secular NGOs tend to be smaller in

number, but perhaps more committed to the substance of refugee work.

All NGOs need funds to carry out their programmes and the pressures of fund-raising are inevitably linked to the type of programmes the NGOs develop. Southern NGOs dependent on contributions from Northern governments, Northern NGOs, Northern churches or UNHCR often tailor their programmes to meet the perceived priorities of the donors. This leads at times to a certain "trendiness" of programming. When Northern donors talk of the need for refugee self-sufficiency, Southern NGOs develop income-generating programmes for refugees. When Northern governments and UNHCR make repatriation a priority, Southern NGOs may develop programmes — or reorient existing programmes — to focus on training for repatriation. This pressure has both negative and positive results. Southern NGOs presumably know the needs of the refugees with whom they work better than distant donors. The fact that they have to develop their programmes to respond to the demands of donors — rather than the demands of refugees — is seen as another manifestation of Northern pressure and paternalism. At the same time, there are cases where Southern NGOs would prefer to continue with programmes which are essentially charity-oriented and assistential in nature. But under pressure from the donors, they move to work in areas which may better meet the needs of the refugees in the long-term. Sometimes the record is mixed. For example, in recent years, there has been increased donor interest in supporting activities which benefit refugee women. In some cases, Southern NGOs resent this pressure and often use cultural arguments to explain why such programmes cannot be carried out. Sometimes in response to this pressure, they develop programmes which are not very effective. And yet because of the pressure from donors, Southern NGOs have not only developed programmes for refugee women but, more importantly, have undergone some conceptual changes in the way they approach the issue. And those staff of Southern NGOs who have tried for years to focus on refugee women may feel supported when pressure is exerted by Northern agencies.

Another consequence of the dependence on funds from Northern NGOs has been the need to devote significant resources to fund-raising — resources which most Southern NGOs would rather put into assistance for refugees. Northern agencies complain about the high administrative expenses of their Southern partners, but the reality is that when representatives of Southern NGOs devote more resources to travel in the North, their requests for financial support are more likely to be successful than when they stay at home and work with refugees. At the World Council of

Churches, for example, partners who are well-known to WCC staff are more likely to receive increased funding than those who are known only through correspondence — or who are unknown.

The pressure to raise funds is similarly a major determinant of Northern NGO decision-making. Fund-raising has become big business. An international NGO needs to demonstrate to its funders that it is doing something important. In times of emergencies, this often means that NGOs need not only to be present in a given situation, but they need to be visible. Media coverage of a particular emergency situation may lead to constituency pressure to "do something" — even when the NGO has little expertise in a particular country or when the implementing structures in the country don't have the capacity to manage a large-scale programme. Thus in the Ethiopian crisis of 1984/85, Northern NGOs and churches were under pressure to transfer funds to the region; some Northern church agencies reported receiving cheques from individuals who wanted to help the famine relief even when those agencies had no programmes in the country. In response to the spontaneous income, programmes were developed and channels identified for transferring the funds. Catholic Relief Services, which did have major programmes in Ethiopia at the time, also came under constituency pressure to do more. Thus, while CRS received 80,000 individual contributions by mail in all of 1983, in the two months following the first media coverage of the Ethiopian famine some 250,000 individual contributions flooded into their office. [19]

The pressure of fund-raising is one reason why NGOs want "their own people" in the country. The visibility that comes from a Northern NGO presence is perceived as important for fund-raising; even when the funds would be more responsibly spent by going directly to a local NGO, the international NGO perceives that it needs the visibility of a Northern NGO presence. Sometimes the international NGO presence is perceived as necessary in order to demonstrate that the money is being responsibly spent. NGOs seek to reassure their constituency that the funds raised for a particular emergency situation are indeed going to those in need; one way of doing that is to demonstrate that "our man on the scene" is overseeing the spending of funds.

The imperative of fund-raising also means that agencies are under pressure to become more "professional". For Southern NGOs, this may mean investing in computers and spending hours on funding proposals. For Northern NGOs, it may mean hiring professional "fund-raisers" who have the expertise to develop and implement large-scale funding campaigns. The techniques of fund-raising vary greatly. In the United States, direct-mail solicitation and television appeals are major techniques for large NGOs — but these are expensive strategies. Not only do they take a lot of money away from programming, but they also create a dynamic for certain kinds of programming — for programmes which can be demonstrated on television, for high media-impact stories, for programmes related to media coverage of emergency situations. The amount of money raised, for example, to support assistance to Iraqi Kurds in the aftermath of the Gulf war was substantial. While the needs of the Kurds were desperately real, there was an imbalance in the funds made available to such a high-visibility emergency and those made available in countries, such as Liberia, where media coverage has been minimal.

It is generally easier to raise funds for famine relief or refugee emergencies than for development and long-term programming. There are cases where NGOs raise more money for such emergency situations than they can responsibly spend. When they try to act responsibly and use these funds for longer-term rehabilitation or reconstruction, they may be criticized for misuse of funds. Thus in the mid-1980s, Catholic Relief Services (CRS) collected large amounts of money for famine relief in Ethiopia, but used these funds in support of its ongoing programmes. One critic wrote that while CRS collected between US$50 and $67 million for famine relief in Ethiopia, by November 1987, only $17 million had been spent — of which $7-8 million was for regular CRS programmes. [20]

The need to raise funds among the general public can also lead an agency to de-emphasize politics and to avoid the risks that come from identifying with a particular political cause (especially when such a cause is politically unpopular). As Lissner says, ambiguous positions increase the number of potential contributors and political neutrality can be a device to increase the number of NGO supporters. [21] In the United States, the National Council of Churches is still feeling the consequences of media exposés that funds raised for humanitarian purposes were being channelled to African liberation movements. Although the NCCCUSA and Church World Service, in particular, tried to explain the significance of the grants (through the WCC's Programme to Combat Racism), the damage done by the perception that the organization was taking a political stand was substantial.

Constituency pressure and the fund-raising imperative play a major role in shaping both church and secular NGO priorities for action. NGO priorities are also shaped by governmental pressure, particularly in those cases where governmental funding is needed. Lissner notes that NGOs often feel an "inferiority complex" vis-a-vis governmental organizations.

They have less staff, time and resources than governmental aid agencies; sometimes, he reports, they try to adopt a government style and a professional image. He notes that churches in particular are susceptible to this inferiority complex, perhaps because of the missionary tradition. Often they try to disassociate themselves from concepts of evangelism in order to increase their access and credibility with governments. [22] In looking at refugee resettlement agencies, Lanphier finds that in order to fulfill their function as buffer between governments and refugees, "of necessity... larger NGOs will resemble in organizational infrastructure the very governmental organization which they buffer!" [23]

Another determinant of NGO priorities and decisions is their past record. In particular, NGOs tend to see operations in terms of what they are good at doing and this specialization creates conflicts. "An NGO that specializes in a particular form of assistance has a vested interest in promoting that expertise." [24] Similarly, NGOs that have always worked in a certain manner are likely to continue to work in that way unless challenged by outside forces. Thus Smith studied US and Canadian NGOs and found that while all NGOs talk about long-term development as opposed to immediate suffering, there are very different methods of implementation and a continuing reliance on traditional assistential mechanisms. Two-thirds of US NGO assistance is still largely relief and it is far from clear that such actions are contributing to system transformation. "PVOs [private voluntary organizations] may very well be surrogates for, or complements to, these other larger institutions in a region, but not necessarily innovators of new and replicable techniques nor even precursors for them to do more." [25]

The fact that NGOs have limited resources and staff means that they are often unable to "process" the information which arrives in their offices. Sometimes there is so much information about so many different situations that the NGO response is simply to continue with business as usual. Staff are over-burdened with information; to figure out what to do in Sri Lanka or Guatemala, even when the available information indicates that something needs to be done, is simply overwhelming. It is easier to concentrate on administering existing programmes than on sorting through the new information to determine new projects. And it is easier to administer an existing programme than to engage in a full-scale evaluation of what has been done.

Within NGOs, as within governments and UN bureaucracies, factions and personal/political conflicts emerge as determinants of refugee policies. Conflicts between field staff and headquarters, or between partner agencies and the umbrella co-ordinating body are often tense — and shaped not by differences of opinion on substantive issues, but by the personalities and power struggles involved. An ambitious junior official may seek to use a particular refugee programme as a way of advancing his or her career. Thus the programme is built up, resources are committed, and publicity is generated not primarily because of the needs of the refugees, but because of the political interests of the individual. Regional factions within NGOs (as well as among NGOs) may create a peculiar dynamic where, for example, Latin American staff are lobbying within their organization for increased funding of programmes in Latin America — in competition with their African colleagues. Similar dynamics are apparent in Southern NGOs as well, where for example a Christian council may seek an increase in funding for refugee programmes as a way of building up the council as a whole. And there are cases where funds made available to refugee departments of Christian councils are used to support the councils' other programmes and infrastructure.

NGOs are often perceived by both refugees and wider society as possible change agents. But the demands on NGOs leave little time for dealing with broader issues or the causes of refugee flows. Moreover, there is a strain between advocating collective change in society and trying to get specific benefits for a particular group of refugees. [26]

Responding to emergencies

NGOs often become involved in a particular refugee situation when an emergency develops. International NGOs with development programmes in a given country may learn of the developing emergency from their field staff or from partner agencies working in the area. In fact, NGO personnel are often the first to warn of impending refugee emergencies. Or they may be pressed to act by their constituencies or by governments seeking a channel for distribution of assistance. The relief of human suffering through relief assistance is the primary mission of most NGOs and their perhaps instinctive reaction to news of a disaster or refugee emergency is to consider how they can respond. For churches and NGOs in the countries affected by a disaster, the initiative to respond may come from the human desire to help hungry or homeless people. They may collect food or blankets or bring refugees into their homes. Often, as the emergency continues, they appeal to Northern donors for assistance.

Some observers of the system of disaster response are more cynical in their interpretation of NGO motivation. Kent's classic work on disaster relief maintains that the emphasis on disaster relief is a direct result of international NGOs' need for funds. NGOs see the drama of disasters as a way of generating funds — funds which can also be used for development work. While NGOs serve as convenient channels for public sympathy, in fact they share most of the assumptions of governments. Kent finds that often they have little experience in countries; even when they have been involved in development work in the country, these skills and experiences are often not relevant in the creation of an effective response to the disaster.[27] Cuny sees a major problem in the fact that "many of the international agencies are very amateurish". They don't do research and many don't learn from previous experiences by conducting in-depth evaluations. Only a few have participated in international training programmes or have developed disaster preparedness approaches. This leads to duplication and overlapping in relief operations.[28]

The problems in co-ordination of NGO activity increase in disaster situations when new NGOs enter the scene and when there is little incentive for co-ordination. The greater the number of outside agencies converging on a scene, the greater will be the interorganizational conflict. In 1989 as the number of Romanian refugees arriving in Hungary increased, numerous churches throughout Western Europe began collecting and transporting used clothing and food to Hungary. These actions sprang from the desire of many individual Christians and parishes to do *something* to respond to the emergency; however, their lack of co-ordination, particularly with the Hungarian churches, created problems in the field. Sometimes the clothing wasn't appropriate or needed and all of it had to be sorted and stored by Hungarian volunteers. In light of growing media attention to the Ethiopian famine in 1984-85, new Northern NGOs were created to raise funds and to provide assistance in the region. But many of them lacked experience in the logistics of moving relief items to the Horn of Africa and horror stories abound of vehicles or medicines sitting for months waiting for customs clearance.

Some of these new groups may be "filling gaps" in the existing international system of relief. Some may develop expertise and emerge as major new NGOs. Some come into being around a particular disaster and then, when the funds dry up (as they inevitably do), the NGO also fades away. The lack of co-ordination among NGOs in emergency situations is legendary. The most successful examples of co-ordination appear to be in situations where the UN takes the upper hand in "forcing co-ordination" — force which is backed by control of funds. NGOs are often criticized for being in such haste to respond to a given emergency — and to spend funds raised for that purpose — that they don't plan effectively. On the

NGO response to the 1984-86 Ethiopian famine, Clay says that NGOs did not carry out research into the causes of the famine before implementing their programmes. Such research needn't be expensive or time-consuming, he argues, but is vital if NGOs are to develop programmes which meet the needs of affected people — and don't make the situation worse. Because of their lack of understanding of the causes of the Ethiopian famine and the political sensitivities of working within the constraints of an authoritarian regime, the agencies were manipulated by the government. He concludes that "during the Ethiopian famine of the 1984-86 period, Western humanitarian agencies collaborated with the government, both actively and passively, in programmes that both intensified the famine and extended it to new areas". [29]

The Ethiopian case was a particularly difficult one for NGOs because of the political controversies surrounding the government's resettlement scheme. In a widely publicized move, Médecins sans Frontières withdrew from Ethiopia in protest over the government's policy of forcibly resettling people — a policy which contributed to death, trauma and hundreds of thousands of separated families. But most other NGOs continued to work in the country — even while recognizing that their work provided some legitimacy to the government — because they considered the positive results of their programmes to outweigh the negative consequences of leaving. Larry Pezzulo, head of the large Catholic Relief Services, defends a CRS decision to continue to work in Ethiopia, though it deplored the government's limited resettlement policy, because their feeding programme, which was providing food to 2 million people, was alleviating suffering. [30]

These political conflicts are present in both emergency and long-term refugee situations. Thus on the Thai-Cambodian border, NGOs continued to provide assistance to Khmer refugees — even though the camps were controlled by military factions and some of the relief assistance was supporting military forces. Although espousing policies of humanitarian, non-partisan assistance, in fact all assistance can be and often is politicized. Sometimes NGOs are unaware of the political implications of their work; more often they are aware of the implications, but hesitate to confront them openly or to address them publicly for fear of harming ongoing programmes. Perhaps most NGOs working with refugees see themselves as motivated by humanitarian ideals — to respond to human need regardless of political considerations. But increasingly, NGOs are recognizing the importance of considering and addressing political issues.

The move from charity to politics

The dominant characteristic of NGOs working with refugees today is their movement towards a more political stance — from charity to politics. This move isn't a uniform one. Some NGOs are going very slowly in this direction, others more quickly. Sometimes this move towards more active political engagement on behalf of refugees is resisted by an NGO's members; while the constituency may support provision of relief to refugees, they may be less enthusiastic about the NGO's lobbying efforts to address the causes of the violence. [31]

Nonetheless, NGOs and churches are playing increasingly political roles in their work with refugees. One reason for this trend was the growing awareness of human-rights violations in the late 1970s and the subsequent development of broad-scale effective human-rights networks which challenged the refugee-serving agencies to become more involved with larger political issues, particularly questions concerning the root causes of refugee flows. Initially agencies resisted getting involved in questions of root causes; given UNHCR's reluctance to deal with these issues and their own self-perceptions as non-partisan agencies, consideration of root causes did not come easily to voluntary agencies. But as human-rights groups became more active in publicizing the horrible violations of human rights going on and as it became politically acceptable in Western countries to talk about human-rights abuses occurring in third-world countries (while often ignoring their own human-rights situations), refugee-serving agencies began to draw the connections with their own work.

Often an agency's involvement with refugees and other victims of wars will lead it to adopt more politicized positions. Frank Judd, then director of Oxfam, explained the emergence of Oxfam's political role, with particular reference to Nicaragua: "In our over-riding concern to relieve poverty we must look beyond the symptoms to the underlying causes and inform public and political debate about them. We have tried to encourage political power-brokers to listen." [32]

Within the churches, over the last two decades, the humanitarian/political dichotomy has begun to break down. Progressive elements within the churches began to talk about solidarity with the poor, the need for just and participatory societies and the preferential option for the poor. It soon became clear that if churches were to be on the side of the poor and the marginalized, they would come into conflict with the powers supporting the status quo. A Lutheran World Federation consultation concluded that the notion of charity is rooted in a vision of society as stable and hierarchical. Aid policy which concentrates only on the relief of suffering reflects this right-wing view and supports the status quo. [33] Structural change is needed to address the causes which uproot people — wars and societal violence, economic disparities and environmental degradation.

The emphasis on the need for structural change also meant a change in the methods and orientations of the refugee-serving church agencies — from assistance to advocacy, from a goal of working *for* to working *with* refugees.

These trends have combined to produce pressure on churches and church-related agencies to adopt more openly political strategies in their service to refugees. [34] Yet the transition from non-partisan to politically active roles is one fraught with difficulty for the churches and related agencies. Perhaps most fundamentally, the transition is impeded by the self-perceptions of Christians and agency personnel. The consequences of overt political involvement by churches can be at best unsettling and at worst personally dangerous.

The political culture of the country determines in large part the extent to which politicization of churches is viewed as acceptable. Thus while there is a long tradition in the United States of churches openly challenging civil authority, in most European countries, such behaviour is not politically or socially acceptable. In fact, the legal status of church-related agencies may be jeopardized by overt political activity.

Political involvement is particularly difficult in some third-world countries where refugee agencies are already viewed with suspicion by their governments. The more repressive the government — and thus the higher the costs of political involvement — the less local agencies will be able to tackle political issues without putting their lives at risk. This reality makes it imperative that such local agencies work in conjunction with churches and agencies outside the country which may enjoy greater protection from the consequences of their political involvement.

Church-related agencies in the North have found it easier to become politically active and many — though not the majority — have begun to draw the connections between the needs of the refugees they serve and the role of their own governments in contributing to the violence which forces refugees to flee their homes. Some NGOs recognize the importance of development education or awareness-raising in their home countries, but the process is uneven. Smith studied 22 NGOs in Canada and the US and found that since 1968 Canadian NGOs have been much more committed to public education on global issues, spending from 2 to 20 percent of their budgets on information activities at home. US NGOs were found to be much less likely to devote resources to public education campaigns.[35]

The type of political involvement by NGOs takes many forms. Most commonly perhaps, church-related agencies engage in advocacy work vis-a-vis their own governments for better treatment of refugees and asylum-seekers. The Canadian churches have taken the lead in pressing their government to adopt refugee determination policies which guarantee the rights of asylum-seekers. Japanese churches protested their government's deportation of a Chinese asylum-seeker who had hijacked an airplane to come to Japan. Tanzanian churches have worked with their government and UNHCR to try to find solutions for Burundian refugees imprisoned for their political activities. Ecumenical groups in Mexico have not only publicized abuses of asylum-seekers by government officials but played a role in bringing about a change in the government's asylum policies. In Central America, the churches' support for refugee organizations and for their demands was a politically controversial move, particularly during the repatriations of the late 1980s. In Namibia and South Africa, the Christian councils not only developed programmes to receive returning refugees, but lobbied with the government to establish the political conditions of their return. There are many cases where NGOs, churches and related groups are undertaking political advocacy to change governmental policies towards asylum-seekers and refugees and the evidence is that such policies are increasing.

Fifteen years ago, Lissner concluded that NGOs are most likely to resort to pressure activities when their own financial interests are threatened, less likely on third-world issues with no direct bearing on their own activities and least likely to speak out on issues that touch on the political and economic self-interest of the high-income countries.[36] While that pattern may still hold, the evidence is that churches and NGOs in Northern countries are becoming much more involved with advocacy efforts vis-a-vis their own governments on the treatment of refugees and asylum-seekers.

To a lesser extent, NGOs and churches advocate specific issues within UNHCR and express solidarity with other like-minded NGOs, particularly those working in third-world countries. Perhaps most significantly, they are beginning to co-ordinate their political efforts with other agencies, both religiously-based and secular, on national, regional and international levels.

While recognizing the importance of increasing such co-operation, in fact it has been difficult to achieve. Even among church-related agencies which have more in common with each other than do secular agencies, there are differences in orientation and in priorities. Different constituency pressures make it difficult to co-ordinate political strategies, particularly in the absence of many successful models of inter-agency collaboration.

For local organizations working in the South, suspicion and sometimes competition with each other for UNHCR contracts or funds from outside donors limit co-operation. The realities of aid flows from North to South may mean that local agencies are more tied to their particular donor than to other local agencies which are also dependent on other foreign donors. Different political philosophies, ethnic conflicts or personal disputes may make local agencies reluctant to co-operate with each other in areas as sensitive as political advocacy.

In looking at NGO co-ordinating bodies in Africa, Asia and Latin America, Stremlau found that the advocacy role of such bodies is limited. While co-ordinating bodies are organizations of NGOs, in fact "few NGOs want to be represented by another organization nor do they want to have another organization impinge on their programmes or activities". [37] This dynamic appears to be true on the international level as well where NGOs often resist efforts for more active joint advocacy when they are perceived as limiting the scope of action for individual agencies. Stremlau goes on to note that "when co-ordinating bodies have been advocates, it has more often been in regard to policies or regulations directly affecting NGOs, such as registration procedures or duty-free privileges, than in regard to more general economic and social policies of government". Moreover, rather than serving as advocates vis-a-vis governments, it is far more common for such co-ordinating bodies to serve as a forum or point of contact for government ministries. Governmental bodies may view such co-ordinating bodies as useful vehicles for keeping track of NGO activities. [38]

The trend towards more active involvement in political issues, and particularly in determining root causes, can be illustrated by a brief look at two of the largest NGO networks involved with refugee assistance: the International Federation of Red Cross and Red Crescent Societies and the World Council of Churches.

The Red Cross movement has been an important actor in the provision of humanitarian assistance to victims of natural disasters and other emergencies for over one hundred years. The International Committee of the Red Cross (ICRC), as we have seen, has played a central and unique role in conflict situations. The International Federation of Red Cross and

Red Cross Societies works with its national member societies in a range of areas, particularly related to emergency relief. In the last decade, the Federation has developed specific programmes to respond to the needs of refugees and other uprooted people. The role of the Federation and of the national societies "is to provide assistance to refugees, asylum-seekers, returnees and displaced persons in accordance with its guidelines". Presently the national Red Cross and Red Crescent societies are active in most countries where refugees and asylum-seekers are present. In recent years, the Federation has sought to increase its training programmes of national society staff by organizing seminars on working with victims of torture and trauma and through workshops on the legal dimensions of refugee policy. [39] Moreover, the Federation — in spite of its humanitarian, non-partisan principles — has moved towards a recognition that governmental political action is necessary in order to address the causes of refugee movements.

When one looks for example at the resolutions passed by the international conferences of the Red Cross and Red Crescent, this evolution is obvious. In its 1981 conference in Manila the resolution on international Red Cross aid to refugees did not mention root causes. In 1986, at its 25th international conference in Geneva, the resolution begins by calling "upon states, in the search for lasting solutions, to address first and foremost the causes of movements of refugees from their countries of origin". In 1991, the council of delegates, meeting in Budapest, included a call to seek actively the support of governments with a view... "to address first and foremost the causes of people fleeing their homes, and to promote peace and respect for human rights and to intensify co-operation in socio-economic development, particularly among low-income countries". The statement continues by calling on governments "to ensure that a decision to deny asylum is taken only within the framework of fair and proper procedures and that the principle of return in safety and dignity of rejected asylum-seekers is reaffirmed and, if assistance is given by national societies, to respect their adherence to the fundamental principles of the movement". The latter statement is particularly important for national societies working on advocacy efforts in Northern countries to ensure that procedures are followed which uphold basic guarantees for asylum-seekers.

The World Council of Churches "in process of formation" was involved in refugee work even before its official formation in 1948. During the second world war, churches in different countries worked together to assist those displaced by the violence, and this co-operation increased in the post-war period. In the first two decades of its work with refugees, WCC developed a large international structure, with dozens of field offices to facilitate the resettlement of refugees. In fact, for a while, there were more staff in the refugee department than in the rest of the Council put together. Over the years, emphasis shifted from WCC-administered resettlement programmes to support for local ecumenical initiatives.

Unlike most other large international NGOs, all of WCC's support for refugees goes through local partner churches, Christian councils and ecumenical groups. Programmes are developed and administered by local churches and ecumenical bodies. The WCC channels funds from church-related agencies to these local initiatives. But support for local church work with refugees is much more than financial. Training opportunities and human-resource development play an important role in international ecumenical support for church-related refugee activities. Increasingly, WCC has worked with ecumenical partners to develop an expanded role in advocacy on behalf of refugees, asylum-seekers and displaced people. In particular, for the past decade, WCC and its partner church bodies have devoted substantial energies to fostering greater co-operation between churches on issues of asylum and protection.

Meeting in Stony Point, New York, in 1981, church representatives began a process of consultation which has grown steadily over the past decade. In May 1986 an ecumenical consultation on asylum and protection held in Zurich brought together one hundred participants from countries of asylum and countries of origin. Participants at the Zurich meeting identified several areas for joint action, including:

1) the establishment of a systematic means of sharing information on root causes of refugee flows, governmental policies towards refugees, and church refugee programmes;
2) the establishment of mechanisms for joint advocacy vis-a-vis UNHCR and governments;
3) the express commitment to work more closely with other NGOs on questions of asylum and protection;
4) the establishment of a mechanism for co-ordinating and disseminating studies of root causes;
5) the creation of an ongoing consultative committee to follow up and implement these recommendations.

Since then the WCC has moved to encourage regional co-ordinating bodies in Africa (where the All Africa Conference of Churches has had a refugee committee since the early 1980s), Latin America, Asia and

Europe. Working with other Christian agencies, particularly Caritas Internationalis, the Lutheran World Federation and the International Catholic Migration Commission, WCC has worked to create the mechanisms to provide co-ordination of growing advocacy efforts in the regions. It is perhaps too early to assess the impact of these changes in policy, but they offer a clear orientation of how the churches are beginning to develop a more sophisticated approach to advocacy issues.

Conclusions

The record of NGO involvement in the international refugee system is a mixed one. As we have seen, in the formative years of the 1920s-1950s, NGOs played an important role in lobbying for the creation of a United Nations agency, while at the same time mobilizing tremendous quantities of material resources to meet the needs of people who were unassisted by the international community. Since then, while NGOs have played important roles in mobilizing aid and needed services to uprooted people and in advocating changes in governmental policies, for the most part they have remained on the sidelines of the refugee *system*. Major decisions about the structure of the system are not made by NGOs, but by governments and UN structures which command far greater financial and human resources than NGOs. Their lack of professionalism, difficulties in co-ordinating their efforts, individual NGO concerns about fundraising and satisfying constituent demands have limited their effectiveness in bringing about structural changes in the *system* of refugee assistance and protection.

And yet there is evidence that some NGO efforts to challenge the system are beginning to have results. It was largely a church initiative which raised the issue of internally displaced people and ensured that it was taken seriously by the United Nations system. NGOs have taken the lead in raising public awareness about injustices in national refugee policies as in the campaign for "temporary safe haven" in the United States.

But the potential exists for NGOs to have a far greater impact on the international system. NGOs and church-related agencies in particular, have access to information collected at the grassroots level which can be used to challenge restrictive government policies in both the industrialized world and the developing countries. The ability to mobilize public opinion to put pressure on governments is an NGO resource which is increasingly being used. The churches have a particular role to play in reconciliation efforts to bring some conflicts to an end. In this respect co-operation over refugee issues may lead to co-operation in resolving the conflicts which produce refugees.

Most of all, NGOs are often seen by the other actors in the system as raising ethical and moral concerns which governments and UN agencies, by virtue of *their* constituencies, are unable to raise. These concerns must be raised if the international system which emerges is to meet the needs of uprooted people.

The rules of the game

As we have seen in these chapters, the rules of the game for responding to uprooted people were established largely as a result of the historical experience of the second world war. A UN convention was established, setting out the definition of those people in need. A UN agency, the UNHCR, was set up to implement the convention and to provide protection and assistance to those deemed needy by the international community. The set of norms and rules of behaviour of the international community towards refugees now includes some thirty regional agreements, hundreds of pieces of national legislation, international conventions and other agreements. This international regime has emerged in response to changing international conditions. The UNHCR was gradually given more authority. The convention and definition itself were applied in accord with national needs, particularly those of the major powers. And by the mid-1980s, the whole international system was in crisis. The carefully-constructed system of international protection established in the aftermath of the destruction caused by the second world war was being undermined — by the very governments which had played the leading role in its creation.

Before looking at that crisis in more detail, we examine the causes of the massive uprooting of people which is presently taking place.

NOTES

[1] Mark Raper, "Research and Teaching in the Service of Refugees", paper prepared for the seminar "Development Strategies on Forced Migration in the Third World" sponsored by the Institute of Social Studies, The Hague, Netherlands, 27-29 August 1990, p.8.

[2] Randolph C. Kent, *Anatomy of Disaster Relief: The International Network in Action*, London, Pinter, 1987, p.35.

[3] *Ibid.*, p.36.

[4] *Ibid.*, p.37.

[5] Louise Holborn, *Refugees, A Problem of Our Time: The Work of the United Nations High Commissioner for Refugees* (2 vols), Metuchen, NJ, Scarecrow Press, 1975, p.524.

[6] Cited by Bruce J. Nichols, *The Uneasy Alliance: Religion, Refugee Work and US Foreign Policy*, New York and Oxford, Oxford University Press, 1988, p.68.

[7] Kent, *op. cit.*, p.46.

[8] Brian Smith, "US and Canadian PVOs as Transnational Development Institutions", in *PVOs as Agents of Development*, ed. Robert F. Gorman, Boulder, CO, Westview Press, 1984, p.115. Smith also notes that in the OECD countries governmental contributions accounted for 33 percent of total revenues of NGOs (p.116).

[9] Landrum R. Bolling with Craig Smith, *Private Foreign Aid, US Philanthropy for Relief and Development*, Boulder, CO, Westview Press, 1982, p.235.

[10] C. Michael Lanphier, "Bureaucratization and Political Commitment: Challenges for NGO Refugee Assistance", in *Refugees in the Age of Total War*, ed. Ann C. Bramwell, London, Unwin Hyman, 1988, p.313.

[11] *Ibid.*, p.314.

[12] Kent, *op. cit.*, p.172.

[13] Lanphier, op cit., p.322.

[14] Robert Gorman, "Private Voluntary Organizations in Refugee Relief", in *Refugees and World Politics*, ed. Elizabeth G. Ferris, New York, Praeger, 1985.

[15] Smith, *op. cit.*, p.149.

[16] Robert C. Wright, "Voluntary Agencies and the Resettlement of Refugees", in *International Migration Review*, vol. 15, no. 1, 1981, p.172.

[17] Brian Smith points out that "... the unevenness of evaluations of PVO [private voluntary organizations] projects does not help to prove PVO claims that they are more effective than governmental agencies in certain areas of development assistance — e.g. innovation and replicability of techniques, extensive involvement of recipients in decision-making, enhancement of the bargaining position of low-income sectors with other institutions in their environment." *Op. cit.*, p.146. He goes on to cite Judith Tendler's study in 1981 of 75 evaluations of PVO projects in the files of the US Agency for International Development. She found that the projects tend to be insular in focus and the evaluations indicate few interviews with recipients or other actors. Tendler's study found that many PVOs aren't doing what they say they are doing — e.g. reaching the poorest groups — and, in fact, they are doing a lot of the same things that governments do. Smith, *op. cit.*, pp.146, 151.

[18] Leon Gordenker, *Refugees in International Politics*, London, Croom Helm, 1987, p.105.

[19] Laurence A. Pezzulo, "Catholic Relief Service in Ethiopia", in *The Moral Nation: Humanitarianism and US Foreign Policy Today*, eds Bruce Nichols and Gil Loescher, Notre Dame, IN, University of Notre Dame Press, 1989, p.218.

[20] James MacGuire, "Scandals in Catholic Relief", in *National Review*, 3 July 1987, pp.26-30.

[21] Jorgen Lissner, *The Politics of Altruism: A Study of the Political Behaviour of Voluntary Development Agencies*, Geneva, Lutheran World Federation, 1977, pp.83-85.

[22] *Ibid.*, pp.107-110.

[23] Lanphier, *op. cit.*, p.315.

[24] Kent, *op. cit.*, p.104.

[25] Smith, *op. cit.*, pp.117,155.

[26] Lanphier, *op. cit.*, p.319.

[27] Kent, *op. cit.*, p.41.

[28] Frederick C. Cuny, "Politics and Famine Relief", in *The Moral Nation: Humanitarianism and US Foreign Policy Today*, *op. cit.*, p.282.

29 Jason Clay, "Ethiopian Famine and the Relief Agencies", in *The Moral Nation: Humanitarianism and US Foreign Policy Today*, *op. cit.*, p.267.

30 Pezzulo, *op. cit.*, p.229.

31 Lissner, *op. cit.*, p.275.

32 Frank Judd, "Why Peace in Nicaragua Is a Catalyst in Conquering Poverty", in *The Independent*, 13 July 1989, p.28.

33 Lutheran World Federation, *The Politics of Church Aid: Report of the LWF Consultation on Church Agencies: Fund-Raising, Education and Advocacy*, held in Aarhus, Denmark, 25-29 April 1977, Geneva, Lutheran World Federation, p.21.

34 See, for example, Elizabeth G. Ferris, "The Churches, Refugees and Politics", in *Refugees and International Relations*, eds Gil Loescher and Laila Monahan, Oxford, Oxford University Press, 1989, esp. p.167.

35 Smith, *op. cit.*, pp.130-133.

36 Lissner, *op. cit.*, p.224.

37 Carolyn Stremlau, "NGO Coordinating Bodies in Africa, Asia and Latin America", in *Development Alternatives: The Challenge for NGOs*, special issue of *World Development*, vol. 15 (supplement), autumn 1987, pp.213-221.

38 *Ibid.*, pp.216-217.

39 League of Red Cross and Red Crescent Societies and the International Committee of the Red Cross, *The Movement and Refugees*, Geneva, 1991.

4. Root Causes
The Interplay between Politics, Economics and Violence

The present international system for dealing with uprooted people is undergoing major changes, but before analyzing current and future trends, it is necessary to consider *why* there are so many uprooted people. Why do people leave their communities? Why do they abandon their families and leave their possessions behind for the difficult and uncertain life of exile? The answers to these questions go to the heart of the present crisis of uprooted people. At one level, they are simple: people leave because they are afraid or unable to survive at home. At another level, the answers are complex. Determining the causes of individual behaviour is always tricky; in the case of the uprooting of people, many causes come into play.

Why do people leave? Individual decisions
On an individual level, people decide to leave their home countries because they perceive that they are in danger and that their lives may be more secure elsewhere. This same dynamic operates for both internally and externally displaced refugees. Individuals leaving their home communities for other, presumably safer, areas of the country are motivated by the same fears and aspirations as those who cross a national border in search of refuge. The search for security and peace is the fundamental driving force behind all refugee migrations — regardless of the ultimate destination of the refugee and in spite of important differences in refugee situations.

Individuals make the decision to leave in different ways and under different conditions. Stein, for example, distinguishes between acute and anticipatory refugees, depending on the amount of time available for making the decision.[1] The degree of alienation from the national system as well as the immediacy of the threat affects individual decisions to leave the country.

How does an individual make that decision? Research on the process of individual decision-making is scanty. One can hypothesize that perceptions of danger come from personal exposure to violence, from personal experiences with the government or with the agents of violence, and from friends and family members who have experienced such violence first-hand as well as from more generalized fears and rumours. Studies of trauma, for example, among Mozambican refugees in Zambia and Central American refugees in the US show that a substantial percentage of refugees had been personally touched by violence, either by witnessing a violent act or by having a relative or friend victimized by violence, or by personally having been targeted by violence or persecution.[2]

People also leave when they perceive that their ethnic identity is threatened and fear that further persecution will be forthcoming. This seems to be the case of those uprooted in the former Soviet Union as well as those emigrating from the Middle East. In both cases, there is a perception that conditions will get worse for people and their families. Interviews with Christians from the Middle East, for example, reveal that a major motivating reason to leave is the declining space for Christians in the face of Islamic resurgence. And of course, the larger the number of Christians who leave, the smaller the Christian presence and the harder the conditions for those who remain.

We know that people are more likely to leave when there is a loosening of repression. When conditions are at their most difficult, it may be impossible to get out of the country. When conditions become somewhat better, people take the opportunity to leave. This has certainly been the case in the migration of Soviet Jews in the last five years. While there are alarming reports of growing anti-Semitism in the (former) Soviet Union and Eastern Europe, at the same time, political conditions are improving and individual persecution is declining. People leave because they are afraid and because they feel that they *can* now get out of the country.

People leaving their country because of economic reasons also make an individual decision to leave because they perceive that their chances for survival are better elsewhere. Sometimes it is a family decision to send one or more members abroad with instructions to send back remittances to ensure the family's survival.

But individual decisions are the product of conditions and developments at the national — and increasingly at the international — level.

Why do people leave? National factors

The root causes of refugee and migration flows are complex interactions of political, economic and social forces shaped by both indigenous conditions and external pressures. Examining root causes is a bit like peeling an onion. For example, people often leave their communities because they are afraid of an escalating war. So war or violence may be seen as the immediate cause. The violence may be made more brutal by foreign intervention or by international supplies of arms. Those are contributory factors to the violence, but usually are not the sole explanatory factor. The question then becomes: Why is there violence in the first place? The answer may involve a range of economic, social and political factors: because there are deep-rooted ethnic conflicts, for example, or unmet nationalist expectations. Political systems are often unable to resolve the inevitable conflicts in complex societies without resort to violence. Some have argued that violence and human-rights violations are a necessary part of the process of state-formation and of political change. The violence may be the result of particular governmental policies, such as resettlement policies, or may be affected by international economic institutions and policies. The sections which follow discuss some of these factors and then attempt to relate them to each other.

Economics and migration

During the nineteenth century, most of the world's major migration flows were initiated by colonial powers and by governments of the then so-called traditional receivers: the US, Canada, Australia, New Zealand, Argentina, Brazil, South Africa and Rhodesia.

> Colonial powers were responsible for an estimated 15 million slaves being transported from Africa for work in the Americas prior to 1850, and during the century following the official end of slavery (i.e. from 1834 to 1937), over 30 million persons were shifted from the Indian sub-continent to work in other colonies in Asia, the Indian Ocean and the Caribbean, although about 24 million ultimately returned home. In Eastern Asia, Chinese populations in Hong Kong, Indonesia, Thailand and Malaysia exceeded 16 million by the end of the second world war. An estimated 50 million Europeans simultaneously emigrated to the traditional receivers between 1846 and 1924.[3]

Historically, people have always sought to move when they were unable to survive because of drought, famine or widespread unemployment. Usually poverty in the countryside leads to rural-urban migration. Desperate economic conditions in the cities may in turn lead to international migration. But situations of extreme economic deprivation (e.g. Burkina Faso, India) have not generated massive cross-border migration. Rather internal migration increases and even when people do leave their countries, the poorest are the last to leave.[4]

Migration has become a key factor in the economies of many regions. The Caribbean islands together send more migrants to the United States than any other place in the world, including Mexico. George cites a senior World Bank economist for Jamaica who said "there is no doubt that emigration is an essential part of any development strategy for that region", and a USAID official referring to the Caribbean who said "none of these islands is viable. The best way to solve their problems is to subsidize their exports and allow the people to emigrate. Other than that, their best shot is tourism."[5]

On a family level, the decision to send a relative abroad may be a sound economic decision. A representative of a Salvadoran NGO explained at a 1988 international meeting that Salvadorans have three options for survival: developing a micro enterprise, getting involved in narcotraffic, or migrating to the US. And foreign remittances represent major transfers of hard currency to poor countries. Central Americans remit more than $2 billion annually from the US; Filipinos send back some $3 billion per year from around the world. The Gulf war produced serious hardships for many countries dependent on the foreign remittances from their nationals working in the Gulf. India, for example, lost more than $2 billion.[6] In addition to the 3 million Asians working in the Middle East at the time of the Gulf war, millions more work in other Asian countries, often illegally. The funds they send home help their families to survive; their governments are dependent on this transfer of hard currency. This labour migration is also useful for the countries where the labour is performed. From the late 1950s until 1974 over 30 million people were given "temporary" status in the European labour force. By the early 1970s, over one-third of the Swiss work force was foreign. Guest workers numbered more than 2.6 million in Germany and 200,000 in Sweden. In 1973, the year before labour immigration policies changed, worker remittances to home countries was between US$4 and 6 billion.[7] Even when European policies changed and the workers were encouraged to return home, many stayed in Europe. And because of policies favouring family reunification, migration continued. Some 150,000 people moved to the United Kingdom between 1985 and 1988 to join family members living there; 235,000 moved to France between 1983 and 1989. And the remittances back home continued. In 1988, Turks in Germany sent home over US$1 billion while Moroccans remitted nearly the same amount to their families.[8]

Migration for economic reasons has thus become big business for many third-world countries. Frequently political and economic factors interact to uproot people. In 1991-92, Haitians fled their country in the aftermath of a military coup. But they also left because they could not survive economically. The economic embargo, which was intended to pressure the government into accepting a democratic regime, caused serious hardships for the bulk of the population. Shortages of food, fuel and consumer products and the closing of many industries meant that many people had no jobs and no way to survive except through migration. The desperate poverty in which so many Haitians live is a product of political decisions; violence and poverty are inter-related. The US government maintained that all the Haitians seeking to enter the US were economic migrants — not refugees — and deported them to Haiti, even after some evidence emerged that those returned faced persecution by the authorities there.

While deteriorating economic conditions may be a consequence of violence and governmental repression, economic underdevelopment by itself is not a major cause of refugee flows.[9] Rather, it seems to be the interaction of economic and political factors which has generated most of the world's refugees. The damages to infrastructure and the environment caused by war make reconstruction costly and may inhibit the return of the refugees. Another economic-political connection is that refugee movements have historically tended to follow existing routes of economic migration. Thus, when the violence in El Salvador escalated in the early 1980s, hundreds of thousands of Salvadorans sought to escape by travelling to the US — the traditional destination of economic migrants. Because of the large Salvadoran communities, cities such as Los Angeles were now more attractive destinations for refugees.

Furthermore, as will be discussed later in this chapter, international economic structures and foreign debt contribute to economic decline and to the political conditions which uproot people.

Wars and violence: immediate causes of flight

Most recent wars have been internal conflicts, not wars between countries. With the exception of the Gulf war, it is almost as if governments have discovered more effective and less costly ways of forcing other governments to do what they want short of going to war with them. As tools of foreign intervention have become more sophisticated, including, for example, economic and social means of control as well as political and military ones, war no longer seems to play a big role as an instrument of "diplomacy". In fact, some have argued that war as an institution for resolving interstate conflicts is becoming obsolete. [10] But even as interstate wars have declined in intensity and scope — again with the exception of the Gulf war — internal conflicts have increased in severity and casualties. At the beginning of 1991, there were 48 wars in the third world, involving 39 countries. Of these 46 were civil wars in which some 5 million people died. About two-thirds of these wars have lasted for over a decade. [11]

But the relationship between wars and refugee flows depends on the type of conflict. As Suhrke states, "some types of conflicts (protracted warfare, international wars, and certain kinds of ethnic tension) seem to produce major outflows; other conflicts (typically elite rivalry, coups d'etat, governmental suppression of critics) tend to produce a trickle of a few, highly politicized individuals". [12] A change in the type of national conflict thus produces a change in the type and number of individuals seeking refuge. In Guatemala, for example, frequent military coups and sporadic silencing of opposition leaders over the past thirty years led to a steady stream of exiles from the region — exiles who were typically well-educated, middle-class, and politically active in Guatemalan political parties and popular organizations. But when governmental policies changed in favour of mass counter-insurgency campaigns conducted in rural areas, so too did the nature of refugee flows. Instead of a few educated political leaders, hundreds of thousands of mostly illiterate indigenous peasants streamed across Guatemala's borders in search of security.

The nature of warfare is also changing as governments turn to more sophisticated counter-insurgency strategies which deliberately target civilian populations as a way of confronting guerrilla forces. Mass bombing, use of terror to intimidate communities into not supporting rebel forces, and forced relocation (see also below) have all become tools in the arsenal of governments seeking to eliminate armed opposition. The decisions to turn to this type of counter-insurgency campaign are not isolated ones; as Klare notes, by the early 1980s, the fostering of low-intensity conflicts was a part of the Reagan administration's policy of waging war by proxy. [13]

It is also important to note the impact of modern weapons and weapon systems as a cause of population displacement. The widespread use of mines, for example, renders vast areas of territory uninhabitable. Mines are targeted at civilian populations. Not only do they force people to flee their homelands, but they also prevent their return. Clearing of mines is expensive and often hindered by a lack of maps, suspicion between contending groups, and inadequate funds. The widespread marketing of weapons and other military goods by arms salesmen (and they are usually men) is a direct cause of the widespread casualties of modern warfare and thus of the forced displacement of people.

These strategies of warfare are, of course, not only used by governments (although primarily so), but also by insurgent forces. Sendero Luminoso in Peru, the Khmer Rouge in Cambodia and Renamo in Mozambique terrorize rural communities as a way of destabilizing governments and pursuing the armed struggle.

Governments are not only becoming more sophisticated in their rural counter-insurgency campaigns, but also in the persecution of opponents. The use of death squads and disappearances, for example, has become a common way of ensuring that there are no popular alternatives to authoritarian governments. In Guatemala, the systematic repression against popular leaders — whether of trade unions or churches or popular movements — ensures that an organized opposition will not challenge the ruling sectors. Sometimes these policies are carried on under a facade of democracy through the use of paramilitary death squads or henchmen to intimidate — or kill — opponents of a regime.

Prolonged civil conflict and the absence of a central government able to assert control create a generalized climate of violence. In Sri Lanka and Angola, Mozambique and Ethiopia, armed groups ravage the country and fight rival armed groups, creating a climate of terror and fear which has led to the displacement of hundreds of thousands of people. In these countries, civil strife has resulted in a breakdown of societal norms and violence has acquired a seemingly random nature. In this respect, the forced recruitment of young people, sometimes *very* young people, into the competing armies or groups is a cause for flight. In Sri Lanka and Mozambique, irregular forces have terrorized young people into joining their ranks. Many have tried to escape to other countries.

Finally, prolonged violence — whether the result of civil war, government counter-insurgency campaigns or invasions — has a high economic cost. Crops are burned, homes destroyed, schools closed and employment opportunities eliminated. Even those personally untouched by the physical violence suffer the economic consequences.

Governmental policies of control

Governments use not only military means to control their populations. Other governmental policies often directly affect the propensity — and the ability — of their populations to flee. Most obviously, governments can control the ease with which their people are able to travel or to permanently emigrate. At one extreme they can prohibit all travel through military control of borders and regulation of passports. At the same time, they can also expel dissenters or simply facilitate their departure as a sort of safety valve to relieve the pressure of opposition.

Governments may force emigration as a means of achieving cultural homogeneity or for asserting the dominance of one ethnic community over another. As Weiner notes, "many third-world countries also expelled their ethnic minorities, especially when the minorities constituted an industrious class of migrant origin in competition with a middle-class ethnic majority",[14] and concludes that "to view refugee flows simply as the unintended consequences of internal upheavals or economic crises is to ignore the eagerness of some governments to reduce or eliminate from within their own borders selected social classes and ethnic groups and to affect the politics and policies of their neighbours".[15]

As Zolberg notes, governments always face a dilemma in deciding whether to expel dissenters or to keep them within the nation. When political repression is high, governments may seek to prevent refugees from leaving the country. Conversely, during times of reduced international tension "the costs of repressing dissidents may outweigh those of allowing them to leave".[16]

Nowhere has this been more evident than in the events over the past two years surrounding the break-up of the Soviet Union and the transformation of Eastern Europe. For example, Brubaker traces the vacillation of the East German government's use of repression and exit policies — and ultimately their impact on domestic political change. "For years," he says, "East German citizens had voiced demands for freer exit, including both travel and emigration rights. In response the government markedly liberalized exit in January 1989." People began to leave. "Hundreds of thousands, perhaps millions more began to think more or less seriously about leaving. The government faced a dilemma: approve emigration requests and allow a slow bleeding of the country, or refuse them and aggravate popular discontent. Thus even before the dramatic events of last fall [1990], the spectre of mass emigration had convinced the more open-minded party leaders that reform was necessary." The opening of the borders, the outpouring of East Germans was the "decisive catalyst for change. If citizens would no longer be compelled to remain, they would have to be induced. Reform was urgently needed in order to avert a hemorrhage.... Finally, the borders were thrown open in a desperate attempt to persuade citizens not to leave. The Wall that was erected in 1961 was breached 28 years later for the same reason: to keep East Germans from fleeing to the West."[17]

At the other extreme are those cases where governments decide to expel people from their countries. Building on resentment and discrimination, Idi Amin in August 1971 announced that Uganda's Asian population would have to leave the country. Officially, 40,000 Asian Indians were expelled from Uganda in three months in 1972; unofficial figures are as high as 80,000. But as Jain notes, the Ugandan Asian population had experienced discrimination for years; however, they did not leave until they were expelled by Amin who accused them of sabotaging the country's economy and encouraging corruption. About 23,000 people, a little over half of the expelled Indian population, had Ugandan citizenship by Ugandan birth or by personal choice. The rest had British passports. [18]

Expulsion of particular ethnic groups may also create major difficulties in relationships between governments. As Weiner notes, "where one state promotes or compels emigration to a state that limits or prohibits entry, the situation is fraught with a high potential for armed conflict". [19] This situation has occurred in the flow of refugees from East Pakistan to north-eastern India, from Vietnam, Cambodia and Laos to Thailand, from Burma to Bangladesh and from Bangladesh to India.

Often a governmental decision to expel a particular group is linked to its process of state-building, a process which also usually includes appeals to nationalism.

Nationalism and state-building

There is a lot of talk these days about the growing forces of nationalism, religious identity and ethnic aspirations. These three inter-related phenomena occur in all regions. As Frankel says, "in fact, most of the nation-states we know today are jerry-rigged contraptions that owe their existence to the twentieth-century collapse of the Ottoman, Hapsburg, British and French empires and derive most of their powers from distinctly nineteenth-century models. More than 90 of the UN General Assembly's 159 member states were born after world war II. Analysts say the problems of virtually every world trouble spot can be traced in part to defects in the nature of those states."[20]

The "defects" referred to by Frankel include the fact that most of today's nation-states are multi-ethnic, multi-national creatures. During the colonial period, colonizing powers often exploited ethnic rivalries as a means of maintaining control. The political institutions which they left behind upon independence were usually unable to deal with the pressures of multiple ethnic demands. Clay cites the example of Rwanda and Burundi where Belgian colonial administrators ruled through the dominant Tutsi group. But just before granting independence in 1959, Belgium switched its political backing from the Tutsi to the numerically dominant Hutu. As the Hutu majority consolidated its power — after years of oppression under the Belgian-backed Tutsi — some 100,000 Tutsi were killed; perhaps 300,000 fled as refugees. In Burundi, the Tutsi minority was able to retain its position of power, in spite of the lack of Belgian support. In 1972, the Tutsi, fearing that the Hutus were planning a revolt similar to that in Rwanda, struck back. Over 200,000 Hutus were killed after an alleged coup attempt and larger numbers fled to neighbouring countries as refugees.[21]

In the post-colonial period, the most typical pattern has been for ruling groups to try to centralize power and to deny the legitimacy of competing ethnic claims to power. The process of state-formation and creation of the modern nation-state often involves discrimination against minority groups for the goal of creating a national identity. When ruling elites seek to strengthen national unity, "they tend to turn on groups whose language, ethnicity, religion, culture, political beliefs or socio-economic status do not fit in".[22] This process took place in Europe over a period of several hundred years; discrimination and repression of ethnic minorities was an essential ingredient in the process of national state-formation. "Since world war II, struggles for political power between various groups within new states, centralization of power within a state by a dominant group, and persecution or discrimination as a result of competition for limited resources have been at the root of refugee flows."[23] National boundaries, often set by colonial rulers, do not often correspond to lines of ethnic population distribution. The suppression of ethnic or nationalist claims is thus the only way to build a nation-state. In Yugoslavia, for example, we have seen the tragic consequences of the creation of such artificial nation-states, with the violence between Serbs, Bosnians and Croats. When these tensions are intensified by foreign intervention, the costs can be very high.

But as Dowty notes: "If the consolidating monarchies of Europe produced refugees in thousands or tens of thousands, flows now are measured in millions. Some of this is due to larger populations, the greater efficiency of modern warfare in uprooting civilians, and the 'pull' effect of refugee assistance programmes that did not exist in the past. But some of it is due to basic social and political conditions."[24]

In a perceptive essay, Halliday challenges the assumption that nationalism is natural and inevitable in this century. Nationalism is based on the idea that there is a latent community "waiting to be discovered". However, he argues that while communities and ethnic groups have existed for thousands of years, nationalism itself is a modern phenomenon associated with the French Revolution. "Nations", he says "are groups of people who, at some point in the nineteenth or twentieth centuries, decided to proclaim themselves as such."[25] A second myth surrounding the nationalism debate is that there is something real that corresponds to a nation — such as history, tradition, language, race. But as Halliday notes, while there are only 170 recognized states in the world, there are 4,000 languages. The assumption that language defines a nation could thus mean the emergence of 4,000 nation-states. Finally, he critiques a third myth of nationalism, that in some way we all belong to a nation. He notes that the claim to belong is also a claim to control. The simplest way to discredit opponents is to call them traitors. Halliday argues that "what constitutes tradition is defined by those in power".[26] Nationalism is thus often used as a tool to silence opposition and to assert control over a group of people.

In asserting the rights of people to independence and cultural identity, nationalism has been a powerful, positive force. As Stålsett says, "a sense of nationalism enables peoples to be secure in their own identities and assures them of belonging. It gives them courage to be themselves so that they may take part alongside others in a rich and diverse world. National identity in and of itself does not provide solutions, but the assurance of knowing where one comes from enables some to live in peace and security in a pluralistic society."[27] At the same time, nationalism has been a force leading to hatred and conflict. "Integral to nationalism is the inability to understand any *other* nationalism, and indeed the lack of any *desire* to understand it."[28] Nationalism can lead to suppression of minority rights, to anti-democratic behaviour and to wars — as we see now in the republics formerly associated with Yugoslavia and the Soviet Union. Moreover, as Halliday reminds us, the dangers of nationalism aren't confined to oppressor states. It was the Kurds who killed many of the

Armenians in the first world war. Lithuanians, Byelorussians and Ukrainians played an important part in the extermination of Jews in the second world war. [29]

Nationalism is undoubtedly a factor in many of the world's wars; given present trends, it is likely to lead to more rather than less violence in the future. Nationalism is often supported by religious values and ethnic and nationalist movements alike have been quick to use religious traditions to support their claims. [30]

Along with the state-building process, it is sometimes argued that conflicts and wars are necessary to bring about political change. Thus Elshtain writes that wars have played essential roles in forging national identity, in shaping political culture, and in developing stable political systems. [31] Zolberg goes even further, saying that efforts to address the root causes of refugee movements are essentially conservative efforts to maintain the status quo as conflicts are necessary to bring about social change. "A revolution, for instance, should not be judged merely by the tragic but historically necessary fact that it produces refugees." [32]

But certainly while wars may bring about political change, there is ample evidence of their negative impact, most obviously on human beings, but also on the development of social structures. And indeed some of the most profound societal changes are brought about by economic and cultural forces — not military ones.

Foreign intervention

Foreign intervention takes many forms. As mentioned above, in many countries, colonialism resulted in the imposition of foreign political structures with little base in the domestic society. These institutions often lack legitimacy — that is, people do not see them as having the right to resolve conflicts. The destruction of indigenous structures for conflict-resolution, coupled with weak national political institutions, has meant that violence has become a common and even accepted means of resolving conflicts. If means do not exist for the peaceful resolution of conflicts — such as those involving competing demands of different ethnic groups — then violence breaks out. The violence appears to be ethnically-based, but is really indicative of the weakness of political institutions for resolving conflicts.

Northern governments intervene in the South to protect their presumed strategic interests and their economic interests. Intervention to protect economic interests is frequently justified in terms of strategic concerns. Thus the US government justified its intervention in Central America on the basis of a "communist threat to peace".

The long tradition of intervention by the US, the USSR, and other former colonial powers was often rooted in security doctrines of the cold war. Troops were sent, economic assistance extended, and political pressure exerted to prevent the other power from increasing its influence in a given region. During the forty-year cold war, many regional conflicts were intensified and prolonged as a result; Angola, Afghanistan, Nicaragua and Somalia are all examples of wars whose long duration can be attributed in large measure to the cold war.

With the end of the cold war, there is hope that some of the long-standing civil conflicts can be resolved. And indeed that seems to be the case in places such as El Salvador and Cambodia where peace processes have been negotiated. At the same time, it may be that the cold war, while intensifying some regional conflicts, also acted as a restraining influence in other cases.

Moreover, there is little prospect that the arms trade will come to an end. Fierce competition among manufacturers and defence industries in the North will probably lead to more aggressive efforts to find new markets in the third-world. "There are also reports that many countries are seeking hi-tech weapons from the USA in the wake of the Gulf war. It remains to be seen if US industry will let this newly emergent market go unexploited, and if US strategic considerations can avoid the temptation to build up political influence in the third world through arms sales."[33] Also, the emergence of significant arms industries in the third world are changing the pattern of international arms trade; countries such as Brazil, China, Egypt, India, Israel, Pakistan, Syria and Taiwan have developed major export-oriented arms industries. "The end of the cold war does not signal any sales restraints for these third-world arms exporters. Quite the contrary, it provides encouragement to those countries to export more."[34] However, the removal of the Soviet Union as a major arms merchant and the increasing economic constraints facing third-world governments may set limits to a major expansion of the arms trade.

The existence of large refugee populations may serve to mobilize international support for the rebels' cause. "Refugee warrior communities" are a major characteristic of today's refugee situations. The Afghan mujahidin in Pakistan, Khmer-controlled camps on the Thai-Cambodian border and the Nicaraguan Contras are all examples of the way in which refugee populations can serve to support fighting rebel groups. Zolberg notes that while such groups have existed throughout the ages, today's situation is different in that there is a highly developed international refugee regime that can sustain a large-scale civilian population in exile for years as well as a dominant ideology of democratic nationalism which makes a civilian refugee population a necessary adjunct for the warriors. Even when the civilians and warriors are physically separated, they remain linked in that refugees constitute both a legitimizing population for the warriors and a recruitment pool.[35]

Thus, the presence of refugees may actually make it more likely that rebel groups will receive international assistance either directly or indirectly through refugee relief.

Connections: relocation, resettlement and land

By looking at the relationships between governmental resettlement policies and the uprooting of people, some of the interconnections between the causal factors of refugee movements can be explored. Resettlement of local populations in other areas is one tool used by governments around the world. The pattern is a common one. A government decides to resettle a particular ethnic group in another region of the country because it needs or wants the land for other purposes. Sometimes it wants the land for economic reasons — such as export agriculture to generate foreign exchange to pay the service on its foreign debt. Sometimes the reason is political — to dissipate a potential or actual separatist movement. Sometimes such a movement is justified by an environmental rationale, such as "overpopulation" in one region while other regions have ample land. And sometimes it is out of a genuine desire to improve the accessibility of services to a dispersed population or to provide protection from a guerrilla insurgency.

Although the reasons vary, the reaction of the people to the idea of being moved or resettled is remarkably similar. They resent the prospect of being separated from their connection to the land — land which for them is much more than a means of livelihood. For most ethnic groups, land is life, culture, religion. To be torn from their land is to be uprooted from a way of life. In many such resettlement schemes, people leave the country rather than accept resettlement in another region. Another frequent consequence is that some of those to be resettled rebel and either form or join armed resistance groups. The activities of guerrilla forces in turn lead the government to adopt harsher policies towards the population, including scorched earth policies, bombing, terror and intimidation — which forces still more of the population to flee the violence in their countries.

In Guatemala, the military began seizing the land of indigenous groups on a large scale in the late 1970s and relocating the people in strategic villages as part of a counter-insurgency plan (and also as a way of increasing the wealth of some military leaders). But the massive relocation led only to massive displacement of communities, increased violence by the government, a more active armed opposition, virtual civil war, human-rights violations on a large scale and millions of displaced people and refugees. As long as the Guatemalan government refuses to address the causes of the violence, return the land to those to whom it belongs, and guarantee their ability to live and work there in peace and justice, there can be no solution to the pain of exile and displacement for millions of uprooted people.

Also in Latin America one can look at the situation in countries as diverse as Haiti, El Salvador and Nicaragua and see the relationship between land and refugees. In Haiti and El Salvador the pressure on land is tremendous; these are densely-populated countries where small farmers have a deep attachment to the land, and efforts by the oligarchies to gain control of the land led to a massive displacement of population. Without their land, without a means of survival, and living in a repressive political situation without recourse to a legal system to regain their land, many millions of Haitians and Salvadorans left their countries. Although the violence took different forms, in both cases the seizure of land and the repression of civil liberties were reinforced by vigilante squads in collaboration with government military forces, provoking terror which also led to the uprooting of communities.

In Nicaragua, the reasons for resettlement were different, but the results were similar to other Latin American examples. The escalating Contra war, coupled with a lack of understanding of the Atlantic Coast culture, led the Nicaraguan government in the early 1980s to embark on a resettlement programme to protect the indigenous population from an increasingly vicious Contra war. Using persuasion at first and then force, indigenous communities were resettled away from their homes in central villages. This action, coupled with a pattern of historic grievances against the Spanish-dominant government, led many of the indigenous to flee into neighbouring countries, and some to join the Contra forces. Only when the government started returning land and rebuilding their homes did the refugees begin to return. While the process of restoring trust will be a long one on the Atlantic Coast, the fact that indigenous communities are being involved in the planning and that the land has not been given to other groups makes reconciliation more likely.

Policies of relocation rarely occur in a vacuum; they are usually accompanied by policies to repress culture. Thus, in Romania, the Ceaucescu government's policy to move Hungarian-speaking populations out of their traditional areas into new villages with "modern" facilities was widely viewed as part of a larger effort to suppress the Hungarian-speaking minorities. The result was a large-scale flow of refugees from Romania into Hungary, the first major "East-East" refugee flow since the immediate post-war period. Perhaps the best-known example of the political effects of such relocation policies is that of Israel's occupation of the West Bank and Gaza, forcing Palestinians into camps and taking active measures to suppress Palestinian culture. Land and culture go hand in hand.

One of the most controversial cases of forced resettlement is Ethiopia where the Mengistu government's scheme to resettle hundreds of thousands of people from the north on more productive agricultural land in the south and west provoked vocal opposition from relief agencies. The fact that those to be resettled were from northern areas with active insurgent movements led to charges that the Ethiopian government's plan was intended primarily to weaken a rebellion which had gone on for almost thirty years. The presence of Western relief agencies and media focused attention on the forcible nature of the resettlement plan as people were rounded up, families separated, and casualties mounted as a result of inadequate logistical arrangements. Less well-known than the resettlement plan was the government's villagization scheme in which some 10 million people, or 25 percent of the country's rural population, were moved into villages where their movements could be monitored and their agricultural production controlled by the government. The villagization scheme, like the relocation plan, displaced millions of Ethiopians and Eritreans both within and outside the country.

Environmental factors are sometimes cited by governments to justify such relocation efforts. In the mid-1980s, for example, the Thai government decided that hill-tribe farmers, who traditionally practise slash-and-burn agriculture, were responsible for destroying the nation's forests. [36] It adopted a policy to resettle ethnically-distinct hill-tribes — Karen, Hmong, Lahu and others — in the lowlands.

In September 1987, government officials conducted a series of dawn raids on 13 hill-tribe villages in Thailand's northernmost province of Chiang Mai. Houses and granaries were torched; livestock were stolen or purchased at fire-sale prices; and villagers were forced, sometimes at knife-point, to hand over their silver ornaments. Unlike the inhabitants of the wildlife sanctuaries, these evicted highlanders were not scheduled for resettlement; instead they were herded on trucks and dumped at the Burmese border — "repatriation".

The impact of resettlement schemes on local populations is also a cause of displacement and refugee movements. The government's plan to resettle hundreds of thousands of Indonesians from Java in more sparsely populated Irian Jaya provoked a strong reaction from Irian Jayans who feared that their culture was threatened with extinction. The transmigration scheme not only involved settling people of a different culture in the region and giving them land, but the introduction of new agricultural technologies which challenged the whole way of life of the indigenous population. The armed opposition group, the OPM (Free Papua Movement), grew in strength and became more active. The government responded with more repression, often directed at the civilian population in an effort to destroy the guerrillas' base of support. In 1984, 10,000 Irian Jayans crossed the border into Papua New Guinea. Since then many have returned in small groups although information on their condition is almost non-existent. About 7,000 remain in Papua New Guinea living in camps (and probably as many live dispersed throughout the country with varying legal status.) Although the trans-migration scheme has apparently slowed down and migrants are being resettled at a slower pace than originally anticipated, the effects on the Irian way of life make it difficult for the refugees to contemplate return.

The use by governments of resettlement as a means of political control and destruction of indigenous culture is evident in many countries from South Africa to the US treatment of Native Americans and Brazil's development plan for the Amazon basin. While not all of these actions lead to refugee flows, they almost invariably uproot populations from their communities.

Proximity to a national border, traditional migration flows, mobility of the population and receptivity of a neighbouring government and population seem to be the main determinants of whether such resettlement schemes will lead to internal displacement or to external refugee flows.

Connections: debt and displacement

As we have seen, economic factors play an important role in both migration and refugee movements. But economic conditions in particular countries are significantly affected by international economic and political structures.

The present international system is based on patterns of trade established during the colonial era; countries in the South produced raw materials and bought manufactured goods produced in the North. But the terms of trade were determined by the North — the prices for commodities, markets, interest rates — which meant that Southern countries were dependent on the North. And while the prices of manufactured goods steadily increased, the prices of raw materials — food, minerals, oil — were unstable and subject to precipitous decline. If all countries in the South increased their exports of these goods, the prices would inevitably fall.

In an effort to break out of this dependency and this reliance on primary products, most Southern governments have sought to change through "development" — through building up their own industries. But this means they need heavy infusion of capital. The development model they have chosen is not sustainable, particularly when interest rates are high. Increasing numbers of countries which saw industrial development as a potential saviour now find that it means greater debt. By the mid-1980s, the foreign debts of Southern countries had mushroomed and acquired a momentum of their own. In spite of total debt service of more than $1.3 trillion from 1982-1990, the debtor countries as a group began the 1990s fully 61 percent more in debt than they were in 1982.[37] Typically governments borrowed against future export earnings; today many governments face a situation where over half of their country's export earnings must go to pay the servicing of the debt — the interest and fees — while the principal, the original amount borrowed, remains untouched. So the governments borrow more money to pay the interest on the debt — and try to implement the conditions imposed by the lenders. But the conditions are not neutral technical or administrative ones. Typically, the International Monetary Fund requires the imposition of structural adjustment policies which include devaluation of the national currency (making imports more expensive), reduction of public-sector spending, stimulus to exports, easing of restrictions against foreign investment. Cutting public spending means cutting back jobs and services — services usually intended to help the poorer sectors of society. Reducing or eliminating subsidies on food or transport similarly affects the poor much more than the rich. Devaluing currency leads to a spiral of inflation.

As Davison L. Budhoo, who resigned in 1989 as an economist with the IMF, said in an open 150-page resignation letter, the IMF never suggests cuts to defence, police or public-control measures. Austerity packages affect the poorest first and amount to economic suicide for the governments concerned. Hopes of joining what Budhoo dubs the new nobility are enough to gain the compliance of third-world officials who might otherwise oppose the introduction of Fund programmes. [38]

An estimated 10 percent of third-world debt has been spent on arms. Smith reports that of the 41 states involved in wars in 1990-91, data on debt are available for 38. Of these 25 — about two-thirds of the total — have heavy debt burdens. Of the 27 states involved in war for more than a decade, data on debt are available for 24 — of which 18, or three-fourths, have heavy debt burdens. War has been a major cause of heavy debt in twelve countries — El Salvador, Ethiopia, Guatemala, Israel, Mozambique, Morocco, Myanmar, Nicaragua, Somalia, Sri Lanka, Sudan and Uganda. [39] Between 1981 and 1985 Ethiopia spent at least $2 billion on arms and now has a total debt of $2.5 billion, its people have a life expectancy of just 43 years, and only 6 percent of them have access to clean water.

As third-world governments use scarce foreign currency and take on still larger loans to buy arms and spare parts, they are enabled to conduct wars and repression of their populations at the same time that they mortgage the labour of future generations to pay the costs of the wars.

These economic factors clearly have an impact on migration. Most obvious, the burgeoning debt in many countries makes it more difficult for people to survive. With inflation driving up the price of food at the same time that unemployment rates increase and government programmes to help those most in need are cut, more and more people have no option but to leave their communities of origin in search of work and food. Cities throughout the world are growing as people abandon their farms and look for jobs in cities. Meanwhile the farms are being absorbed by agribusiness producing for export which further drives up the price of food available locally. Rural-urban migration is one consequence of the debt crisis — and the phrase covers up a litany of pain and suffering as communities abandon their cultures for the often unrealized hope of survival in the cities. And migration — motivated by the same desire for survival — also occurs between countries. As Manuel Montes testified at the Ecumenical Hearing on the International Monetary System and the Churches' Responsibility in Berlin in 1988: "We've started exporting people. Now there are Filipinos working in illegal jobs everywhere." Migration from the Pacific islands to New Zealand and Australia is decimating whole communities and leading to an irreversible change in the region's cultural traditions.

Migrants who come illegally are particularly vulnerable to economic and social exploitation.

While the relationship between migration and the debt is relatively clear, its effect on refugee movements is more indirect. As governments are forced to implement unpopular policies to meet the conditions imposed by international institutions — to continue to receive funds to pay the interest on the debt — they often implement more repressive measures against their populations. For example, when they must cut government spending by firing public employees, strong public sector unions must be suppressed. As Zambian economist Cosmas Musumali testified at the Berlin hearings: "You cannot freeze wages or cut social expenditures if you have an active trade union movement." Political opposition to the government's policies must also be suppressed for maintaining the necessary control to be able to implement the unpopular measures. Spending on police and military forces, as mentioned above, often increases as a way of maintaining "public order" in the face of public opposition to governmental policies mandated by international economic institutions as conditions for meeting the obligations of the debt. Democratic institutions and popular participation in the political process are made much more difficult, perhaps impossible, by the harsh realities of governmental efforts to acquiesce to the demands of the foreign lenders.

Moreover, there is a process under way in most third-world countries in which an elite within the country benefits from the country's participation in the international economic system and comes to believe that the interests of the country are best served by continued participation — in spite of the obvious social and political cost. This elite, known by different names such as "comprador" class or modernizing elite, identifies more closely with the interests of international capital than with their fellow compatriots and takes the responsibility for implementing politically unpopular measures.

In fact, the debt crisis usually provokes involuntary migration for both political and economic reasons. People leave the country in search of work and food and because of the lack of political freedoms. In today's world, the reasons for which people seek security through flight are usually a mixture of economic and political factors. The "grey area" between economic and political migrants is increasing.

This trend is perhaps most striking when the effects of natural disasters — floods, drought, famine — are intensified because of governmental policies. In fact, the massive movements of refugees today —

Mozambique, Somalia, Sudan — are produced by a combination of brutal war, adverse climatic conditions, and government policies. Environmental degradation is becoming an increasingly significant reason for migration and one which will undoubtedly become more so in the future. About 20 percent of the 43 million people in north-eastern Brazil have left the region, with substantial numbers of other people relocating within the north-east due to drought and soil depletion.[40] Environmental degradation in turn is often exacerbated by a country's foreign debt and the subsequent need to increase export earnings.

At the same time that the debt contributes to an outpouring of people, some governments, particularly in the third world, find themselves with far fewer resources to respond to the needs of refugees and migrants who seek security within their borders. The debt crisis means that public spending declines and resources are simply not available to provide the necessary assistance to refugee populations. Nor is the economy able to absorb large numbers of people in need of jobs. This is most evident in the third world where governments depend on international institutions such as UNHCR to provide the necessary assistance to refugees. But the economic pressures are also manifest in the North where growing unemployment, the political effects of "free-market" economies, and reductions in government expenditures result in more poverty, unemployment and lack of opportunities for those at the bottom of society. In most Western countries, the gap between rich and poor is widening and the incidence of absolute poverty is increasing. Not surprisingly, resistance to large numbers of migrants and refugees is exploited by politicians seeking an easy answer, a scapegoat, to the economic and political problems of their society. Lack of understanding about the causes for which so many come to Northern countries is contributing to the resurgence of racism and xenophobia in countries which have long prided themselves on their liberal democratic traditions.

And to make things still more complicated...

We have considered some of the factors pushing people from their homes — the nature of wars, the policies of governments, the global economic structures — but there are also certain "pull" factors that may attract additional refugees. For example, Suhrke considers those refugees who come in response to the international assistance available as quasi refugees and includes Cubans and Indochinese emigrating in 1980 in this category.[41] She hypothesizes that quasi refugees are likely to appear when a "generous refugee programme is politicized and when refugee routes overlap with increasingly restricted migration routes". Thus quasi refugees are attracted to host countries by assistance and/or resettlement programmes, and are not being forcibly expelled by the governments in their countries of origin. Awareness of the "pull" factors affects national policy in the host country. For example, Thailand's decision to implement a policy of "humane deterrence" was predicated on the premise that making resettlement unattractive and unavailable would reduce the number of refugees.

However, distinctions between refugees and quasi refugees and between the relative impact of push versus pull factors are very difficult to distinguish in practice. In Cuba, for example, an individual refugee deciding to leave the country in 1980 was immediately a target for popular antagonism and political restrictions. The very act of leaving — although not initially triggered by a particular government act of repression — meant that henceforth the individual would be singled out for political persecution.

Addressing root causes: NGOs and churches

There has been growing awareness among the churches and NGOs regarding the vital need to address the root causes which produce refugees and displaced people. In 1984 the All Africa Conference of Churches and the World Council of Churches drew up a statement on root causes for the ICARA conference.

> The tendency that most of us are guilty of is to treat merely the symptoms of refugee movements rather than deal with their root causes... These are refugees from fear, persecution, intolerance, poverty, racial and ethnic hatreds, wars, and civil strife — all reasons whose origins may have complex historical roots but which nevertheless continue to manifest themselves in the countries of independent Africa. It is certainly not our intention to minimize the blame that must be shared by the white minority regimes in southern Africa, or by the legacies left by former colonial rulers, or by the inequities that prevail under post-colonial arrangements, or by the interventions in Africa by rival great powers. But we do insist that any candid and honest examination of the refugee crisis in Africa today leads to the sad but true conclusion that it is the independent African countries which produce and receive by far the greatest number of refugees. Why is this? Why have so many of the high hopes we associated with independence been dimmed? Why is our continent marred by the presence of 5 million refugees?[42]

For churches and NGOs, it is, of course, easier to recognize the need to address the causes than to take the concrete actions which prevent wars and violence. As the AACC/WCC statement implies, addressing root causes often means confronting the complicity of one's own society in the violence. It is suggested here that three steps are necessary for beginning to take action to confront the causes which uproot people. In each of these steps, it is important to involve both local Christian groups and international ecumenical networks. The *local* churches and NGOs have the principal responsibility to identify and address the root causes, but international support can play an essential role in supporting their efforts.

As a first step, *the root causes must be identified*. While there are some general root causes — economic injustice, ethnic conflicts, militarism — national and regional situations differ. We must be careful not to over-simplify the causes of a conflict and not to underestimate the importance of cultural beliefs and loyalties. If we are going to be successful in addressing the root causes of refugee situations, we need to think about potential *future* conflicts as well as about ongoing ones. For example, in the (former) Soviet Union, it is clear that the pressures for social conflict, for violence, and for economic suffering are enormous. We know that the kind of violence which could occur would uproot people and perhaps create massive population displacement. But in order to act in that situation, we have to understand the forces which are operating. To do so, we need the assessment of people in the region; outsiders cannot fully understand the depth or the complexity of such situations. We also see that pressures are building in the Philippines and Peru (to name only two of many examples). In both countries, poverty and disillusionment with the political system, coupled with increasing violence, are rising dramatically. The two situations are very different and steps to address the causes that uproot people must recognize the particular national factors in each case.

Once there is a general understanding of the causes of a conflict — or potential conflict — *specific actions need to be formulated* which will respond to these causes. Again, there are both general steps which can be taken — for example, working to reduce the burden of international debt on countries of the South — and actions in specific cases (e.g. supporting sanctions in South Africa or monitoring elections). Both national and international organizations need to think more creatively about the steps which can be taken to address the causes and must be willing to take some risks in doing so. For example, in a situation where reports of violence between ethnic or religious groups are increasing, we need to think of concrete steps which can be taken to reduce the tension and the violence. In some situations local churches and ecumenical groups have stepped up their efforts to raise awareness about what's happening, to provide forums for dialogue among differing groups, and for church leaders to meet with their counterparts to discuss ways of defusing tensions. There are many steps which could be taken in these situations (and indeed there are many such initiatives under way). But too often, it is easier to mobilize international concern and funds to meet the needs of the victims of violence than to take smaller steps which might have a chance of preventing the violence from occurring in the first place.

It is also true that NGO structures may prevent these steps from taking place. For example, there are many specialized agencies which work with refugees and emergency assistance while there are many other organizations, or departments for development, human rights, international affairs, environment, etc. It is often the case that while a refugee or emergencies department can support refugee programmes in a given situation, responsibility for addressing the human-rights situation or monitoring peace negotiations rests in other departments of the organization. If we are serious about addressing the root causes of refugees and displaced people, organizational change and networking are needed. Refugee groups need to work with human-rights and development groups, with peace and environmental organizations, in order to develop common strategies for addressing root causes. But while many people working in refugee-related NGOs recognize the need for such relationships, the demands of meeting the human needs of refugees make it difficult to take those steps. When there are a dozen asylum-seekers at the door, or when reports of malnutrition among refugees are pouring in, it is hard to find time to think about situations which have not yet become crises. But if churches and NGOs are to be effective in addressing root causes, then priorities must be re-examined and steps taken to find the time to work on the causes of uprooting.

Finally, we need to recognize that peace is not achieved merely by signing a ceasefire agreement; *peace is a process which must be sustained and nurtured.* Too often in the media — and in the ecumenical movement — there is a great deal of interest in a particular crisis until a peace agreement is signed or until elections are held. Once it appears that the crisis is over, attention shifts to other parts of the world. But peace is often very fragile and needs both national and international support. Addressing root causes includes not only a commitment to bring an end to the conditions which caused refugees to flee their homes, but also to continue to support the forces of peace and justice in a particular situation. This means, for example, to maintain pressure in countries such as Chile and Nicaragua where elections have been held and to continue monitoring and advocacy in Cambodia and El Salvador where peace agreements have been signed. Work in reconstructing war-damaged countries, particularly in mine clearance, is essential if refugees are to be able to return to their communities and countries. Less obvious, perhaps, is the need for rehabilitation of people traumatized by the war to enable them to become productive citizens of a new and peaceful society. This need is particularly acute in the case of former soldiers, both the rebel forces and the military. Securing employment opportunities and housing for demobilized troops is essential for building a sustainable peace. In Ethiopia today, the presence of hundreds of thousands of demobilized and unemployed soldiers constitutes a threat to the peace process. When there are large numbers of people with fighting experience and often access to arms who have no alternative means of survival, violence is likely to continue. A commitment to working for peace and addressing the root causes of displacement must be a *sustained* commitment. In comparison with human-rights and peace groups, such sustained commitment is perhaps easier for those who work with refugees. The security and well-being of returning refugees depend on the maintenance of peace and economic justice. A concern with repatriation also means a commitment to ensuring that the conditions which made the repatriation possible are maintained and sustained.

Addressing the root causes is perhaps the key challenge facing NGO work with refugees and displaced people in the future. Wars and injustice produce unspeakable suffering. While we can do more to assist the victims of such wars, we must devote more energies to preventing the violence which displaces people.

NOTES

[1] Barry N. Stein, "The Refugee Experience: Defining the Parameters of a Field of Study", in *International Migration Review*, vol. 15, 1981, pp.320-330.

[2] See, for example, Margaret McCallin, *The Psychosocial Consequences of Violent Displacement*, Geneva, International Catholic Child Bureau, 1991. Margaret McCallin and Shirley Fozzard, *The Impact of Traumatic Events on the Psychological Well-Being of Mozambican Refugee Women and Children,* Geneva, International Catholic Child Bureau, 1992.

[3] International Organization for Migration (IOM), *Migration and Health*, vol. 2, no. 1, January 1992, p.1.

[4] Aristide R. Zolberg, Astri Suhrke and Sergio Aguayo, *Escape from Violence: Conflict and Refugee Crisis in the Developing World*, Oxford, Oxford University Press, 1989, p.260.

[5] Susan George, *The Debt Boomerang: How Third World Debt Harms Us All*, London, Pluto Press, with the Transnational Institute, 1992, pp.118-119.

[6] Saul Landau and David Pedersen, "Third World Labour and the Cold War", in *Paradigms Lost: the Post Cold War Era*, eds Chester Hartman and Pedro Vilanova, London, Pluto Press, 1992, p.165.

[7] George, *op. cit.*, p.123.

[8] *Ibid.*, p.131.

[9] Zolberg et al., *op. cit.*, p.260.

[10] John Mueller, "The Obsolescence of Major War", in *Bulletin of Peace Proposals*, vol. 21, no. 3, September 1990, pp.321-328.

[11] Dan Smith, "Conflict and War", in *The Debt Boomerang, op. cit.*

[12] Astri Suhrke, "Global Refugee Movements and Strategies of Response", in *US Immigration and Refugee Policy*, ed. Mary M. Kritz, Lexington, MA, Lexington Books, 1983, p.164.

[13] Michael Klare and Peter Kornbluh eds, *Low-Intensity Warfare*, New York, Pantheon Press, 1988, esp. chapters 1-4. See also Michael Klare, *The New Pax Americana: US Interventionism in the Post-Cold War Period*, Uppsala, Life & Peace Institute Research Report, 1992.

[14] Myron Weiner, "Security, Stability and International Migration", mimeo, 1991, pp.7-8.

[15] *Ibid.*, p.12.

[16] Aristide R. Zolberg, "International Migrations in Political Perspective", in *Global Trends in Migration: Theory and Research on International Population Movements*, eds Mary M. Kritz, Charles B. Keely and Silvano M. Tomasi, New York, Centre for Migration Studies, 1981, p.24.

[17] Roger Brubaker, "Frontier Theses: Exit, Voice, and Loyalty in East Germany", in *Migration World*, vol. 18, no. 3/4, 1990, pp.13-14.

[18] Sushil Jain, "Expulsion of Asian Indians from Uganda: Or the Color of African Racism", in *Migration World*, vol. 18, nos 3/4, 1990, pp.27-29.

[19] Weiner, *op. cit.*, p.27.

[20] Glenn Frankel, "Decline of the Nation-State", in *Guardian Weekly*, 2 December 1990.

[21] Jason Clay, "Ethnicity: Powerful Factor in Refugee Flows", in *World Refugee Survey 1984*, Washington, DC, US Committee for Refugees, 1985, p.11.

[22] Alan Dowty, "Emigration and Expulsion in the Third World", in *Third World Quarterly*, vol. 8, no. 1, January 1986, pp.152-153.

[23] Clay, *op. cit.*, p.10.

[24] Dowty, *op. cit.*, p.157.

[25] Fred Halliday, "The Siren of Nationalism", in *Paradigms Lost, op. cit.*, p.37.

[26] *Ibid.*, p.38.

[27] Gunnar Stålsett, "Religion and Nationalism", in *Bulletin of Peace Proposals*, vol. 23, no. 1, pp.8-9.

[28] *Ibid.*, p.5.

[29] Halliday, *op. cit.*, p.39.

[30] Elizabeth Ferris, "On the Use and Misuse of Religious Values in Defense of National and Fundamental Values: A Christian Perspective", paper presented to the International Council of Christians and Jews, Southampton, UK, July 1991.

[31] Jean Bethke Elshtain, *Women and War*, New York, Basic Books, 1987.

[32] Zolberg et. al., *op. cit.*, p.262.

[33] S.D. Muni, "The Post-Cold War Third World: Uncertain Peace and Elusive Development", in *Bulletin of Peace Proposals*, vol. 23, no. 1, 1992, p.95.

[34] *Ibid.*, p.95.

[35] Zolberg et al., *op cit.*, p.277.

[36] For additional information on this case and others cited here, see *Cultural Survival Quarterly*, vol. 12, no. 4, 1988.

[37] George, *op. cit.*, p.xvi.

[38] Cited in *The New Internationalist*, November 1988.

[39] Smith, *op. cit.*, pp.146-151.

[40] Susan Forbes Martin, "The Inhospitable Earth", in *Refugees*, UNHCR, May 1992, p.13.

[41] Suhrke, *op. cit.*, pp.164-165.

[42] Cited by André Jacques, *The Stranger Within Your Gates*, Geneva, WCC, 1985.

5. Crisis in the International System

For the past decade, there has been much talk of the "refugee crisis". In December 1989, *The Economist* called 1989 the "year of the refugee", but since then the situation has only got worse. By the late 1980s, it seemed that on every continent, refugee movements were challenging national structures and international norms. The system was being overwhelmed and could no longer cope. This was a problem not just for international lawyers and national bureaucrats working with immigration issues. It meant that the lives of millions of people were placed in jeopardy.

Refugee numbers

As we have seen, it is difficult to define refugees and different groups use different norms and standards. It is also difficult to count refugees, particularly as political considerations enter into such counting exercises. The number of refugees in a given country may affect the amount of international assistance and may also have political repercussions within the country, depending on the ethnic or national origin of the immigrants. And counting of refugees who are not recognized by the government is fraught with obvious difficulties; it is very hard to count people who are trying to hide from authorities. The US Committee for Refugees (USCR) is generally recognized as having the most reliable statistics. Using United Nations statistics, governmental records and other reports, the USCR came up with the following three tables which provide estimates of three groups of people: those considered to be refugees in need of protection and assistance, those considered to be in "refugee-like situations", and internally displaced people. As USCR recognizes, the figures

themselves are of variable quality and, in some cases, significant variations are reported in different sources. Moreover, there have been
changes since these figures were compiled, with considerable increases,
for example, in the numbers for refugees and displaced persons from
Yugoslavia, Colombia and Iraq. The chapters on particular regional
situations include more detailed analysis of numbers by individual
country.

TABLE 1:   REFUGEES AND ASYLUM-SEEKERS
IN NEED OF PROTECTION AND/OR ASSISTANCE, 31 DECEMBER 1991

	1987	1991
Total Africa	3,574,910	5,340,800
Total East Asia / Pacific	560,260	688,500
Total Europe / North America	69,200	677,700
Total Latin America and Caribbean	290,090	119,600
Total Middle East and South Asia	8,802,000	9,820,950
Grand total	**13,296,460**	**16,647,550**

Source: US Committee for Refugees, *World Refugee Survey*, 1987-1992. Note that in some
cases, sources vary significantly in numbers reported. Figures do not include ethnic
Germans admitted to Germany as immigrants, nor do they include 250,000 ethnic Turks
from Bulgaria admitted to Turkey as immigrants. Except for Turkey, 1991 figures for
Europe and North America represent persons who applied for asylum.

These figures include only those who are recognized as refugees or
asylum-seekers. In addition there are also those individuals considered to
be in "refugee-like situations", that is, those who may fear persecution if
returned to their home countries, but who for some reason fall outside the
legal protection mechanisms of host countries and international agencies.

TABLE 2:   SELECTED POPULATIONS IN REFUGEE-LIKE CIRCUMSTANCES

Palestinians	
Jordan	740,000
Kuwait	180,000
Egypt	100,000
Lebanon	40,000
North America / West Europe	281,000
Central Americans	
USA	200,000
Costa Rica	80,000

Honduras	50,000
Belize	28,000
Guatemala	250,000
Mexico	340,000
El Salvador	20,000
Nicaragua	16,000

Haitians
USA	450,000
Dominican Republic	650,000
Canada	30,000
Bahamas	30,000
Caribbean	30,000
France	23,000

Rwandans in Burundi	187,000
Rwandans in Uganda	120,000
Chadians in Cameroon	35,000
Lebanese in Cyprus	10,000
Lebanese in Syria	100,000
Kashmiris in Pakistan	10,000
Pakistanis in Bangladesh	260,000
Burmese in Thailand	160,000
Ethiopians in Saudi Arabia	160,000
Afghans in Saudi Arabia	30,000
Somalis in Saudi Arabia	1,000
Lesotho in South Africa	4,000

Iranians in Turkey	100,000
Iraqis in Iran	500,000
Yugoslavians in Hungary	45,000
Yugoslavians in Austria	8,000
Albanians in Greece	9,800

Source: US Committee for Refugees, *World Refugee Survey*, 1987-1992.
Note that sources vary significantly in numbers reported.

TABLE 3:   INTERNALLY DISPLACED CIVILIANS, 31 DECEMBER 1991

Asia, Europe and Middle East
Afghanistan	2,000,000
Burma	500,000-1,000,000
Cambodia	140,000

Cyprus	268,000
India	85,000
Iran (1989)	500,000
Iraq	700,000
Lebanon	750,000
Turkey	30,000
Philippines	1,000,000
Sri Lanka	600,000
USSR	900,000
Yugoslavia	557,000

Africa

Angola	827,000
Chad (1989)	225,000
Ethiopia/Eritrea	1,000,000
Liberia	500,000
Mozambique	2,000,000
Somalia	500,000-1,000,000
South Africa	4,100,000
Sudan	4,750,000
Uganda	300,000
Sierra Leone	145,000
Rwanda	100,000

Latin America

Colombia	150,000
El Salvador	150,000-400,000
Guatemala	150,000
Haiti	200,000
Honduras	7,000
Nicaragua	354,000
Panama	10,000
Peru	200,000

Source: US Committee for Refugees, *World Refugee Survey*, 1987-1992. Note that estimates for South Africa include persons forcibly relocated in government resettlement programmes.

Analysis of the figures

These figures reveal a number of interesting trends which, when taken together, provide background for understanding some of the reasons for the breakdown of the present system of refugee protection and assistance.

1. The total number of people considered to be refugees in the world is increasing — in spite of the fact that UNHCR has been emphasizing voluntary repatriation, that conditions in exile are deteriorating, that there have been numerous peace initiatives in the world, and that the cold war is over. In 1989 there were one million more refugees than in 1988. In 1990 there were 2 million more than in 1989. In 1991, the numbers remained about the same.

2. While there have been several substantial new refugee flows in the last two years — notably Liberia, Somalia and former Yugoslavia — the increase in overall numbers is largely due to the fact that these numbers are added on to already large refugee populations. The major refugee flows of the 1979-80 period — Afghans, Indochinese, Ethiopians, Somalis and Sudanese —largely remain in exile.

3. Solutions for refugees are becoming more elusive. While the 1990 repatriation of 40,000 Namibians was a joyous event, return of refugees in other areas is more problematic. Although Soviet troops withdrew from Afghanistan four years ago, the vast majority of the almost 6 million Afghan refugees remain in exile. While there is hope for repatriation of refugees to South Africa and Eritrea, their return could well be matched by increases in numbers of people uprooted elsewhere in the continent.

4. As wars drag on, sometimes for generations and with support by outside powers, solutions become less likely for those displaced by the violence. Refugee camps have become a semi-permanent fixture in many regions and, in some cases, the presence of these refugee populations may complicate peace processes.

5. The total number of people who have been forcibly uprooted but who do not fall into the definition of refugee, e.g., those considered to be in "refugee-like situations" or internally displaced people, is also growing. Their situation is becoming increasingly difficult as governments seek to limit the number of refugees or asylum-seekers assisted.

6. These trends of increasing numbers are apparent in various contexts, but the political and economic implications of each are different. There are growing numbers of refugees going from third-world countries to other third-world countries where they place substantial economic and political burdens on host countries and make development, environmental protection and democratization more difficult.

7. Perhaps most important for the international refugee *system*, there are growing numbers of people moving from South to North and seeking asylum in Northern countries. For example, up to a million Central American refugees have entered the US over the past decade seeking

security from the ongoing political violence in El Salvador and Guatemala. Most live without any legal status whatsoever. In 1975, the Federal Republic of Germany had 9,627 asylum-seekers. By 1985 that number had grown to 110,000 and by 1989 to 350,000 (most of them Central Europeans.) Many European governments have experienced a 300 or 400 percent increase in the number of asylum-seekers over a three-year period. Improved transportation and communication coupled with deteriorating conditions in countries of first arrival seem to be the major reasons for this flow.

8. This has led to increasingly restrictive policies by Northern governments. Governments are making it more difficult for asylum-seekers to receive asylum or to remain in their countries, even as they use ever more sophisticated methods to limit the number of asylum-seekers reaching their territory. Questions about accelerated refugee determination procedures, visa requirements and airline sanctions have become controversial political issues in most European countries. And along with increasingly restrictive governmental policies has come a rise in expressions of racism and xenophobia. From Sweden to Switzerland, expressions of hatred and fear of foreigners are becoming more evident. Most recently, outbreaks of violence against foreigners in former East Germany raise questions about the political impact of migration and popular response in the context of rapid political change in Central Europe.

9. There are growing numbers of people moving from East to West, as a result of the political and economic changes taking place in countries which were once part of the Eastern bloc. Perhaps more important than the number of people who have arrived in the West from the East is the fear that this is a harbinger of future mass movements.

10. Many of these people cannot be considered refugees in the sense of the United Nations definition or even in the broader terms of the OAU or Cartagena declaration. Many are economic migrants in search of a better life, or simply survival. But since the opportunities for legal immigration are so limited, particularly in Western Europe, they enter via the asylum system. In the process they are overwhelming this system, which was created in Western countries to handle a small number of cases and to provide relatively generous assistance in the process. For example, Great Britain received about 2,000 asylum-seekers in 1980. In 1991, the figure was expected to be about 50,000. The system set up to process 2,000 has been somewhat modified in light of the changing numbers, but basically remains the same. But it doesn't work with 50,000.

Breakdown of the system

These trends are indications that the international system of refugee protection — a system built up so carefully in the post-second world war period — is breaking down. This system was characterized by a consensus that refugees had a special claim on the international community and that it was the responsibility of the international community to provide protection and assistance to refugees — not just the responsibility of the governments of the countries in which they happened to arrive. Today that consensus appears to be in trouble. All three components of the system — the legal definition of refugees, the Convention itself, and UNHCR, the principal actor in the system — are undergoing change. Specifically, we see:

— a more restrictive application by national governments of the classic definition of refugees embodied in the 1951 UN Convention and the 1967 Protocol;

— increasing questions about the suitability of the definition in an age where most refugees are displaced by war and violence, not by individual persecution, and where the line between economic and political motivations for flight is blurred; and

— a weakening of the United Nations High Commissioner for Refugees' (UNHCR's) leadership role in refugee protection and assistance (discussed in more detail below).

The increase of people in "refugee-like situations" illustrates some of the difficulties in the international response. While uprooted people in these categories are often assisted, such assistance is carried out on an ad-hoc basis which depends on the good will and political interest of the principal actors (governments and UNHCR). This somewhat ad-hoc basis for responding to uprooted people means that there are glaring regional disparities. Western governments have encouraged a broad interpretation of the Convention definition for refugees in third-world countries even while applying strict Convention criteria when the same individuals apply for asylum in their countries.[1] Thus, an individual considered as a refugee and provided protection and assistance in a country of first asylum is often not considered as a refugee in another country or region.

Moreover, in spite of growing understanding about the importance of addressing root causes, there have been few systematic efforts (for understandable reasons) to integrate work with refugees with efforts to resolve the conflicts that displace populations. UN agencies are limited in this respect because of the need to respect national sovereignty and to work on the basis of humanitarian (e.g. non-partisan) principles. Although there have been repeated calls for early-warning mechanisms, for example (and some good work has been done on the technical side of this issue), the question remains: what can be done once the early-warning signs are present (as, for example, today in Armenia or Peru)?[2] Similarly, while refugee-serving NGOs have been important advocates in calling for root causes to be addressed, their concrete efforts in this area have been largely invisible.

Governments frequently see refugee/migration issues in terms of foreign-policy and security interests and seek to use the international system in pursuit of their national interests. This is not a new phenomenon. But the inconsistencies are creating increasing difficulties for the international *system* of refugee assistance and protection. For example, US policies of interdiction of Haitian refugees have always been at odds with its stated denunciations of Thai and Malaysian pushbacks of Vietnamese boats of asylum-seekers. While deplored by human-rights and refugee groups, the inconsistency was largely accepted or ignored. But when the US protests the deportation of Vietnamese from Hong Kong, who have been found not to be refugees under the terms of the Convention, while interdicting Haitians who have no recourse to an asylum procedure, more serious questions are raised.

The end of the cold war has given rise to hopes for peace agreements to settle long-standing disputes in third-world countries — Cambodia, Angola, Western Sahara, Mozambique, El Salvador, Ethiopia, etc. In these and other countries, efforts are well under way to resolve the conflicts between warring parties and to repatriate the refugees. But there is growing awareness that repatriation is a good deal more complicated and less of a panacea then generally recognized. Most importantly, peace is a process, often a fragile process, which requires the sustained attention and commitment of the international community.

The stakes in such an erosion of the international system are high. Ninety percent of the world's refugees come from countries in the South and 90 percent of them remain in the South. Governments of countries far poorer than those of Western Europe or North America — countries which host far larger numbers of refugees — are questioning why they should be expected to provide for refugees when richer countries are closing the doors. The failure of the three traditional solutions to refugee situations has implications for both North and South.

Failure of traditional solutions

The three traditional solutions for refugees — voluntary repatriation, local integration, and resettlement in a third country — are all becoming more difficult.

Repatriation: Voluntary repatriation has always been considered the optimal solution for refugees — to enable people to return home once the causes for their displacement have been resolved. After a five-year study of voluntary repatriation, Stein and Cuny underline the importance of the issue: "In any given year, less than one percent of the world's refugees escape the limbo of refugee status either by resettlement in third countries or by obtaining citizenship in their country of asylum. *If the number of refugees is to be reduced significantly, it will be by means of voluntary repatriation.*"[3]

The UNHCR has declared 1992 the "Year of Voluntary Return" and estimates that ideally 3 million refugees can return. Plans are under way to launch organized repatriation for 1.7 million people and to provide assistance to an additional 720,000 who return on their own. The budget for this repatriation is estimated at $400 million in 1992 which includes funds for assistance to 620,000 people who returned home in 1991, but who need further assistance.[4] For the past several years, repatriation has been the hope and the principal interest of UNHCR and the governments which support its operations.

As Stein and Cuny note, from 1985 to 1990 over one million refugees have voluntarily repatriated and most of these people have returned to areas of conflict. Refugees returned to El Salvador although the violence in that country was widespread. They are returning to Liberia even though the country is divided and the fighting goes on. This raises special concerns for UNHCR which seeks to ensure the protection and safety of the returnees. In the case of El Salvador, for example, UNHCR has a responsibility to monitor the returnees' safety for a period of two years, although in practice this responsibility may become an indefinite one. Monitoring the safety of returnees, particularly when they return to areas of conflict, often puts UNHCR deep into the political issues of the day in that country. Moreover, it often involves UNHCR in providing assistance and/or protection to other groups, including internally displaced people who are also returning to their community of origin, as well as local populations.

Although the emphasis in repatriation is on its voluntary nature, in practice the "voluntariness" of return is ambiguous. There are times when conditions in refugee camps are so bad that refugees prefer to take their chances in a war back home. In most cases, the choice for the refugee is continued life in a refugee camp or return to a conflict situation. Other options are closed for them, such as local integration, and resettlement for the vast majority of the Cambodian refugees in Thailand or the Vietnamese in Hong Kong. In the worst cases, refugees return home when war breaks out in their country of asylum, as was the case for Ethiopian refugees in Somalia.

While UNHCR often takes the lead in planning for repatriation, working closely with the governments of both the country of origin and the country of asylum, in fact most refugees return on their own, without international assistance. This spontaneous repatriation, which has been well-documented by Stein and Cuny, occurs in different phases. A few people may return to their communities and then go back to their country of asylum. [5] Decisions about repatriation take place on both the individual and community levels. As will be seen in the chapter on Central America, the return of whole communities can pose special protection and assistance problems.

Repatriation exercises are complicated to arrange and involve a whole range of activities from planning transportation to negotiations with armed factions in the country of origin. Co-ordination among a range of actors, including governments, other UN agencies, and a host of NGOs is often difficult.

Even when conditions at home have changed significantly, and the violence or repression which provoked flight has diminished, there are still difficulties for returnees. Their land may be occupied by someone else. Relations with people who remained during the years of war or repression may be strained. In Chile, for example, the return of large numbers of refugees after ten or more years in exile posed particular problems of adaptation for the refugees and particularly for their children. The country had changed dramatically in their absence and it was difficult to pick up where they had left off. Jobs were difficult to find and low-paying, particularly for those Chileans who returned from European countries where they had professional occupations.

Local integration: While voluntary repatriation is the desired option and will probably be the eventual solution for most refugees in the world, varying degrees of integration into a country of asylum remains an option for many refugees. At one extreme is the case where refugees are allowed to become citizens of the host country and to live among the local population as citizens. At the other extreme are cases where the refugees live illegally, without government recognition, and are subject to deportation by the security forces. In between are the many cases of refugee camps and settlements where the degree of freedom of movement varies widely.

When a sudden mass influx of refugees arrives on a national border, the government concerned and the international community react more or less typically to the emergency dimensions of the problem. Food is provided, shelter arranged and basic medical care is secured for the refugees. But often, too often, the temporary influx becomes a semi-permanent settlement and decisions made in the emergency phase of response may have effects for years on the way the camp is administered and on the well-being of the refugees themselves.

The issues involved in local integration include: legal status, ability to work, settlement in camps, the degree to which refugee self-sufficiency is encouraged and/or attained, relationship with the local population, access to education and so on. Governments first of all decide whether or not the refugees can enter the country; this occurs on an individual level in the case of individual asylum-seekers. It also occurs when a large number of people arrive and the government decides to consider them as a group to be refugees, that is, without individual refugee determination procedures. Often a government will allow the refugees to enter the country but will demand that they be confined to camps or to a particular region of the country. Given the variety of refugee backgrounds, many refugees may seek to move to urban areas where they live illegally. Although most of the research has focused on refugees living in camps, in fact the number living illegally in large cities probably exceeds the total camp population.

The survival strategies of urban undocumented refugees may include working, often in exploitative conditions, mini-businesses, petty trade, prostitution and so on. Their lack of legal recognition often makes them vulnerable to exploitation. Women in particular seem to be particularly vulnerable.

Education has been a particular concern for refugee populations. While the UN Convention guarantees the right of refugees to basic education, that has been interpreted by UNHCR in most cases to mean primary education. And when funds are short, educational programmes are among the first to be eliminated. In a few countries, governments allow the refugees to attend national schools and universities. But in cases where there are insufficient schools for nationals and/or high school fees, education remains out of reach for most of the refugees. University placement is particularly difficult for refugees. In camps, efforts are often made to encourage the self-sufficiency of refugees, but the major factor here is access to land. In many places, from Honduras to Hong Kong, such self-sufficiency is impossible because of restrictions on refugee movement.

For the past decade, the international community has emphasized that refugee aid and development must go together. Refugee populations must be taken into consideration by development planners; infrastructure created to serve refugees can be used by the local community when and if the refugees return home. But host governments usually do not have the resources to provide this infrastructure for major refugee populations, particularly when their own populations need support. In Malawi, for example, a recent World Bank-sponsored study of uncompensated public expenditures arising from the refugee presence found that the Malawi government had invested US$25 million to provide infrastructure for the more than one million Mozambican refugees in that country. The World Bank recommended an emergency assistance programme to offset the impact of such expenditures.[6] But such funds have been difficult to mobilize. While the international community has been relatively generous in providing financial support for the emergency phases of refugee assistance, it has been notably less generous when it comes to long-term development-oriented planning. ICARA I and II were two major conferences which sought to place the issue of aid to African refugees in a development context, but the funds for the many projects never reached the objectives.

Increasingly too, governments are beginning to worry about the environmental impact of refugee movements. According to current estimates, some 333 hectares of land need to be cleared to provide for the construction of new homes for 100,000 refugees upon their arrival. Annual consumption of fuelwood by the same refugee population may reach some 85,000 metric tons. In the case of Somalia, estimates are that "the average refugee camp would deplete 600 hectares of land in the first year of its establishment and 400 hectares every year thereafter. In and around refugee camps, entire settlements have been completely cleared of all trees and shrubs, and the destruction of the surrounding woody vegetation progresses at a rate that confirms the above estimates. The inhabitants of three- or four-year-old camps have to walk for several hours to find trees and shrubs to eat."[7] Honduras and Turkey, to cite two examples, have used the environmental damage caused by refugees as a reason for limiting their freedom of movement in the country.

Resettlement: The least desirable of the three options has always been resettlement to a third country. But this has been an extremely important option in several refugee situations — most obviously in the case of East Europeans and Indochinese refugees. The UNHCR's programme of resettlement gives priority to refugees who need to be moved out of the country or region for security reasons. A second category consists of those who need to be moved as "humane protection cases or vulnerable groups". This latter category includes women at risk, victims of violence, the physically or mentally disabled, those requiring medical care not available in the country of asylum and long-stayers.

In 1990, of the world's then global refugee population of 15 million, UNHCR requested resettlement assistance for just under 150,000 persons or approximately one percent. In relative terms, Troeller reports, 1990 was a good year for UNHCR resettlement, due in large part to the exceptional success of refugee admissions under the Comprehensive Plan of Action for Indochinese refugees. But in that year, UNHCR registered only 52,000 departures — a 65 percent shortfall in meeting the office's stated needs.[8] Resettlement has been a highly politicized governmental response to refugees. The United States, which admits by far the largest number of refugees for resettlement, has traditionally used the resettlement option as a way of pursuing its foreign and domestic policy objectives. Thus, programmes were set up in the post-second world war period to admit victims of communism; in the 1970s the resettlement policy shifted to favour those who were fleeing communism in Southeast Asia.

Troeller notes that of the 159 member states of the UN, only ten governments establish and announce refugee resettlement quotas.

TABLE 4:   REFUGEE RESETTLEMENT QUOTAS

US	125,000	New Zealand	800
Australia	14,000	Denmark	500
Canada	13,000	Finland	500
Sweden	1,250	Netherlands	500
Norway	1,000	Switzerland	250

Total   156,800

Source: Gary Troeller, "UNHCR Resettlement as an Instrument of International Protection: Constraints and Obstacles in the Arena of Competition for Scarce Humanitarian Resources", in *International Journal of Refugee Law*, vol. 3, No. 3, July 1991, p.569.

The US, Australia, Canada and New Zealand admit many refugees who are processed independently of UNHCR. The other countries have much smaller quotas but reserve admissions almost solely for UNHCR resettlement submissions. Countries such as the United Kingdom and France do not announce annual quotas as such but will admit a certain number of refugees and will accept submissions from UNHCR on a case-by-case basis, with preference to family reunion and UNHCR priority groups.

Selection criteria used by the four traditional receivers — US, Australia, Canada and New Zealand — often include immigration criteria. That is, governments look for people who are judged to be capable of integrating into — and contributing to — the host society. In practice, that means preference is given to those with family connections in the resettlement country, those who speak English, those who are young and healthy, and those with needed skills. In some cases, it appears that humanitarian considerations take a back seat to economic needs of the host country.

The table below provides data on numbers of refugees admitted for resettlement in proportion to population.

TABLE 5:   REFUGEES RESETTLED AND PERSONS GRANTED ASYLUM
IN RELATIONSHIP TO INDIGENOUS POPULATION, 1990

Country	1975-1990 cumulative	Ratio refugees/ population
Sweden	121,154	1/71
Canada	325,045	1/82
Australia	183,104	1/96
USA	1,478,184	1/171
Denmark	29,480	1/173
Norway*	21,708	1/198
New Zealand	11,428	1/306
France	203,030	1/283
Switzerland	22,295	1/305
Austria	24,249	1/318
Netherlands	21,880	1/686
Germany	91,478	1/869
Spain	38,713	1/1007
United Kingdom*	14,897	1/3860

Source: US Committee for Refugees, *World Refugee Survey 1992*, Washington, DC, USCR, p.36. * = statistics unavailable for 1975-81. Note that figures for Germany do not include 220,000 ethnic Germans from the former USSR, Poland and Romania.

Extensive research has been done on the problems and successes of integration of refugees resettled. In most of the large resettlement countries, substantial support has been given to the individual refugee in terms of financial and language assistance and in finding housing, jobs, etc. In the US and Canada, sponsorship of refugees by community and church groups has been an important component of the programme. Such community sponsorship has been an important factor in the successful integration of the refugees and has also served to mobilize popular support for refugee programmes. However, in the case of the US, it may also have served to prolong the conflict in Southeast Asia and Eastern Europe in that large numbers of Americans came to see the refugees as the human victims of communism.

As the number of asylum-seekers arriving on the borders of many of the traditional resettlement countries increased, governments moved to restrict refugee admissions. Blurring of economic and political distinctions of refugees, as in the case of Vietnamese, further complicated issues. As Troeller says: "There are already signals in certain sectors of traditional resettlement countries, reflecting the feeling in some quarters of public opinion, that with so many direct arrivals at their frontiers why should governments continue, at least at present levels, with overseas refugee resettlement admissions?"[9]

In some cases, notably Australia, commitment to a multicultural society appears to be waning. The economic difficulties in that country are leading to some degree of scapegoating of refugees for economic and cultural problems. In the US, the end of the cold war has meant a re-evaluation of resettlement admissions policies and an overall decrease in the number of people admitted.

Thus, all three traditional solutions are becoming more difficult. The UNHCR, as we have seen in chapter 2, has been in crisis for the past five years as a result of some of these pressures as well as factors related to administrative competence and leadership. The weakening of the definition, the crisis at UNHCR, governmental fears, and the failure of the traditional solutions to provide lasting opportunities for people to rebuild their lives have all produced a sense that the system itself is in crisis. Moreover, the pressures are increasing as more people are being uprooted even as few of those previously displaced find lasting solutions.

As might be expected, this crisis has had an impact on NGOs and churches. When UNHCR cuts a scholarship programme for refugees, for example, the refugees often turn to churches and NGOs for assistance. As UNHCR cut its budget in various parts of the world, NGOs reported increasing requests for assistance from their partners and field staff. While in some cases NGOs tried to respond, they did not have the resources to make up for such reductions. Moreover, they insisted, it was the responsibility of governments, working through UNHCR, to meet the basic needs of refugees. Thus, they sought to advocate with governments that they fulfil their obligations to support UNHCR and tried to raise awareness about what was happening to refugees as a result of changes at the international level.

While NGOs and churches were working to strengthen UNHCR by lobbying for increased funding of its operations, they were also increasingly pushing UNHCR to do more to meet the needs of two particular groups of refugees, women and children. While women and children make up the majority of the refugee population, UNHCR and governments frequently treated their concerns as "marginal" to the larger issues of refugee well-being. By raising awareness about the needs and resources of the majority of the refugee population, NGOs and churches were able to bring about some policy changes at UNHCR and to underscore the need for still further change to translate UN rhetoric into action.

Refugee women[10]

> The war in Somalia is an anarchist war. It is a war on the women. Any woman between the ages of eighteen and forty is not safe from being forcibly removed to the army camps to be raped and violated. And that's only the beginning. If her husband finds out, he kills her for the shame of it all. If they know that he has found out, they kill him too. If he goes into hiding instead and if she won't tell where he is, they kill her.[11]

> The topic I most want to talk about is the women and children. The young women in the camps suffer more than we do. They are raped by Thai soldiers, across the Mekong river. When they get to the border, Thai soldiers stand just alongside the Mekong river and sometimes take a group of women away. They don't know where they are going but they say they will take them to a safe place. But it's not right. Sometimes we couldn't find that young woman till five or ten months later. I've got my friend who is still missing. They are raped by the Thai soldiers or treated by them like prostitutes. If the young people escape together the men and women have to have their rooms separate. The women are raped. It happens all the time, but nobody notices this.[12]

For the past few years awareness has been increasing about the specific needs of refugee women and girls who constitute the majority of the world's 30 million refugees and displaced people. Like all refugees, women face problems as a result of their displacement. Like all refugees, they face physical dangers in flight from their community, stress in adapting to a new cultural environment, questions about their identities, and guilt and worry about those left behind. They face uncertainty about both their long-term future and about their survival in the immediate camp situations. All refugees, men and women, young and old, face difficulties as a consequence of their uprooting. But refugee women face particular difficulties in their experience of exile; because of the central role which refugee women play in their communities, their difficulties have consequences for society as a whole.

The roles which women play vary enormously from situation to situation, but a number of roles can be identified which apply to most situations.

1. *Women as mothers:* As mothers, women bear and nurture children, provide support for their husbands and seek to hold the family together. For most women, the family is the centre of their life and their efforts are devoted to ensuring the well-being of their children, husbands, and other relatives. They are responsible for the physical maintenance of the family, securing food, cooking and serving it, providing clothing for the family, keeping the home clean. They are in the real sense the first providers of primary health care — and make important household and family decisions such as about the way in which wastes are disposed of or how to seek medical treatment for a child.

Women are largely responsible for the transmission of cultural beliefs to the next generation, for instilling pride in one's culture, for learning the norms and rules of community life. For refugees, this role of transmitting culture is a particularly important one. Women, in many cases, also maintain religious traditions within the family. Although they are rarely religious leaders, they are often responsible for fostering and developing the religious practice of the family, for ensuring that children receive religious education, and trying to maintain proper religious rituals to the extent possible. [13] Women are often responsible for the education of the children within the family and, where possible, for ensuring that they go to school.

These roles often become more difficult in exile. Families are separated, social support systems are weakened, and there are new and different ways of securing the family's well-being. Sometimes an older daughter tries to keep the family together when the mother is not present. Women's struggles to keep families together become more difficult as a result of these changes. Moreover, women are frequently forced to assume new roles in exile.

2. *Women have economic responsibilities:* These are often heavier in exile than back at home. This is particularly the case for mothers who arrive without their husbands and who face the task of providing for the economic well-being, and survival, of their children. The need to ensure the survival of the family leads to various survival strategies — such as developing ways of getting increased rations from a food distribution system or entering the work place or working with other women to produce household goods and handicrafts. Survival strategies may also involve turning to the black market, finding a man for protection or even resorting to prostitution.

In many refugee situations it is difficult for men to resume their traditional responsibilities of providing for the economic well-being of the family. Dependence on food rations may mean that the husband of the family has little to do, even as the woman's domestic responsibilities continue or even increase as a result of exile. The new situation often leads to changed roles within the family. This is perhaps most apparent where women arrived in refugee settlements without their husbands and were forced to assume the unaccustomed role of family bread-winner. When the husband returns, there is thus a new dynamic in the marital relationship which can lead to conflicts within the family.[14] In other situations, such as that of Afghan women in Pakistan, exile may mean a decrease in their economic activity outside the home and more restrictions on their movement within the community.

3. *Women are community organizers:* Although usually not recognized as such in terms of formal power (and indeed many women would not see themselves as politically powerful), women play a central role in terms of making and implementing decisions which affect the well-being of the community as a whole. This power is exercised in many ways — by influencing the men in the community to take particular decisions, by developing informal networks of support, or by simply ignoring decisions with which they disagree. Too often women are not consulted about community decisions and yet their support is essential to the success of particular programmes. For example, decisions about where to place a water pump or how to secure access to firewood or how to encourage the use of latrines, must all involve women. Although systematic research is lacking, it seems that women are more likely to exercise political power openly and to be acknowledged in that role in situations where they play important economic roles.

4. *Women as reconcilers:* Refugee women are usually seen as victims to be assisted or even as resources to be used in the improvement of

refugee communities. Little attention is paid to their potential role in *resolving* the conflicts which led to the displacement of people.[15] It is true that women have largely been outside the decision-making circles which produced the conflicts; it is rarely women who decide to go to war or to institute counter-insurgency policies intended to displace communities. But women do play a role in this regard. Within the family, they play a central role in instilling attitudes in their children which can either make future reconciliation possible or nourish the desire for revenge. The way in which the causes of exile are explained can influence the perceptions of the future generation.

When you talk with refugee women, the issue of root causes comes up over and over again. When asked, for example, about what a particular agency could do to improve the situation of refugee women in a given situation, the answer is often "stop the violence back home so that we can return. That's more important to us than a health care programme or literacy classes."

Particular problems facing refugee women

While women face specific, and often serious, problems it is important to keep in mind that, in spite of these problems, refugee women are strong and resourceful people. As the 1991 Australian Refugee Day theme reminds us, they are *survivors*. They have managed to escape, often by dangerous routes, from the violence of their home community; often they have been able to protect their children along the way. So the focus on the particular problems which refugee women face should not obscure their strengths and resources which can contribute to the well-being of their children, their families and their communities.

Protection: Virtually every article or study on refugee women begins with the problem of the violence they experience. Refugee women are vulnerable to violence at every stage of their flight. In the conflicts which produced the uprooting, women are often victims. As we have seen, the wars which have produced most of the world's refugees frequently target civilian populations. Bombing, torture, massacres and rape mark many of the world's wars, from Liberia to Peru, from Mozambique to El Salvador. The systematic rape of women is sometimes used as a tool of warfare, as for example indicated in recent reports from Bosnia-Herzegovina. Sometimes women are singled out for persecution, simply because they are women. Women may be captured or tortured as a way of punishing male relatives. Or women may be harassed or abused because of their failure to follow traditional norms for women's behaviour in a given society.[16]

During flight, refugee women face particular problems of rape and abuse, from those from whom they are fleeing, but also sometimes from those from whom they seek protection. [17] At borders, they are more vulnerable to sexual abuse and intimidation. [18] Once they arrive in camps, they face the possibility of violence from camp officials, from other refugees, and from their own families. Women living as urban refugees, particularly when they are undocumented, are often subjected to sexual abuse.

It is increasingly recognized that women's protection needs are related to their assistance needs. When they cannot obtain sufficient food for themselves or their families, they may turn to prostitution. [19]

While the international community has become aware of the problems of violence against refugee women, designing effective action to prevent it has not been easy. A survey of NGOs in 1987 found that most respondents knew that there was violence against refugee women in the camps in which they worked, but there were few programmes to deal with the consequences. "No one takes action if it happens between the refugees themselves, but if the case is caused by a national, it will be investigated by the authorities." One respondent wrote: "In cases where culturally sensitive counselling can be given to all involved [in family violence], there are positive results, but in too many cases such help is not available." Another respondent wrote of the physical and psychological consequences of such violence: guilt feelings, low self-esteem, fear, loneliness, rejection by family members.

As one NGO representative said: "I meet some refugee women with their faces swollen and beaten, but they are ashamed to tell their problems." [20]

Assistance questions: In the area of assistance, women refugees, like men refugees, have specific needs for education, health, cultural support and economic activities. Although services may be made available for the whole community, women seem to make less use of them. For example, women often lack access to education because programmes aren't available or are scheduled at inconvenient times, because there is no provision for child care, or because the educational programmes are perceived as irrelevant to their needs. They may be discouraged from participating in them because of social or cultural pressures. And since they often face heavy family responsibilities in the camps, they simply may not have the time to participate. [21] Given the fact that women tend to have less education than men in their countries of origin, the lack of educational opportunities in refugee situations may further increase the gap between male and female educational levels.

There is also evidence that women's needs are often not taken into consideration in the planning of health programmes. [22] Nutrition is one area with definite consequences for refugee women. As the *Practical Guide for Working with Refugee Women* states: "Refugee camps are not run according to democratic principles. Power tends to be concentrated in the hands of a few, and it is usually attained through the control of food aid. Generally men are in charge of food distribution which gives them enormous power at the expense of the most vulnerable in the community; women, and particularly women who head households and who do not have male protection, suffer the most." [23] When food is insufficient or nutritionally poor, women suffer most. Women's greater needs for iron, calcium and iodine make them particularly vulnerable to nutrition-deficiency diseases. Moreover, cultural traditions can lead to inadequate rationing within the family. Women may give their share of food to their husbands or children because their well-being is more important to them than their own. Krummel, in reviewing the literature on refugee women, notes: "Malnutrition is a potential problem among all refugees living in camp situations, but it is especially acute among women restrained by the traditions of purdah from being seen by men not related to them. Afghan women in Pakistani camps are dependent on men for protection and in the distribution of food, and often receive less than their due. Especially in camps comprising several different tribes or clans, women heads of families are sometimes unable to acquire sufficient food for themselves and their children, because of the high risk of being seen by male strangers if they queue for food themselves." [24] Furthermore, women face problems of trying to prepare strange food in strange conditions and may not know about the nutritional value of new foods.

It is well-recognized that women have particular health needs related to pregnancy and breast-feeding. In refugee situations, traditional ways of giving birth may no longer function as traditional midwives may not be with the community or because the particular setting for childbirth is not available. The family and social support systems for childbirth may have been destroyed as a result of the factors which produce the uprooting. With insufficient prenatal care and inadequate nutrition, the chances of mothers giving birth to healthy babies diminish.

Available health services may not meet the needs of refugee women because of a lack of female examiners; disregard for traditional health care; absence of care and treatment for problems specific to women; and inconvenient clinic hours. [25]

Economic problems may lead women to seek alternative ways of increasing family income, but here too there are problems. In some cases, programmes of income generation or agriculture are directed towards the men in the community. Where available, women tend to use such programmes less than men for the same reasons they use educational services less. They lack time and child-care or they perceive that the programmes are irrelevant to their situations.

There have been few systematic studies of the psychological or mental health problems of women; those that have been conducted have tended to focus on the particular problems facing refugee women in resettlement countries — experiences which are probably not applicable to women living in camp situations or as urban refugees in third-world cities.[26] Some of the studies point to serious psychological problems among women: depression, psychosomatic ailments, nightmares, loneliness, apathy.[27] It is known that stress weakens a woman's resistance to disease and adversely affects her ability to undertake essential economic and family activities. Mental health problems of refugee women include those arising from torture, loss of traditional support systems, difficulties in cultural adjustment, overwork, nutritional imbalance, sexual abuse and domestic violence.[28]

All of these obstacles limit the ability of refugee women to play active, positive roles within their communities and their families.

The NGO community and, within the NGOs, the churches have played a vital catalytic role in raising awareness on the international level about the issues facing refugee women. In 1986, the NGO Working Group on Refugee Women was formed as a loose association seeking both to pressure UNHCR to take women's issues seriously and to work within their own organizations to bring about change. When they realized that NGOs frequently didn't know how to go about changing their programmes to meet women's needs and that positive examples were needed, they organized a consultation on refugee women in 1988. At that consultation, women refugees and NGO staff working with refugees shared concrete experiences of how refugee women's needs are met. The publication that came out of that consultation, *Working with Refugee Women: A Practical Guide*, details many case studies of successful programmes to meet the needs of refugee women. The common theme that emerges from this guide, and indeed from virtually all studies of programmes benefitting refugee women, is the importance of including refugee women in the planning and implementation of any programme. If refugee women are involved in a meaningful way from the beginning, the project's chance of success is much higher. Often agencies see them as recipients of welfare assistance rather than as actors in resolving their own situations.

Once women have been asked to identify their problems and to come up with solutions, there are usually many ways of meeting the needs. For example, we know that women will make greater use of health care facilities when there are female practitioners and provision for child care, and the hours are convenient. There are ways of incorporating traditional health practices, including childbirth practices, into health programmes. Providing information to women about nutrition and health is essential — but it is important that the information is provided in such a way that women can use it.

There are many positive examples of ways in which programmes can be designed to meet the needs of refugee women.[29] And there are many useful "guidelines" and checklists developed by UNHCR to help policy planners respond to women's needs when programmes are being considered. By including refugee women in the planning process, by listening to their needs and their suggestions, it is possible to design programmes which are much more responsive to their needs. Once people in positions of responsibility are aware of the needs and committed to addressing them, there is much that can be done. But the problem is developing the awareness of the situation and the commitment to action.

In the past few years, awareness has increased about the specific needs of refugee women. Studies have been carried out, recommendations carefully formulated, new organizations of refugee women created, gender-awareness training undertaken, meetings held and new governmental policies implemented.[30] But in spite of the apparent awakening of the international community to issues concerning refugee women, there are major obstacles to be overcome at the policy level. Specifically:

1. Those in positions of responsibility often do not *see* the problems or the resources of refugee women. Violence, for example, is often invisible to those who have not been sensitized to it. For a variety of reasons, women in virtually all cultures are reluctant to talk about violence which they have experienced unless they are reasonably confident that they will get a sympathetic hearing. And sometimes a sympathetic disposition is not enough. Women may be reluctant to talk with men or with foreigners. They may resist speaking of their experiences in a foreign language or in front of other refugees or in the presence of camp officials.

2. Officials must be willing to take actions to address the problems of women. To take the case of violence again, when it is a question of

putting up extra lights in a camp or even hiring female interpreters, such decisions may require only the expenditure of additional funds (which of course is difficult enough these days). But the more problematic issues involve political decisions — decisions which may mean hard choices. For UNHCR the problem may be to decide whether to push for disciplinary actions against border guards known to routinely abuse women seeking asylum, when to do so might mean further restrictions in other areas important not only to UNHCR but also to refugees. It is often a risk to offend a camp commander when that commander has the ability to make conditions much worse for all refugees in the camp. For NGOs, the difficulties may be in taking actions which may reduce violence against refugee women but alienate refugee camp (male) leadership. For international NGOs it may mean taking positions that run counter to the wishes of indigenous organizations. And for all refugee-serving organizations, addressing the causes of violence against refugee women may mean committing substantially more resources — to ensure that women aren't forced into prostitution in order to survive, or aren't vulnerable to exploitation by officials.

3. In order for people within international and national agencies to *see* the problems and resources of refugee women, there must be commitment on the part of the top leadership of the organization. Depending on a few sensitive individuals within the organization isn't enough to effect major change. People will begin to *see* the problem and to feel confident enough to take action only when they perceive that to do so is expected by the leadership. I would argue that this is true among NGOs and churches as well as UNHCR and other UN agencies.

4. There is a relationship between women in senior management positions and steps being taken to address the situation of refugee women. Certainly there are many sensitive men and there are many women who are not able to see problems related to women. But it seems that in UNHCR and among the NGO community, initiatives to support refugee women are usually undertaken by women staff who then enlist the support of male colleagues.

Angela Berry, UNHCR nutritionist, notes that there is a relationship between decisions made at the international level and the well-being of refugee women in local situations. Because diet is the responsibility of administrative organizations and not usually the specialized agencies, this essential aspect of assistance to refugee women can be overlooked. For example, in the case of nutrition, "it is clear that improvement must be instigated at an institutional level. In the absence of thoughtful planning, health services will be only marginally effective in addressing women's health needs. For example, unless food aid contains enough vitamins, minerals and calories to sustain good health, malnutrition and related diseases will continue to afflict thousands of refugees, primarily refugee women... One reason advanced for the slow institutional response to women's health needs is the lack of women with decision-making authority. For example, in 1981 only 16 percent of the membership in the Nutrition Subcommittee of the United Nations Administrative Co-ordinating Committee were women. Within seven years this figure has risen to 33 percent. Given that nutrition has traditionally been regarded as principally within a woman's domain, the relatively small proportion of women serving on the United Nations' highest nutritional body is noteworthy."[31]

5. The issue of refugee women is closely related to that of making the rhetoric of refugee participation a reality. And this is often a difficult issue — particularly as the refugee community may not be sympathetic to the woman who has been raped, or to the mother who seeks income from prostitution to feed her children, or even to the suggestion that refugee women should be listened to in a culture where males traditionally speak for the community. A commitment to refugee women's participation often puts an outside organization at odds with the male hierarchy.

6. Often international and national agencies justify their lack of programmatic involvement with refugee women on cultural grounds. Thus the extremely low percentage of Afghan refugee girls in schools (in comparison with boys) is explained by the fact that this reflects Afghan cultural beliefs and outside agencies cannot impose their values in this situation. Certainly, it is difficult to argue *in favour of* cultural imposi-tion, particularly imposition of Western cultural values in this day and age. But at the same time, we must recognize that by virtue of being refugees and receiving assistance, intervention is taking place — inter-vention which may challenge traditional cultural beliefs on a number of levels. In many, many situations, refugee women find themselves assum-ing new responsibilities which they would not have had to assume back home and which sometimes run counter to their traditional cultural beliefs. Decisions made by outside actors challenge cultural traditions in many areas — a decision to provide beans that require eight hours of cooking or to insist that children be inoculated or that people with infectious diseases receive special treatment. One rarely hears the argu-ment that "we couldn't vaccinate children because it's not part of their cultural tradition" although it is frequent to hear statements like "we can't

interfere in the practice of female circumcision because it is part of the refugees' culture".

Many of these issues also apply to the experience of refugee children and young people.

Refugee children

Over half of the world's 16.5 million refugees are children. They flee their homes for the same kinds of reasons adults do, but their experience of exile is often different. While they have certain identifiable needs, refugee children and young people are also a source of hope for the future. In some cases, children receive education and training which they contribute to the rebuilding of their country when conditions change and they return home. Leaving one's country and living as a refugee, either in camps or among the local population, is a new experience for children — an experience which is often painful, but which also can build strength and independence among children who live through it. [32] But in order for the pain of exile to be minimized, and for the potential of refugee children to be realized, their basic needs must be met and opportunities for growth provided. Too often, this has not been the case.

At the international level, awareness is growing about the needs of children. After ten years of work begun during the International Year of the Child (1979), the Convention on the Rights of the Child was adopted by the General Assembly of the United Nations on 20 November 1989 and came into force on 2 September 1990, having been ratified by the required twenty countries. Its approval marked the culmination of efforts to define children's rights that began soon after the turn of this century.

The approval of the Convention was followed in September 1990 by the World Summit for Children. More than seventy world leaders signed the World Declaration on the Survival, Protection and Development of Children. They committed themselves to a ten-point programme to protect the rights of children and improve their lives.

But while world leaders are saying the right things and while the Convention on the Rights of the Child is an important sign of progress, children are still being killed in wars and deprived of basic assistance in exile.

The conditions that produce refugees, uproot children, cause families to become separated and scar young people. Children have always suffered from the political violence waged by adults, and they continue to suffer in exile. For young people, flight from home and friends is a phenomenon over which they have little control; decisions to leave are usually made by others. Although they may not understand the reasons why they had to flee, they suffer the consequences. For children living in camps, the refugee experience means a disruption of their traditional ways of living and changes in their hopes and plans. Educational opportunities change; for some, life in exile may offer a chance to attend primary school, but all too often young people's hopes for secondary and university education are destroyed. For those travelling without their parents, the trauma of life as a refugee is particularly difficult. For refugee children resettled with their families in a third country, the experience of exile may bring about alienation from their culture as well as tension within their families.

Children in armed conflict

It is estimated that 750,000 children have been killed and another 250,000 severely traumatized within Mozambique due to the guerrilla activities of the Mozambican National Resistance, RENAMO.

The number of "child soldiers" in the world is estimated at 200,000 — in spite of international statements, resolutions and conventions designed to protect children in situations of armed conflicts. The Cambodian army forcibly recruited boys as young as 14 in "conscription drives" which took place in the streets of Pnomh Penh.

The Inter-American Children's Institute estimates that about 420,000 Salvadoran, Guatemalan and Nicaraguan children were affected by the armed violence in 1987-88. This figure includes half of Guatemalan orphans and children with psychological damage resulting from the violence.

Children and youth are usually innocent bystanders in armed conflicts, but in some situations they have played active military roles. Armed children and youth have never been extended protection; rather, they are usually treated as adult combatants. In the Israeli-occupied territories, this role is perhaps most visible.

The direct and personal experience of violence leads young people in many parts of the world to become militarily active. Refugee workers in the Sabra and Shatila camps in Lebanon, the site of brutal massacres in 1982, report the hopelessness of young people and the development of a fierce desire for revenge. In other cases, such as Mozambique, young boys are recruited by guerrilla forces and undergo a period of training which socializes them to kill and desensitizes them to violence. [33]

But although there are many cases in which young people have turned to violence, the vast majority of the world's young refugees have not played such an active role. Rather, they have been victims of violence not of their own making. They have suffered from bombings, they have seen family members tortured and killed, they have been coerced or persecuted themselves, and, either alone or with their families, they have fled for their lives.

Violence takes its toll on children in many ways. Psychologists at the 1984 Rädda Barnen conference described the effects of the violence on young people in Beirut. Normal life was disrupted, schools were often closed or occupied by displaced people. Parks, playgrounds and other gathering places for youth had become dangerous. Parents were afraid to let their children go outside unaccompanied and so the normal activities of teenagers were limited. Family members became separated as relatives moved away from the violence and as travel became more difficult. At the same time, the separation was not only physical but also emotional as parents struggled to understand the turbulent politics and to adapt to life under fire. The parents' energy goes into survival; too often they have little time to respond to the emotional needs of their children. At the same time, there may be too much physical closeness as restrictions on children and adolescents prevent them from leading more independent lives and from having privacy within the family. [34]

The children deal with the situation in a variety of ways: by repressing the fear, escaping into a world of fantasy, or taking drugs. Children in Lebanon as in other war-torn countries face an early end to their childhood. They are forced to become adults — with the fears and responsibilities that entails — from far too early an age. In Lima, Peru, children displaced by the violence in the highlands are usually forced to work in order to provide income for their families' survival. The children's opportunities are limited, like the adults', by their lack of documentation. Many times the children do not have birth certificates or identity cards, which prevents them from attending schools where the majority of nutrition programmes are located.

Children in exile

Children who flee with their families into exile also face trauma. Young children may not understand the reasons for the flight while older children may be all too aware of the situation back home. As children in the process of growth and development, they have special nutritional needs — needs which are often not met. Currently almost 7 million refugees are dependent on food aid provided by UNHCR and the World Food Programme. Recent surveys show that an average of 10-15 percent of refugee children under the age of five are malnourished, with rates in some countries as high as 30 percent. By comparison, malnutrition rates among other populations range from 2-5 percent in Asia and Central America and 5-10 percent in Africa.[35] Refugee children are affected, sometimes the most affected, by cuts in budgets for refugee assistance and by declining international support for refugees.

One of the principal needs of children and youth is education. But even though the need is clearly recognized by UNHCR and the agencies, resources are seldom available to provide anything more than minimal educational opportunities. Schools in camps are often inadequate to meet the tremendous needs of children and young people. For refugees living in cities without access even to the rudimentary schools provided in the camps, the high cost of providing an education for their children, particularly at the secondary and post-secondary levels, are often beyond the parents' capacities. Churches and other NGOs have been providing scholarships to many students. These scholarships not only offer educational opportunities to individual young people, but can also serve to help maintain hope in an environment that too often frustrates young people.

Due to UNHCR's financial difficulties, education programmes were seriously curtailed in the late 1980s. Less than one in ten of the children receiving assistance from UNHCR were enrolled in schools. Funds for education programmes were reduced by another 23 percent in 1990. In Malawi, only 70,000 of the more than 300,000 refugee children have an opportunity to go to primary schools. The primary schools which exist are overcrowded and ill-equipped. Only 9-14 percent of Ethiopian refugees are receiving education — in comparison with 36 percent in Ethiopia itself. In Pakistan about 12.5 percent of Afghan refugee children are in school, compared with 18 percent in Afghanistan and 47 percent in Pakistan.

The situation of refugee girls is particularly bad. In Pakistan in 1990, only 8,123 Afghan girls were enrolled in school (out of a total enrolment of 125,000). This figure represented less than one tenth of one percent of the school-aged girls. A study of two camps in Somalia showed that approximately 4,000 children were enrolled in primary school, but only 40 percent were in attendance, almost all of them boys.[36]

In countries of resettlement, the experiences of children and young people in exile may differ from that of their parents. One study of adolescent Chilean exiles in France examined the psychological impact of exile on this group. Ana Vasquez found that the Chilean youth used a range of defence mechanisms — from forgetfulness to idealization of the past — to cope with the pressures of being uprooted to a strange land. [37] Many of them experienced downward social mobility and both overt and covert racism. Their self-image suffered from exposure to a different culture and values. Problems in French schools were commonplace as the young Chileans were forced to adapt to foreign values and educational methods. What had been valued back home was no longer appropriate in France. Thus creativity in arguing viewpoints and egalitarian norms were no longer appropriate behaviour. These cultural conflicts created problems at home as well as in school. Difficulties in reconciling Chilean and French standards of behaviour for young people frequently led to conflicts between parents and children. For the Chilean young people, the problem of struggling to define their own identity was central to the conflicts they experienced. Although they were considered by society to be political refugees, in fact they had not been politically active. While adults drew support from their identity as exiles, young people did not have this experience and therefore it was harder for them to understand who they in fact were.

Children alone in exile

While most children and young people flee violence and war accompanied by at least some members of their families, many arrive alone. Sometimes children are abandoned by their families in flight, sometimes they run away on their own, and often they get lost in the confusion of flight. In some cases, children may be sent ahead for their own protection or to increase chances for the family to gain admission in a resettlement country. Young men in particular face special dangers in situations of civil war as they may be conscripted into the army or targeted for persecution. In countries such as Iran and Nicaragua, young people leave their homes to evade military service or because they were urged by family members to seek safety abroad. But in exile, they face problems of acceptance. As young men, they may be perceived as threatening to the local population — both because of the possibility of their being involved in anti-social behaviour, and their competition with local youth for scarce jobs.

Unaccompanied minors raise difficult issues for NGOs, UNHCR and governmental officials trying to provide for their well-being. There are differences in definitions of the age of majority, which may be much lower in the country of origin than in the host country. Many minors assumed to be orphans and without close relatives may in fact simply be lost. In Mozambique, posters with the photographs of missing children are circulated throughout the country and the refugee camps in neighbouring countries to help trace relatives separated in the violence.

The development of appropriate policies regarding the placement of unaccompanied minors has been difficult. Standard interviewing procedures for adults may be inappropriate for children travelling alone. Many young people may not know their exact age and may have difficulties in articulating their past experiences and their future hopes. UNHCR and NGOs have worked together to develop procedures that better meet the needs of the child. [38]

At the Rädda Barnen Conference on Children in Armed Conflicts, Lars Gustafsson urged participants to consider some of the following questions:

— What does it mean to children, in the long run, to lose their childhood, to become adults — responsible persons — at the age of eight or ten?

— What does it mean to children to lose for ever, already by the age of three or four, faith in their parents' ability to protect them?

— What does it mean to children to lose members of their family temporarily or for ever, without understanding why?

— What does it mean to a child not to learn any other methods of solving a conflict than killing?

— What does it mean for children to grow up in exile? What are the long-term effects of exile on their development? How do they balance their need to maintain ties with their own cultures with the need to adapt to a new environment? [39]

From rhetoric to action: progress on refugee children

As awareness increased about the particular needs of refugee children, UNHCR worked with NGOs to develop a set of comprehensive Guidelines on Refugee Children which survey some of the many factors to be taken into account in working with refugee children — such as determination of refugee status, questions of nationality and birth registration, physical health, and education and treatment of disabilities. The guidelines point to three groups of particularly vulnerable children — unaccompanied children, children living with families other than their own, and children staying for extended periods in camps. The guidelines offer an impressive guide to action in a variety of situations. And yet a study of the implementation of the guidelines in Malawi revealed that they are neither widely disseminated at the field level nor especially effective at an operational level. [40]

UNHCR has created a new post of co-ordinator for refugee children in order to monitor progress in implementing the guidelines and to emphasize that children are a priority issue.

But in spite of the fact that the international community has developed plans and guidelines for action — in spite of the fact that many know what *should* be done — the fact remains that growing numbers of children are living in desperate conditions. Their basic physical needs are not being met, they don't have the opportunity to go to school, and they carry deep emotional wounds as a result of the experiences they have gone through. This reality challenges the churches and other religious traditions to reassess their actions and their programmes to see that the needs of children are given the priority they deserve.

Given the fact that women and children are a majority in most refugee situations (in even larger proportions than in non-refugee populations), it can be argued that all assistance and protection programmes should be tailored to meet their needs with special programmes designed for particular adult male needs as circumstances dictate. The needs of refugee women and refugee children are not "special interests" or "marginal" to other refugee concerns. Their needs and resources are central to all work with refugees and cannot be responded to with special projects labelled "refugee children" or "refugee women" tacked on to other programmes which largely ignore these concerns. Once this reality is recognized and incorporated into our thinking as well as our programmes, the resources of refugee women can more effectively be mobilized to meet the needs of their communities, and particularly their children.

* * *

We shall return to some of these concerns in the last two chapters. But now we turn to an examination of the situation of uprooted people in the regions. While space precludes the detailed analyses which each of the cases merits, it is important that we consider some of the specific situations before trying to draw out the common threads. Each regional situation is unique and while it is useful to see global trends, it is also necessary to ground such an understanding in the complexities of the regions. We begin our regional survey with the case of Africa where the number of uprooted people and the complexity of their situations have challenged individuals and organizations for decades.

NOTES

[1] Barry N. Stein, "The Nature of the Refugee Problem", paper presented at a conference on the international protection of refugees, sponsored by the Canadian Human Rights Foundation, Montreal, Canada, 29 November-2 December 1987; Dennis Gallagher, "The Evolution of the International Refugee System", in *International Migration Review*, vol. 23, no. 3, pp.579-598.

[2] See, for example, Lance Clark, *Early Warning of Refugee Flows*, Washington, DC, Refugee Policy Group, 1989; Leon Gordenker, "Early-Warning of Disastrous Population Movement", in *International Migration Review*, vol. 20, no. 2, summer 1986.

[3] Barry N. Stein and Fred C. Cuny, "Introduction", in *Repatriation Under Conflict in Central America*, ed. Mary Ann Larkin, Washington, CIPRA, Georgetown University, p.2, emphasis in the original.

[4] *Refugees*, UNHCR, no. 88, January 1992, p.6.

[5] Stein and Cuny, *op. cit.*

[6] UNHCR, *Refugees: A Challenge for Least Developed Countries*, document submitted to the UN General Assembly, A/CONF.147/PC/3/add.20, July 1990, p.5.

[7] *Ibid.*, pp.7-8.

[8] Gary G. Troeller, "UNHCR Resettlement as an Instrument of International Protection: Constraints and Obstacles in the Arena of Competition for Scarce Humanitarian Resources", in *International Journal of Refugee Law*, vol. 3, no. 3, July 1991, p.568.

[9] *Ibid.*, p.577.

[10] Adapted from Elizabeth G. Ferris, "Refugee Women and Family Life: The Context of Intervention", paper presented at the meeting on psychosocial needs of refugee children, organized by the International Catholic Child Bureau, Geneva, September 1991.

[11] A Somali woman who escaped to Canada after her husband disappeared, leaving her young baby with her sister. Reported in *Canadian Women Studies*, vol. 1, no. 1, spring 1989, p.28.

[12] Thongsy Vanitory, reported in *Refugee Resettlement and Wellbeing*, ed. Max Abbott, Wellington, New Zealand, Mental Health Association of New Zealand, 1987.

[13] For example, several studies have found that the practice of purdah seemed to be more widespread among Afghan refugees in Pakistan than in Afghanistan. Many women who had been educated, urban professionals back home, were now wearing the veil for the first time. The researcher speculated that the reason for the increased use of purdah was that the refugees, especially the men, felt their cultural identity was being eroded by the pressures of exile. The return to purdah was a way of providing continuity with traditions in a new situation. See, for example, Hanne Christensen, "Afghan Refugees in Pakistan: From Emergency Towards Self-Reliance", Geneva, United Nations Research Institute for Social Development, 1984, pp.43-46.

[14] One researcher found that the marriages of Angolan refugees in Zambia, for example, came under heavy pressure as a result of poverty, hard work and deprivation. Both men and women refugees were dependent on the generosity of local people for their survival and worked long hours for local families with little pay. Though some marriages, especially longer-lived ones, survived, tensions often arose and sometimes led to divorce. See, for example, Anita Spring, "Women and Men as Refugees: Differential Assimilation of Angolan Refugees in Zambia", in *Involuntary Migration and Resettlement: The Problems and Responses of Dislocated People*, Boulder, CO, Westview Press, 1982.

[15] The Life & Peace Institute is presently involved in research on the ways in which women use non-violence to resolve conflicts within their own communities.

[16] See for example work done by Marijke Meier, *Sexual Violence: You Have Hardly Any Future Left*, Dutch Refugee Council, 1987; "Guidelines for the Asylum Claims of Women", in Ninette Kelley, *Working with Refugee Women: A Practical Guide*, Geneva, NGO Working Group on Refugee Women, 1989.

[17] See, for example, the work done by Tu-Khuong Schroeder-Dao, "Study of Rape Victims among the Refugees on Pulau Bidong Island: An Experience in Counselling Women Refugee 'Boat People'", Geneva, November 1982; and also "Victims of Violence in the South China Sea", pp.18-38 in *Refugees — the Trauma of Exile: The Humanitarian Role of the Red Cross and Red Crescent*, ed. Diana Miserez, Boston, MA, Martinus Nijhoff, 1988. In these and other works, she details the severe psychological problems experienced by Vietnamese women raped by pirates during flight and the consequences for the community.

[18] See, for example, Roberta Aitchison, "Relevant Witnesses: The Sexual Abuse of Refugee Women in Djibouti", in *Cultural Survival Quarterly*, vol. 8, no. 2, 1984.

[19] There is also some evidence that women who have been raped during flight are more likely to turn to prostitution. Aitchison cites the case of a refugee woman in Djibouti who turned to prostitution because she was certain she would be raped anyway so she thought she might as well earn some money in the process (*op. cit.*, p.27). The dissolution of traditional social norms coupled with dire economic need can give rise to a feeling that the old values against prostitution no longer apply.

[20] Elizabeth Ferris, "NGO Survey of Refugee Women", Geneva, NGO Working Group on Refugee Women, mimeo, 1987, p.4.

[21] These same factors emerge over and over again in discussions among NGOs about women's use of existing programmes. Whether health clinics or adult literacy classes or vocational training, the issues of child care, lack of time, inconvenient schedules, repeatedly come up as the main obstacles to women's participation in assistance programmes (see *Working with Refugee Women: A Practical Guide*, *op. cit.*). The results of the 1987 NGO survey indicate that refugee women tend to be best served by material assistance programmes and to play a more active role in food distribution systems than other social programmes.

[22] In Sudan in 1982, for example, only 10 percent of the beneficiaries of medical counselling services were women. Not a single one of these women was the head of a family. United Nations Economic Commission for Africa, "Refugee and Displaced Women in Africa", paper presented at the third regional conference on the integration of women in development, Arusha, 1984, p.10.

[23] Kelley, *op. cit.*, p.27.

[24] Sharon Krummel, *Refugee Women and the Experience of Cultural Uprooting*, Geneva, WCC, 1989.

[25] Kelley, *op. cit.*, p.28.

[26] See for example, R.A. Pirollo, "Value Systems and Depression Levels of Vietnamese Refugee Women", MS thesis, Denton, TX, Texas Women's University, 1983; I. Walter, "One Year after Arrival: The Adjustment of Indochinese Women in the United States", in *International Migration*, vol. 19, nos 1-2; *Fluchtingsfrauen*, Stuttgart, Diakonisches Werk, 1987; *Puis, la porte s'est ouverte: problèmes de santé mentale des immigrants et des réfugiés*, Groupe chargé d'étudier les problemes de santé mentale des immigrants et des réfugiés au Canada, Ottawa, Santé et Bien-Etre Social, 1988; also Nogues L. Rodriguez, "Psychological Effects of Premature Separation from Parents in Cuban Refugee Girls: A Retrospective Study", Boston University, School of Education, 1983.

27 See, for example, Christensen, *op. cit.*, on Afghan refugee women. M. Sundhugal, "Situation and Role of Refugee Women: Experiences and Perspectives from Thailand", in *International Migration*, vol. 19, nos 1-2, found that the emotional stresses of Khmer refugee women in Thailand contributed to a deterioration of their physical health as they became apathetic and consequently careless about hygiene and health.

28 See *Working with Refugee Women: A Practical Guide, op. cit.*, pp.31-33, for further exploration of these themes.

29 One of the most interesting examples is that of the International Catholic Child Bureau's work in Ukwimi refugee settlement where research and action were used both to identify problems and to devise appropriate measures of intervention. See Margaret McCallin and Shirley Fozzard, *The Impact of Traumatic Events on the Psychological Well-Being of Mozambican Refuge Women and Children,* Geneva, ICCB, 1990.

30 See for example, UNHCR statements on refugee women adopted at executive committee meetings in 1988, 1989, 1990; Susan Forbes Martin, *Refugee Women*, London, Zed Press, 1991; Ninette Kelley, *Working with Refugee Women: A Practical Guide, op. cit.*; Elizabeth Ferris, "Refugee Women: Lively Debates in Nairobi and Beyond", in *Refugees*, WCC, no. 68, 1985, and "Refugee Women: Reflection and Action", in *Refugees*, WCC, no. 87, 1987. Also see Women's Commission for Refugee Women and Children, *Report on the Situation of Women and Children in UN and UNHCR-Administered Refugee Operations*, New York, IRC, 1989; Helen Callaway and R. Gauna, *Women Refugees: Their Specific Needs and Untapped Resources*, London, Third World Affairs Foundation, 1986; G. Rais de Lerner and I. Tapia de Peralta, *La mujer latinoamericana y la migración forzada*, Caracas, Servicio Social Internacional, January 1981.

31 *Working with Refugee Women: A Practical Guide*, *op. cit.*, p.33.

32 For further information on refugee children, see especially the work of the International Catholic Child Bureau, including Margaret McCallin, *The Psychosocial Consequences of Violent Displacement,* Geneva, ICCB, 1991; Margaret McCallin and Shirley Fozzard, *op. cit.*; *Children Worldwide*, the regular publication of ICCB. Also see John Gabarino, F.Scott and Faculty of the Erikson Institute, *What Children Can Tell Us: Eliciting, Interpreting and Evaluating Information from Children*, Oxford, Jossey-Bass, Inc., 1990; C. Dodge and M. Ranudalen eds, *Reaching Children in War: Sudan, Uganda and Mozambique*, Uppsala, Scandinavian Institute of African Studies; E. Ressler, N. Boothby and D. Stinbock, *Unaccompanied Children: Care and Protection in Wars, Natural Disasters and Refugee Movements*, Oxford, Oxford University Press, 1988; special issue of *Refugee Participation Network* (Refugee Studies Programme, Oxford University) on "Refugee Children", no. 2, March 1992; also see *Refugees*, WCC, "Refugee Children and Youth", no. 74 and "Refugee Children: Hope for the Future", no. 112, March 1991.

33 See, for example, Neil Boothby, Peter Upton and Abubacar Sultan, "Boy Soldiers of Mozambique", in *Refugee Participation Network*, no. 12, March 1992, pp.3-6.

34 Rädda Barnen, *Report: Child Victims of Armed Conflicts*, NGO Forum, Rome, 28 April 1984. For a brief description of some of the trauma facing Mozambican children as a result of the war, see Neil Boothby, "Living in the War Zone", in *World Refugee Survey 1988*, Washington, DC, US Committee for Refugees, 1989.

35 Cited by Elizabeth Ferris, "Refugee Children: Hope for the Future", in *Refugees*, WCC, no. 112, March 1991, p.2.

36 Figures for 1990. Cited by Ferris, *ibid.*, p.2.

[37] Ana Vasquez, "Adolescents from the Southern Cone of Latin America in Exile: Some Psychological Problems", in *Mental Health and Exile*, London, World University Service-UK, 1981.

[38] See, for example, Jan Williamson and Audrey Moser, *Unaccompanied Children in Emergencies*, Geneva, International Social Service, 1987.

[39] Barnen, *op. cit*. For an overview of some of the problems facing refugee children in Europe, see the report of the European Seminar on Protection of Refugee Children, held in Stockholm and Åland Islands, 4-8 September 1989.

[40] See D. Tolfree, "Refugee Children in Malawi: A Study of the Implementation of the UNHCR Guidelines on Refugee Children", London, International Save the Children Alliance and UNHCR, 1991.

6. Refugees in Africa
Too Many, Too Long

As heavy fighting breaks out in Southern Ethiopia, Sudanese refugees are forced to return to their country — a country where a brutal war is raging. Half of Liberia's population has been displaced by the violence. People in neighbouring countries welcomed them warmly when they arrived. But now the welcome is wearing thin.

A peace agreement in Angola has been signed, but before the refugees and displaced people can return, something has to be done about the countless mines which have torn so many bodies apart.

Change is coming to Southern Africa. 40,000 Namibians were able to return home in 1990 and to participate in their country's elections. Now it's the turn of South African exiles to travel home and to adapt to a new situation in their country.

More than a third of the world's refugees and displaced people are in Africa. The situations which led to their flight are different; the causes of the violence vary by regime and by specific national characteristics. The refugees from Burundi flee a different sort of violence from the Saharoui refugees living in Algeria. But in another sense, the situations are tragically similar as people are forced to leave their communities and abandon their homes because of violence. African generosity in receiving the strangers is legendary; while some European governments complain at being "overwhelmed" by a few thousand asylum-seekers, most African countries have provided a generous welcome to far larger numbers of refugees seeking protection and security. But host African governments have paid a price for their generosity — an economic, political, social and environmental cost. As the refugees stay longer and longer, the welcome becomes more difficult to sustain.

It is impossible in a single chapter to include descriptions of the complexities of the various African refugee situations. This chapter provides a survey of only three of the largest refugee movements on the continent: the Horn of Africa, Liberia and Southern Africa. Although a focus on these situations enables us to consider three very different groups of refugees, we barely scratch the surface of the dilemmas of African refugees.

Most studies on African refugees focus on the burden they present to host governments and host populations. And the burdens are real as governments seek to balance competing economic, political, ethnic and humanitarian demands. But refugees are not only a burden; they are also a factor in resolving conflicts and in reconstructing war-damaged societies. The exiles who returned to Namibia in 1990 brought with them skills and experiences which the new government needed in bringing about the transition to democracy. Exiles who are preparing to return to Eritrea and South Africa, to Mozambique, Angola and Western Sahara want to be a part of the rebuilding of their homelands. Refugees are — or can be — a resource for development and democracy.

Africa has historically been a scene of forced migration — from the slave trade of the nineteenth century which robbed the continent of millions of their people to patterns of forced labour established by colonial rule. National borders established by colonial authorities never stopped the pastoralists from travelling their historic routes in search of agricultural goods and grazing for their herds. Many borders are notoriously porous; routes across borders are followed not only by traders and nomads, but increasingly by people searching for work or fleeing drought or political violence. Sometimes their stay abroad is temporary: the drought recedes and people return home, or an agreement is reached to bring about an end to hostilities. Sometimes they are forced back home because the host government changes its policies or because new violence erupts in the country of exile and the refugees do not feel safe. Sometimes these happen at the same time. In December 1991 the Congolese government decided to expel Zairians living illegally in that country. The Congolese government estimated that as many as a million Zairians were living in the country — in comparison with the country's indigenous population of 2 million. But the expulsion came at the same time that Zaire was racked with internal political turmoil and economic desperation. [1]

One 1983 study showed that of the 433 million people in Africa, over 3 percent or 13.4 million were immigrants. When one adds refugees and people outside their countries of origin, the overall estimate of 35 million is a plausible one — a figure which represents 8 percent of sub-Saharan Africa's population.[2] Today when one includes internally displaced people, the figure would undoubtedly be higher. While most of the immigration occurs within Africa, the region has been hit particularly hard by emigration of skilled workers to countries outside the region. By 1987, nearly one-third of Africa's skilled people had moved to Europe. Sudan lost a particularly high proportion of professional people with 17 percent of its doctors and dentists, 20 percent of university teaching staff, 30 percent of engineers and 45 percent of surveyors lost to emigration in 1978 alone.[3]

Refugee flows: causes

While Africa has a long tradition of migration, the present wave of refugee flows dates from the mid-1960s. The independence movements resulted most immediately in refugees who had supported the former colonial system. But the process of consolidating the state has also produced subsequent flows of refugees. As discussed in the chapter on root causes, colonial policies largely contributed to the modern refugee phenomenon: most obviously in drawing up borders with little correspondence to the ethnic and political make-up of the inhabitants. More fundamentally, the difficulties which independent African governments have faced in consolidating the state have led to political turmoil, human-rights abuses, and wars — all of which have led to refugee flows. Some of these difficulties are the result of colonialism and neo-colonialist policies (particularly in countries such as Angola, Burundi, Chad, Rwanda, Sudan, Uganda and Zaire) where colonial policies created intense political competition for economic and social resources and set the stage for an open battle for exclusive control of the state.[4] But there is increasing realization that the instability and wars in independent Africa have more complex roots than colonial policies. Rather the process of consolidating the state, coupled with authoritarian leadership and the creation of one-party states in societies marked by deep economic and ethnic cleavages has led to conflicts — and to refugees.

The causes of specific refugee flows — as discussed in the sections below (pp.136f.) — are unique to each case and yet there are certain common themes which will be examined further in the concluding section of this chapter.

TABLE 1:   REFUGEES AND DISPLACED PEOPLE IN AFRICA, 31 DECEMBER 1991

Country of origin		Total refugees	Internally displaced
Algeria		204,000	
West Sahara	165,000		
Mali	35,000		
Others	4,000		
Angola		10,400	
Internally displaced			827,000
Zaire	10,300		
South Africa	100		
Benin		15,100	
Togo	10,500		
Chad	100		
Botswana		1,400	
South Africa	1,000		
Angola	200		
Others	300		
Burkina Faso		400	
Chad	200		
Burundi		107,000	
Rwanda	80,600		
Zaire	20,900		
Somalia	100		
Others	400		
Cameroon		6,900	
Chad	6,500		
Others	400		
Central African Republic		9,000	
Sudan	8,000		
Chad	1,000		
Congo		3,400	
Chad	2,300		
Zaire	400		
CAR	300		
Others	400		
Côte-d'Ivoire		240,400	
Liberia	240,000		
Others	400		

Country of origin		Total refugees	Internally displaced
Djibouti		120,000	
Somalia	105,000		
Ethiopia	15,000		
Egypt		7,750	
Palestinians	5,500		
Somalia	1,300		
Ethiopia	600		
Others	350		
Ethiopia/Eritrea		534,000	
Internally displaced			1,000,000
Sudan	519,000		
Somalia	15,000		
Gabon		800	
Gambia		1,500	
Senegal	1,000		
Liberia	500		
Ghana		6,150	
Liberia	6,000		
Guinea Bissau		4,600	
Senegal	4,600		
Guinea		556,000	
Liberia	397,000		
Sierra Leone	169,000		
Kenya		107,150	
Somalia	92,200		
Ethiopia	11,800		
Rwanda	2,000		
Uganda	700		
Others	450		
Lesotho		300	
South Africa	300		
Liberia		12,000	
Internally displaced			500,000
Sierra Leone	12,000		
Malawi		950,000	
Mozambique	950,000		

Country of origin		Total refugees	Internally displaced
Mali		13,500	
Mauritania	13,000		
Niger	500		
Mauritania		40,000	
Senegal	22,000		
Mali	18,000		
Morocco		800	
Mozambique		500	
Internally displaced			2,000,000
Namibia		30,200	
Angola	30,000		
Others	200		
Niger		1,400	
Chad	1,400		
Nigeria		4,600	
Chad	3,300		
Liberia	1,000		
Others	300		
Rwanda		32,500	
Internally displaced			100,000
Burundi	32,500		
Senegal		53,100	
Mauritania	53,000		
Others	100		
Sierra Leone		17,200	
Internally displaced			145,000
Liberia	17,200		
Somalia		35,000	
Internally displaced			500,000-1,000,000
Ethiopia	35,000		
South Africa		201,000	
Internally displaced			4,100,000
Mozambique	200,000		
Lesotho	1,000		

Country of origin	Total refugees	Internally displaced
Sudan	717,200	
Internally displaced		4,750,000
Ethiopia/Eritrea	690,000	
Chad	20,000	
Zaire	4,500	
Uganda	2,700	
Swaziland	47,200	
Mozambique	39,500	
South Africa	7,700	
Tanzania	251,100	
Burundi	131,000	
Mozambique	72,000	
Rwanda	22,300	
Zaire	16,000	
South Africa	9,600	
Others	200	
Togo	450	
Tunisia	50	
Uganda	165,450	
Internally displaced		300,000
Rwanda	87,000	
Sudan	75,500	
South Africa	2,000	
Zaire	600	
Others	350	
Zaire	482,300	
Angola	310,000	
Sudan	104,000	
Burundi	45,000	
Rwanda	12,000	
Uganda	10,000	
Others	1,300	
Zambia	140,500	
Angola	103,000	
Mozambique	25,000	
Zaire	9,000	
South Africa	2,000	
Uganda	1,500	

Country of origin	Total refugees	Internally displaced
Zimbabwe		198,500
Mozambique	197,000	
South Africa	1,000	
Others	500	
Total		**5,340,800**

Source: US Committee for Refugees, *World Refugee Survey 1992*, Washington, USCR, 1992.

The Horn of Africa

The refugee situation in the Horn of Africa has been one of the world's largest, most intractable, and most complex human tragedies. The countries of the Horn — Ethiopia, Sudan, Somalia and Djibouti — have different colonial backgrounds, different ethnic and religious characteristics, and different political issues. Yet they are linked — not only by traditional trading patterns, but increasingly by the mass movements of large numbers of people. A survey of the principal movements of refugees provides a dizzying array of refugee situations: there are Somalis in Ethiopia and Djibouti, Ethiopians in Sudan, Somalia and Djibouti; and Sudanese in Ethiopia. This movement of people also spills into other countries as well with Sudanese in Uganda, Ugandans in Sudan, Somalis and Sudanese in Kenya, and Sudanese, Ethiopians and Somalis in Egypt. And Chadians have come to Sudan in large numbers as well.

The wars and violence which have forced so many into exile have also displaced millions within the borders of their own countries. The war in southern Sudan has resulted in an influx of refugees into neighbouring countries, but an even larger outpouring of southerners into other parts of Sudan — where their conditions of life are generally much worse than those of the people who live in exile. The situation of uprooted people in the Horn of Africa is also a dynamic one. In the past two years, the departure of the Mengistu regime in Ethiopia and the success of the struggle for Eritrean independence has opened possibilities for the return of large numbers of refugees — many of whom have lived in exile for more than a decade. At the same time, a new round of particularly savage violence in Somalia is producing new waves of refugees and an increasingly desperate situation for the far larger numbers of internally displaced. And the war in Sudan goes on, while the United Nations appeals for assistance for the 9 million Sudanese at risk of starvation and death.

The causes of the mass population movements in the Horn include wars, ethnic rivalries, religious conflicts, secessionist movements, human-rights abuses, political repression, and environmental causes such as drought and famine. Usually most of these factors occur simultaneously, making it difficult to separate out "political", "economic" and "environmental" causes of population displacement. The suffering produced by a drought, for example, is exacerbated by political conditions; when a drought occurs in a war-torn area, relief assistance is difficult, and people are forced to walk long distances in search of food. They leave their countries and their communities because there is no food; but the reasons for the unavailability of food are both environmental and political. In practice, most of those uprooted because of famine and drought are received as refugees by the neighbouring countries and are treated as refugees by UNHCR. The complexities of legal definitions seem almost irrelevant in light of human need. But when those same individuals seek asylum in Western countries, they are often found not to be refugees fleeing political persecution, but economic migrants who choose to leave their country because of economic difficulties.

Sudan: another decade of civil war

Sudan became independent in 1955 and was almost immediately engulfed in civil war between the northern and southern regions of the country. The differences between north and south are many: the northerners are Muslim, ethnically closer to the Arab nations, and in control of the government. The minority southerners, both Christian and animist, come from different ethnic groups and are closer to the black African nations of the continent. But the conflict is more than just Christians versus Muslims: issues of economics, culture and political power are also involved. Questions about the form of the state, the degree of autonomy to be enjoyed by regions of the country and the distribution of the state's resources have led to conflicts between north and south — conflicts which are often reduced to religion or ethnicity but which are intensified by the political and economic climate of the country.

The war came to an end in 1972 as a result of a political settlement, but was resumed in 1983 when the Sudanese government imposed Shar'ia — Islamic law — on the whole country. In southern Sudan it has led to the region's isolation as the government has virtually prohibited transportation to the region. Roads have been cut off, blockades imposed on rivers, airplanes have been banned from the area. The Sudanese govern-ment has given arms to nomadic groups that live in the zone between north and south who are traditionally hostile to the southern Sudanese and these groups have carried out massacres of civilian populations. The war has caused hundreds of thousands of casualties, as a result of the fighting and of the isolation. The displacement of millions of southern Sudanese has been the human result of the fighting and the food shortages.

Sudanese refugees and displaced

Since the war broke out in 1983, Sudanese refugees have fled into southern Ethiopia as well as to Zaire, Uganda and the Central American Republic. A disproportionate number of refugees arriving in Ethiopia in the late 1980s were young boys and adolescents who had suffered severe physical and emotional trauma as a result of the violence and their flight. In addition to the problems of 40,000 unaccompanied minors, the 300,000 Sudanese refugees faced difficulties in Ethiopia because of overcrowding, poor transportation, and inadequate planning for them.

Following violence in Ethiopia, during the year after Mengistu's overthrow, 270,000 Sudanese refugees in Ethiopia returned to southern Sudan. Their return was carried out under the worst possible conditions: they decided to return not because they judged that conditions in Sudan had changed, but because they feared for their lives in Ethiopia. The returnees were attacked and bombed as they made their way to the Sudanese side of the border, and once inside Sudan conditions were desperate in the hastily-established camps. And the war in Sudan con-tinued.

According to the US Committee for Refugees, some 4.5 million Sudanese have been displaced within their own country as a result of the violence — 4 million of whom are southerners (out of a total southern Sudanese population of 5 to 6 million). An estimated 1.8 million displaced people live around Khartoum, another 350,000 are located in the so-called "transition zone" between north and south and 2.35 million are displaced within the south, both in rebel-held areas and in the few government-held garrison towns in southern Sudan, principally Juba.[5]

The conditions of the displaced southerners in Khartoum are terrible. They live in the poorest areas of the city, sometimes on garbage dumps, with little access to water, health care or other social services. In fact, the government makes it difficult for NGOs to provide any such services to the displaced and has prohibited international agencies from assisting them. Reports in early 1992 are that Islamic relief agencies make aid to the displaced conditional on their conversion to Islam. The government has repeatedly warned the displaced southerners to return and, since 1987, has conducted periodic campaigns to forcibly move the displaced away from Khartoum. In late October 1990, for example, the Sudanese military burned the homes of 30,000 displaced people at Hillat Shook displaced camp and forcibly moved some 4,000 to 5,000 of them to a site thirty miles south of Khartoum — to an area described by a UN report as completely unsuitable for human habitation. The government's policy is to rid Khartoum of the southern Sudanese. The government maintains that the city does not have the resources to support this population (which is undoubtedly true) and that it wants Khartoum to be an "Arab" city.

The displaced who remain in the south of Sudan are vulnerable to violence from government forces pursuing the Sudan People's Liberation Army forces and seeking to destroy their civilian bases of support, to forced recruitment by the SPLA and, above all, to widespread hunger as a result of the war and the drought. In 1988, an estimated 250,000 southern Sudanese died, largely as a result of war-induced famine. A report by Africa Watch traces the connections between the war and the famine which killed so many.

> The famine was created by war. The most important causes for this famine are the results of deliberate policies adopted by both the government and the Sudan People's Liberation Army (SPLA). The most significant governmental policies included using militias and paramilitary forces. The army and SPLA tactics included "scorched earth" policies and the SPLA also resorted to siege of government-held towns. Both the government and the SPLA denied food to the civilian population in the war zones. The policies of denying relief did not create the famine, but made it much more severe when the famine occurred. These tactics included obstructing relief supplies, obstructing or distorting commercial food markets and preventing famine stricken populations from following "coping" strategies (for instance, searching in the bush for wild foods). [6]

Beginning in early 1990 the international community again began warning of a massive drought and impending famine in Sudan. Although the Sudanese government denied the impending famine and prohibited international relief supplies from reaching the region, the signs of famine were clear to most observers. A USCR visit to southern Sudan in March 1990 led to testimony before the US Congress: "There are *no* buffer stocks of food in any of the areas we visited... we could routinely see old women forty feet up in the tops of trees, picking leaves to eat; they had nothing else." [7] By the end of 1991, the international estimates were that

9 million people in Sudan were at risk because of severe food shortages. A report by the World Health Organization and the Sudanese ministry of health on nutrition status in the Red Sea province indicated a total absence of children between six months and three years of age. Presumably they had all died. [8]

In 1989, the Sudanese government and the SPLA co-operated in allowing a UN-led effort known as Operation Lifeline Sudan to deliver assistance to hundreds of thousands of Sudanese at risk. The project was criticized for its bias towards the government and for the expense of the operation, but nonetheless it was able to supply food to about 250,000 people. In 1990 efforts to continue the programme met with resistance from the government and it came to a halt.

In 1990 and 1991, the government not only denied the famine and consistently impeded efforts by relief agencies, including the UN, to provide food to the south, but also spent scarce foreign currency to purchase arms to continue the war in the south. The present economic situation of the country could not be more desperate. Much international aid to Sudan has been cut off, the IMF has declared Sudan — the Fund's largest debtor — to be a "non-co-operative state" which means that Sudan will not be eligible for most large-scale economic assistance from major donors. The drought has led to food shortages throughout the country, the war has caused hundreds of thousands of deaths, and refugees from Ethiopia and Eritrea remain in the eastern parts of the country in large numbers.

Unless there is a peace agreement and an end to the war in southern Sudan, it is hard to see any possible positive outcome for the people of the region.

Ethiopia and Eritrea: Africa's longest war

From 1975 until 1991, Ethiopia was ruled by Lt Col. Haile Mariam Mengistu, a dictator who seized power in a military coup and who ruled with absolute authority. Under the Mengistu regime, opposition was silenced, human-rights abuses were widespread and the war against the Eritrean and Tigrayan insurgent groups intensified. As seen earlier, the government's plans for relocation and villagization led to massive displacement of people and to further refugee flows.

The violence in Ethiopia produced three distinct groups of refugees: primarily urban Ethiopian dissidents fleeing the human-rights violations of the Mengistu regime; Ethiopian refugees fleeing to Somalia as a result of war with Somalia, the villagization programme, and drought; and

Eritrean, Tigrayan and Ethiopian refugees fleeing into Sudan as a result of the war and famine.

With the fall of Mengistu, a new refugee flow was produced. In early June 1991 around 50,000 Ethiopian soldiers and their dependents arrived in Kassala, fleeing the forces of the new government. Although they had arrived in fairly healthy condition, within three months they were dying of disease and malnutrition. "For weeks, botched logistics and poor co-ordination between humanitarian agencies resulted in the delivery of rations consisting of little but wheat, much of it infested." The lack of fresh produce led to scurvy as well as dysentery. By the time UNHCR learned of their plight many of those who survived could barely walk. [9]

The urban Ethiopian dissidents left in the aftermath of the 1975 coup; some had been associated with the Haile Selassie regime, most fled as a result of the crackdown on human rights by the new administration. Some of the Ethiopians who fled remained within the region, but most went further abroad, particularly to the US and Europe. Washington DC is said to house over 60,000 Ethiopian and Eritrean refugees.

Flight to Somalia

The earliest Ethiopian refugees to enter Somalia were relatively small numbers of Oromos who fled the 1976 fighting between the government and the Oromo Liberation Front. But the war between Ethiopia and Somalia in 1977 over the Ogaden, an area of Ethiopia inhabited mainly by ethnic Somalis, led to further flows of ethnic Somali refugees from Ethiopia. With Somalia's 1978 defeat in the war and reprisals by Ethiopian troops against the Somali and Oromo populations of the region, large numbers of Ethiopian refugees entered Somalia. Although the numbers are recognized as "large", and increased periodically as a result of repression and drought in Ethiopia, the whole question of numbers of refugees in Somalia has been an extremely difficult and contentious one.

The Somali government recognized early on that the amount of international relief from UNHCR and other UN agencies depended on the number of refugees in the country: the more refugees claimed by Somalia, the more assistance from the international community. Thus, the Somali government in 1978 claimed that there were one million Ethiopian refugees in the country — a figure disputed by UNHCR and others. In 1982, after exhaustive consultations between the two sides, a planning figure of 700,000 was accepted. In 1986 a revised figure of 840,000 was negotiated between the two sides — in spite of the fact that some 400,000 Ethiopians had repatriated to Ethiopia with UNHCR assistance. The US

Committee for Refugees estimates that the actual number of refugees at that time was probably below 200,000. [10]

The question of the numbers of refugees has made providing assistance difficult. Another difficulty was caused by persistent reports that the Somali government was arming and recruiting Ethiopian refugees to fight in its own civil war. In 1988, Somalia and Ethiopia agreed not to host each other's liberation movements. Thus the Somali guerrilla group, SNM, was pushed back into Somalia from its Ethiopian base. The Somali military under Siad Barre's presidency in turn recruited soldiers among Ethiopian refugee camps in Somalia. With the intensification in 1988 of the Somali war, this forced recruitment increased, leading UNHCR to cut off assistance to refugees in northern Somalia in late 1989 (although food assistance was later resumed for a six-month period at the UN Secretary General's request.) In late 1989, in southern Somalia, UNHCR registered all Ethiopian refugees and gave them the option of returning voluntarily to Ethiopia (about 30 percent of the refugees chose this solution), local integration with a cash and food grant (some 70 percent chose this option), or continued refugee status (less than 1 percent). But international funds to support this programme did not materialize. And in December 1990, as fighting within Somalia intensified, UNHCR — and most of the refugees — left Somalia. A month later, Siad Barre fled the country as well. By March 1991, only some 15-35,000 Ethiopian refugees remained in Somalia, mostly in Mogadishu and Qorioley. Some 3,000 Ethiopian refugees, mainly Oromos, fled from Somalia to Kenya.

Ethiopian/Eritrean refugees in Sudan

The largest number of Ethiopian/Eritrean refugees have been those fleeing into Sudan. Since 1967 when clashes between Eritrean and Ethiopian forces intensified, refugees have come to Sudan. But following the devastating drought in Ethiopia, particularly northern Ethiopia, in 1984, the numbers jumped dramatically. As was the case elsewhere in the Horn, the combination of drought, war and a repressive government proved to be deadly. The 1984-85 famine was brought home to the Western public by widespread media coverage which resulted in an outpouring of attention, funds, and Western aid agency programmes in the country. [11] Relief operations were marked by enormous logistical difficulties compounded by serious political problems as the government was more concerned with fighting the war against the Eritreans than with facilitating provision of relief assistance to hungry people.

Some of those who fled the famine returned home as conditions improved. The intensified fighting in 1989-90 led to a further wave of refugees from Eritrea and Tigray. Presently the Sudanese government and UNHCR list some 700,000 Ethiopian/Eritrean refugees in the country of whom about 370,000 are assisted in reception centres and agricultural settlements.

The war for Eritrean liberation, Africa's longest liberation struggle, was a bitter and bloody one. In May 1991, opposition forces to the Mengistu regime brought down the government, forcing Mengistu into exile and establishing a new transitional government which represented various ethnic and political groupings in the country. A conference two months later agreed to hold a referendum in Eritrea within two years which would determine the region's future. Although Eritrean independence has thus been effectively postponed for two years, it is now widely expected to become a reality and most observers now recognize Eritrea's de facto independence. The long war has come to an end, but the return of the refugees will depend on the reconstruction of Eritrea and the establishment of peace and security in the region. In autumn 1991, some 1,000 families a month were returning spontaneously to Eritrea, but conditions are difficult and the Eritrean Relief Association estimates that approximately 80 percent of Eritrea's population is in need of food assistance. Difficulties in mobilizing sufficient funds to provide for the reintegration of returnees and in reaching agreements with UNHCR have meant that repatriation efforts have been delayed.

The end of the war also meant the demobilization of the former army and the return of prisoners. An estimated 300,000 prisoners of war began to move south from former conflict regions. Most are concentrated in urban centres in Tigray, Gondor and Welo although some are continuing to walk to their areas of origin. Associated war-displaced civilians, whose numbers may be as high as 150,000, mostly mothers and families, are also moving south and putting pressure on food stocks and community resources. The demobilization of the military and the displacement of people affected by the war create strains on resources; one-third of the former soldiers are injured or disabled. They need jobs and food; without these, the de-mobilized and displaced are a threat to the maintenance of peace. [12]

Somalia: violence and more violence

The outbreak of civil war in northern Somalia in mid-1988 and the Somali government's brutal retaliation against the civilian population (including, as we have seen, the forced recruitment of Ethiopian refugees in the country) led more than 700,000 Somalis to flee to Ethiopia, Kenya and Djibouti, and displaced hundreds of thousands of other Somalis within the country. The war also forced the Ethiopian refugees to go back to Ethiopia where they faced perilous conditions in camps hastily constructed in eastern Ethiopia. The government of Mohammed Siad Barre sought to contain the rebellion, but the pressures mounted.

In December 1990, the violence escalated. Fighting in the capital led to widespread destruction of the city and to the evacuation of most foreigners and international agencies operating there. Siad Barre and his troops were forced to leave Mogadishu in January 1991, and a new government under the leadership of the United Somali Congress was formed. But it was unable to bring about an end to the violence and fighting continued throughout the year. Gangs of armed men terrorized the city, looting and killing at random. People trying to understand the political differences between the warring factions were frustrated as the violence seemed to have acquired a momentum all its own. By the end of 1991, the fighting seemed to be dominated between two strong men intent on fighting each other to the death over issues related to intra-clan rivalry rather than ideology or even economics. Social norms and values degenerated as hospitals were attacked, children killed, and everything of value stolen. Life in Mogadishu became dominated by rival gangs and unorganized looters, all heavily armed. The ICRC and a few NGOs continued to provide very limited assistance, but were hampered by lack of supplies and, above all, by the growing desperation of the city's population. In spite of efforts by the United Nations and others to provide relief assistance and food, the violence in the port led fully-laden ships to turn back from Mogadishu because they couldn't unload. Meanwhile hundreds of thousands of Somalis faced starvation because of lack of food. By early 1992, it was estimated that between one-quarter and one-third of all Somali children under the age of five had already died.[13]

Peace initiatives were undertaken, a few UN missions sent to the country, but given the random nature of the violence, a solution to the violence and even a limited cease-fire proved to be elusive. As in other wars, indications are that it was the civilian population, particularly women and children, who are paying the heaviest price for the violence between the Somali strongmen.

In May 1992, the UN and the Red Cross began importing the first significant food shipments since internecine warfare erupted in Mogadishu. To protect the grain, the organizations have hired small armies of mercenaries who are meant to forestall attack from the thousands of hungry armed men who roam the streets.

> The shipments are the product of tortuous negotiations in which the United Nations and Red Cross met daily for more than a month with clans, subclans, militias and families. The negotiations underscored the profound divisions within Somali society, as did the two organizations' need to hire gunmen to escort their relief convoys. [14]

In response to the increasing violence, by mid-1992 the ICRC was devoting 50 percent of its entire worldwide emergency budget for its relief operations in Somalia. Four other NGOs remained in Somalia throughout this period — despite the extraordinarily difficult situation — to provide assistance while the United Nations remained largely on the sidelines. [15] In April the UN Security Council agreed to establish a UN Operation in Somalia to promote a political settlement and fifty UN observers were dispatched. In August the Security Council approved the deployment of 3,000 additional troops although only 500 Pakistani troops had actually arrived by the end of the year — and the widespread violence prevented them from playing an active role.

By late 1992, 1.5 million people faced imminent starvation; almost 5 million were totally dependent on external food aid. While the crisis had been building over a long time period, the political response was much slower. As pictures of the Somali tragedy were shown on Western television sets and as public pressure mounted, in December the UN Security Council accepted the US offer of military troops to establish a "secure environment for humanitarian relief operations" in Somalia. In resolution 792, the Security Council determined that the "magnitude of the human tragedy caused by the conflict in Somalia constituted a threat to international peace and security". By early 1993, US troops were in Somalia, actively trying to establish a "secure environment for humanitarian relief operations" even as plans were advanced for replacing US troops with UN peace-keeping forces.

While it is unlikely that the crisis in Somalia will be resolved rapidly, the response of the international community to the tragedy is being seen as a possible precedent for further UN intervention in support of humanitarian goals. Like other UN humanitarian action, however, its success will ultimately depend on the extent to which peace and security are re-established.

Since 1990 over one million Somalis have fled the country in the aftermath of the violence, seeking protection and food in Ethiopia,

Kenya, Yemen, Djibouti and Saudi Arabia. But even in exile, they faced serious problems.

In Ethiopia they arrived in areas without water, far from roads to facilitate delivery of water and relief supplies. While UNHCR sought to transport water to the camps, the logistical and bureaucratic difficulties meant that water and food were insufficient. Violence in the refugee camps has continued to be a major problem; many of the refugees are armed, and foreign relief workers are not allowed to spend the night in the camps. The further influx in April 1991 of an additional 200,000 Somali refugees into Ethiopia stretched UNHCR's capacity to breaking point. Reduced rations and increased malnutrition led some Somalis to return to Somalia — in spite of the brutal war going on in that country.

The Kenyan government reacted to the new Somali arrivals with dismay; facing its own ethnic conflicts and a growing popular reaction against Somalis, it did not want to encourage the arrival of large numbers of Somali refugees. On the other hand, the widespread suffering in that country as well as the relative inaccessibility of the border meant that it was reluctant to be too aggressive in keeping Somalis out. But the arrival of large numbers of Somalis, often in desperate physical condition, posed a severe strain on the Kenyan government and society. In early 1991, Kenya hosted 14,000 refugees with relatively few problems. By the end of the year, nearly 200,000 were jammed into overcrowded camps and more were expected. The Liboi camp, for example, near the Somali border was intended for 3,000 refugees. By early 1992, it housed 68,000 Somali refugees. The lack of water meant that people had to queue for up to 48 hours to get their ration of three litres. At the same time the Somalis were arriving in Kenya, refugees from southern Ethiopia poured into Kenya. Some of the refugees had walked for more than 600 kilometres to reach the border; many were wounded, and weakened by the long trip. In mid-1992 UNHCR estimated that at least 300,000 people in southern Ethiopia were in dire need of assistance. Without that assistance, they will continue to arrive in Kenya. Conservative estimates said that the refugee population in Kenya would have reached 340,000 by the end of June. [16]

The Horn of Africa: drawing the connections

Although we have followed tradition by describing the refugee situations in terms of the countries of origin of the refugees, such a description inevitably oversimplifies what is a more complex phenomenon. In particular the countries hosting each other's refugees are not disinterested observers; rather, they often seek to use the refugees or the presence of refugees as a way of enhancing their political claims. Thus there are claims that the Ethiopian government, by allowing the Sudanese refugees to remain in their country, was supporting the SPLA. And there are corresponding claims that the Sudanese government provided a haven to the various Eritrean liberation movements, allowing them to mount cross-border relief operations intended to alleviate Eritrean famine and to support the war efforts. Without the safe haven of a nearby country, both the SPLA and the Eritrean People's Liberation Front, the Tigray People's Liberation Front and other groups would undoubtedly have had a harder time in sustaining their struggles. Sudanese policies towards the Ethiopian/Eritrean refugees were shaped in part by its perceptions of Ethiopian support for Sudanese refugees. On occasion the two governments would agree to ban the political activities of each other's refugees, but these agreements would eventually be broken by one side or the other. Similarly the war in Somalia between and within clans has generated fears that the conflict will spread outside the country's borders.

Moreover, as we have seen in this all-too-brief survey, the refugee situations in the Horn of Africa are not recent phenomena. The wars have gone on for years, in some cases for decades. Many in the West have the suspicion that regardless of international assistance and massive aid programmes, the problems will remain and the suffering will continue. A sort of "compassion fatigue" is apparent among the major donor governments and the general public as well. And yet the recent changes in Ethiopia and Eritrea do offer grounds for optimism. A dictatorial and repressive government was overthrown and conditions laid out for resolution of the Eritrean struggle for independence. The new government is far from perfect and monumental problems remain in forging a new political system in a context with few democratic traditions and an immense task of reconstruction. But the Ethiopian example demonstrates that political change can occur and offers a space, a "window" of opportunity for bringing about political change that may result in an end to the bloodshed which has forced so many into exile.

In the spring of 1991 as the rebel forces were advancing on Addis Ababa, some observers attributed the rebels' victory to their superior discipline and military force. But others pointed to the fact that Ethiopians were tired of war, tired of sacrificing their young people and their resources for a war which could not be won. This weariness with war was perhaps as important a factor in explaining Mengistu's downfall as the political and military strength of the rebels.

The Ethiopian case also points to the necessity of finding ways of sustaining peace. The overthrow of a dictator, the signing of a peace agreement, the establishment of a transitional government are all important steps to bringing about an end to war. But peace in Ethiopia — as in a dozen other places — remains a fragile and elusive process. Questions, for example about the future of the demobilized Ethiopian soldiers, are crucial for the country's future. Similar pressures are evident in Eritrea. Although the great armies have been disbanded, if the soldiers have no way to survive economically, the potential for violence remains. Indeed, reports of renewed fighting in Ethiopia in mid-1992 are a cause for deep concern.

The issue of conflict-resolution is central. Undoubtedly tension in Ethiopia will surface between the claims of competing ethnic groups; such tension is inevitable, given the country's history and the natural clashes of groups seeking divergent objectives. But the central question, the question which will determine whether peace is lasting in Ethiopia and Eritrea or simply a pause in the fighting, is whether mechanisms can be established to allow for the resolution of conflicts without resort to violence.

One mechanism which offers some hope is that of the Ad Hoc Peace Committee. The Committee was formed in 1991 by Ethiopian and Eritrean exiles living in the US as a way of mobilizing help for the peace process, with the help of the Life & Peace Institute, the Mennonite Central Committee and European agencies. The Committee, composed of nine "elders", people respected for their position and their moral stature, was drawn from most of the major ethnic groups and religions in the country. In the year preceding the change in government, the Committee met a number of times and had discussions with competing liberation movements and the government in an effort to provide a neutral ground for the conflicting parties to meet to try to reconcile their differences. With the overthrow of Mengistu, the Committee continued to play a role in the July 1991 peace conference, looking for ways to facilitate agreements and resolve conflicts in order to ensure a stable transitional process. Since 1991, the Committee has served a different function by opening an office in Addis Ababa and working to provide alternative — non-violent — means of conflict-resolution. Because they are respected in the society, and because the Committee is drawn from all sides in the conflict, Committee members have a certain credibility and status which can be used to facilitate the resolution of conflicts short of war.

NGOs have played a very important role in responding to refugee needs in the Horn of Africa. In Sudan and Ethiopia literally hundreds of NGOs have participated in providing famine and emergency relief to refugees. At times co-ordination of their activities has been difficult and an obstacle to the timely provision of relief needs. At times their presence has caused serious and unexpected problems. In eastern Sudan, for example, the presence of large NGOs operating more or less independently in specific refugee camps meant wide inconsistencies in the level of care and facilities available in different places. Thus, one NGO might have facilities for performing surgery in a particular refugee camp while refugees in a neighbouring camp have no such facilities. Tension between the government of Sudan and the NGOs, particularly the foreign NGOs, has been more or less constant for the last decade. By operating directly with the refugees, and bypassing the government's own relief ministry, the NGOs may have helped to weaken the government's capacity to provide assistance and co-ordination. [17] The government has often accused NGOs operating in the south of sympathizing with and supporting the SPLA. In 1987, for example, the government accused 16 US and European relief agencies of supporting the SPLA and ordered them to leave the country. [18] In all of the countries, governments have provoked the anger of foreign NGOs by restrictions on currency exchange and have sporadically limited visas to their employees.

But in spite of the problems, the NGOs continue to provide important services. In Somalia, when the UN agencies and foreign governments withdrew their personnel, the ICRC and NGOs continued to provide medical services to the many wounded civilians. In Sudan, the Sudan Council of Churches has over the years organized large-scale relief programmes for refugees, even as it has spearheaded advocacy efforts to bring about a resolution of the conflict which has caused so much suffering. Christian relief and development agencies worked together to mount cross-border operations into Eritrea when famine threatened the country and it was difficult to get supplies through Ethiopia. This initiative, through the Emergency Relief Desk, has grown from a programme channelling less than $400,000 per year to channelling $100 million in 1991. Inside Ethiopia, the Mekane Yesus Church, in co-operation with the Lutheran World Federation, mounted a major relief programme in northern Ethiopia to transport food by trucks to the war-torn region. In doing so, the Joint Relief Programme, as it was called, had to negotiate safe passage with both the liberation movements and the Ethiopian government.

West Africa: new refugee crises

Unlike the Horn of Africa and Southern Africa, West Africa does not have a long tradition of refugee emergencies. Most West African countries host a small number of refugees from neighbouring countries, particularly Chad, and even smaller numbers from other African regions. But migration, not refugee movements, has characterized population movements in the region. In 1983 and 1984, Nigeria expelled over a million migrants, most of them from Ghana, giving them short notice to return home. In April 1989, a minor incident on the border between Mauritania and Senegal led to violent clashes and to a decision, taken by the two governments, to evacuate each other's citizens. More than 90,000 Senegalese living in Mauritania were returned to Senegal and about 100,000 Mauritanians living in Senegal were returned to Mauritania. Moreover, about 10,000 black Mauritanians (in contrast to the lighter skinned Arab/Berber population in the country) were either forcibly deported or fled to Mali during the same time period. And about 22,000 Senegalese, most with ethnic links to Senegalese ethnic groups, also fled (or were deported) to Mauritania in 1989. Since then, continuing human rights abuses in Mauritania have led to smaller flows of refugees from the country. In Senegal a little-publicized civil war in the south of the country between government troops and rebels led to thousands of refugees fleeing to Gambia and Guinea Bissau in late 1990.

But in spite of these cases, the situation in West Africa seemed quite different from that in other parts of Africa. The number of refugees was relatively small, UNHCR's presence was minimal, few NGOs were working with refugees, and the world's attention was focused on the great emergencies to the South and the East of the region.

Liberia: destruction of a people and a country [19]

The Liberian civil war, which erupted in December 1989, caught the international community by surprise. Unlike the cases of the Horn of Africa and Southern Africa, there was little warning that what started as an effort by a rebel group to overthrow a corrupt president would result in a bloodbath in Liberia and to the displacement of half of that country's population.

In December 1989, a rebel force led by Charles Taylor invaded the country in an effort to overthrow the then-President Samuel Doe. The ensuing war produced a climate of widespread terror for hundreds of thousands of non-combatants caught between the warring factions. What had begun as an effort to seize power from a dictator turned into an ethnic war. By mid-1990, people from all parts of the country, including Monrovia, poured across the borders seeking to escape the bloodshed. Large numbers of displaced persons from the countryside fled to Monrovia itself. Hunger and malnutrition increased throughout the country.

As the violence escalated, the Economic Community of West African States (ECOWAS) sent a peace-keeping force known as the ECOWAS Monitoring Group (ECOMOG) to Monrovia in August 1990 to protect civilians and try to restore order in the capital. The intervention by ECOWAS was an attempt by countries in the region to put an end to the bloodshed and to prevent the conflict from spilling over Liberia's borders. But the ECOWAS process was marked by political division between different West African countries and ECOMOG forces were perceived as playing a political role within the country. Unlike other peace-keeping forces working to implement a peace agreement, the ECOMOG forces were drawn into the conflict and had to fight to establish a modicum of stability. By October 1990 ECOMOG forces had driven Taylor out of Monrovia. Tens of thousands of Liberians fled to Monrovia where the city faced a desperate food shortage. Little was known about condition of those civilians living in Taylor-controlled areas.

Today, Liberia is a divided country. Charles Taylor's forces, the NPFL, control some 95 percent of the country, limiting access and travel from Monrovia. Their capital is Gbarngu. The interim government in Monrovia, led by Amos Sawyer, depends on ECOMOG's 8,000 troops for security and controls an area limited to a 15-mile radius of the capital. The swollen population of Monrovia exists on free food distributed through SELF (Special Emergency Life Food); employment opportunities are limited, there is little money in the country, there are large numbers of orphans and traumatized children. Although the food and security situation has greatly improved, looting and harassment of civilians continues on a sporadic basis. The population of Monrovia continues to wait for a political resolution of the crisis.

In the countryside, few outsiders are able to report from the Taylor-held part of the country. Travel in the region is difficult, but indications are that there are large numbers of internally displaced people, continuing human-rights violations (although reportedly on a lower level than earlier), hunger and inadequate access to health care. One of the widely-reported problems is the use of child soldiers by Taylor's forces.

Liberian refugees: the limits of cohabitation

When the first wave of Liberians spilled into Guinea, Côte d'Ivoire and Sierra Leone in late December 1989, the local villagers opened their homes and their communities to the refugees. The generosity of the local population was remarkable and meant that the Liberians were not placed in refugee camps but rather "cohabited" with the local populations. Given the very slow response of the international community to the refugee emergency, this generosity undoubtedly enabled many to survive. But two years later, the honeymoon had worn off. The lack of food, the strain of large numbers of refugees on health and education services led to tension and resentment among local populations. Some refugees reported that relations with the local population were good when food was available; but when the relief supplies didn't arrive, conflicts arose.

In March 1991, Liberian rebels invaded Sierra Leone and occupied the eastern sections of that country. Even now the reasons for the invasion are unclear and there is speculation that the invading forces included Sierra Leoneans opposing their own government. The occupation of large areas of eastern Sierra Leone uprooted several hundred thousand Sierra Leoneans; their plight as displaced people has received little international attention. More than 96,000 Sierra Leoneans as well as some 10,000 Liberian refugees who had been living in the region left the country for Guinea. By early 1992 these numbers reached 170,000. As a result of the invasion, the Liberian refugees faced increased harassment and discrimination. Refugees reported being thrown out of their housing by Sierra Leoneans. After consultation with family and friends in Monrovia, many concluded it was safer to risk return to Liberia than continued harassment in Sierra Leone.

As a result of the violence and the harassment from Sierra Leoneans, many refugees approached UNHCR for assistance to return to Monrovia. However, UNHCR declined to organize a mass repatriation, maintaining that conditions in Liberia did not yet make it possible for large numbers of refugees to return in secure conditions. But given the fact that many Liberians wanted to return, the interim government in Monrovia arranged for the repatriation of Liberian refugees by ship (and UNHCR facilitated travel to Freetown). The Liberian Council of Churches, assisted by the Lutheran World Federation and UNHCR, co-ordinated the repatriation of refugees from Freetown. By June 1991, they reported that about 12,000 had repatriated.

While initially welcoming the refugees with warmth and generosity, the presence of so many refugees for three years strained the economic and social resources of Sierra Leonean communities. But it was the invasion and the fears that the Liberian conflict would spill over into Sierra Leone that proved to be the catalyst for a negative reaction towards the refugees. Charles Taylor's forces, the NPFL, were repelled by Sierra Leone troops fighting alongside ULIMO, the force of Sierra Leone-based Liberians. But after pushing the NPFL out of Sierra Leone, ULIMO crossed into Liberia and battled the Taylor forces there. Continuing clashes across the border and continued fear on the part of Sierra Leoneans not only affected the country's receptivity to refugees, but also the internal politics of the country as evidenced in the April 1992 military coup.

Although military conflict has been avoided, the situation for Liberian refugees in Guinea and Côte d'Ivoire has deteriorated as well. Relations between refugees and the local populations (particularly those living far from the border) have become strained as a result of the pressure on social services and limited food supplies. In May 1991, the Ivorian government stopped granting automatic refugee status to newly arrived Liberians and instituted a procedure for determining refugee status on an individual basis. Reportedly only about half of those cases screened by the government resulted in positive decisions. The Ivorian government has tried to discourage new arrivals of refugees; like representatives of UNHCR and the US government, there seems to be a feeling that those Liberians now leaving their country are doing so in order to take advantage of increased food and economic opportunities in Côte d'Ivoire rather than fleeing the violence. In January 1992, UNHCR reported there were 566,000 refugees in Guinea (397,000 Liberians and 169,000 Sierra Leoneans) and 240,000 in Côte d'Ivoire (almost all Liberians). [20]

Peace and future repatriation?

Since the November 1990 cease-fire, ECOWAS has arranged several meetings between interim President Sawyer and Charles Taylor in a search for a lasting Liberian peace agreement. The latest round of talks, held in Yamassoukro, Côte d'Ivoire, in November 1991, resulted in agreement for a process of disarmament of troops, establishment of an election commission for elections to be held by April 1992, withdrawal of hostile forces from Sierra Leone and establishment of a buffer zone on the Liberian side of the Liberian-Sierra Leonean border. The results of this latest round of talks were greeted with great enthusiasm. Unfortunately, implementation has been slow. The fact that the INPFL, Prince Johnson's forces, and ULIMO were not invited to the talks is another limitation.

Unlike peace accords in other parts of the world, the November 1991 Yamassoukro IV talks do not provide for the repatriation of Liberian refugees before elections, even though they represent a significant percentage of the Liberian electorate. The issue of assisting and facilitating repatriation is thus left to UNHCR. While in December 1991, UNHCR indicated that it would not at this stage actively promote repatriation to Liberia because of unsettled conditions there, the agency is preparing a plan for eventual repatriation. UNHCR anticipates that some 176,000 Liberian refugees, particularly those settled near the border, will return home on their own, either before the official plan is under way or at the same time. Another 356,000 refugees would be provided transportation to Liberia and receive repatriation assistance.

Liberia, a country which since independence had never experienced large-scale civil conflict, became engulfed in a war which resulted in over 50,000 deaths and forced more than one-half of the 2.3 million population from their communities. The country's economy, infrastructure and environment have all been seriously damaged. According to a report in *The Guardian* the rebels under Charles Taylor are selling off timber from the rainforest to buy arms. From October 1990 to March 1991, Liberian rebels earned $3.6 million from three companies operating in areas of Liberia under rebel control. [21] The costs of rebuilding the country's infrastructure are huge, but the efforts required to heal the hatred and fear among the population are even greater. International assistance for Liberia has been slow to materialize. In July 1991, the UN Secretary General appealed for $135.5 million for the period July 1991 through July 1992 to provide both for emergency and reconstruction; however, by November 1991 donors had only contributed $78.3 million. Traditionally the US has played an important role in Liberian political and economic development. Indeed, the US government provided over $450 million in economic and military assistance in the first five years of Samuel Doe's regime and has provided the bulk of emergency relief supplies during the war. But US commitment to the country seems to be waning; in the light of new foreign policy interests and a changing world order, it seems that the US now considers Liberia "irrelevant". [22] The task of reconstruction and reconciliation will have to be carried out largely by the Liberians themselves.

In a 1991 report on the situation, a Catholic priest reported: "Everything we have known in Liberia — including the church — is finished." In a list of challenges to be faced in future planning, the report cites:

1) a people (Liberia) devastated and abandoned;
2) the biggest trans-coastal West African refugee problem in our history;
3) a country which has been almost totally destroyed;
4) a people whose inner wounds are so deep that hatred and revenge will be a part of their being for a long time;
5) a nation in which there are no longer any settled communities. [23]

The churches, working through the Liberian Council of Churches' relief co-ordinating committee, channel relief supplies to congregations of 17 participating denominations as well as to clinics and orphanages. But even more than the provision of relief, the churches in Liberia are challenged to play a role in reconciling the disparate groups in the country and helping them learn to live in peace — after so much bloodshed.

Southern Africa

After decades of war, violence and oppression, change is coming to Southern Africa. The independence of Namibia meant the return of 40,000 exiles. Political change in South Africa itself offers hope for an end to the brutal apartheid system established in 1948 and hope for an end to the exile of some 40,000 South African refugees. A political agreement in Angola has been reached and finally there seems to be a chance for a political settlement to end the long war in Mozambique. The neighbouring states of Zimbabwe, Tanzania, Malawi, Lesotho, Swaziland, Zambia and Botswana have long born the burden of hosting the refugees from the violence in Southern Africa. They too will undoubtedly undergo major changes in the coming years.

The violence in Southern Africa, like the wars which have uprooted millions of refugees throughout the continent, has complex roots. The apartheid system in South Africa, the foreign and military policies of the South African state towards neighbouring governments, the cold-war manipulation of Angola, the bandits of RENAMO in Mozambique, ethnic rivalries compounded by economic hardship, colonial legacies and political authoritarianism have all played a role in uprooting millions of citizens of Southern African countries. While the process of change is far from complete and the forces of reaction remain strong, there is a sense in Southern Africa that a "corner has been turned", and that the changes so far are irreversible. The pace of change has been so rapid that sometimes it is easy to minimize the extent of the transformation taking place. Nelson Mandela negotiates with the South African government for a new constitution and a new political system. The Namibian government struggles with problems facing all African governments but does so as a free and democratic government — after decades of repression and rule from Johannesburg. In Angola, a country bruised and torn apart by a bloody war supported and financed from abroad, the political settlement holds out the possibility of a return of the refugees, the establishment of a multi-party political system and rebuilding of the country's ravaged infrastructure. Mozambique's long and violent war continues but halting steps towards a peace agreement offer some hope for a political agreement.

Why, after so much violence for so many years, is change taking place now? The altered international climate and the demise of the cold war have undoubtedly played major roles in bringing about the change. With the collapse of the Soviet Union, the white South African government became less important to Western powers as a bulwark against communism in Africa. It became harder for the South African government to present itself as standing against Marxism in the region. Moreover, the collapse of the Soviet Union also meant a decrease in Soviet support for the Mozambican government and perhaps contributed to its willingness to institute political reforms. Some of the change is undoubtedly due to the personality of South African President F.W. de Klerk whose willingness to negotiate and consider alternatives which would have been unthinkable a few years ago has been widely praised in the Western press. But perhaps more important as a change agent than de Klerk's political skills and orientations is the fact that the popular forces in South Africa have worked and struggled for years to bring about this new situation. Their patient work through the years deserves most of the credit for the monumental changes taking place in South Africa today — changes which have been supported and encouraged by the shifting international political climate and by the particular political personalities of de Klerk and his advisers.

Today Southern Africa is a region caught up in change and the hope is emerging that the suffering brought about by apartheid may come to an end.

South Africa

Since the establishment of apartheid in 1948, South Africa's minority white government has dominated politics throughout Southern Africa. The apartheid policy at home was parallelled by activist policies throughout Southern Africa designed to support the maintenance of white rule, to prevent exiles from organizing resistance to the South African regime, and to maintain South Africa's economic domination of the region. These policies of "pax Pretoriana" had the effect of destabilizing governments which were "unfriendly" to the South Africans and, in the process, generating huge numbers of internally displaced people and refugees.

South African refugees in neighbouring states

Although the violence and repression in South Africa have not generated massive movements of refugees, over the years thousands of refugees have fled the violence in South Africa. Some, particularly educated urban individuals, travelled to Europe and elsewhere outside the region in search of safety. Others have sought to continue the struggle against the South African regime from exile in neighbouring countries.

Refugees associated with liberation movements have been treated differently than refugees caught in the crossfire of political violence. Typically, governments in the region — because of South Africa's active opposition — preferred them to live elsewhere. Politically, the liberation movements kept the struggle against South Africa alive by providing information to the international media and to dozens of different NGOs and governments about actual conditions in South Africa. In doing so, they were able to mobilize significant international opposition to the South African government. Following the 1960 Sharpeville massacre, the African National Congress (ANC) and the Pan-Africanist Congress (PAC) left South Africa to set up activities in nearby countries. In 1963-64 the ANC formed its armed wing (Umkonto we Sizwe) and the PAC formed its own (Poqo). Tom Lodge estimates that in the mid-1980s there were about 10,000 members of the armed wings — all but a few hundred living outside South Africa.[24] Until 1984, the armed wing of the ANC had its base in Maputo; following its expulsion from that country, its military headquarters were based in Angola.

In addition to the members of the liberation movements, students and families were also in exile, with some 1,500 students, for example, living in Tanzania and receiving their education from ANC schools.

But the South African government's policies towards neighbouring countries were designed to confront the threat of the armed movements as well as to intimidate their governments. Gasarasi outlines the elements of South African policy in the region as follows:

1) negotiation of unequal non-aggression pacts with the host countries in the region, often conditional upon the host country's expulsion of freedom fighters;

2) creating and extending military support to dissident movements in order to destabilize and if possible remove the unco-operative governments of the host countries;

3) carrying out trans-border military raids in the unyielding host countries; and

4) destabilizing the economies of such countries. [25]

These were brutal policies. South African raids in Angola killed hundreds of refugees; at one time or another the South African air force strafed the capitals of all the seven countries bordering South Africa and Namibia. In December 1982, a South African force destroyed 34 oil storage tanks valued at $40 million in the Mozambican port of Beira, causing severe oil shortages in Zimbabwe as well as Mozambique. [26] South African economic pressure has also been extensively used. Between 1982 and 1987, destabilization policies cost the member countries of the Southern African Development Co-ordination Conference (SADCC) at least US$25 billion — three times the total amount of foreign assistance they received in the same time period. [27]

The policies were successful in intimidating governments in the region and dissuading them from openly supporting the liberation movements, although governments of neighbouring countries were faced with the need to respond to individual South Africans seeking refuge. Swaziland has been reluctant to offer refuge to South Africans believed to be affiliated with the ANC although approximately 7,000 South African refugees, primarily of ethnic Swazi origin, live at Ndzevane settlement. Only 25 of the estimated 4,300 refugees living in Lesotho are officially recognized and assisted by UNHCR. Most are South Africans who have on their own settled in Lesotho. Since 1986, when a military government took power in Lesotho, newly-arrived South African refugees are only offered temporary asylum until their resettlement in another country can be arranged. During 1990 the number of arrivals and departures was about the same. About 3,500 South Africans live in Zambia, whose policy is that South Africans should be transferred to other countries and not settle permanently in Zambia. There are about 2,200 South Africans living in 16 ANC camps in Angola, located in the north-western quarter of Angola, presumably further from the reach of South Africa. Botswana hosts about 1,000 South African refugees, but is reluctant to allow its territory to be used as a base for attacks against its neighbours. The South African Defence Force launched raids against suspected ANC targets in 1985 and 1986 resulting in the deaths of a number of Botswanan civilians; bombing incidents in 1987 further heightened Botswanan concern. Perhaps 9,000 South African refugees live in Tanzania.

The unbanning of the African National Congress followed by the release of Nelson Mandela in February 1990 heralded political change.

Since then some of the worst laws of South Africa's government have been repealed and a process is under way to create a new constitution and a new political system which will better reflect the needs of the black majority.

However, the change process has also brought about violence. Ethnic rivalries between the country's black population have been exploited by South African security forces with clashes occurring almost daily. Fights between supporters of the ANC and Inkatha, the ethnic Zulu organization, have taken hundreds of lives since the process of political change began.

As a result of this process and of the expressed desire of many South African refugees to return home, UNHCR entered into a long process of negotiation with the government to facilitate the repatriation of an estimated 40,000 South African refugees. The process has been marked by considerable difficulty, because of the political sensitivity of the issues and the lack of any UN presence in the country. Following more than a year of negotiations, an agreement was signed in September 1991 in which UNHCR was permitted to establish a small temporary presence in the country to facilitate the return. The agreement with UNHCR was limited to assistance to returnees; in spite of demands by NGOs, churches and others, UNHCR was not permitted to work with the large number of Mozambican refugees in the country. UNHCR developed a plan for the voluntary repatriation of 30,000 refugees with a budget of nearly $29 million. However, once registration of refugees began, it was clear that there were would be far fewer returnees. The original estimate of the number of South African exiles was too high and it turned out that many refugees wanted to wait before deciding to go back. By March 1992, it appeared that the final number would be between 13,000 and 15,000 with an overall budget of $26.7 million. Unlike other UNHCR repatriation plans, the agency received a surplus of funds for its revised budget. By late April 1992, more than 3,100 of the 7,170 who had applied for voluntary return had come back home.[28]

The actual support for the repatriation and reintegration process is being provided by a group known as the National Co-ordinating Committee for the Repatriation of South African Exiles which includes representatives of the liberation movements, the churches, and representatives of other faiths. The Committee is charged not only with facilitating the physical return of the refugees, but with developing programmes for their reintegration into South African society — a society that has undergone major changes since the exiles left. The first South African returnees under the UNHCR programme arrived in the country in December 1991. The programme is scheduled to be completed by late 1992. Although the programme of organized repatriation is now under way, it is expected that many South African refugees will return on their own, without organized assistance. While the exiles are welcomed as a sign of the changes which have taken place and while most are eager to be a part of the transition to black majority rule, the experience of Namibia suggests that the economic barriers to their successful reintegration will be considerable. Most returnees are going back to urban areas where the unemployment rate is 40 percent; the few returning to rural areas face a countryside devastated by the worst drought in thirty years.

Namibia: end to exile

Namibia's struggle for independence came to a successful conclusion in March 1990 with the support of the United Nations. Following an agreement in December 1988, UN forces began to implement the peace process designed to culminate in elections for a constituent assembly in September 1989. The return of the refugees was an integral part of this plan. In June 1989, the repatriation process began; in the course of a few months, some 40,000 Namibian refugees from forty countries were returned to Namibia. The repatriation process was not an easy one; UNHCR was under pressure to return the refugees in time for their registration and participation in elections scheduled by the peace agreement. The Christian Council of Namibia was given primary responsibility for receiving the refugees and supporting their reintegration into Namibian life. In practice, the returnees faced difficulties in tracing their relatives, and the assistance for food and housing was insufficient. One of the biggest problems was finding jobs; almost three years after their return, most of the repatriates remain unemployed.

In spite of these problems and in spite of the mammoth difficulties facing the new government in Namibia, progress has been substantial. The refugees returned, elections were organized, SWAPO leader Sam Nujoma became the country's first president, and the task of rebuilding the country began in earnest. SWAPO which for 24 years had been leading the military struggle against South Africa now became the largest party in the country's parliament.

But while a political settlement led to peace and the return of refugees in Namibia — and a similar momentum is evident in South Africa — the situation for the victims of the violence in Angola and Mozambique is less hopeful.

Angola: war and displacement

Since Angolan independence from Portugal in 1975, the country has been racked by violence. Studies estimate the number of casualties in the millions: 40,000 to 50,000 amputees as a result of the land-mines, 330,000 child deaths as a result of the conflict, and perhaps as many as 2 million civilians — roughly 22 percent of the entire population — uprooted by the violence.[29] Of those uprooted, about 827,000 Angolans have been internally displaced; an additional 600,000 moved from the countryside into government-controlled cities and towns and about 500,000 have fled to neighbouring countries. About 30,000 Angolan refugees live in Namibia, over 103,000 are in Zambia and some 310,000 are in Zaire. The uprooting of Angola's rural population has produced major food shortages in the cities, shortages compounded by the current drought. While the government provides some limited assistance to the displaced in rural areas, the urban destitute have virtually no access to assistance. The effects of the war have been catastrophic.

The roots of the violence go back to the colonial era when various liberation movements fought the Portuguese for independence. The struggle for independence was long and costly, with more than 100,000 Angolan deaths and some 500,000 forced into exile.[30] After independence, more than 300,000 Portuguese left Angola. But the conflict continued between the government's ruling party, the People's Movement for the Liberation of Angola (MPLA) and the opposition National Union for the Total Independence of Angola (UNITA), a US-backed rebel group under the leadership of Jonas Savimbi. It was intensified by foreign intervention: Cuban troops and Soviet aid supported the government and South Africa and the US supported UNITA. US funding of UNITA was done illegally between 1981 and 1985 and legally thereafter. In many ways, the tactics of UNITA resemble those of RENAMO in Mozambique, with destruction of the country's economic infrastructure, extensive use of land-mines and policies designed to provoke terror.

In 1990, famine caused by drought and continued fighting threatened millions of people. Food shortages intensified and levels of malnutrition increased dramatically throughout the country. There were some efforts to negotiate an agreement for the provision of relief supplies with both UNITA and MPLA — but an initial agreement was in fact not implemented. "Observers speculate that the relief agreements broke down because both the government and UNITA wanted to achieve as much military gain as possible before a cease-fire, and relief efforts inhibited their abilities to achieve these aims."[31]

Finally in mid-1991, a Portuguese-mediated peace settlement was signed between the Angolan President José Eduardo Dos Santos and Jonas Savimbi, leader of UNITA. The agreement includes a cease-fire, the creation of a new, integrated national army, and a multi-party electoral transition to a new democratic order by late 1992. A joint political-military commission is made up of the government and UNITA as well as representatives from the United States, the Soviet Union and Portugal. Building on the Namibian experience, the peace agreement also established the United Nations Angola Verification Mission to oversee the process. UNHCR is planning for repatriation of Angolan refugees from neighbouring countries; however, such plans depend on the establishment of peace and stability throughout the country. In 1989-90, UNHCR began a repatriation programme from Zaire; but in its first year of operation only about 6,000 refugees returned to the country before it was suspended. In 1991, another 15,000 Angolans repatriated from Zaire, primarily as a result of the developing political crises in that country.

Hopes for an early peace and for the return of refugees and internally displaced are presently at risk because of the widespread drought in Southern Africa. Once again, Angolans are threatened with hunger and malnutrition — as well as with the war's legacy of a destroyed infrastructure and thousands of land-mines in rural areas. But a peace agreement has been signed in the country — which offers more hope than in the case of Mozambique.

Mozambique

The struggle for Mozambican liberation began in 1962 with the formation of FRELIMO; 13 years later Mozambique achieved its independence. Throughout its war of liberation, FRELIMO operated from neighbouring countries which suffered reprisals by the Portuguese colonial authorities, including incursions and trans-border operations. With independence in 1975, Mozambique returned the favour, giving sanctuary to liberation movements in Rhodesia, particularly Zimbabwe Africa National Union. By 1980, 60,000 refugees from Rhodesia/Zimbabwe were living in Mozambique.

But although independent, Mozambique suffered from reprisals and intervention from its neighbours. In 1974 the Movement of National Resistance (MNR), known as RENAMO, was formed by the Rhodesian secret service in collaboration with some Portuguese settlers. Later RENAMO received support from the South African government as part of its regional policy of destabilization. Throughout the late 1970s and the decade of the 1980s, RENAMO sought to destabilize the FRELIMO government by conducting military actions designed to provoke terror among the population. RENAMO targeted the country's infrastructure — roads, electric generating pumps, schools, health centres — causing immense damage to the country and to FRELIMO's programme for rural development. Raids on remote villages displaced thousands of Mozambicans, the figure subsequently rising to the millions as the level of brutality and violence increased. By late 1989, the number of deaths attributable to the violence was over 600,000, almost 500,000 of whom were children whose deaths could have been prevented had peace prevailed. The atrocities of RENAMO have been well-documented, including its practice of mutilation and torture of civilians and forced recruitment of civilians, including children, to fight or to serve as porters for its forces. While the brutality of RENAMO has been widely acknowledged, the situation is complicated by the general breakdown of social norms and mores. Bandits operating on their own, the existence of many RENAMO factions, the brutality of FRELIMO forces and charges of corruption within the government are all indications of the disintegration of the social fabric of the country.

By mid-1983, the conflict in Mozambique had already seriously affected close to 2 million of the country's 14 million population. By the end of 1987, the figure was 4 million — with 2 million physically displaced within Mozambique and some 800,000 in exile. By the end of 1991, there were over one million refugees in neighbouring countries, particularly in Malawi.

Today, there are almost 1.5 million Mozambican refugees in neighbouring countries, almost a million of whom are in Malawi. According to the government, an additional 2 million Mozambicans are internally displaced and another 2.5 million have been affected by the conflict and are dependent on international assistance. As in other parts of the world, the internally displaced are particularly vulnerable to the continued violence and to hunger and malnutrition. As a result of the fighting only 5 percent of Mozambique's arable land is now under cultivation. [32]

The violence of RENAMO and the devastation of the war are rooted in South African policies of support for the bandits, part of its regional policy of destabilization in the region.

In the early 1980s the government of South Africa expressed its concern about the presence of South African exiles in Mozambique and carried out a number of raids and bombing attacks against South Africans living there.

Just as devastating for the Mozambican government was South African economic pressure. Through a series of agreements with South Africa, a system had emerged in which Mozambique became the main supplier of mine workers to South Africa and in which the remittances of these miners became a major source of foreign exchange for Mozambique. Between 1904 and 1973, Mozambique supplied an average of 38 percent of South African mine workers. But from the time of independence, South Africa began to use the mine workers as a lever on the country. Between 1975 and 1982, Mozambique lost $3.2 billion as a result of South Africa's reducing the number of mine workers from 120,000 to 45,000 and overturning the long-standing practice of remitting part of their wages in gold to the Mozambican government. This economic pressure was intensified when South Africa cut the amount of its traffic moving through the Maputo port from 600 to 100 million tons, a move which cost Mozambique $250 million in fees. [33]

The pressure worked. Beginning in 1983 the Mozambican government began negotiating with the South African government, resulting in the signing of the Nkomati accord in March 1984. The accord included a Mozambican pledge to stop its support for the ANC in exchange for South Africa's pledge to end its support for the MNR. But while Mozambique generally kept its side of the bargain, expelling ANC activists, confiscating weapons and money from ANC, and closing their offices, the evidence is that South Africa continued to support the RENAMO guerrillas, albeit in a more clandestine form. South Africa also resumed its incursions into Mozambique, such as the attack by South African commandos on a Maputo residential area in 1987.

The war in Mozambique affects all the countries in the region — most obviously by the presence of the refugees. But its economic impact is also substantial. Zimbabwe has sent 12,000 soldiers to Mozambique to help protect the railway through the Beira corridor and contain the MNR insurgency. The refugees in Tanzania, Zambia and Zimbabwe as well as smaller numbers in other countries of the region have been settled in camps and are assisted by UNHCR, the governments and the churches of those countries. Zimbabwe, for example, hosts about 100,000 Mozambican refugees in camps and another 100,000 live outside the camps where they face a particularly precarious position as they are not permitted to work. For Zimbabwe, which has experienced a number of raids by RENAMO forces across the border, the presence of the refugees is a security problem. Over the years, there have been many cases where Zimbabwean soldiers have forcibly repatriated Mozambicans back to Mozambique.

The government and people of Malawi have generally responded with generosity to the arrival of around a million Mozambican refugees, many of whom were in desperate conditions. One of Africa's poorest countries, Malawi presently hosts the largest number of refugees on the continent and while international assistance has played a major role, the costs for the Malawian government have been substantial. The refugees in Malawi live in difficult conditions; the funding crisis at UNHCR has meant cuts in budgets for food, water and education.

Ironically, perhaps, hundreds of thousands of Mozambicans have sought protection in South Africa where they face rejection, and hostility from the authorities. "The South African authorities try to prevent the entry of Mozambican refugees into South Africa, hunt down those who manage to cross the border and deport those whom they catch." [34]

For decades, Mozambicans have entered South Africa in search of work and today some 50,000 Mozambicans work legally in South African mines. But an additional 200-250,000 Mozambicans have entered the country illegally as a result of the violence in Mozambique. In 1986 the South African government installed an electrified fence along its border with Mozambique which, together with the animals in the Kruger game park, killed many would-be refugees. Although the fence was eventually de-electrified, the government continues to deport those whom it finds. In 1990, South Africa deported over 37,000 Mozambican refugees. In contrast to this treatment, many Mozambicans have been given shelter in the homelands, particularly in Gazankulu and Kangwane whose leaders have defied the South African government in providing some assistance. But the economic and social situation remains desperate for the refugees there. The South African Council of Churches' refugee department has organized assistance to the refugees as have a few other South African NGOs.

Efforts to negotiate an end to the war in Mozambique began in the late 1980s with informal meetings mediated by the Roman Catholic Church. Many rounds of peace talks followed between RENAMO and the Mozambican government. Finally, in late 1992 an agreement was negotiated between the government and RENAMO and there were renewed calls for UN peace-keeping forces to oversee the transition. Although the peace process will undoubtedly face many obstacles, for the first time in years there is hope that the long Mozambican war will come to an end. Even before the peace agreement was finalized, around 200,000 Mozambican refugees have reportedly returned from Malawi to their home communities and UNHCR is finalizing plans for large-scale repatriation.

Just as the UNHCR is making plans for large-scale repatriation, so too the church bodies in the region are planning assistance to the returnees and to the victims of the violence. The Ecumenical Co-ordination Office for Emergencies and Rehabilitation in East and Southern Africa (ECOERSA), now based in Maputo, works with Christian councils in 12 countries. Its programme of "Repatriation, Resettlement, Rehabilitation, and Reconciliation for Refugees and Returnees" in the region includes training workshops for countries which may receive large numbers of returnees (Angola and Mozambique) and working with host countries to develop ways of developing church support for the repatriates. Perhaps most important, the programme is planning workshops around the theme of "peace, national unity and reconciliation" in helping the churches to play a more meaningful role in healing the divisions produced by the conflict.

But in order for UNHCR to assist refugees to return and for the churches to play a role in their reception and in reconciliation efforts within their countries, there must be peace in Mozambique.

* * *

We began this section by talking about the winds of change in Southern Africa, and indeed, in comparison with many regions, prospects for peace and justice have improved here in the last two years. In spite of the continued potential for violence the difficulties of developing democratic institutions, and the economic challenges facing the region, there are genuine grounds for hope that conditions will change in Angola, South Africa and Namibia. At the same time continued violence in Mozambique has forced Mozambicans to flee their country (there were 81,000 more Mozambican refugees in Malawi in January 1992 than in the preceding March). People continue to be displaced by the violence; and there are signs that the violence is increasing in parts of the country — possibly as a negotiating tool for the peace talks. The country has been devastated by the war and is dependent on international relief. In spite of the Nkomati accord of 1984 and the political changes in South Africa, knowledgeable observers continue to accuse South Africa of supporting the RENAMO forces.

Given South Africa's central economic, military and political role in the region, change in South Africa can be expected to have repercussions throughout the region. As one Mozambican church worker said in an AACC meeting: "If you want to help the victims of Mozambican violence, you have to work on South Africa." Transition to majority rule in South Africa will undoubtedly result in a different set of foreign policies in the region; but such a change in governmental foreign policies could be accompanied by the growth of paramilitary groups only tenuously linked to democratic processes.

In both Angola and Mozambique, the signing of peace agreements must be accompanied by efforts at reconciliation and reconstruction. In the case of Angola, if the urgent need for large-scale mine clearance programmes and for assistance in rebuilding destroyed infrastructure is not met, displaced people will not be able to return to their communities. In both countries, efforts will be needed to heal the physical and psychological wounds of the long wars — wars where civilians and especially children were often the first casualties.

NOTES

[1] *International Herald Tribune*, 14-15 December 1991.

[2] Cited by Reginald T. Appleyard, *International Migration: Challenge for the Nineties*, published for the 40th Anniversary of the International Organization for Migration, Geneva, IOM, 1991, p.45.

[3] United Nations Development Programme, *Human Development Report 1992*, New York, Oxford University Press, 1992, p.57.

[4] Constance G. Anthony, "Africa's Refugee Crisis: Statebuilding in Historical Perspective", in *International Migration Review*, vol. 25, no. 3, 1991, pp.574-591.

[5] US Committee for Refugees, *World Refugee Survey 1992*, Washington, DC, USCR, p.53.

[6] Africa Watch, *Sudan: A Human Rights Disaster*, Washington, DC, Africa Watch, 1990, p.103.

[7] US Committee for Refugees, *World Refugee Survey 1990*, Washington, DC, USCR, 1991, p.55.

[8] *Ibid.*, p.56.

[9] *Refugees*, UNHCR, no. 87, October 1991, p.8.

[10] *World Refugee Survey 1990, op. cit.*, p.52.

[11] See, for example, Jason Clay, "Ethiopian Famine and the Relief Agencies", pp.232-288 in *The Moral Nation: Humanitarianism and US Foreign Policy Today*, ed. Bruce Nichols and Gil Loescher, Notre Dame, IN, University of Notre Dame Press, 1989. Laurence A. Pezzulo, "Catholic Relief Service in Ethiopia", pp.213-231 in *The Moral Nation, ibid.* Randolph Kent, *Anatomy of Disaster Relief*, London, Pinter Publishers, 1987.

[12] Jeffrey Clark, "Beyond Famine: New Dynamics in Post-War Ethiopia and Eritrea", pp.24-30 in *World Refugee Survey 1992, op. cit.* Also see *CRDA News*, August 1991.

[13] Jeffrey Clark, *Famine in Somalia and the International Response: Collective Failure*, USCR Issue Paper, Washington, DC, US Committee for Refugees, November 1992, p.13. For further information on the background to the Somali conflict, see also Africa Watch, *A Government at War with Its Own People: Testimonies about the Killings and the Conflict in the North*, New York, Africa Watch, 1990.

[14] Todd Shields, "In Somalia, No Refuge from Starvation", in *International Herald Tribune*, 8 May 1992, p.6.

[15] Clark, *Famine in Somalia...*, *op. cit.*; for further criticism of the UN's role, see also Rakiya Omaar, "Somalia: At War with Itself", *Current History*, May 1992, pp.230-234. Clark cites Mohamed Sahnoun, then UN Special Representative for Somalia, who questioned how it could be that Save the Children-UK, a relatively small private relief agency, had delivered more food to Somalia in 1992 than had UNICEF. In October 1992, Sahnoun resigned after being rebuked by the UN Secretary-General for his public criticism of UN operations.

[16] Christiane Berthiaume, "Kenya: The Birth of a Crisis", in *Refugees*, UNHCR, May 1992, pp.26-28. Also see Lucia Ann McFadden, "Report from Church World Service Trip, Refugee Camps in Kenya", 29 February-13 March 1992, mimeo, New York, Church World Service, 1992.

[17] Barbara E. Harrell-Bond, *Imposing Aid: Emergency Assistance to Refugees*, Oxford, Oxford University Press, 1986.

[18] US Committee for Refugees, *World Refugee Survey*, Washington, DC, USCR, 1987, p.42.

[19] Most of the discussion of the Liberian war and refugee situation is taken from the excellent study by Hiram Ruiz, *Uprooted Liberians: Casualties of a Brutal War*, Washington, DC, US Committee for Refugees, 1992.

[20] *Refugees*, UNHCR, January 1992, p.31.

[21] Cited by Liberia Working Group, July 1991.

[22] Ruiz, *op cit.*

[23] Reported by the Liberia Working Group, July 1991.

[24] Tom Lodge, "State of Exile: The African National Congress of South Africa", in *Third World Quarterly*, vol. 9, no. 1, 1987.

[25] Charles Gasarasi, "The Effects of Refugees on Inter-state Relations in Southern Africa: Conflict and Co-operation", mimeo, Dar es Salaam University, p.16.

[26] Okechukwu Ibeanu, "Apartheid, Destabilization and Displacement: The Dynamics of the Refugee Crisis in Southern Africa", in *Journal of Refugee Studies*, vol. 3, no. 1, 1990, p.57.

[27] *Ibid.*, p.58.

[28] Michael Keats, "South Africa: Facing Reality", in *Refugees*, UNHCR, May 1992, pp.34-36.

[29] Hiram A. Ruiz, *Peace or Terror: A Crossroads for Southern Africa's Uprooted*, Washington DC, US Committee for Refugees, 1989. *World Refugee Survey 1992, op. cit.*

[30] Ruiz, *ibid.*, p.7.

[31] US Committee for Refugees, *World Refugee Survey 1991*, Washington, DC, USCR, 1991, p.38.

[32] *World Refugee Survey 1992, op. cit.*, p.47.

[33] Ibeanu, *op. cit.*, pp.56-57.

[34] *World Refugee Survey 1991, op. cit.*, p.53.

7. Refugees in Asia
Victims of War and Instability

Asian complexities

The uprooting of people has a long and complex history in Asia. The variety of regimes and national circumstances in the region makes generalizations difficult and dangerous. The violence which displaces people has many causes — ethnic conflict, economic disparities, authoritarian regimes — all exacerbated by a long history of foreign intervention. The uprooting of people because of violence and persecution takes place in a context characterized by a complex panorama of economic migration.

Within the Asia-Pacific region, there is intra-regional migration of both unskilled and highly skilled workers. Bangladesh, India, Indonesia, Malaysia, Nepal, the Philippines, Sri Lanka and Thailand all export large numbers of workers in the region as other countries such as Brunei, Japan, Hong Kong, Pakistan, Singapore, Korea and Taiwan face labour shortages and import labour. Some countries do both. Malaysia, for example, exports skilled labour to Singapore and imports large numbers of unskilled workers from the Philippines, Indonesia and Thailand. Many of the migrants work illegally in their host countries. In Japan, for example, between 100,000 and 300,000 illegal immigrants work without legal protection, and are exploited by unscrupulous employers. In the Pacific, patterns of migration towards the "rim" countries of Australia, New Zealand and the US are changing the demography of some islands and resulting in erosion of cultural values. Some countries facing labour shortages and large numbers of illegal immigrants are relocating labour-intensive firms abroad to countries with an abundance of labour. [1]

In addition to intra-regional Asian migration, over 3 million Asians have worked in the Middle East since the mid-1970s; their remittances home have been an important source of foreign exchange for their countries. As was seen in the aftermath of the Gulf war, governments of those countries faced serious financial difficulties when these remittances came to an end.

As in other regions, many of those displaced from their communities are uprooted by a combination of economic and political factors. Wars and violence disrupt economic production and cause unemployment, as in the case of Sri Lanka. People flee because they are afraid of the violence, but also because they are unable to survive owing to the disruption of the economy.

Table 1 presents a listing of the current refugees and displaced people in Asia. It is obvious that refugees are unevenly distributed throughout the region and tend to be concentrated in the poorer countries. Rich countries such as Japan and Korea host relatively few refugees.

TABLE 1:   REFUGEES, INTERNALLY DISPLACED PEOPLE,
AND PEOPLE IN "REFUGEE-LIKE SITUATIONS" IN ASIA, 1991

Country of origin	*Total refugees*	*Internally displaced*
Afghanistan		
Internally displaced		2,000,000
Bangladesh	290,150	
Burma	30,000	
Pakistan (Biharis)	260,000	500,000-
Internally displaced		1,000,000
Cambodia		
Internally displaced		180,000
China	14,200	
Burma	10,000	
Laos	4,200	
Hong Kong	60,000	
Vietnam	60,000	

Country of origin		Total refugees	Internally displaced
India		402,600	
Sri Lanka	210,000		
China (Tibet)	100,000		
Bangladesh	65,000		
Bhutan	15,000		
Afghanistan	9,800		
Burma	2,000		
Others	800		
Internally displaced			85,000
Indonesia		18,700	
Vietnam	17,000		
Cambodia	1,700		
Japan		900	
Vietnam	900		
Korea		200	
Vietnam	200		
Macau		100	
Vietnam	100		
Malaysia		12,700	
Vietnam	12,500		
Indonesia	200		
Nepal		24,000	
China (Tibet)	14,000		
Bhutan	10,000		
Pakistan		4,604,000	
Afghanistan	3,591,000		
Others	3,000		
India (Kashmiris)	10,000		
Papua New Guinea		6,700	
Indonesia	6,700		
Philippines		18,000	
Vietnam	18,000		
Internally displaced			1,000,000
Singapore		150	
Vietnam	150		
Sri Lanka			
Internally displaced			600,000

Country of origin		Total refugees	Internally displaced
Taiwan		150	
Vietnam	150		
Thailand		512,700	
Cambodia	370,000		
Laos	59,000		
Burma	70,000		
Burma (refugee-like situation)		160,000	
Vietnam	13,700		
Vietnam		21,000	
Cambodia	21,000		
Total		**6,146,250**	

Source: US Committee for Refugees, *World Refugee Survey 1991*, Washington, DC, USCR, 1992. Figures as of 31 December 1991.

The presence of large numbers of refugees complicates relations between governments and creates hardships to governments already struggling to provide for their people. The presence of refugees also creates security concerns for the governments involved. Several of the large Asian refugee populations are known for their "armed warrior" communities, such as the mujahidin in Pakistan and the Khmer resistance movement on Thailand's border with Cambodia. But other groups of refugees also include members of insurgent groups as in the case of Sri Lankan refugees in India and the Burmese Karen refugees in Thailand. The security concerns of governments often have an international component as well. The government of Pakistan, for example, was able to use its support for the mujahidin refugees to increase its strategic importance to the United States.

Unlike the case in Africa and Latin America, Asian governments have not developed specific Asian legal instruments to respond to the situation of uprooted people in the region. Nor have they been in the forefront of efforts to shape an international response to refugees. In fact, most of the governments which host large numbers of Asian refugees have signed neither the 1951 UN Convention on Refugees nor the 1967 Protocol — including Afghanistan, Bangladesh, India, Indonesia, Malaysia, Pakistan, Singapore and Thailand. Although UNHCR is active in all of these countries, governments in the region have retained the right to decide under what circumstances and for which groups UNHCR will be allowed to work. Thus, Thailand allows UNHCR to work with Vietnamese, Laotian and a small percentage of the Cambodian refugees in the country while not permitting it to operate with the large Cambodian border population (except in preparing for the repatriation of the refugees) nor with the Burmese refugees on the border. Similarly, the government of India has refused to allow UNHCR to play an operational role with the Sri Lankan refugees in the state of Tamil Nadu.

Asian governments have responded in different ways to different groups of refugees. South-east Asian governments saw the Indochinese refugees as the product of the US war in Vietnam and demanded that the US and the international community take responsibility for the refugees as the human by-products of that war. For the large Afghan refugee population, the solution was seen as putting them in camps until the situation stabilized and they could return home. Internally displaced people usually exist on the margins of the societies in which they live; sometimes they live in government-administered camps for displaced people, sometimes they crowd into the homes of relatives, sometimes they are "invisible" among large urban populations.

International non-governmental organizations have been quite active in working with Asian refugees but, with a few notable exceptions, Asian churches and NGOs have been less involved. As Clement John of the Christian Conference of Asia points out, church involvement with Asian refugees has been mainly through Western churches.

> The Asian churches on their part have remained content to act as conduits for relief and material assistance to the refugees. Consequently, all major policy decisions and operational activities are often handled by expatriates with little or no sensitivity to and knowledge about local conditions. The main actors, therefore, are the state and the outside funding agencies with the local church acting as the passive partner in this enterprise. A classical example of this are the refugee operations carried out in Pakistan by Western churches and partner agencies for Afghan refugees. There is little or no involvement of the National Council, the UP Church or the Church of Pakistan. There are other similar situations in Asia.[2]

The sections which follow analyze the situation of three broad groups of uprooted people in Asia: Afghan refugees in Pakistan who fled the Soviet invasion of 1979 and the continuing instability and war; those who were forced to flee as a result of the war in Indochina; and the group which includes those displaced because of internal violence — violence which often has ethic components.

Although the war in Indochina formally ended in 1975, the human consequences of that war have displaced millions of Vietnamese, Cambodians and Lao. Some of the uprooted people have been considered as refugees by the international community and have been resettled in distant countries. Many still languish in camps waiting for an end to the violence; their repatriation is linked to questions of peace and economic stability in their countries of origin.

The specific groups considered in the third category are the Sri Lankan displaced people and refugees, Burmese refugees, and displaced people in the Philippines. There are, of course, many other situations of uprooted people in Asia. The treatment of tribal hill people in the Chittagong tracts in India, displaced Bangladeshis, Tibetan refugees in India, Bhutanese refugees in Nepal, the vast transmigration schemes in Indonesia, the treatment of illegal immigrants in Japan, the whole question of sex tourism and forced prostitution, the impact of migration on culture and identity in the Pacific islands — these are all issues which are related to peace, justice and security in the region. The cases selected for analysis not only account for most of the region's uprooted people, but also illustrate some of the complexities of the situation.

Afghan refugees: victims of the cold war?

The Afghan refugees are the world's largest refugee population, with about 3.5 million living in camps in Pakistan and another 2 million in Iran. In addition, an estimated 2 million Afghans are internally displaced. Between the exiles and the internally displaced, almost half of Afghanistan's pre-war population of 15.5 million has been uprooted. Some Afghan refugees left in 1978 following the coup in Kabul. Most fled after the Soviet invasion of 1979. The repressive anti-Islamic policies of the government led to armed uprisings throughout the country which in turn led to harsh Soviet counter-insurgency campaigns. The ensuing war with widespread bombings of rural areas led to the flight of millions of Afghans from their homes.

In April 1988, the United Nations facilitated an agreement providing for the withdrawal of the Soviet troops, and the prohibition of intervention in Afghan and Pakistani affairs, including the continued arming of resistance groups. Soviet troops began their withdrawal in May 1988 and completed their pull-out, as foreseen in the agreement, by February 1989.

But more than four years after the agreement and three years after the Soviet troop withdrawal, the vast majority of refugees remain in exile. Political instability and violence continue in Afghanistan and the legacy of the war will live on for decades, in the continued fighting between guerrilla factions and, perhaps most concretely, in the presence of millions of mines which make resettlement of agricultural communities difficult. About 75 percent of the refugees in Pakistan live in camps in the North West Frontier Province; an additional 20 percent of them live in Baluchistan. While the refugees come from many different ethnic groups, the majority are Pathans — as are most of the population on the Pakistani side of the border. Almost half of the refugees are children; a little more than half of the adults are women. Many of the men have been killed or remain behind to continue the struggle — many more leave the camps periodically to fight inside Afghanistan.

The Afghan resistance forces, the mujahidin, are a disparate group of fighting men organized into some 300 guerrilla fronts throughout Afghanistan's 28 provinces. For years they carried on the war against the Soviet-supported Afghan government. But when the government fell in early 1992, the divisions between the mujahidin intensified. Fighting continued in Kabul and other cities as guerrilla forces struggled for control of the country and for power. Shifting alliances, the presence of contending private armies and the desperate uncertainty in the country make it difficult to foresee the establishment of necessary conditions of peace and security which would enable the large-scale return of the 5.5 million refugees in the near future.

The conflict in Afghanistan is a clear example of the human costs of the cold war. US military aid to the mujahidin between 1980 and 1987 was estimated at well over $2 billion — the largest undeclared US military action since Vietnam.[3] These military supplies were supplemented with additional arms from China and Saudi Arabia. On the other side, Soviet involvement in the conflict included commitment of troops, air support, and massive military supplies to particular factions. The war dragged on for over a decade in large part because of such super-power involvement.

Pakistan's involvement with the refugees has also been shaped by the super-power conflict. By allowing the refugees to live in Pakistan and by allowing the mujahidin to carry out military operations inside Afghanistan from Pakistani territory, it increased its importance to the United States as "holding the line against Soviet expansion". US support for Pakistan was manifest in many ways. The current six-year aid package, approved in early 1987, is for over US$4 billion. US concerns about nuclear nonproliferation and evidence of Pakistan's nuclear progress were over-shadowed by the need to continue the war in Afghanistan. Within Pakistan, the military became stronger.[4]

The creation of large refugee camps, large *armed* refugee camps on the border of Afghanistan was a major obstacle to the establishment of peace in the country. Perhaps in no other refugee situation in the world was the presence of armed refugees across a border such an obvious security risk to the government of Afghanistan. The refugees, the armed guerrilla groups, posed a threat to the continued existence of the Afghan government — a threat which was eventually realized with the government's overthrow by the guerrilla forces. A lasting settlement in the country will be largely determined by the mujahidin groups which were supported in exile, which carried on the armed struggle and which are now fighting with each other in the streets of Kabul.

The central role of the mujahidin groups in Pakistan presents many contradictions. Although armed groups or individual combatants are not considered to be refugees, in fact in the Afghan case such distinctions are difficult. Many of the Afghan men are away from the camps for long periods of time as they continue the armed struggle back home. The mujahidin and the Islamic religious leaders make virtually all decisions in the camps, limiting the role of UNHCR and the hundred or so international NGOs providing services in the camps. In comparison with most other refugee situations, the Afghan refugee situation is one where the armed groups have significant control over camp life. Before refugees are eligible to be registered for assistance, the Pakistani government requires that they belong to one of the mujahidin parties. (Actually, as will be shown below, the situation is similar to that of the camps along the Thai-Cambodian border.)

But the security considerations of Afghan refugees go beyond the actions of the armed groups. The vast majority of the refugees come from rural backgrounds (like the vast majority of Afghans), but they have been living in urban or semi-urban settings and in the artificial life of camps for more than ten years. Most of them have not been involved in farming for the past decade and there is fear that they are losing their knowledge and experience in the area where they will have to make their future livelihoods.

The provision of food rations and the availability of basic services within the camps have led refugees to become dependent on relief. Although training programmes and income-generating projects have been initiated, they are not a substitute for the agricultural work to which most of the refugees will return. On the other hand, access to medical care and other health services has resulted in improved material conditions for the refugees. For example, the mortality rate for refugee children under the age of five is 130 per 1,000 — high by standards of developed countries but low in comparison to the corresponding 300/1,000 rate in Afghanistan.[5] Since 1979, UNHCR has spent over $600 million in aid to the Afghan refugees in Pakistan alone — and the costs of repatriation will be substantial.

The role of NGOs in providing relief assistance to the refugees has led to some serious questions about the extent to which they were, albeit indirectly, assisting the guerrilla forces and strengthening the mujahidin leadership. While most NGOs affirm the importance of working with refugee leaders, the dominance of the mujahidin leadership meant that programmes were developed and implemented under their control, limiting the ability of the NGOs to, for example, provide adequate educational opportunities for women and girls.

The vast majority of the Afghan refugees are eager to return to their country and their lands. With the signing of the peace accord in 1988, hopes were raised that repatriation to Afghanistan would occur on a large scale. But while a few refugees returned in 1989, there were 70,000 new arrivals and additional camps had to be constructed. UNHCR came under increasing pressure to speed repatriation — for financial reasons, but also for political ones as the agency desperately needed to show that assistance to refugees is not a permanent requirement and that lasting solutions are possible. Prince Sadruddin Aga Khan was appointed by the UN Secretary General as the co-ordinator for UN Humanitarian and Economic Assistance Programmes related to Afghanistan in 1988 (a post he relinquished in 1990 to assume responsibility for the movement of people in Jordan as a consequence of the Gulf war).

In July 1990, UNHCR initiated a pilot project to provide incentives for up to 250,000 refugees to return home. Opposed by most mujahidin factions, the programme had only limited success. While UN Operation Salaam estimated that more than 200,000 would return to Afghanistan in 1990, ration cards for only about 78,000 people were turned in. As in other situations, it is estimated that larger numbers returned on their own, without international assistance. And it appears another 36,000-60,000 Afghan refugees returned from Iran.[6]

In preparation for repatriation, UNHCR plans to cut back its spending in the camps and is talking with the Pakistani government about consolidating the camps, reducing staff and integrating services to refugees with services to Pakistanis.[7]

Until 1992 repatriation of Afghan refugees occurred at a slow pace, but during 1992, over 1.4 million refugees returned to Afghanistan. And yet the Afghan repatriation has received relatively little attention and meagre international aid.[8] Questions about repatriation and about the prospects of future large-scale return of the refugees inevitably raise questions about the conditions to which they are returning.

Since the overthrow of the Afghan government and the return of the mujahidin to the country, there are reports of refugees returning in relatively small numbers. It seems that in many cases refugees want to re-establish their land ownership and to survey the situation quickly — even if they are not yet ready to bring their families from the camps in Pakistan and Iran.

But while the refugees continue to wait and while the guerrilla forces continue to battle over the country's future, the attention of the world has shifted elsewhere. With the break-up of the Soviet Union and Afghanistan's subsequent decrease in strategic value to the West and with new conflicts in Eastern Europe, there is decreasing Western interest in the situation of Afghan refugees. Pakistan, for example, finds that its importance as a US ally has diminished as a result of global changes. The US finds itself (as it so often does) in the somewhat uncomfortable position of trying to formulate policies towards the disparate guerrilla groups which it supported for years.

One of the lessons learned from the Afghan case is that peace is a process and must be carefully nurtured and sustained in order to allow for the return of displaced populations. Although the cold war is over, in Asia it is still evident in the fact that over 5 million Afghan refugees are not yet able to return home. Improved relations between the US and the Soviet Union and even the withdrawal of Soviet troops from Afghanistan have not been sufficient to permit the establishment of peace in the country. The presence of millions of mines throughout the country is a formidable obstacle — not just to the return of the refugees and other displaced populations, but to the country's potential to become self-sustaining in the future. The presence of hundreds of thousands of guerrilla forces who, for at least a decade, have learned that violence is the way to resolve conflicts and to stand up for their nationalist aspirations, is bound to be a destabilizing force for Afghanistan — even after the refugees return home.

Indochinese refugees: the consequences of war fifteen years later

The war in South-east Asia produced a whirlwind of movements of people — people torn from their lands, forced into exile, setting off for other countries by boat and on foot. The human consequences of the war are still being felt throughout the region. Vietnamese boat people, Cambodian refugees living as political pawns on the Thai-Cambodian border, Lao refugees — each of these situations is unique and each poses a somewhat different set of problems for host governments. But like the Afghan refugees, the Indochinese uprooted from their homes are a lasting human consequence of the cold war; like the Afghan refugees any durable solution to their plight will most likely be long and painful.

The Vietnamese

The exodus of boat people from Vietnam reached its peak in 1979 when as many as 50,000 people were fleeing by sea every month. [9] At the same time, the violence of the Khmer Rouge and the aftermath of the Vietnamese occupation of Cambodia uprooted millions from their home communities. Many poured across the border into Thailand. As the numbers escalated, the Thai government felt abandoned by the international community. It didn't want the refugees and, although it was being pressed by the international community, particularly the United States, to adopt generous policies towards the new arrivals, the government felt that it could no longer cope.

In mid-1979, the Thai government began towing Vietnamese vessels back out to sea. Similarly the Malaysian government began pushing Vietnamese boats out to sea; by one estimate some 40,000 Vietnamese were pushed away from Malaysia in 1979 alone. [10] In June 1979, the Thais rounded up 40,000 Cambodian refugees and forced them at gunpoint to return to their country, via a deep escarpment into a heavily mined field. Some 10,000 people died in this exercise, either from exploding mines or from Thai gunfire when they tried to turn back. The inhumanity of the actions was roundly condemned, but the international community responded to relieve pressure on the Thai government. A special United Nations session was convened in Geneva in July 1979 to consider appropriate actions for Indochinese refugees.

At that meeting, the basic outlines of a policy towards Indochinese refugees were worked out — a policy which was to last for almost a decade. Thailand and other countries would allow the refugees to come into their countries in return for a promise by the international community that the refugees would be resettled outside the region. Thailand — like

Malaysia, Indonesia, Hong Kong and others[11] — was unwilling to accept the refugees for permanent settlement and argued, with considerable justification, that the refugee situation was the product of the Indochina war — a war that it did not create. So a *quid pro quo* was reached — countries in the region would preserve the right of first asylum, in return for assurances that they would not be "stuck" with the refugees.

One of the most interesting options instituted by the 1979 conference to deal with the Indochinese refugees was the creation of the Orderly Departure Programme (ODP)— a programme without parallel in the world. Through this programme, Vietnamese are allowed to depart legally from Vietnam for Western countries as refugees without recourse to flimsy boats or through uncertain first-asylum countries.

For two years the policy seemed to work with large numbers of refugees resettled by Western countries, principally the United States, Canada, Australia and Western Europe. But growing fears that the resettlement option in itself was serving as a pull factor — and increasing evidence of "compassion fatigue" in the West — created pressures for other actions.

In 1981 Thailand instituted a policy of "humane deterrence" — a policy implemented the following year in Hong Kong. The rationale of the policy was to make life in exile more difficult as a way of deterring further arrivals. So resettlement options were curtailed, the camps were made less comfortable, and freedom of movement was limited. In spite of humane deterrence, by the late 1980s, the number of Vietnamese arriving in both Thailand and Hong Kong had again increased. While over a million Indochinese had been resettled outside the region, the governments of Thailand and Hong Kong feared that they would be "stuck with" the residual cases — those individuals rejected by resettlement countries. By 1989 Thailand and Malaysia again began towing Vietnamese boats back out to sea.

In response to these developments, in June 1989 another international conference was held in Geneva and a Comprehensive Plan of Action (CPA) was adopted by the international community. Under the terms of the CPA, the international community agreed that the Orderly Departure Programme would be expanded and that Vietnam would increase its efforts to discourage people from leaving. As in 1979, the Asian asylum countries would continue to provide temporary asylum while the resettlement countries would intensify their efforts to clear the camps, giving priority to long-stayers. But unlike the 1979 conference, the CPA provided for the establishment of a screening mechanism to determine refugee status under the 1951 Convention. Those who were screened in would be guaranteed a resettlement offer within a specified period. Those who were screened out, that is, found not to be refugees under the terms of the UN Convention, "should return to their country of origin in accordance with international practices". The agreement also stipulated that "in the first instance, every effort will be made to encourage voluntary return".

The CPA was a further international response to protect the right of first asylum in the region by making it clear that it was the responsibility of the international community — and not just that of the country in which the refugees happened to arrive — to provide for their future. But unlike the case a decade earlier, the CPA made it clear that the West's commitment to resettlement was not open-ended. Only those individuals found to be refugees under the Convention would be resettled. While this policy was deplored by many US politicians and by a number of NGOs, in fact it was hard to argue against it. As is the case in all Western countries, refugee status determination by competent government officials is a prerequisite to being allowed to remain in the country. Individuals found not to be refugees are liable to deportation. Unless the rights of governments to deport people from their territories are questioned, the screening procedures in themselves cannot be challenged.

And in both Vietnam and Hong Kong, screening procedures were instituted. Although initially criticized on procedural grounds by Amnesty International and other human rights groups, the screening procedures in themselves were greatly improved over time. And in December 1989, the first group of Vietnamese were forcibly returned, followed almost two years later by a second group of returns with prospects of further forced repatriations to come.

Nonetheless, people continued to flee Vietnam — in spite of the often desperate conditions of exile and in spite of the lack of current resettlement opportunities. The debate over the reasons for their flight is crucial to understanding what will happen to them. Some argue that they are fleeing poverty and economic suffering which are the result of the international isolation of the country. Others, particularly in the United States, see those who choose to leave as individuals fleeing the persecution of a communist regime. The latter group wants to prevent forced repatriation, the former see such returns as necessary for the survival of asylum for those few who do have legitimate fears of persecution.

But perhaps because of the high emotional feelings generated by the Vietnam war, the situation of the Vietnamese asylum-seekers, refugees or economic migrants continues to provoke international interest and concern. It has become a security issue for many governments. The fact that resettlement was developed as the most likely option for most of the Vietnamese undoubtedly acted as a "pull factor". That is, Vietnamese were not only leaving their country because conditions were bad, but also because there was an option (until the various cut-off dates) to leave the country. Under the CPA procedures for encouraging voluntary return of Vietnamese, financial assistance was granted for returning refugees. And there have been some cases of so-called "double-takers", that is, Vietnamese who collect their money by returning to Vietnam and then again make their way to Hong Kong (presumably to collect another grant).

Presently the situation in Hong Kong appears to be moving towards a solution in light of the determination by the British and Hong Kong governments to deport Vietnamese, found not to be refugees, back to Vietnam. But such deportations are highly charged events. The Vietnamese in Hong Kong's closed camps are adamantly refusing to go quietly. Demonstrations, hunger strikes and violence have increased. Opposition by the US to such deportations seems to have given way to a grudging acceptance that there are no other feasible alternatives. Moreover, Vietnamese continued to arrive in Hong Kong, as many as 14,000 in the first half of 1991 — a 300 percent increase over the same period in 1990. [12] In 1992, however, the numbers decreased substantially. While Hong Kong receives the most media attention, the situation is the same in other Southeast Asian countries where, sooner or later, such deportations will also have to take place. [13]

In May 1992, the governments of Great Britain and Vietnam signed an agreement providing for the forced return of the 50,000 Vietnamese detained in Hong Kong camps. The agreement states that the forced returns will be "conducted under conditions of order, safety and dignity". The Vietnamese are to be returned at the rate of 1,000 per month which means it could take four years for the camps to be emptied — assuming that more Vietnamese do not arrive.

Following relatively low numbers in the early years, by 1989, a record 39,000 Vietnamese left via ODP (with 29,000 of those cases going to the US). Bilateral agreements between the US and Vietnam provided for the regular departure of family members (including AmerAsian children) and former re-education camp prisoners. But these programmes have not stopped Vietnamese from leaving. And some estimates place the number of people on the ODP waiting list at close to one million.

Lao refugees

Policies towards the Vietnamese boat people were shaped by the presence of hundreds of thousands of other Indochinese refugees — the Lao and the Cambodians — both in Thailand. Events in those two countries were profoundly affected by the Indochinese war and, like the Vietnamese, the Lao and the Cambodian refugees are victims of political developments beyond their control. In all three countries, changes of regime took place in 1975 and in all three cases these changes were accompanied by the massive displacement of people. First those who had worked with the former regime took flight, followed by a broader range of people.

In Laos, the Pathet Lao proclaimed the Lao People's Democratic Republic on 2 December 1975. A policy of national unification was carried out by the government with the guidance of Vietnam. The rapid socialist transformation of Laos's economy and society was carried out and a climate of fear and suspicion combined to lead many to flee to neighbouring Thailand.

From 1975 to 1986, approximately 325,000 Lao left their country for Thailand — a figure representing 10 percent of that nation's population. By 1992 about 300,000 Lao refugees have been allowed to resettle abroad, two-thirds going to the United States. The Lao refugees represent two different ethnic groupings: the lowland Lao and the hill-tribe Lao. The Thai government's policy was to place the lowland Lao into camps but as the stream of lowland Lao continued, it adopted a number of measures designed to curb the influx. Informally, there were many reports of "push-backs" occurring along the Thai-Lao border in which would-be refugees were prevented from entering. Also in 1980, an agreement was reached between UNHCR and the Lao government providing for voluntary repatriation.

As in the case of the Vietnamese, in 1981, the Thai government instituted a policy of "humane deterrence" to reduce the influx of refugees. Humane deterrence included several policies. Most significantly, no Lao entering the country after a specific date (August 1981) was considered a refugee or as eligible for resettlement. Rather, they were considered to be illegal immigrants and were transferred to less attractive closed camps in which services were restricted to an essential minimum. Moreover, foreigners were generally denied access to the camps as the government felt that the refugees might associate their presence with resettlement possibilities.

These measures led to an immediate drop in the number of Lao refugees entering the country in 1982. During 1983, the Thai government began relaxing its restrictions, allowing processing of resettlement cases — first the difficult cases (e.g., handicapped refugees) and then individuals by order of arrival date. This precipitated another surge in new arrivals during 1984 and the first half of 1985. In July 1985 the Thai government, in collaboration with UNHCR, instituted a screening procedure for new Lao arrivals. Following interviews with the newly arrived Lao, decisions were reached to accept some and reject others. The screening procedure was designed to reduce the number of people leaving Laos for economic reasons while granting asylum only to people with genuine fears of persecution. But then the question of what to do with the "screened-out" Lao came up; following long negotiations, the Lao government finally agreed to accept the returnees. In the last ten years over 3,000 Lao returned to Laos (1,700 in 1989 alone) under UNHCR auspices; reports also indicate that over 17,000 Lao have returned unofficially without international assistance. Reports claim that the voluntary repatriation has been successful, in part because of improved Thai-Lao relations, economic and political reforms in Laos and a growing confidence on the part of refugees in the Thai camps that they won't face government reprisals. The CPA also provided for full access by all Laotian asylum-seekers to the Laotian border screening programme which was established in July 1985. About 90 percent of the lowland Lao who were interviewed in 1989 were screened in and allowed to enter a camp where they would be eligible to apply for resettlement.

The situation of the hill-tribe Lao has been quite different. The first arrivals in Thailand were those individuals who had fought for the US Central Intelligence Agency before the change of government. The majority of the hill-tribe Lao arrived in 1975, and there was virtually no resettlement of this group until 1979-1980. Between 1975 and July 1986, about 125,000 more hill-tribe Lao arrived; over half of those were resettled. The Thai government has always treated the hill-tribe Lao more leniently than other groups. Because of their closer identification with the US government and the fact that their resettlement outside the region is not a realistic option, the highland Lao have been considered to be more "bona fide" refugees than the lowland Lao. But in spite of the fact that large numbers of highland Lao have been resettled, the future is difficult in that cultural adjustment of these people in resettlement countries has been enormously difficult. Only about 750 hill-tribe Lao have returned to Laos via official channels.

Cambodians

Cambodia's involvement in the Indochina war produced tragic consequences for its people — consequences still felt today even as the peace
agreement is being implemented. From 1970-73 intensive US bombing
devastated the countryside. By early 1972, 2 million Cambodians were
homeless. By one estimate the war had claimed some 450,000 Cambodian lives by the time the Khmer Rouge came to power in April 1975. At
least one million of Cambodia's total population of 7 million died of
starvation, disease, punishment or murder during the Khmer Rouge
regime. The December 1978 invasion by Vietnamese forces led to an
outpouring of refugees in 1979. During the Khmer Rouge regime few
could get out of the country (from April 1975 to December 1978 only
34,000 Cambodians crossed into Thailand though some 320,000, mostly
ethnic Vietnamese, went to Vietnam). The flight of so many Cambodians
in 1979 was the result of fear of the policies of the new Vietnam-backed
regime, food shortages and the likelihood of famine and perhaps the built-
up suffering produced during the years of Khmer Rouge rule. Well over
500,000 Cambodians came to the Thai border by October 1979. A camp,
Khao I Dang, was opened for them, but was closed to new arrivals in
1980 when the numbers increased. People were confined to the border,
for the most part to the Cambodian side of the border. Relief assistance,
food and medical care were provided under the auspices of the joint
ICRC-UNICEF mission which co-ordinated the work of some 95 NGOs.
But the joint mission couldn't control the growing militarization of the
area. By the end of 1980 both UNICEF and ICRC decided to withdraw
from the joint mission exercise.

The growing presence of the refugees along the border was greeted
with fear and hostility by the Thai government, which not only forced
some to return to Cambodia, as mentioned above, but refused to consider
them as refugees. Instead they were classified as "displaced persons";
UNHCR was not permitted to work with them and in 1982 a new United
Nations agency was created, the UN Border Relief Operation (UNBRO),
to provide assistance. But unlike UNHCR, UNBRO had no mandate to
provide for protection along the border. The ICRC is supposed to provide
that protection, but there are many limits on its operations. In particular
the Thai government forbid international personnel to stay in the camps
after 5 p.m. And there have been cases where ICRC personnel have stood
as helpless witnesses while refugees were killed before their eyes. [14]

The creation of UNBRO coincided with the formation of the Coalition
Government of Democratic Kampuchea, composed of the different politi-

cal and military groupings which controlled the camps. From the beginning the camps were dominated by the military forces; this was recognized, and different camps were openly controlled by one of the three main guerrilla forces.

Thailand saw the refugees as a buffer against Vietnam — a buffer which was necessary now that Cambodia no longer filled that role. "Encouraged by China and with US acquiescence, Thailand adopted the policy of encouraging the growth of guerrilla groups opposed to the Vietnamese-backed government in Phnom Penh along the border it shares with Cambodia."[15] The border was a fluid one. The refugees' — or displaced persons' — camps were on the Cambodian side of the border but the people would flee into Thailand during the frequent military offensives. But in late 1984-85, Vietnamese troops launched their biggest offensive ever, forcing the refugees into Thailand proper and building fortifications right up to the international border in an effort to stop the guerrillas.

The situation of the Cambodian refugees along the border was unique in that it was the population base of a "government in exile" recognized by the United Nations. The UN recognized the unlikely CGDK (Coalition Government of Democratic Kampuchea) as the legitimate Cambodian government. In practice, the military guerrilla groups controlled the camps. The Thai authorities maintained that the CGDK had jurisdiction over the people in the camps. Although material supplies and technical support were provided through UNBRO and the NGOs, the camps were administered by the different military factions of the CGDK. "These factions find it relatively easy to manipulate information and relief goods to their advantage; assistance intended for beneficiaries is routinely diverted for political and military purposes."[16]

The camps along the border were violent places, subject to shelling and frequent artillery fire from troops as close as one kilometer away. Forced conscription by the military forces is commonplace. Given the heavy incidence of mines in the border areas, casualties were high. Abuses and violence by the Thai Rangers (Thai military forces charged with providing security in the border area) were also commonplace and have been well-documented.[17] The guerrilla forces controlled the camps and forced the refugees — many of whom are there because they have no choice — to go to fight inside Cambodia. "Relief officials generally use a figure of 90 percent when quantifying the number of people who have no desire to be part of DK-controlled areas" (DK: Democratic Kampuchea, Pol Pot's forces).[18]

A continuing human-rights abuse is the existence of so-called "satellite" or hidden border camps which are physically close to the UN-administered camps and serve as military bases. Perhaps 100,000 civilians live in those camps, with no access to relief supplies and services, and vulnerable to forced combat. Periodically people would be forced from the UN-administered camps into the hidden camps, in spite of NGO protests and reports from human-rights groups.

Thailand's ambivalence towards the refugees was clear. While the Thai government wished to provide support to the guerrillas opposing Vietnam, it didn't want to be permanently burdened with the Cambodians, and refused to allow the camps to be moved to safer positions within Thailand further from the border. Before 1984-85, Thailand refused to allow Cambodians to stay on Thai soil, except for brief periods following military offensives.

Like the Afghan refugees, the Cambodian refugee population has included a sizeable military component which has posed a security threat to the existing government in Cambodia.

The question of the return of the refugees has become a hot political issue and is linked to developments inside Cambodia and particularly to the implementation of the UN-brokered peace agreement. Since 1979, UNHCR, in co-operation with the Cambodian Red Cross, has facilitated the reintegration of 400,000 Cambodians returning from Thailand, Laos and Vietnam. Most of them returned between 1979 and 1983 before the fighting in the country escalated. But most of these repatriations took place without UN involvement. People either spontaneously decided to return on their own or were forcibly returned by guerrilla forces.

By mid-1992, it was estimated that there were 370,000 Cambodian refugees along the border (and perhaps 150,000-200,000 displaced within Cambodia). The signing of a peace agreement for Cambodia in October 1991, although it had been in process for years, came very suddenly and raised concerns about the safety of the refugees to be repatriated. Under the terms of the peace agreement the refugees are to be repatriated before elections are held, probably in April or May 1993. The pressure to repatriate the refugees quickly in order to safeguard the peace process and allow for elections — as well as to protect the refugees from forced repatriations by resistance groups — has increased the pressure on UNHCR to act quickly. As of 1 November 1991, UNHCR took over responsibilities for the border camps from UNBRO in order to prepare the refugees for repatriation. As one knowledgeable observer commented: "It is both ironic and telling that UNHCR finally has been given responsibility for the entire Cambodian refugee population in Thailand when it is time for them to go home."[19]

The UNHCR initially estimated that of the 370,000 Cambodians along the border, about 100,000 would want to return on their own, without UNHCR support. However, by May 1992, 330,000 of the refugees had registered for UNHCR-supported repatriation; the first returnees began the journey home on 30 March 1992 and repatriation continued through early 1993. From the beginning, UNHCR made it clear that five conditions would have to be met for the returnees:

1) the preferred choice of camp residents;
2) the availability of land;
3) the absence of mines;
4) the availability of water;
5) access to a road to enable the provision of assistance.

But there are problems with all five of these conditions. While the return is to be voluntary, the charged political atmosphere of the camps makes it difficult to provide neutral information to the refugees. The availability of land is perhaps the biggest stumbling block to the returnees. While UNHCR confidently predicted on the basis of satellite mapping and on-site verification that sufficient usable land was available to give each returning family two hectares, in fact, the situation on the ground looks different. Some of the land is flooded, some is mined, some is occupied by others. The widespread presence of mines is a deterrent to the return of the refugees and a rapid de-mining programme is essential. Cambodia already has the highest number of amputees in the world as a result of the widespread presence of land-mines. Less than 5 percent of Cambodia's population has access to safe water; securing safe water supplies for the refugees will be a difficult task. The question of water raises other issues about the repatriation. As Iain Guest notes, there are 65,000 Cambodian refugee children under the age of five who have had access to clean, chlorinated water all of their lives. Their well-being in Cambodia and perhaps their survival depends on their continuing to have access to clean water.[20] And yet, UNHCR and NGOs cannot protect the refugees from the conditions under which all Cambodians live nor treat them like a privileged minority within their own country. But it is difficult to reach the right balance to enable them to return in safety to their home communities — which implies a certain level of international assistance — while not offering them preferential treatment.

Most of all, of course, the safe repatriation of Cambodians is based on the premise that the peace agreement will be implemented under the UN

Transitional Authority, that the guerrilla forces will be disarmed, and that the country will move towards the establishment of stable, democratic institutions. And yet, there are serious problems with Khmer Rouge compliance with the peace agreement, raising questions about the long-term implementation of the plan. Moreover, in Cambodia — as in Afghanistan and Ethiopia — there are large numbers of bandits and men who have been trained all of their lives to resolve conflicts with arms rather than negotiation. But the international attention being given to Cambodia and the presence of large numbers of UN troops and civilian workers make it somewhat more likely, at least in the short term, that peace has a chance to be established. This is not the case in those countries where the principal cause of the population displacement are internal conflicts.

Violence and displacement

Internal conflicts are a major source of population displacement in Asia, as in the rest of the world. The causes of the conflicts differ of course, reflecting the ethnic and political forces in the country. But while the causes differ, the results are distressingly similar. People are displaced, first within their own country, and then in some cases to other countries.

Burma (Myanmar)

The suppression of basic human rights in Burma and outbreaks of ethnic violence directed towards several minority groups have led to the displacement of a large number of Burmese, both within the country and outside its borders. The groups displaced are a disparate mixture of Karens and other ethnic groups, students, and Rohingya Muslims. But they all reflect the consequences of repressive military rule. The country's State Law and Order Restoration Council or military junta has brutally put down pro-democracy movements, continues to hold Nobel Peace Prize Laureate Aung San Suu Kyi under house arrest, and has taken measures to suppress ethnic movements.

The presence of Burmese refugees in the neighbouring countries of Thailand and Bangladesh has created tensions along Burma's borders. In early 1992, there were a number of occasions when the Burmese army used Thai territory to attack positions of Karen rebels and reports of Burmese incursions into Thailand are becoming common. Thai policy towards the incursions is inconsistent; sometimes the government protests and sometimes the Thai forces actively resist. Clashes between Burmese and Bangladeshi forces followed an incursion by Burmese troops into Bangladesh in December 1991 and there are reports that both sides are building up their military forces along the border. [21]

Although recent statistics are lacking (the last ethnic census was in 1931) the Karens are estimated to number approximately 3 million out of a total Burmese population of 35 million. The history of the Karens, and the other ethnic minorities in Burma, is one of tension and conflict. The Karen rebellion started in fact in January 1949, one year after the country's independence. Since the early 1950s, the Burmese government has gradually reduced the Karen-held territory. Part of the traditional homeland of the Karens lies near the Burma-Thai border and until recently the Karens controlled much of the black-market trade between the two countries. Indeed, it was said that 70-80 percent of all consumer goods available in Rangoon markets came through the Karen tollgates from Thailand. Since 1949 the Karens have carried out a guerrilla war against the Burmese government. From 1975 until about 1984 small numbers of Karen refugees would cross into Thailand during government dry-season offensives. When the rainy season began, the Burmese troops would be withdrawn and the Karens would return to their homes. However, in 1984, the situation changed as the Burmese attacked in greater force and on a much wider front and were able to maintain their basic supply lines. The Burmese have constructed roads into the area and give no signs of withdrawing — in fact, the offensives against the Karens, the Karenis and the Mons have only increased in the last five years. In addition to these groups, there are other displaced groups such as the Kachin, the Shan, and the Wa. Recent agreements between the Burmese and Thai governments to increase production of lumber from the border regions have added to the displacement of people — and paradoxically increased international pressure on the two governments. (As one NGO representative sardonically commented, when it was just refugees along the border, there wasn't much concern, but now that the teak forests are threatened, there's much greater interest.)

In 1987-88, the popular uprising against the Ne Win government resulted in virtual anarchy for several weeks and finally led to a military coup in September. The repression which followed resulted in an estimated 10,000 deaths and the flight of thousands of students, with as many as 7-10,000 arriving on the Thai-Burmese border. Many of the students underwent military training with the minority forces. But after a couple of years, many of the students reportedly left the border area and found their way back to Burma. Presently, about 2,000 students live in the border regions while another 1,500 are in Bangkok. On several occasions in the past three years, students have been sent back to Burma. A recent Amnesty International report highlighted the human rights concerns of the students. In September 1991, the Thai government announced its intention to create a "safe camp" in a former police camp near the Burmese border and to transfer all the students there where they would be screened; students found not to fear persecution in Burma would face appropriate legal action. This move is opposed by the students who fear reprisals on members of their families back in Burma and who worry that international guarantees would not apply to the camp. [22]

Today, about 40,000 Karen refugees live inside the Thai border. Politically it is unlikely that the Karen guerrillas will succeed in their struggle for autonomy but so far they have given no indications that they are willing to compromise. So the struggle drags on and the Karen refugees remain in camps. While the camps are for the most part in areas inhabited by Thai Karens, relatively little integration has taken place. They are not recognized as refugees, UNHCR does not assist them (although it does provide some assistance to Burmese students living in Bangkok where they are recognized as refugees.) The Thai government does not wish to make an issue of the Karens as the Burmese-Thai relationship is important to both governments. The Saw Maung regime has moved closer to the Thai government. In opening the country to more investment and economic agreements, Thailand has reportedly secured 75 percent of these agreements, particularly in teak, fishing and gem production. Many of the logging concessions granted by Saw Maung are in Karen territory and there is growing co-operation between Thai and Burmese military forces. [23] While the Thai government has allowed them to stay temporarily, it refuses to allow them to construct any permanent facilities (e.g. school or hospital buildings) or to develop programmes which might encourage them to stay. Rather the Thai government wants them to return to Burma at the earliest possible opportunity. [24]

Today there are about 70,000 Burmese asylum-seekers in Thailand. In addition to the ethnic minority groups and the students, there are about 160,000 other Burmese living in Thailand without documentation.

In addition to the Burmese refugees in Thailand there are some 225,000 Burmese refugees in Bangladesh as well. This current influx began in early 1991 and reached dramatic proportions in December of that year with arrivals of up to 6,000 per day. The refugees reported that the government has mounted a campaign of persecution against the Rohingya

Muslim population in Arakan province, and that they are forced to work for the army, often without pay, while large numbers of women have been raped by government forces. The Rohingyas comprise 1.4 million of the 2.2 million population of Arakan. The Myanmar government denies the allegations and says that the refugees were illegal immigrants and that it won't take them back. Bangladesh is one of the poorest countries of the region and is anxious that the refugees be repatriated quickly. In fact, in 1978 when Bangladesh persuaded more than 200,000 Rohingyas who fled from Burma to return home after the Burmese authorities promised to stop the abuses that caused the refugees to flee, the Burmese government did not keep the promise. The government initially sought to resolve the problem through bilateral negotiations with the Burmese government; but as the numbers increased and a political settlement proved to be more difficult than anticipated, the government accepted UNHCR's offer of assistance. UNHCR reports that the refugees are arriving in very difficult conditions and that the conditions in which they are living are poor and risky. Of particular concern is the lack of shelter for the refugees as the cyclone season is beginning. [25]

As the political situation in Burma worsens, the potential for massive population displacement increases. The US Committee for Refugees at a recent US Congressional hearing warned: "It is entirely possible that before the end of the year [1992], Burmese refugees will be the largest refugee group in Asia... The number of internally displaced people could easily exceed one million." [26]

Sri Lanka

Within Sri Lanka's 16.5 million population, 74 percent are Singhalese (mainly Buddhist), 18 percent are Tamils (mainly Hindu) while Muslims number about 7 percent. The violence in Sri Lanka is often seen as an ethnic conflict, with its roots in the colonial period. [27] Policies of discrimination against the Tamils in the 1960s and 1970s and the failure of traditional political mechanisms to respond to Tamil grievances led to the creation of a Tamil liberation movement dedicated to achieving the establishment of an autonomous state. In July 1983 ethnic tensions escalated with anti-Tamil riots in Colombo and elsewhere. Many Tamils moved north to predominantly Tamil areas of the country. As violence intensified after 1983, escalating into civil war, growing numbers of Tamils fled to the Tamil Nadu state in India where there are about 50 million Tamils with links to the Sri Lankan Tamil minority. By 1987, the war had gone on for almost five years and an estimated 135,000 refugees were living in and outside of camps in India. In addition, many others were displaced within Sri Lanka.

Following various initiatives, a peace accord was signed between the Indian and Sri Lankan governments in July 1987 in an effort to end the five-year civil war. The Indian Peace Keeping Force (IPKF) arrived to replace the Sinhalese-dominated Sri Lankan army in the Northern and Eastern provinces. While the IPKF was initially seen as an ally by the Tamil population, its efforts to destroy the leading Tamil militant group, the Liberation Tigers of Tamil Eelam (LTTE, or Tigers) led to an escalation of conflict. In fact, the IPKF became an active participant in the conflict and the levels of violence increased. The death toll in the north-east section of the country reached 10,000 in the 1983-89 period.

In the expectation that peace would permit the repatriation of refugees from India, UNHCR opened offices in Colombo in November 1987 and at four other sites in the country. In 1988 and 1989, some 43,000 Sri Lankans were returned to their homes and by 1990, UNHCR's programme of reintegration was being phased out and UNHCR field offices were being closed. This repatriation from India was parallelled by small-scale deportation of some Tamils from Europe in 1988-89.

But in mid-June 1990, violence again broke out as the last contingent of IPKF left in March 1990, three years after its arrival. Even as UNHCR was winding up its programme to facilitate the return of refugees from India, new refugee flows were being created. In fact, in a three-month period from June to September 1990, some 140,000 Sri Lankans left the country through Mannar Island. [28] In India, the Tamil Nadu government began reopening camps that had been closed in 1987 and cyclone shelters were used to house the new arrivals. In Sri Lanka, the government set up camps for the internally displaced; by late June 1990 there were 300,000 displaced people in more than 100 camps. By late July, the number had increased to over 880,000, of whom 355,000 were in 350 camps in Jaffna district. By September more than one million were displaced in the north-east province, half of them in Jaffna.

While UNHCR was present in Sri Lanka in order to aid in voluntary repatriation, the escalating violence and large numbers of internally displaced who were often in desperate conditions created a fundamentally different situation. In that situation, UNHCR began to move to provide assistance to internally displaced people — although it has no mandate to do so. UNHCR's actions were explained by the fact that the High Commissioner has a mandate to take "ad-hoc humanitarian measures as may be deemed necessary". Its intervention was also justified on the grounds that internal displacement was fuelling an exodus of asylum-seekers to other countries, principally to India. "Reducing the pressure to leave Sri Lanka in such circumstances could therefore be said legitimately to address some of the immediate causes of the refugee outflow."[29] The UNHCR's response in this situation was to create Open Relief Centres as temporary places where displaced persons on the move could freely enter and leave and where they could obtain essential relief assistance. These ORCs were established in several areas of the country and are estimated to have provided assistance to 30,000 people between September 1990 and June 1991.[30]

In addition to the Tamils who were internally displaced or fled to India, conflicts between the government and the JVP (Janatha Vimukthi Peramuna) and outbreaks of Sinhalese nationalism led to perhaps 30,000 deaths in the south of the country in 1988 and 1989. An estimated 96,000 Tamil-speaking Muslims and ethnic Sinhalese have also fled the violence in the eastern province since 1987. In fact, since 1987, most of the violence has been intra-group, Tamil versus Tamil and Sinhalese versus Sinhalese. According to human-rights organizations, the government encouraged violent actions by right-wing vigilante groups. As the Sri Lankan army and the Tamil Tigers alike began forced conscription of young people, many fled the country to escape the violence and the forced recruitment. Some of these Tamils, particularly young men, found their way to Europe, where they encountered an "uncertain" reception from Western host governments.

Within the past year the situation of Sri Lankan refugees and internally displaced has worsened. After Rajiv Gandhi's assassination, there was a crackdown on Tamils living in the state of Tamil Nadu. All Sri Lankans living outside the camps were ordered by the state government in June 1991 to register themselves at the nearest police station. Some 26,000 people were arrested for failure to register (including a number of persons who had become Indian citizens).[31] Following the order, there were reports of Tamil refugees losing their jobs, being evicted from their accommodations and being denied admission to public schools.

In early 1992, the Indian and Sri Lankan government worked out an agreement providing for the repatriation of refugees from India. The Indian government says that over 30,000 of the 110,000 Sri Lankan refugees living in government-run camps in Tamil Nadu have agreed to return and the government has issued a directive to another 120,000 refugees living outside the camps to register for return. By March 1992, some 12,000 refugees had returned to the country; but faced with the continuing violence, most have been unable to return to their own communities. Many are stranded in makeshift camps and the promised returnee benefits have not materialized. UNHCR has consistently refused to endorse the repatriation, saying that conditions in Sri Lanka are not conducive to safe return of the refugees. [32] UNHCR's lack of access to refugees in the camps in India makes it difficult to verify the voluntary nature of the return operation, although some reports indicate that there is considerable coercion involved.

As if the situation weren't bad enough, there were an estimated 100,000 Sri Lankans in Iraq and Kuwait before August 1990. The forced return of so many Sri Lankans to the country increased both the economic and political pressures on the government.

Connections: international and regional developments

Events in Asia shape — and are shaped by — developments at the international level. In terms of the forced movement of people, for example, the end of the cold war has made possible the negotiation of a political settlement in Cambodia. Although peace in Afghanistan remains elusive, it is certainly more likely in an era characterized by US-Soviet co-operation than in one characterized by "proxy wars". The normalization of diplomatic and economic relations with Vietnam by the US and other Western powers is certainly more likely in the post-cold war era than in the past 15 years. All of these are positive signs and indications that developments at the international level can positively affect the situation of refugees in Asia.

And yet, not all conflicts and not all refugees are the product of super-power politics. Ethnic conflicts and the struggle for democracy in Burma are the prime reasons for the presence of 70,000 refugees on the Thai-Burmese border and for the growing numbers of Rohingya refugees in Bangladesh. The violence in Sri Lanka is the result of a complex mixture of ethnic, political and economic forces which will not be resolved by the passing away of the cold war. While the international community has been able to mobilize pressure for peace in the case of Cambodia, such a solution is less likely (for a number of reasons) in Burma, Sri Lanka and the Philippines.

Of the Asian refugee situations examined here, the Indochinese case stands out for the degree of interest and responsibility assumed by the international community. While Sri Lankan, Burmese and Afghan refugees have been largely cared for in countries of first asylum (although international funds have been provided, particularly for the Afghans), solutions for the Indochinese refugees have been sought from abroad. This is perhaps logical, given the international involvement in the war in Indochina — a war which was the prime cause of displacement. Both the 1979 and 1989 UN conferences on Indochinese refugees saw resettlement outside the region as a vital component to resolving the problem of these refugees.

The forced movement of people in Asia is closely related to the search for peace. The presence of refugees can be an obstacle to peace. Certainly in both Cambodia and Afghanistan, the presence of large armed groups on the borders was and is a political force which must be dealt with in order to bring peace and stability to those countries. But the prospects of the return of refugees also raise larger questions. If and when the refugees return to Cambodia or to Sri Lanka, for example, they must be able to survive economically and not become a destabilizing force in countries recovering from war. The way in which Asian governments respond to foreigners arriving at their borders will depend in large part on national political and economic factors. But ultimately the fate of the refugees and displaced people in Asia depends on progress in achieving peace with justice.

NOTES

[1] C.W. Stahl, "South-North Migration in the Asia-Pacific Region", in *International Migration*, vol. 29, no. 2, 1991, pp.163-193.

[2] Clement John, "Foreword", in *Asian Refugees: A Search for Solutions*, by J. Basil Fernando, Hong Kong, Christian Conference of Asia, International Affairs, 1991.

[3] Task Force on Militarization in Asia and the Pacific, *The Afghan Crisis*, New York, TFMAP, 1988.

[4] David Feith, *Stalemate: Refugees in Asia*, Parkville, Vic., Australia, Asian Bureau Australia, 1988.

[5] *World Refugee Survey 1989*, New York, US Committee for Refugees, 1990.

[6] *World Refugee Survey 1991*, New York, US Committee for Refugees, 1991.

[7] "Afghanistan: A Sad Legacy of the Cold War", in *Refugees*, UNHCR, no. 88, January 1992, p.19.

[8] Hiram A. Ruiz, *Left out in the Cold: The Perilous Homecoming of Afghan Refugees*, Washington, DC, US Committee for Refugees, 1992.

[9] Although Vietnamese had left the country earlier — an estimated 135,000 were evacuated with the last US troops in 1975 — the outflow increased in the 1977-79 period because of the imposition of North Vietnamese authority over the South, increased persecution of ethnic Chinese, the establishment of new economic zones and the incarceration of thousands of political prisoners. Moreover, Vietnam reversed its policy of discouraging deportations in 1978-79 and began realizing some concrete economic benefits by impounding refugees' goods and making them pay in gold for their departure (see Feith, *op. cit.*).

10 Joseph Cerquone, *Uncertain Harbors: The Plight of Vietnamese Boat People*, USCR Issue Paper, 1987. He also asserts, as do others, that a modest estimate is that 100,000 Vietnamese died at sea from 1979-1987.

11 Because they fled by boat, Vietnamese refugees are the most far-flung of the Asian refugees. They landed in Thailand, Malaysia, Singapore, Indonesia, Australia, the Philippines, Brunei, Macau, Taiwan, Hong Kong and Korea and were picked up at sea even further away. Following China's invasion of Vietnam in 1979, about 230,000 mostly ethnic Chinese Vietnamese fled to China where most have become fairly self-sufficient and well-integrated into Chinese life.

12 Steven Muncy, "Assessment of Needs in Indonesia", in *Impact*, no. 3, 1991.

13 From 1975 to 1988, over 100,000 Vietnamese landed in Indonesia, 99,000 of whom were resettled in third countries. More began to come in 1979 when Malaysia began pushing back Vietnamese boats (arrivals in Indonesia jumped from 7,000 to 31,500 in 1989) (Feith, *op. cit.*, p.21). Similar pressure is now building up. Galang camp in Indonesia now has 20,559 persons, about 70 percent (14,000) of whom arrived in 1990. Like their counterparts in Vietnam, screening is a major issue and refugees are traumatized and angry about the procedures.

Singapore has followed a much more restrictive policy. An asylum-seeker is not allowed to enter unless there's a firm guarantee that another country will accept him or her. And since early 1979, Singapore has firmly adhered to a policy that no more than 1,000 refugees will be allowed in the country at any one time. About 35,000 refugees have been given temporary asylum in Singapore and resettled elsewhere (Feith, *op. cit.*, p.24).

For those refugees from Hong Kong and the Philippines who have been "screened in" and are awaiting resettlement, plans are under way for a regional resettlement transit centre in the Philippines. (The centre was formally opened on 4 June 1991, but the volcanic eruption in the Philippines has delayed its operations.)

14 See for example the account in "No Place Called Home", in *Chicago Tribune Magazine*, special supplement on refugees, 1989.

15 Lawyers Committee for Human Rights, *Seeking Shelter: Cambodians in Thailand*, New York, Lawyers Committee, 1987, p.26.

16 Norah Niland, "Report from the Border", briefing paper prepared for the Asia-Pacific Task Force, August 1990.

17 *Ibid.*, p.1.

18 *Ibid.*, p.9.

19 Court Robinson, in "Buying Time: Refugee Repatriation from Cambodia", *World Refugee Survey 1991*, Washington, DC, USCR, 1992, p.20.

20 Iain Guest, "Cambodia: Homeward Bound", *Refugees*, UNHCR, May 1992, p.25.

21 David Arnott, "Offensive in Burma: A Million Refugees?", in *Peace News*, March 1992.

22 Jesuit Refugee Service, *Diakonia*, October 1991.

23 Jack Dunford, "Burmese Refugees in Thailand", in *Asian Refugees: A Role for the Churches?*, report of the CCA/WCC/CICARWS Asian refugee working group meeting, Bangkok, 17-19 May 1989.

24 In addition to these two well-known groups of Burmese refugees, the ethnic minorities and the students, more than 250,000 Burmese refugees, mainly Muslims of mixed Burman and Indian ancestry, fled to Bangladesh in late 1978. This flight followed the large-scale Burmese army persecution of Muslims in Arakan state. Although some were repatriated shortly thereafter, an undetermined number remain in Bangladesh. (*World Refugee Survey 1989, op. cit.*).

[25] See, for example, Fernando del Mundo, "Bangladesh: In the Eye of a Storm", in *Refugees*, UNHCR, May 1992, pp.29-31. Hiram Ruiz, "Soaring Number of Burmese (Rohingya) Refugees in Bangladesh Hampers Efforts to Provide Relief", in *News from the US Committee for Refugees*, Washington, USCR, 19 March 1992.

[26] Cited by Arnott, *op. cit.*

[27] In fact, the ethnic situation is more complicated than that. Sri Lankan Tamil "repatriates" are Tamils born in Sri Lanka but never granted citizenship. Their ancestors came from India in the nineteenth century to provide labour for the British estates. These "repatriates" have always been separate from the indigenous Sri Lankan Tamils. In 1949, this group of nearly a million people, known as Indian or plantation Tamils, were disenfranchized by the Sri Lankan government. In 1964 an agreement for the return of some 525,000 plantation Tamils to India and some 300,000 to remain in Sri Lanka and become citizens was worked out. There are still some 350,000 stateless Tamils in Sri Lanka. It has been particularly difficult for those who have gone to India as they had always lived in Sri Lanka (Feith, *op. cit.*, p.37).

[28] These figures and the description of UNHCR activity are based largely on W.D. Clarance, "Open Relief Centres: A Pragmatic Approach to Emergency Relief and Monitoring during Conflict in a Country of Origin", in *International Journal of Refugee Law*, vol. 3, no. 2, 1991, pp.320-328.

[29] *Ibid.*, p.324.

[30] *Tamil Information*, no. 2, September 1991.

[31] *Ibid.*

[32] *The Sri Lanka Monitor*, January and March 1992.

8. Uprooted People
in Latin America
Political and Strategic Issues

> Without peace, the victims of armed conflict cannot resume their lives. Without democracy, they cannot participate in their societies. Without national reconciliation, they cannot coexist with neighbours who fell on the other side of the lines of combat. [1]

Chileans in exile, displaced Salvadorans and Guatemalans, Central American refugees in the US, Haitian boats interdicted and Haitians sent back to Haiti, uprooted Peruvians and Colombians as a result of the escalating violence — Latin America has had its share of refugees and displaced people. But the mass movement of Latin Americans for political reasons is a relatively recent development. Although Latin America has a long history of legal initiatives on asylum and exile, and in the last century took the lead in developing laws and guidelines for granting of asylum, the last thirty years have challenged that framework.

After the victory of Fidel Castro in 1961, hundreds of thousands of Cubans left their country, most finding a receptive home in the US. The US government welcomed the refugees; politically they seemed to demonstrate the tyranny of Cuban communism which helped to legitimize US opposition to the regime. Over the course of a decade about one-tenth of Cuba's population decided to leave; their departure caused serious economic problems for Cuba as the refugees were drawn, at least initially, disproportionately from the educated middle and upper classes. At the same time, some have suggested that the departure of so many discontented Cubans enabled the Castro regime to consolidate its rule more effectively. The option of expelling one's opponents is attractive to many authoritarian governments, but few have found such a willing host country as the Cubans found in the United States.

After the initial wave of Cuban refugees, the flow diminished until 1980 when some 120,000 Cubans left the country from the Cuban port of Mariel. These "Marielitos" fled for a variety of reasons, some because of the lack of political freedom but most in search of a better economic life. The years of revolutionary consolidation in Cuba continued to be economically hard on the population; the glitter of Miami was a strong attraction, particularly for young people who couldn't remember the hardships of life before the revolution. But the Marielitos faced a diminished US welcome; some were viewed with hostility and suspicion and some imprisoned for their criminal activities in Cuba. Most were eventually integrated into US life where they discovered that Miami's streets were not paved with gold. A decade later, in 1991-92, the number of Cubans escaping by boat (and other devices, such as inner tubes, rafts and tires) increased significantly; for Cuba's government the changes in the Soviet Union meant increasing economic hardship and growing political isolation. Economic conditions in the country, already difficult because of the US economic embargo, demanded increasing sacrifices, with shortages of medicines, oil and consumer goods of all kinds. At the same time, the Castro regime adopted a hard line towards political opponents and many Cubans became convinced that political change would be impossible as long as Castro remained in power.

Although the Cuban exodus was one of the first large-scale movements of politically-motivated migrants, it was seen in Latin America as primarily a US-Cuban issue. The fact that the refugees were generously received by the US government and that the US government used them in support of its foreign-policy objectives made the Cuban migration a special case. While other countries received smaller numbers of Cubans in the 1960s and later, for the most part they didn't cause major difficulties for the host governments. Many of the first wave of Cubans joined relatives or business associates in nearby countries, such as Venezuela and Colombia. But their numbers were small and their economic and social conditions facilitated their integration into their host countries.

The 1973 military coup in Chile and the resulting repression of opponents to the regime resulted in a mass exodus of Chileans which some have estimated to number over 200,000. The Chilean case was most dramatic in South America, as embassies in Santiago crowded with hundreds of people seeking to leave the country, but it reflected the fact that the decade of the 1970s was the decade of military governments in the Southern Cone. Argentina, Uruguay, Brazil and Chile all went through a period where military governments were determined to root out subversives and to establish absolute control. In the process they forced many to flee their countries. Unlike the situation of the 1980s in Central America and the present situation in the Andean countries, the refugees from the Southern Cone tended to be young people with some involvement in politics. In Argentina, the climate of terror created by the disappearances of thousands of Argentine young people led many to leave their country. Many were not recognized as refugees and indeed never sought refugee status. Rather, families sent their young people abroad to study or work "for a while" in light of the widespread violence in the country. The Chileans fled in larger numbers; some were resettled in Canada and European countries with the assistance of the International Organization for Migration. Larger numbers crossed the border into neighbouring Argentina, where in spite of the repression by the military dictatorship in that country they were able to live in greater security than in Chile. The Chilean refugees fleeing to Argentina joined a much larger community of Chilean economic migrants who for decades had sought employment opportunities in the vineyards and industries of north-western Argentina.

Political repression coupled with the infamous death squads led thousands of Uruguayans to leave their country as well. As in the case of the Argentine exodus, some went to Europe and North America while others sought protection in neighbouring countries. The large number of Uruguayans working in Argentina made it difficult to estimate the number of refugees; by 1985 when democracy was restored, many returned, but figures are unavailable precisely because of the ambiguous nature of their exile and because of existing migration patterns.

Over the decade of the 1980s, Argentina, Uruguay, Brazil and finally Chile all established democratic regimes; the military stepped down from government (though not from political power) and human-rights abuses decreased. Even in Paraguay, the Stroessner dictatorship was replaced by democratic elections. In all of these cases, some of the exiles returned. For those, like the Chileans who had been in exile for years — sometimes more than a decade — the decision to return home was a difficult and painful one. Economic conditions in Chile made it difficult to find a job and almost impossible to duplicate the living standards which those who had been in exile in Europe were accustomed to. Many Chilean returnees ended up living with family members for extended periods of time. And, like returnees in all regions, the Chilean returnees found that the Chile to which they had returned was different from the Chile which they had left a decade before. Although the Chileans welcomed back the returning refugees, some felt resentment that while they had spent the decade under Pinochet's harsh rule, their compatriots in exile had lived more comfortable lives. And sometimes there was resentment when the returnees wanted to engage in political activities or seemed critical of those who had stayed behind.

But the South American case also illustrates the difficulties of return after long periods of exile. After almost twenty years, many of the Chilean exiles had established new lives in other countries. They had become established in their jobs, their children had grown up speaking another language, often marrying nationals of other countries. It became more difficult to return; sometimes family members urged them *not* to return as they provided security for the family in Chile by living and earning a living elsewhere. Many of the Chilean exiles have not yet permanently returned, and it is likely that with the passage of time even fewer will do so.

In contrast to the refugees from the Southern Cone, the violence in Central America and the Andean countries has displaced large numbers of rural communities (as well as urban activists). In spite of peace agreements in El Salvador and Nicaragua, continued uncertainty impedes the return of most of those uprooted by the violence in Central America.

Central America

The fate of the approximately 2 million Central Americans uprooted by the violence of the last decade depends on the establishment of peace, reconciliation and stability in the region. This reflects the fact that the Central American refugees and displaced people were a product of the political and military developments in that region. Displacement of civilian populations has become a deliberate strategy of counter-insurgency campaigns in many countries around the world; in Central America it became almost institutionalized.

The presence of so many Central American refugees and displaced people is not simply a humanitarian challenge of providing protection and assistance to a vulnerable group of people, although that task is certainly an urgent one. Rather, analysis of the situation of Central America's uprooted people also offers an opportunity to explore the relationship between their situation and the larger questions of peace, justice, security and economic recovery. The presence of large numbers of refugees has posed a high political and economic burden on host governments and has complicated relations between governments of the region. The political and economic costs of large numbers of uprooted people have been considerable for the countries of Central America. But as peace agreements are negotiated and peace is maintained, the return of the refugees and displaced also entails substantial political and economic costs.

In early 1991, UNHCR recognized about 150,000 Central Americans as refugees and provided assistance to about 123,000 of them. But the actual number of individuals displaced within their own countries or living in another country without legal recognition is far greater. Current estimates of the number of uprooted Central Americans range from 2 to 3 million. But there are wide variations in the statistics, reflecting both the dynamic nature of forced migration and difficulties in counting people who seek anonymity. Refugees and displaced people return to their communities when the violence abates — and then may leave again if it intensifies. Many Central Americans in Mexico are probably "in transit" to the United States, although the journey may take months, and many end up remaining in Mexico.

In preparation for the 1989 International Conference on Central American Refugees (CIREFCA), governments in the region made a concerted effort to identify the number of refugees and displaced people in their countries. In some cases, such as Mexico, the government accepted estimates by NGOs that there were over 300,000 undocumented Central Americans living in Mexico City alone. In other cases, such as Costa Rica, the government's estimate of "externally displaced" Nicaraguans in the country was over 200,000 — about twice the number estimated by NGOs. Given CIREFCA's emphasis on the presentation of projects by the governments to address the needs of these groups, it may be that the figures are somewhat inflated.

The following table presents a summary of some of the estimates for refugees and displaced people in the region. Although the figures are only approximations, they reveal that significant numbers of people have been uprooted in and from Central America.

TABLE 1:   REFUGEES AND DISPLACED PEOPLE IN LATIN AMERICA,
31 DECEMBER 1991

Country of origin		Total refugees	Internally displaced
Argentina		1,800	
Belize		12,000	
El Salvador	8,500		
Guatemala	3,100		
Nicaragua	400		
Bolivia		100	
Brazil		200	
Colombia		700	
Internally displaced			150,000
Costa Rica		24,300	
Nicaragua	20,000		
El Salvador	4,000		
Others	300		
Ecuador		4,200	
Colombia	4,000		
Others	200		
El Salvador		250	150-450,000
Internally displaced			
French Guiana		9,600	
Suriname	9,600		
Guatemala		8,300	
Internally displaced			150,000
Nicaragua	4,900		
El Salvador	3,400		
Haiti			
Internally displaced			200,000
Honduras		2,050	
Internally displaced			7,000
El Salvador	1,700		
Guatemala	100		
Nicaragua	100		
Mexico		48,500	
Guatemala	43,500		
El Salvador	4,000		
Others	1,000		

Country of origin		Total refugees	Internally displaced
Nicaragua		2,800	
El Salvador	2,600		
Others	200		
Internally displaced			354,000
Panama		1,300	
Internally displaced			10,000
Peru		600	
Internally displaced			200,000
Cuba	400		
Others	200		
Uruguay		100	
Venezuela		1,700	
Cuba	1,000		
Chile	350		
Others	350		
Total		**118,500**	

Source: US Committee for Refugees, *World Refugee Survey 1992*, Washington, DC, USCR, 1992.

The recent refugee situation in Central America reflects the political crises of the last decade as well as much older patterns of labour migration. In the final years of the Somoza regime, about 250,000 Nicaraguans sought protection in Costa Rica. After the 1979 revolution, over 90 percent of them returned to Nicaragua. Traditionally, Nicaraguans have migrated to Costa Rica for economic reasons just as Salvadorans have gone to Honduras and Guatemala and Guatemalans to Southern Mexico. And as is well-known, the trail for Central American economic migrants frequently leads to the United States. One of the characteristics of refugee movements in the region is that they tend to follow established lines of economic migration.

This large-scale displacement reached its peak in the early 1980s in El Salvador and Guatemala — a period corresponding to the outbreak of widespread violence and the imposition of harsh counter-insurgency measures; the large outflows of Nicaraguans occurred several years later, in response to the ethnic conflict in the eastern region of the country and particularly to the effects of the Contra war.

Guatemala and Mexico

Political violence in Guatemala has been widespread for years. Amnesty International estimates that between 1966 and 1976, 20,000 Guatemalans were killed by death squads. [2] But even that high level of violence was further intensified in the late 1970s and early 1980s. In response to growing popular support for Guatemalan opposition groups and in the shadow of the successful Sandinista revolution, President Romero Lucas Garcia (1978-82) launched what Amnesty International has called a "government programme of political murder". During 1980 and 1981, a number of massacres took place in indigenous communities and the war between the government and the opposition forces intensified with high casualties among the civilian population. In order to consolidate control of the rural areas and to deny guerrilla forces the support of the indigenous population, the government adopted a policy based on mass displacement of the rural indigenous population. This was a deliberate strategy, intended both to sever the guerrillas' ties with the community and to depopulate areas considered vital from a military viewpoint. Between 1981 and the end of 1982, the Guatemalan army forcibly uprooted over one million people in the indigenous highlands through the use of forced relocation, massacres and scorched earth policies. Some 17 percent of the total Guatemalan population fled their communities, at least temporarily. [3] About 70 percent of the 1.5 million displaced between 1980 and 1981 returned under the amnesty provisions of President Rios Montt. But their return was carefully monitored and controlled by the Guatemalan government which established development poles and model villages to ensure that the peasant population could no longer provide support to the guerrilla movement.

Displaced communities seeking to return to their villages were directed to these government-designed villages and carefully monitored. Of particular concern was the fact that the peasants were forced to participate in civil defence patrols, which at their height had some 900,000 members. Although they have since been renamed, the voluntary civil defence committees are still obligatory and, according to the government, include over 600,000 members. [4] As will be seen in the sections below, the existence of the model villages and forced participation in the civil patrols, and the military's central role in the resettlement of displaced Guatemalans, have served as a powerful obstacle to further return of uprooted Guatemalans.

At the same time that Guatemalans were fleeing the massacres in the highlands by seeking refuge within their country, an estimated 250-

350,000 Guatemalans fled the country between 1978 and 1983, with some 200,000 going to Mexico. For the refugees, the journey was often a nightmare as they faced harassment and military attack during flight. In June 1983, the Comité de Ayuda a Refugiados Guatemaltecos estimated that at least 8,000 Guatemalans had died trying to reach Mexican territory.[5] The arrival of large numbers of Guatemalans on the Mexican border created problems for the Mexican government which has historically had difficult relations with the Guatemalan government and which at that time was critical of the governmental repression going on in Guatemala. But the response of the Mexican government to the refugees was ambiguous during the first couple of years. On several occasions, there were deportations of large numbers of Guatemalans, but at the same time, limited efforts were made to provide assistance and some form of legal status for others in the border area. The refugees were alternately depicted as poor victims of the bloodshed in Guatemala and as threats to Mexican society and economy. The fact that the refugees arrived in one of the poorest regions of Mexico — Chiapas — and that they followed long established traditions of labour migration, coupled with the undeniable violence in the Guatemalan highlands made it difficult for the government to develop a consistent policy. This difficulty was compounded by the fact that US treatment of undocumented Mexicans in the US was a highly politicized issue in Mexico.

Moreover, security concerns were paramount. From 1982-83 the Guatemalan-Mexican border was violated on several occasions by the Guatemalan army which maintained that it was pursuing guerrillas. Presently, there are some 46,000 recognized refugees of whom about 19,000 live in the camps in Campeche and Quintana Roo and the remainder in approximately 127 dispersed camps in Chiapas. These groups receive assistance form COMAR, the Mexican agency set up to assist refugees, in co-operation with UNHCR. However, UNHCR is phasing out all assistance to Guatemalan refugees in Mexico, encouraging them either to become self-sufficient in Mexico or to return to Guatemala.

Far larger numbers of refugees live without any legal status on the margins of Mexico City and other urban centres where they are vulnerable to exploitation and deportation. At the 1989 CIREFCA meeting, the Mexican government accepted the estimates of NGOs that the number of undocumented Central Americans in the country could be as high as 385,000 of whom 250,000 were Salvadorans, 110,000 Guatemalans living outside the camps and at least 25,000 Hondurans and Nicaraguans.

Many of these Central Americans are presumed to be "in transit" through Mexico to the United States. Although there has always been co-operation between US and Mexican immigration authorities, there is evidence that such co-operation is taking a more active form. A recent study documents the increase of apprehensions and deportations of Central Americans from Mexico from about 14,000 in 1989 to an estimated 160,000 in 1990. According to the study, published by the US Committee for Refugees, this increased co-operation is the result of US campaigns to prevent Central Americans from reaching the US border and is reflected in a decrease of 21 percent in the number of apprehensions of Central Americans at the US border. [6] In the past year there have been a growing number of reports of Mexican deportations of Central Americans to Guatemala; estimates vary from the 35,000 cited by the Mexican government to the figure of 150,000 used by NGOs. [7]

Other changes are taking place in Mexico's policies towards the Central Americans. Although Mexico has not signed the 1951 UN Convention on refugees, in July 1990, for the first time, a definition of "refugees" was added to its general population law. Regulations for implementation of this law have been slow in coming and it is uncertain how the law will affect the large numbers of undocumented Central Americans in Mexico. There is concern among the NGOs and the refugee communities about the effect of the new law and the proposed amnesty, and fears that, once implemented, the law will mean increased deportations of those found not to meet the criteria. The July 1990 changes to the general population law also include a provision (article 118) mandating a ten-year prison sentence and a large fine for those who "bring or intend to bring illegally foreigners into Mexico or house or transport them with the purpose of hiding them from migratory inspection". [8] This would have the effect of making many of the NGOs providing services to undocumented Central Americans vulnerable to charges of illegal activity.

Over the last few years there have been varying trends in the issue of repatriation of Guatemalans from Mexico. In 1986, in the expectation that refugees would be returning as a result of the restoration of civilian government in Guatemala, the Guatemalan government established CEAR (the Special Commission on Assistance to Repatriates) to facilitate the return of refugees. CEAR, an interministerial agency, gave the military a key role in organizing the repatriation. Meanwhile, Guatemalan refugees living in camps organized the permanent commissions in 1988 and developed a set of conditions under which they would return. The Guatemalan bishops' conference in 1986 spelled out three general conditions for Guatemalan return: it should be voluntary, the government must guarantee the refugees' security, and the refugees must be able to choose the communities they wish to settle in.[9] Agreements were worked out between the Guatemalan and Mexican governments and UNHCR on the modalities of return. Between 1986 and 1989 about 3,000 Guatemalans returned to their country with assistance from UNHCR. But as it became clearer that the democratic election of a president was not to be accompanied by a dramatic improvement of the human-rights situation, interest in repatriation among the refugees waned.

A study of those who returned between 1986 and 1989 found that the refugees had based their decisions on fairly good information about conditions back in their communities of origin and that a main reason for their return was the desire to recover their lands. Moreover, the study found that evangelical Christians were much more likely to return than Catholic refugees, although Catholics form a large majority of the refugee population. Although repatriates have not been targeted for attack by death squads, the challenge of providing for their personal security — given the widespread violence in the areas to which they return — is substantial. Presently CEAR meets refugees at the border, provides documentation, transport and some food and tools to the returnees. UNHCR is mandated to monitor the conditions of the returnees, but the terrain and isolation of the communities make such monitoring on a regular basis very difficult. Two of the principal difficulties facing the returnees are the ongoing violence in their communities of origin and access to land. The Guatemalan army reportedly continues to believe that refugees are giving logistical aid to the guerrillas, especially those living near the Mexican border, and views them with suspicion. Since the military is the principal actor in the repatriation process, obviously this intensifies the security concerns of the returnees. In March 1987, for example, the Guatemalan minister of defence specifically accused the guerrillas of preparing the refugees for repatriation.[10] Moreover, there is considerable opposition to repatriation by local communities. In 1987 Sergio Aguayo reported that mayors in over fifty towns had written to President Cerezo expressing their total opposition to any repatriation.[11]

While the Catholic church is virtually the only institution with an extensive infrastructure and networks at the rural level, it cannot guarantee security for the returnees. Nor does the church have an alternative plan for solving the problems of civil patrols and access to land.[12]

The issue of returnees' access to land in their communities of origin has been a serious problem for many of the 3,000 or so refugees who have returned to Guatemala. In the communities of Ixcan and Chacaj, for example, the military governments had declared that the refugees had abandoned their lands "voluntarily" and therefore the lands could revert to state ownership under Guatemalan law, thus permitting the state to repopulate the areas. As a result, in both areas there are great tensions over land between the "antiguos" who fled the army and the "nuevos" who were brought there by the army. But the pressure on land — the conflicts between returnees and those who have remained or been resettled — will only intensify in the event of a large-scale return. Given Guatemala's extremely unequal distribution of land and the desperate economic conditions of the rural highlands, a massive return of refugees could create severe stresses on the infrastructure. Nonetheless, by late 1992, many Guatemalan refugees in Mexico were planning to return to Guatemala and seeking support from churches and NGOs to facilitate their return.

El Salvador

In El Salvador the violence erupting in the country in 1979 led the opposition to intensify the armed struggle and the government to begin a strategy of systematic bombing of areas suspected of harbouring guerrilla forces. At the same time, the death squads increased their activities, human-rights violations rose dramatically, and torture and disappearance became a way of life. In 1979 about 1,000 Salvadorans a month were killed by death squads. By 1985, casualties in the war reached 50,000. This widespread violence and fear displaced a million people — 20 percent of El Salvador's population. About half remained within the country as internally displaced people, about 100,000 crossed into Honduras, of whom 20,000 ended up in government-controlled camps, and others sought security in more distant countries.

Salvadoran refugees began entering Honduras in 1980; by June of that year they numbered 4,000, and by January 1981 the figure had climbed to about 18,000 and the Honduran government moved to regularize their status, placing them in camps near the border. But the Honduran government viewed the refugees with suspicion, seeing them as guerrillas or as providing support to the guerrillas. It feared the revolutionary potential of the upheaval in El Salvador for the region as a whole and worked closely with the Salvadoran military authorities. Close co-operation between the Honduran and Salvadoran military authorities was tragically evident in the massacre of 600 Salvadorans at the Rio Sumpul in May 1980. [13]

The military was particularly concerned about the refugees' proximity to the border, and in November 1981 11,000 refugees were forcibly relocated from the border to Mesa Grande, a camp about forty kilometres away, while about 9,000 refugees remained in the camps of Colomoncagua and San Antonio near the border. The camps were kept under close military surveillance and over the years there have been numerous incidents of military harassment of refugees in the camps. There have also been several efforts to relocate the camps further from the border, but these efforts were prevented by international pressure.

Honduras, like Mexico, is not a signatory to the UN Conventions although a memorandum of understanding was signed with UNHCR in 1987. Of all the refugee situations in Central America, the Salvadorans in Honduras have received the most international attention. The refugee communities in these camps were well-organized and responsible for much of the camp management. Almost from the beginning, the Honduran government viewed the refugees as a security issue and believed that the camps provide a safe haven and a supply line for the Frente Farabundo Martí de Liberación (FMLN).

Beginning in 1987, the refugees began to organize their repatriation back to El Salvador and several mass repatriations have been carried out. Each of the repatriations has been marked by tension and disagreements — in part because of the refugees' clear and insistent demands, in part because of the degree of their international support, in part because of the highly politicized context in which the return operations were carried out.

The refugee repatriations took place in a context in which many internally displaced people in El Salvador were also beginning to return to their communities of origin — in spite of the fact that these communities were located in zones of continuing conflict. This *repoblación* movement was undoubtedly a factor in the decision of refugees living in Honduras to return to their communities and begin rebuilding their lives. But the decision to return was also undoubtedly influenced by a general fatigue with camp life. Many of the refugees had been there for almost ten years and, although they had managed to initiate many programmes and acquire many skills, there was a feeling that there was no future for them in the camps. UNHCR budget cuts in the late 1980s were interpreted by the refugees as efforts to force them back, although in fact the budget cuts affected refugees in other regions more dramatically. But one study asserts that the mass repatriations had little to do with refugees' individual desire to go home.

Rather they went home because they believed that the moment had come when, as organized communities in El Salvador, they could contribute to the political struggle against the government and the military. They had never ceased to support this struggle when they were in the remote, military controlled refugee camps in Honduras.[14]

One of the most controversial aspects of the situation of Salvadoran refugees in Honduras was the issue of their links to the FMLN, the principal insurgent group in the country. Salvadoran, Honduran and US government representatives saw the refugees as channelling supplies to the guerrillas and accused refugee leadership of being directed by the FMLN in El Salvador. While the refugees categorically denied reports of FMLN activities in the camps, in fact there was considerable sympathy for the FMLN and refugee leadership was in contact with both the FMLN and other popular organizations in El Salvador.[15] But the important factor is that the authorities *believed* that the refugees were under the direction and control of the guerrillas and treated them accordingly, increasing the tension between the refugees and the governments.

The repatriations of over 30,000 Salvadorans from Honduras to El Salvador faced many of the same obstacles as the far smaller number of Guatemalans who returned to their country. Security concerns continue to be paramount. Although UNHCR has the responsibility to monitor the security of the returnees, this is difficult to carry out because of the continuing violence in the regions to which refugees have returned. As a way of increasing their security during the return operations, the refugees asked church and NGO representatives to accompany and assist them. This accompaniment did have the effect of providing additional protection and publicity to the returning refugees, but it also created serious tensions at times with both UNHCR and the governments. The church and NGO groups saw their responsibility as being for the refugees and supporting their demands; they often viewed UNHCR as a tool of governmental interests. UNHCR's position was that they were unable to act without the consent of the Salvadoran government. On several occasions, violent confrontations at the border were narrowly averted.

As in the Guatemalan case, the Salvadoran military authorities view returnees as well as the organizations which seek to assist them with suspicion. One of the particularly difficult issues has been that of documentation for the returnees who find that without identity papers security and routine issues in daily life become more difficult. It is estimated that some 80 percent of the returnees have no official identity papers. In the last four years there have been numerous incidents in which returnee communities have been harassed and even bombed by the military, and NGOs seeking to provide humanitarian assistance to the returnees have also been harassed. CRIPDES, a Christian organization working with repatriates and displaced people, reported in October 1990 that more than 150 people from repatriated communities had been killed, wounded or captured in the previous ten months as a result of military operations. [16]

Although virtually all of the Salvadoran refugees living in the Honduran camps have returned (even Mesa Grande was closed in early 1992), the Honduran government estimates that there are some 50,000 Central Americans still living illegally in the country (and perhaps 7,000 internally displaced Hondurans). In addition to the Salvadorans in Honduras, there are perhaps 250,000 in Mexico, perhaps 70,000 in Guatemala, smaller numbers in Belize, Costa Rica and Nicaragua, and estimates of the number of Salvadorans in the US range from 200,000 to 700,000. The prospects of large-scale return of Salvadorans to El Salvador, as in Guatemala, raise serious challenges to the ability of the government to meet the basic human needs of the returnees. Such a return depends, of course, on the implementation of the peace agreement. This was signed on 31 December 1991 and, in spite of many obstacles and delays, has largely been implemented. Many questions remain, particularly concerning the composition of the military leadership, but there is hope that the peace agreement will serve as a basis for the country's reconstruction. But peace — and the ability of the displaced and repatriates to return — depends on economic factors as well. Unemployment is estimated to be between 48 and 50 percent in urban areas and as high as 71 percent in rural areas. [17] In such a context, the return of several hundred thousand refugees would pose an unbearable strain on the economy.

But the potential economic costs of such a repatriation go beyond the direct costs of aiding their reintegration into the economy. Although data are lacking, it is well known that the foreign remittances of the Salvadorans living abroad are an important asset for the Salvadoran economy. Segundo Montes estimated that Salvadoran refugees in the US, although 30 percent of them are unemployed, send an average of US$110 per month to relatives in El Salvador. Annually this represents about US$1.4 billion — a substantial contribution overshadowing US foreign aid and efforts by international agencies to provide assistance to the country. Moreover, Segundo Montes estimated that the funds sent to relatives living in El Salvador provided 60 percent of the income of those groups. [18] If the foreign remittances were to come to an end, those families would undoubtedly be worse off. Given present measures of poverty and malnutrition (with 50 percent of children under five and 75 percent of those under one year malnourished), the economic impact of a decrease in foreign remittances would be substantial. When added to the economic pressures of large numbers of Salvadorans seeking employment and requiring public services, the pressures might well be unbearable.

Internally displaced: Guatemala and El Salvador

In both Guatemala and El Salvador, large numbers of people were displaced within the country as a result of the violence. And in both countries, the displaced were viewed with suspicion by governmental authorities. But quite different patterns of assistance to these groups developed in response to their political and strategic contexts. In El Salvador, the small size of the country, the high population density and the availability of roads made it possible for the internally displaced to go to cities where they frequently lived with other members of their displaced communities. Also in El Salvador, the open state of warfare between the government and the armed opposition meant that the existence of the internally displaced was officially recognized and assistance was organized. Camps were created for them and both governmental and NGO initiatives were undertaken to provide assistance to them. In 1981, the government created CONADES (National Commission for Assistance to the Displaced) under the ministry of the interior, with funding from US AID. By 1986, AID's programme for displaced families was the third largest employer in the country — after the civilian government and the Salvadoran armed forces.[19] But the existence of these official programmes meant that in order to receive assistance, displaced people had to register with the government and their names were checked by local military commanders. In many cases, displaced individuals were afraid to provide the required information for fear that relatives back in their communities would suffer reprisals. But there were alternatives to receiving governmental assistance through the many non-governmental organizations and church groups which ran programmes. These organizations have operated openly, but have also faced serious pressure from both government and para-governmental forces. After the November 1989 FMLN offensive and the smaller offensive in November 1990, church and NGO groups suffered threats and reprisals.

In Guatemala, the displaced tended to go to other rural communities, or to the mountain jungles, with relatively fewer going to the cities than in the case of El Salvador. The Guatemalan government's response was to begin programmes of model villages and development poles to encourage those displaced by the violence to return and settle in more "controllable" settings. Decisions about assistance and relocation of displaced people were left in the hands of the military. Although in 1988 CEAR was also given responsibility for co-ordinating aid to the displaced, the institutional mechanisms for providing such assistance were relatively undeveloped in comparison with the Salvadoran organizations. Moreover, few NGOs and church groups work with the displaced, also because of their physical dispersion throughout the country, in part because of the risk involved, and also because of the difficulties of identifying the target population. "Those who fled before army sweeps through the Guatemalan countryside, as well as the people who have assisted them, have become a prime target of killings and 'disappearances' in recent years. Displaced people were apparently considered 'subversive' because they came from areas where there had been armed conflict between the government and the armed opposition."[20] The labelling of displaced people as subversive creates a climate of fear among the displaced population who are reluctant to identify themselves in this way, and also creates enormous pressure on the NGOs which seek to provide some assistance to them.

Further pressure is put on the NGOs working with the displaced Guatemalans by the fact that the military controls the operations; to work with the displaced usually means accepting military directives and compromising NGO independence. Some NGOs work with the military, others try to maintain their independence and some avoid service to displaced people because they don't want to compromise their independence. The limits to independent NGO activity in working with the displaced are considerable as the following statement by a government official illustrates: "The NGOs work on their own and do horrible things. We don't want them coming in and doing whatever they want unless it's within the general framework of our work."[21] The author of that report was subsequently murdered by unidentified men when she left her office one day in 1991.

Nicaragua

The Nicaraguan pattern was somewhat different. In the decade of Sandinista rule in Nicaragua, two inter-related kinds of political violence combined to displace large numbers of people both within the country and as refugees to neighbouring Honduras and Costa Rica (as well as to the United States and Mexico). First was the long-standing ethnic violence in the Atlantic coast region where indigenous groups struggled with the

Sandinista government to preserve their autonomy and way of life. As negotiations over autonomy bogged down, and as violence broke out, the Nicaraguan government forcibly relocated 12,000 indigenous people into settlements further from the border. In response to this displacement, some 14,000 Miskitus, Sumu and Rama fled into neighbouring Honduras in 1982. A second group of refugees and internally displaced people consisted of non-indigenous or *ladino* population who were displaced by the fighting of the Contras. The Contras, supported by the US, carried on a violent war from Honduras and Costa Rica, against the Sandinista government, causing thousands of casualties and contributing to the downfall of the Sandinista government in the February 1990 elections. Some of those displaced by the Contra fighting had links with the Contra struggle, a fact which has made their repatriation much more difficult. A third group, the Contra fighting forces, remained in Honduras until the peace agreement was reached in the spring of 1990.

Unlike the case of Salvadoran refugees in Honduras, the Nicaraguan refugees in Honduras had comparatively greater freedom of movement. But once the US government approved humanitarian aid to the Contras and relief operations began at the border, refugees began to leave the UNHCR-administered camps. The Nicaraguan refugees in Honduras faced numerous protection problems, particularly from Contra forces seeking additional recruits. The presence of the Contras was also largely responsible for the displacement of over 20,000 Hondurans from around the border area.

The defeat of the Sandinistas in the February 1990 elections led to the return of the Contras and about 30,000 refugees. On 27 June 1990 between 15,000 and 19,000 Contras turned over their weapons to the UN forces overseeing the peace agreement's implementation. The number was higher than expected but suspicion persists that not all arms have been turned over. The return of the Contras was to be facilitated by financing for schools, hospitals and other infrastructure as well as land for resettlement as the result of an accord signed on 30 May 1990. The land was to be divided into eleven "development poles" intended to become autonomous economic communities. Disbanded Contra forces were given the right and the weapons to form autonomous rural security forces to police those areas. But in the ensuing months, many of the promises made by the government to the ex-Contras haven't been kept. Moreover, the deterioration of the Nicaraguan economy has made it difficult for the Contras to find jobs. The lack of genuine reconciliation among the population has hindered the reintegration of the Contra forces and created fear among those refugees still living outside the country. As one human rights group reports:

> The antagonism between Sandinista soldiers, supporters and the Contras who returned to civilian life, is natural. The situation is severely aggravated, however, by the fact that the promises of land, housing and pensions to the demobilized Contras have not been honoured and the suspicion that the Contras are being manipulated and used by some to promote their own well-being. [22]

The return of over 40,000 Nicaraguans from Honduras created serious economic pressures at a time when the country was already ravaged.

President Chamorro formed the Institute for the Development of the Atlantic Region and named Miskito insurgent leader Brooklyn Rivera as minister in charge, thereby placing him in a position of compliance with the central government. The economic and social difficulties in the region, however, appear to be the main obstacle to the return of refugees to Nicaragua. Natural disasters such as the hurricane damage in 1989 and increased flooding as a result of up-river deforestation intensify the difficulties of housing thousands of returning refugees.

The US connection

The United States has played an important role in the development of the region's response to displaced and refugee communities. It has provided funds for various assistance programmes, such as humanitarian assistance to the Contras and support for El Salvador's CONADES as well as other bilateral and multilateral programmes. The US has also played a role by influencing governmental perceptions of refugees in particular situations. In the case of Salvadoran refugees in Honduras, for example, the US embassy in Tegucigalpa was widely recognized as playing the dominant role in Honduran refugee policy; clearly the embassy accepted the view that the refugees were FMLN supporters. [23]

But the US is also an important country of residence for many undocumented Central Americans, and has had an interest in preventing further arrivals of Central Americans on its borders.

Repatriation, economics and CIREFCA

Successful repatriation in Guatemala, El Salvador and Nicaragua depends on an end to the violence in the communities of origin.

The example of the Salvadoran repatriations over the past few years demonstrates some of the political considerations in carrying out such exercises. In the case of repatriations from Mesa Grande, Colomoncagua, San Antonio and, more recently, from Nicaragua, the refugee communities were extremely well-organized. They received delegations of community and church representatives while still in the camps; they identified the sites to which they wished to return; they planned the routes they wished to take; and they enlisted national and international NGOs to support them in the process. Far from being passive objects of others' decisions, they were active participants in the repatriation process. This inevitably put them, as well as the NGOs, into conflict situations with the Salvadoran government and often put UNHCR in the difficult position of negotiating with the government on the basis of demands prepared by the refugees. Seemingly simple logistical details such as which road to take and whether to celebrate a homecoming mass in one church or another became major political questions. Some observers of these repatriations view the refugees as responding to political decisions made by the FMLN, on the basis of strategic calculations. While that seems to overstate the case, it is clear that such returns were motivated in part by the large repopulation movement in the country and that political considerations were taken into account by the refugee leadership.

The Guatemalan refugee organizations are also quite strong in the camps in Mexico; the Comisiones Permanentes have prepared their list of conditions for return (which seem very difficult to meet as they demand return to their communities of origin as well as restoration of their land). And should there be a large-scale return of Guatemalans, it seems likely that the same kind of conflict experienced by Salvadorans will also emerge. However, the role of NGOs is likely to be different as local NGOs are not as strong in Guatemala as in El Salvador and they do not have the political space that the Salvadoran organizations have.

While the refugees can be expected to play an important role in repatriations from camps where refugee organizations are strong, it is much less likely that they will be significant actors in planning spontaneous returns particularly by undocumented refugees living in other countries.

In addition to political concerns about the safety of returnees, economic factors are crucial in understanding possible future scenarios for the refugees. In all three countries, the question of land for returnees is linked with political decisions. In all three countries, the refugees living in the US are sending remittances back to relatives which represent an important source of foreign exchange which would be lost with the return of the refugees. Although data were only cited for the case of El Salvador, it is likely that Nicaraguan and Guatemalan refugees living in the United States are also sending funds back to relatives. The economic and human impact of a decline in these foreign remittances would be considerable.

In all three countries, it is clear that the returnees will need assistance in order to become productive members of their societies. Communities need to be rebuilt and assistance to refugees cannot be separated from assistance to internally displaced people or indeed to local communities.

It was in this climate of the search for a durable solution to what has become a long-standing refugee situation for all countries in the region and the recognition that the financial support of the international community would be needed, that the International Conference on Central American Refugees, CIREFCA, was convened in Guatemala City in May 1989. The conference was convened by the governments of Central America in co-operation with UNHCR to analyze the situation of refugees, returnees and internally displaced people and to formulate concrete plans for resolving the problem. The governments of the region prepared detailed studies of the population movements which had taken place in the region and drew up project profiles which were presented to the conference.

CIREFCA emphasized the importance of development-oriented assistance and the need for reintegration of the internally displaced. But the CIREFCA process depends on the establishment of lasting peace agreements which are still in the process of being tested. Moreover, the CIREFCA process depends on the commitment of Northern governments — governments which, as we have seen, are thinking about other priorities.

To follow up CIREFCA, national committees were established in each of the seven CIREFCA countries to co-ordinate the work of the separate ministries that normally dealt with development issues and assistance to uprooted peoples. In a parallel process, NGOs in each of the countries have also established national co-ordinating mechanisms for the NGOs working with those groups. At the June 1990 follow-up meeting in New York, about 150 participants — governments, UN agencies and NGOs — reviewed the progress made since the initial CIREFCA meeting and expressed their support to the continuing process. About US$156 million was pledged to the 59 CIREFCA projects and to other initiatives related to the tasks of reconciliation, reconstruction and development in the region. Although CIREFCA was not intended to be solely a funding mechanism, certainly some observers see its main emphasis to be the mobilization of funds. But CIREFCA marked an effort to address the problems of uprooted people on a regional basis and its convening was an encouragement for NGOs to organize.

Through their work with refugees and internally displaced people, NGOs throughout the region have become much more politically active, and have emerged as important actors. Presently there are about 100 international NGOs and 600 indigenous NGOs in Central America and Mexico, channelling about US$250 million per year to the region. Diakonia in El Salvador played a major role in the repatriations of Salvadorans from Honduras, negotiating with the government, UNHCR and the refugees, and co-ordinating assistance to the returnee populations.

At the 1989 CIREFCA and its follow-up meetings, it was clear that donor governments respect the work of NGOs, especially in comparison with the governments of some of the countries. Specifically, some governments insisted that their contributions would depend on project implementation by NGOs. This attitude not only recognized the contributions which NGOs have made in the past, but also explicitly supported NGOs struggling to preserve or widen their political space for action. The direct links between refugee communities and international NGOs have enabled international pressure to be exerted on governments undertaking policies opposed by the refugees themselves. This occurred in Honduras over efforts to relocate the refugee camp of Mesa Grande as well as in the various repatriation efforts and it is also evident in relations between international NGOs and the Comisiones Permanentes in Mexico. In comparison with refugee situations in other parts of the world, the Central American case stands out for the independence and advocacy of NGOs.

At the same time, by providing humanitarian aid to refugees, many international NGOs have become much more conscious of the root causes, and have adopted more political stances vis-a-vis their own governments. This is the case in the United States where, for example, church involvement with Central American refugees has been strong. It has also been evident among NGOs in other countries, such as Mexico, which have emerged as important advocates on behalf of refugees as well as service providers.

Violence in the Andean countries

For the past decade, Peru has experienced an escalating spiral of violence as the Maoist guerrilla group, Sendero Luminoso ("Shining Path"), and the Peruvian army has used ever more violent tactics in a war over control of the country. The victims of this war, as in most wars, are mainly peasants and civilians. Since Sendero Luminoso embarked on the armed phase of struggle in 1980, some 18,000 people have been killed, 3,000 have disappeared and over two-thirds of the national territory is under virtual military rule. [24] At least 200,000 people have been displaced from their communities, mainly leaving the Andean highlands for already-crowded Peruvian cities.

In carrying out its armed struggle, Sendero targeted peasant communities, carrying out violence with increasing brutality. People were tortured, killed, raped as a way of instilling terror and control in the highlands. Collaborators were killed and local political leaders were systematically assassinated for their participation in the system. The National Evangelical Council of Peru reports that evangelicals, particularly Pentecostals, are specially targeted by the guerrillas, and reports that more than 300 evangelical pastors have been killed by Sendero Luminoso since 1980. [25] Large areas of the Peruvian highlands came under Sendero control.

In response to the escalating violence and as Sendero demonstrated that Peruvian cities were also vulnerable to their terrorism, the Peruvian military was given increased authority in the highlands and it responded with more violence. As one army general, Luis Cisneros, said: "In order for the security forces to be successful, they will have to begin to kill Senderistas and non-Senderistas alike... They will kill sixty people and at best three will be Senderistas, but they will say that all sixty were Senderistas." [26] At least half of the 18,000 deaths are attributable to army violence.

Displaced people began fleeing their highland communities in large numbers in 1983 as a result of the escalating violence. Young people were particularly at risk as potential recruits for Sendero Luminoso forces. In some areas, the military authorities set up camps and encouraged or (forced) displaced people to live in them. "Unlike in Guatemala, where in theory the military combats guerrillas by promoting development from village-like *polos de desarrollo* or development poles, these refugee camps had a purely strategic function: fortified encampments to repel Shining Path attacks and a ready source of reserve troops for military-led incursions." [27] But most of the desplazados eventually found their way to Lima where they lived in shantytowns, often in areas with other migrants and desplazados from their home communities.

Life for the displaced in Lima is extraordinarily difficult. Not only do they face the problems of poverty and living on the margins of society, but lack of legal documentation makes them vulnerable to round-ups by government officials and prevents them from taking formal employment.

Moreover, violence is endemic in the shantytowns and many desplazados continue to fear Sendero's increasingly active presence.

Work with those displaced in the highlands is also dangerous as the
few NGOs working with the displaced are viewed with suspicion by both
Sendero and the army. Robin Kirk reports that in 1990 Caritas-Peru and
the Ayacucho Archdiocese Office of Social Action fed more than 100,000
people in mothers clubs, orphanages, and other church-affiliated institutions, a large proportion of whom were desplazados. But church
authorities have since restricted that work. While individual church
workers continue to minister to the displaced, official church policy
prevents them from working on issues considered controversial or critical
of the security forces. [28]

While most of those displaced from the violence struggle for survival
in Lima's shantytowns, increasing numbers are making their way to
Bolivia and Ecuador in search of safety. Rosario Sanchez, director of
CESEM, an ecumenical agency working with refugees and migrants,
reports that a major problem is that the Peruvian refugees live in a climate
of fear. They are afraid of other Peruvians living in Bolivia which makes
it difficult to organize collective self-help initiatives such as day care for
refugee women seeking work.

And the violence goes on. Few observers of Peruvian politics are
hopeful that the war between Sendero and the army will come to an end in
the near future.

In neighbouring Colombia, violence is also displacing people from
their communities. Violence in Colombia takes a different form as
paramilitary forces struggle over the lucrative narcotics trade and as
clashes between guerrilla groups and the army cause casualties. However,
human-rights groups are concerned that this interpretation of the violence
obscures the massive human-rights violations taking place. Most human-
rights organizations working in Colombia attribute the main responsibility
for the bloodshed to the military, paramilitary groups, security police and
"hired agents". When the violence is seen as the result of the drug trade
and common criminality, the international community has an excuse not
to pressure the government on human-rights issues.

While human-rights organizations are cautious about figures of
refugees, it is believed that 200-300,000 have been internally displaced
by the violence within Colombia and another 150-200,000 are in exile in
Ecuador. Only a few thousand of those uprooted by the violence are
officially registered. [29] Little is known about the conditions of the
uprooted Colombians.

Early reports from both Colombia and Peru suggest that the Andean countries could experience a major refugee flow in the coming years.

Haitians in exile

More than a million Haitians — about one-sixth of the population — are estimated to live in exile. About 500,000 live in the Dominican Republic, 450,000 in the US, 45,000 in Canada, 15-30,000 in France, and some 65,000 in Venezuela and the Caribbean.[30] The desperate poverty and environmental degradation in Haiti have led many to seek work — and survival — elsewhere. Those who work in the bateys of the Dominican Republic are particularly vulnerable to exploitation; recent reports by human-rights groups have documented the use of coerced adult and child labour and the sub-standard living and working conditions of the Haitian work force.[31]

Haiti's poverty has been compounded by political repression and instability. In 1991, hopes were raised when President Jean-Bertrand Aristide was elected in popular elections; but on 30 September he was overthrown in a military coup. Repression in Haiti intensified as the military sought to consolidate its power and to eliminate opposition. Human-rights groups report that at least 1,000 people were killed in the first two weeks after the coup.[32] In spite of international condemnations of the violence, the situation remained unchanged and Haitians began to leave the country in greater numbers, by boat.

Over the past decade, thousands of Haitians have sought to escape the poverty and repression in their homeland by setting sail in small boats for the US coastline. Unlike its policy towards Cubans seeking the same destination by the same means, the US has followed a policy of preventing Haitians from entering US territory to apply for asylum. The US Coast Guard has interdicted Haitian ships and, after a brief screening interview, returned those found not to have reasonable grounds for pursuing an asylum request in the US. This policy has long come under criticism from human-rights groups who charge that the procedures under which the screening is carried out are not within the spirit of international law. Between 1981 and 1990, only 11 Haitians out of more than 22,000 who were interdicted were "screened in" to pursue their claims for asylum in the US.[33] This US interdiction policy came under increasing attack in late 1991 as growing numbers of Haitians fled the violence of the military coup's aftermath.

The US government reacted with alarm, charging that they were economic migrants — not refugees — and interdicting their boats before they had a chance to land. After six months of vacillating policies, the US government decided to return all Haitians intercepted by boat, charging that they are all economic migrants. It remains to be seen whether a change in the US administration will result in different policies towards Haitian asylum-seekers.

In October 1991, in response to the military coup and the ensuing wave of repression, the Organization of American States imposed an economic embargo on Haiti as a way of pressuring the military regime to enter into negotiations to allow Aristide's return. But the embargo has been incompletely applied, and the regime has been able to trade with countries outside the Western hemisphere. While the country's elites are able to find imported luxury items and oil, the embargo has taken its toll on Haiti's poor majority as factories and businesses have closed their doors — and dismissed their employees — because of lack of oil and raw materials. Food is in short supply and reports from Haiti indicate that many urban dwellers have gone to the countryside in search of food. But the Haitian countryside has been devastated by deforestation, and there is insufficient land for the rural population. Some 200,000 Haitians have been displaced by the violence within their own country.

Violence in Latin America, as in other regions, comes in many forms; the different situations of uprooted people in the region reflect that diversity.

NOTES

[1] Washington Office on Latin America (WOLA), *Uncertain Return: Refugees and Reconciliation in Guatemala*, Washington, DC, WOLA, 1989.

[2] Amnesty International, "Memorandum Presented to the Government of the Republic of Guatemala, Following a Mission to the Country from 10 to 15 August 1979", London, Amnesty International, 1979.

[3] AVANCSO, *Assistance and Control: Policies towards Internally Displaced Populations in Guatemala*, Washington, DC, Hemispheric Migration Program, 1990.

[4] WOLA, *op. cit.*, p.8.

[5] Comité de Ayuda a Refugiados Guatemaltecos, *Boletín*, junio 1983.

[6] Bill Frelick, *Running the Gauntlet*, Washington, DC, US Committee for Refugees, January 1991, p.5.

[7] US Committee for Refugees, *World Refugee Survey 1992*, Washington, DC, USCR, 1992.

[8] Frelick, *op. cit.*, p.5.

[9] Beatriz Manz, *Repatriation and Reintegration: An Arduous Process in Guatemala*, Washington, DC, CIPRA, Georgetown University, 1988, p.30.

[10] *Ibid.*, p.26.

[11] *La Jornada*, 17 August 1987.

[12] Manz, *op. cit.*, p.31.

[13] Gil Loescher, "Humanitarianism and Politics in Central America", in *Political Science Journal*, vol. 103, no. 2, summer 1988, p.307.

[14] *Ibid.*, p.174.

[15] *Ibid.*, p.129.

[16] Cited by Inter-Church Committee on Human Rights in Latin America, *1990 Annual Report on Human Rights in Latin America*, Toronto, January 1991.

[17] *Ibid.*, p.11.

[18] Segundo Montes. *Refugiados y repatriados: El Salvador y Honduras*, San Salvador, Universidad Centroamericana José Simeon Canas, 1989.

[19] AVANCSO, *op. cit.*

[20] Amnesty International, *Guatemala: The Human Rights Record*, London, Amnesty International, 1987.

[21] AVANCSO, *op. cit.*, p.77.

[22] Inter-Church Committee on Human Rights in Latin America, *op. cit.*

[23] Loescher, *op. cit.*, pp.305-308.

[24] See Jo-Marie Burt, "Counterinsurgency = Impunity," in *NACLA Report on the Americas*, vol. XXIV, no. 4, December-January 1990-91, pp.30-31. Also see the articles in this special issue focusing on "Fatal Attraction: Peru's Shining Path", and Gustavo Gorriti Ellenbogen, *Sendero: Historia de la Guerra Milenaria en el Peru*, Lima, Editorial Apoyo, 1991. APEP, *Siete Ensayos sobre la Violencia en el Peru*, Lima, APEP, 1987.

[25] US Committee for Refugees, *World Refugee Survey 1992*, Washington, DC, USCR, 1992, p.88.

[26] Cited by Burt, *op. cit.*, p.30.

[27] Robin Kirk, *The Decade of Chaqwa: Peru's Internal Refugees*, Washington, DC, US Committee for Refugees, May 1991. This is the single best summary of the problems facing Peru's large displaced population.

[28] *Ibid.*, p.31.

[29] På Flukt, *Nyheter*, no. 10, November 1991.

[30] US Committee for Refugees, *World Refugee Survey 1991*, Washington, DC, USCR, 1991, p.85.

[31] See for example reports by the National Coalition for Haitian Refugees, Americas Watch and Caribbean Rights. For regular information, see *Haiti Insight*, a bi-monthly publication on refugee and human rights issues in Haiti.

[32] *Haiti Insight*, vol. 3, no. 7, March-April 1992, p.2.

[33] Bill Frelick, "The Haitian Boat People", in *Christian Science Monitor*, 20 November 1991.

9. The Middle East: Refugees, Land, Identity

Throughout history, the movement of people in the Middle East has been associated with war, politics, power and land. Jewish emigration to Palestine following the second world war, the subsequent creation of the state of Israel, and the ensuing wars displaced hundreds of thousands of Palestinians. The support of the Jewish diaspora has been of vital importance for Israeli development and strength. In the last few years the emigration of hundreds of thousands of Jews from the former Soviet Union has increased Palestinian fears of a strengthened — and larger — Israel. The Palestinians, living in camps and urban areas in the Occupied Territories, Jordan and throughout the Middle East, have been able to keep their identity and to keep alive their hopes of return to their homeland while raising their children in exile. A solution to the Palestinians' dreams lies with the peace process, a fragile and tortuous route. The Israeli invasion of Lebanon in 1982 displaced hundreds of thousands of Lebanese and Palestinians, both within the country and outside Lebanese borders. The Turkish invasion of Cyprus led to the uprooting of a majority of that country's Greek population; in the absence of a political solution, the island remains divided, and displaced people continue to live in temporary housing, waiting for the day when they can return to their homes.

The Iraqi invasion of Kuwait displaced Kuwaitis and hundreds of thousands of immigrant workers in the Gulf states. The interconnectedness of the region with the rest of the world was amply demonstrated as the economies of Sudan and Bangladesh, as well as Jordan and many other countries, were devastated by the return of the migrants. The war against Iraq and the Kurdish uprising led to millions of displaced people, the consequences of which are still not fully understood.

Throughout the Middle East, the movement of people is closely tied to questions of land and identity. Of particular concern to the churches is the migration of Christians from the region, a migration which weakens the Christian presence in the area. Individual Christian families are deciding to leave for a number of reasons: weariness with the ongoing violence and repression, fears of resurgent Islam, and a desire to give their children a better life. But each time a Christian family leaves, the position of the remaining Christians in the region becomes a little more fragile. The churches are worried about this out-migration and have sought to persuade their members to stay and to witness in the region, in the towns and countryside where Christianity was born. But until there is peace and justice in the region, Christians will probably continue to leave.

Given the complexity of migration patterns in the Middle East, this chapter considers only a few of the major population movements: the Kurds, the large number of displaced people as a result of Iraq's 1990 invasion of Kuwait and the subsequent Gulf war, and the current waves of emigration to Israel. Although the story of the Palestinians largely falls outside the scope of this chapter, and indeed that story has been much more comprehensively told elsewhere,[1] this chapter must begin, as do all analyses of the Middle East, with the relationship between the Palestinian diaspora and the larger issues of peace and justice in the region. The fate of the Palestinians is wrapped up in the current peace negotiations, but to a larger extent it will depend on the struggle for land and for identity. As Lex Takkenberg says: "The Palestinian problem is one of the most tragic and compelling refugee crises of the post-war era. In quantitative terms, it is overshadowed only by the Afghan refugee crisis; in terms of duration, complexity and political sensitivity, it is without precedent in modern history."[2]

The Palestinians

Palestinians number about 6 million: almost a million Palestinians live under Israeli rule in the Occupied Territories of Gaza and the West Bank. About a million more live in Jordan with around 300,000 in Syria and 400,000 Lebanon. The rest are dispersed throughout the region and the world. The history of the Palestinians over the last fifty years is the history of two peoples and two cultures competing for a single piece of territory. The history of the Palestinians is also the history of a population forced to migrate: in 1948 after the partition of the state of Palestine and the ensuing war, in 1967 after another Arab-Israeli war, and yet again in the aftermath of the Iraqi invasion of Kuwait and the ensuing Gulf war.

By 1986, Israel ruled over 2 million Palestinian refugees in Israel and the Occupied Territories. The rule became increasingly authoritarian. Palestinians in the Occupied Territories have no rights, no representation in any body that enacts laws governing their lives, and no access to appeal when they feel they have suffered legal or physical injury from the Israeli military government. The economic well-being of the Palestinians is linked to Israel. Some 40 percent of the population of the territories, around 100,000 people, work in Israel, the vast majority in the areas of construction, industry and services.[3]

Throughout these years of exile, Palestinian nationalism remained strong. The development of Palestinian liberation organizations and fluctuating patterns of support from Arab governments and Arab nationalist movements in the Middle East transformed the issue of Palestinian refugees from a question of charity for refugees into a question of peace and justice for the entire region.[4] The outbreak of the intifada in December 1987 transformed the nature of Palestinian resistance to continued Israeli rule in the Occupied Territories. Frustrated by the inability of Arab governments to successfully take up their cause, and impatient with the leadership of their organizations, Palestinians in the Occupied Territories took matters into their own hands. The intifada was a young people's movement, a grassroots movement, and one in which women were active participants. Palestinian political groups in the Occupied Territories gained more power in comparison with organizations based elsewhere. And the costs were high. In the first three years of the popular uprising, more than a thousand Palestinians were killed by the army, Israeli settlers in the West Bank and the Gaza Strip and collaborators; 100,000 arrests were made and around another 100,000 people injured.[5]

The intifada also brought about changes in the role of the United Nations Relief and Works Agency for Palestinian Refugees in the Near East (UNRWA) in the Occupied Territories. As we have mentioned, UNRWA was set up to provide humanitarian assistance to Palestinian refugees in the Middle East — not to play a role in protecting them from the brutality of Israeli rule. Over the years, UNRWA has earned the respect of the Palestinians for its humanitarian work and the commitment of its staff. At the same time, some observers note a certain ambivalence towards the agency. "Both the refugees and the Palestinian population as a whole remain sceptical towards UNRWA itself. It is seen primarily as an organization which has been selected by the international community to perpetuate the status of the Palestinians as refugees."[6] Like other UN agencies, UNRWA depends on the support of the governments with which it works. "Palestinian criticism of UNRWA reduces to the fact that UNRWA does not have the power to articulate and represent Palestinian interests."[7]

At the time of the intifada, some 2.5 million Palestinians were registered as refugees with UNRWA, one-third of whom lived in 61 refugee camps throughout the Middle East. About two-thirds of UNRWA's budget and most of its 17,000 employees were devoted to education and vocational training; some 350,000 pupils attended UNRWA schools throughout the region. UNRWA's health services, which account for 20 percent of its expenditures, include over one hundred health installations where registered refugees receive services.

But with the intifada, the Israelis closed schools, sometimes for long periods of time. UNRWA estimates that about half the teaching time for the first two years of the intifada was lost because of school closures and the less frequent strikes. Casualties of Israeli repression and the generalized violence strained the capacity of UNRWA to provide health services. In response to the widespread violence, UNRWA began providing health services to non-registered inhabitants of the Occupied Territories. But it was unable to prevent the violence. Under international humanitarian law, it is the International Committee of the Red Cross which is charged with overseeing the protection of civilians in times of warfare. But in the case of the Occupied Territories, ICRC action depended on the co-operation of Israeli authorities. At times the Israelis were willing to have ICRC play this role; at other times, they prevented its performing even minimal services.

In 1988, as casualties and abuses mounted during the intifada, the UN Secretary General asked UNRWA to increase its international staff "to improve the general assistance provided to the refugee population". As a result of this request, UNRWA hired international staff as "refugee affairs officers" who were to monitor the human-rights situation in the Occupied Territories and report on violations. By their presence and their monitoring, the refugee affairs officers were able to provide some limited protection to the Palestinians. It was difficult work for the officers as they sought to prevent brutality without provoking the Israeli military merely by their presence as observers. But there is some evidence that their presence served to deter violence in some cases.[8] The Israeli authorities resisted this new role and have been increasingly unco-operative and sometimes hostile. But the shift in UNRWA's activities towards an increasingly visible protection role was the result of the human need triggered by the intifada.

As a result of the Gulf war, conditions for Palestinians in the Occupied Territories became much worse. Palestinians welcomed Iraqi leader Saddam Hussein's support for their cause; moreover, they "welcomed and even applauded the Iraqi missiles landing in Tel Aviv. After all, this was the first time since 1948, when Palestine was dismembered with UN approval, that Israelis experienced the fear of being bombarded and being unable to retaliate."[9] At the same time Israeli fears of the expected Iraqi bombardment, coupled with their anger at Palestinian reaction to Saddam Hussein, led to draconian measures against the Palestinian population. Most obviously, the Israeli authorities refused to issue gas masks to all but a small number of Palestinians living under their rule — even though the Israelis were convinced that chemical weapons would be used. The Israeli government imposed a 24-hour curfew on the Gaza Strip for four weeks, causing immense suffering. Economic conditions in the territories deteriorated sharply as Palestinians were unable to work, because of the curfew and later because of restrictions on their travel to Israel. Because of restrictions and new requirements, Israeli statistics indicate that of the 80-100,000 Palestinians who used to work inside Israel, only 20-25,000 were working at the end of March 1991. Economic difficulties were intensified as the remittances from Palestinians working in the Gulf states ceased.

But the consequences of the Gulf war went far beyond its impact on the Palestinians living in the Occupied Territories; the large-scale emigration/expulsion of Palestinians from the Gulf states had a disastrous effect on Palestinians in the Occupied Territories and Jordan.

The Middle East Council of Churches and others estimate that some 350-400,000 Palestinians were living in Kuwait, which had a total population of 2 million people before the Iraqi invasion in August 1990. By 1992, fewer than 50,000 Palestinians are believed to remain in Kuwait. Half of the Palestinian population fled in fear of the invading Iraqi troops. After Iraq's defeat, thousands more fled because of Kuwaiti retribution for perceived support of Iraq during the war.

Jordan, which already had a population of 1.7 million Palestinians (out of a total of 3 million), was particularly hard hit by the Gulf war and by the "return" of an additional 300,000 Palestinians expelled by Kuwait and the Gulf states. Many of these returning Palestinians had lived in Kuwait for more than twenty years; their return meant overcrowding and a strain on social services. Estimates say that 60 percent of the migrants have been unable to obtain housing on their own and that 80 percent are unemployed in a country whose unemployment ranges between 20-30 percent. Although some of the Palestinians were able to bring their savings with them from Kuwait, their return also meant that their remittances of foreign currency ended — remittances which had reached almost US$1 billion. Moreover, the war and the return of the Palestinians were accompanied by a suspension of economic aid to Jordan from Kuwait and Iraq which had amounted to $185 million per year before the war. To make matters worse, US assistance to Jordan was cut in the aftermath of the Gulf war. While Israel sought US$10 billion in loan guarantees to provide housing to Soviet immigrants — numbering 380,000 (Israel's total population is 5 million) — Jordan has seen its pleas for assistance for a proportionately larger influx fall on deaf ears. [10] Housing shortages in Jordan were exacerbated and fears grew of a future water shortage.

The returning Palestinians have changed the country's political balance, aligning it even more closely with the Palestinian cause. Perhaps because of the desperate economic situation and the volatile political conditions, Jordan's Prince Hussein has been an enthusiastic supporter of the peace negotiations in the region. The 25,000 Palestinians returning to the West Bank and Gaza exacerbated the tremendous economic difficulties in those areas.

Historically, the churches have played a major role in providing services to the Palestinian refugees. The Middle East Council of Churches initiated work with the refugees upon their arrival in 1948 and in 1951 created the department on service to Palestinian refugees which has major programmes for refugees throughout the region. At its first assembly in 1948, the WCC stated: "The World Council of Churches, recalling that the origin of its refugee division was the concern of the churches for Jewish refugees, notes with especially deep concern the recent extension of the refugee problem to the Middle East by the flight from their homes in the Holy Land of not less than 350,000 Arab and other refugees." And even more than the channelling of financial resources, the churches have consistently supported the Palestinians' efforts to regain their homeland. [11]

The Palestinians' struggle for a homeland has been the central axis of the Arab-Israeli conflict; their struggle for independence and their success in maintaining their culture in the face of repression have inspired refugees in many parts of the world. But fears are also growing in other parts of the world of a future "Palestinization" of other refugee situations, reflecting the pain of long-term exile and the fear that questions about the return of refugees will become enmeshed in intractable negotiations.

The Gulf war was the latest in a series of migrations of the Palestinians — and one with far-reaching consequences.

The Gulf war: the exodus

The August 1990 invasion of Kuwait and the Gulf war led to the outpouring of over a million Arab and Asian guest-workers from Kuwait and Iraq and some 800,000 Yemenis from Saudi Arabia. Some 750,000 were sent to Jordan, 300,000 to Saudi Arabia, about 70,000 to Syria, 60,000 to Iran and 40,000 each to Turkey and the United Arab Emirates. About 25,000 Palestinians were forced to return to the West Bank and Gaza, aggravating already crowded conditions. The numbers are huge. Almost 2 million people were uprooted by the invasion; they were to be followed by an equally massive uprooting in the months following the defeat of Iraq's troops. But behind the mass numbers and the political and economic impact they provoked is a great deal of human pain.

The drama of September 1990 was centred on a barren stretch of desert along the Iraq-Jordanian border where migrants, mostly third-country nationals, were stranded after being expelled from Kuwait or fleeing from Iraq. In the first week of September 1990, some 75,000 migrants waited in the desert. The Jordanian government, facing a deteriorating economy, refused to allow the migrants to enter its territory without assurances that they would be moved quickly out of the country. But the governments of the migrants' countries of origin generally did not have the funds necessary to repatriate all of their nationals.

In this crisis, the International Organization for Migration assumed a leading role in organizing repatriation for the migrants. On 3 September 1990, 182 Sri Lankan women left Amman for Colombo, beginning one of the largest orderly mass movements of persons in recent history. Altogether IOM moved over 155,000 people — most (133,525) from Jordan, but also from Turkey, Iran and other locations — and raised over US$82 million during the emergency phase.

The actions by IOM were parallelled by NGOs and church organizations. The Middle East Council of Churches, for example, set up an emergency relief service in Jordan which provided food, clothing, temporary shelter and social services to thousands of the migrant workers forced to flee. The World Council of Churches channelled over $1 million dollars in resources from national churches and agencies to the MECC. The

Lutheran World Federation organized several repatriation flights to Asian countries.

Between November 1990 and 16 January 1991, the number of third-country nationals crossing into Jordan had fallen to 10,000. The borders with Turkey, Syria and Saudi Arabia were virtually closed.

The mass migration of foreign workers from the Gulf states demonstrates the close inter-relationships between different parts of the world — an interdependence brought home by the migration of people. In the wake of this first wave of migrants, Saudi Arabia forced between 500,000 and 750,000 Yemeni workers out of the country in apparent retribution for Yemen's support of Iraq. "The flood of returnees disrupted an already struggling economy, raising the prospect that Yemen, in turn, would expel tens of thousands of foreign workers to make room for their own returning citizens."[12] Jordan, Egypt, Yemen, Pakistan and a dozen other countries had become highly dependent on remittances from their nationals working in the Gulf states and are still suffering from the expulsion of their nationals. But probably no group in the Middle East was as affected by the Gulf war as the Kurdish population of Iraq.

The Kurds

There are today about 20 million Kurds who live in Kurdistan, which encompasses territory in the present-day states of Iraq, Iran, Turkey, Syria and the former Soviet Union. The Kurds migrated to the region some 5,000 years ago and over the years have been periodically (although for short periods of time) successful in establishing an independent homeland. After the first world war, Britain and France promised through the Treaty of Sèvres to give the Kurds an independent state. But in 1923 this was forgotten as the Treaty of Lausanne demonstrated that the allies were more concerned with supporting the anti-communist Turkish regime than with autonomy for the Kurds.

Historically, the Kurdish people have been pawns in the rivalries and domestic politics of the region. In recent history, their revolts and movements for independence have been manipulated by governments in the region and are testimony to a terrible litany of suffering — and resilience. Since 1961, the Iraqi government has engaged in widespread repression of its Kurdish population, including forced relocation, use of chemical weapons and destruction of villages. In 1988, more than 100,000 Kurds fled to Turkey and Iran. A succession of uprootings, fighting, and denial of basic human rights, which has characterized Kurdish life for decades, was repeated in the aftermath of the Gulf war.

The Kurds, for a short time, became important to the Western powers — just as they had been important to Iran during its war with Iraq. For a time, the Western powers lifted up the struggle for Kurdish autonomy as a way of mobilizing support for their own foreign-policy objectives in Iraq. But just as the Kurds had experienced on many occasions over the years, the interest was short-lived and when the Western powers turned their attention elsewhere, the Kurds were again the victims of repression.

With the end of the UN-sanctioned war against Iraq, a third wave of refugees was created; three months after the war ended, some 1.4 million Iraqi refugees had fled to Iran and approximately 500,000 were in Turkey or on the Iraq-Turkey border. In response to this displacement, the US called for a Security Council resolution to aid these refugees and to work inside northern Iraq. Resolution 688 was adopted on 5 April 1991, demanding an end to the repression of Iraq's civilian population and noting that the "massive flow of refugees towards and across international frontiers" consisted a threat to "international peace and security in the region". The resolution demanded Iraq to "allow immediate access by international humanitarian organizations to all those in need of assistance in all parts of Iraq". Even before UN operations could begin, the US, France and Britain began sending troops into northern Iraq to create a safe haven zone for refugees about 100 miles long and 25 miles deep, stretching along the western end of the Turkey-Iraq border. The allied forces secured routes from the mountain encampments on the Turkish border, built way-stations for returnees and assisted in transporting people back to their villages in the safe territories. The Western powers responded to the images of desperate Kurdish refugees in the mountains bordering the Turkish frontier. Massive aid programmes were launched and supplies were airlifted to isolated populations. But the Western countries responded differently to the refugees in Iran and those on the border with Turkey, which had supported the UN-sponsored war against Iraq.

Iran

During the past decade of war and austerity, Iran hosted more than 2 million Afghan refugees, and about 500,000 Iraqis as a consequence of the Iran-Iraq war. For a time, Iran hosted the largest refugee population — about 4.16 million — of any country in the world. From 1982-90, UNHCR spent $406.5 million on 3.3 million Afghan refugees in Pakistan while it spent $81.8 million for 2.35 million refugees in Iran during the same time period. In other words, for every dollar spent on an Afghan refugee in Iran, $3.54 was spent on an Afghan refugee in Pakistan. [13] For years Iran has received less assistance in working with the refugees on its territory than other third-world countries hosting far fewer numbers of refugees. These differences were to intensify in the wave of refugees from Iraq in 1991.

In March there were reports of movements of people into Iran, but not much Western attention paid to them, perhaps because of the West's relative indifference to Iran. During the first week of April, 700,000 refugees poured into Iran. Although the total number of "second wave" refugees in Iran swelled to 1.3 million by mid-May, the number in Turkey and northern Iraq stood at about 340,000 and was rapidly subsiding. "Despite hosting three times as many refugees, however, less than half as much international assistance money went to Iran. For every dollar spent on a refugee in Iran, $7.60 was spent for a refugee on the Turkish border." This discrepancy was largely due to the US contribution — of $200 million for this phase of the crisis, less than $20 million went to Iran. Iran meanwhile was spending $10 million a day to sustain the refugees. [14]

By the end of August 1991 only about 69,246 of the 1.4 million Kurdish and Shiite people who sought refuge in Iran remained. Another 50,000 were living with relatives and friends. Although most of the Iraqi Kurds returned to Iraq by the end of 1991, more than 700,000 Iraqis remained displaced within the country, some because of fear of returning to their homes, others because their communities had been destroyed, and still others because of renewed fighting. In the aftermath of the war and the Kurdish resistance, the Baghdad regime imposed an economic embargo on Kurdistan. Medicines were in short supply because of the international embargo on Iraq. This internal blockade has also made it more difficult for Kurdish leadership to organize and resist pressures from Saddam Hussein. Government services broke down as the central government cut salaries to government workers when they refused to quit working after being ordered to do so by Saddam Hussein, who stopped all payments to government pensioners as well. [15]

The future of the Kurds remains uncertain. It is probably most likely that their struggle for autonomy and self-determination will continue in the background until another crisis emerges — or until another power in or outside the region determines that it is in their interests to take up the Kurdish cause. While the Western media were full of stories about the brave Kurdish fighter and the struggle for self-determination in mid-1991, a year later, Kurds face serious reprisals and extensive bombing from the

Turkish government as well as repression by the Iraqi government. And there is little international outcry.

Much has been written about the precedent-setting action of the UN in deciding to assist the displaced Iraqi Kurds without the approval of the Iraqi government. In justifying the action, US President Bush said: "Some might argue that this is an intervention into the internal affairs of Iraq, but I think the humanitarian concern, the refugee concern, is so overwhelming that there will be a lot of understanding about this." [16] While there was considerable "understanding" about this UN action, the particular circumstances of the war and the UN's involvement in that war make it a unique case. Although few argue that the Iraqi case creates a precedent, growing concern about the notion of "humanitarian intervention" is leading to increased discussion, within and outside of the United Nations, about the conditions under which such intervention is justified. This is a theme to which we shall return in the final chapters of this book.

Although the war against Iraq has come to an end, the human consequences throughout the region are still considerable. In Kuwait, the reconstruction programme has had a human consequence as well. Iraqis, Bidoons (stateless people) and Palestinians, most of whom hold Jordanian passports, have been forced to leave the country. About 23,000 Iraqi refugees remain in the Rafha camp in Saudi Arabia. Some sought asylum directly in Saudi Arabia; most, however, were resettled there from the demilitarized zone during the occupation of that area by coalition forces. There is also another group of 13,000 Iraqi prisoners of war who refused to be repatriated to Iraq. [17] Iraq also hosted a number of Iranian refugees during the Iran-Iraq war, perhaps nearly 65,000. Most lived in camps round Baghdad. As a result of the war and strife, many of the refugees have returned to Iran or have moved to Jordan or live as displaced persons within the country.

Soviet Jews

The in-gathering of exiles, *aliyah*, has been central to Israel's life as a nation-state. Under Israel's "law of return", Jews are granted the exclusive right to immigrate to Israel and automatically receive Israeli citizenship. Before the massive Soviet immigration of the late 1980s, Israelis had expressed concern about the "demographic danger" presented by Palestinians. "The main argument was that a high natural increase among the Palestinians compared with the slow natural growth of the Jewish population might endanger the Jewish character of Israel, with Jews eventually becoming a minority."[18] But the prospects of large-scale immigration from the former Soviet republics is changing that.

The annual trickle of some 1,000 Soviet Jews and Armenians allowed to emigrate from the Soviet Union in the mid-1980s, suddenly and unexpectedly rose in 1987 to almost 11,500, swelled to over 30,000 in 1988 and became "unmanageable" in 1989.[19] In 1990, about 200,000 Soviet Jews arrived in Israel and 400,000 were expected in 1991.[20] Prospective numbers for future immigration were similarly large as the Israeli authorities predicted that 2 million Soviet Jews would be immigrating to Israel in the space of 15 years. These figures represent dramatic increases in the out-migration from the Soviet Union, with profound consequences not only for Israel but indeed for the whole Middle East.

The easing of travel restrictions in the former Soviet Union, deep economic crises in that country and the increased visibility of anti-Semitic political groups in Russia, such as the well-known Pam'iat', were the principal reasons for the exodus. Unlike earlier times, when most of the emigrating Soviet Jews wanted to go to Israel, for most of those emigrating in the late 1980s, Israel was a second choice. Beyer states that while 96.4 percent of Soviet Jews in 1971 opted to go to Israel (rather than to the US), by 1980 only 32 percent opted for Israel, only 6.5 percent in 1988, and in early 1989 only 2.2 percent.[21]

For the United States, the emigration of Soviet Jews has caused major changes in US policy. Traditionally, the US government has pressured the government of the Soviet Union to allow Jews to emigrate and has had an open-door policy towards Soviet Jewish emigration. In fact, until 1988, the US admissions programme had accepted all Soviet Jews for resettlement without their having to go through a refugee determination procedure. In September 1988, Secretary of State Shultz said: "Persons given permission to emigrate from the Soviet Union should have the freedom of choice as to where they want to go... If you are against freedom of choice, you are inconsistent with the Universal Declaration of Human Rights."[22] But as the number of Soviet Jewish emigrants increased and as more expressed a preference for settlement in the US rather than in Israel, US receptivity to Soviet Jewish immigration decreased. From 1988 to 1989, only about 70 percent of Soviet Jewish applicants were approved by the Immigration and Naturalization Service. In 1990, the US government closed the door, maintaining that Soviet Jews could — and should — migrate to Israel. This represented a dramatic change in US policy — and one which was perceived to be beneficial to Israel.

In Israel the arrival of so many immigrants has caused serious strains on housing and employment as well as concern about the potential political impact of the immigrants. Israelis are being forced out of apartments because rents are going up as a result of the immigration and the subsidies made available to them. More than half of the Soviet Jews are university graduates with good training, but by the end of 1990 only about half of those looking for jobs had found them. Of 3,000 Soviet scientists, only 160 had found positions. Israel's 10 percent unemployment rate seriously slows down the absorption of the immigrants. There are also fears among the Sephardic Jews, mainly from Arab countries, who presently number over half of the population and comprise most of the Jews living below the poverty line. The demographic balance between Sephardim and Ashkenazim (Jews of European origin) may be completely changed. [23]

Current reports are that many Soviet Jews are dissatisfied with conditions in Israel and especially with their 40 percent unemployment rate. Poll results in November 1991 indicated that 29 percent of all Soviet immigrants want to leave Israel. While most would rather live in a Western country, 3,000 or more of the newcomers will return to their homeland. The same poll indicated that 52 percent of new arrivals are advising people back in the Soviet Union not to come to Israel. By the end of 1991 immigration was lower than anticipated. [24]

Perhaps the biggest impact of the settlement of Soviet Jews in Israel is a psychological and political one for the Palestinians living in Israel and the Occupied Territories. Palestinians fear that the large number of Soviet immigrants will mean Palestinian displacement, including in Israel and expulsion from their lands. Fears that Soviet immigrants would be settled in the Occupied Territories are compounded by statements from some Israeli leaders of the need for the Judaization of areas heavily populated by Arabs. So far, the number of Soviet Jews settling in the Occupied Territories is small and most have indicated a preference to live elsewhere. However, given the pressure on housing in Israel, their presence could increase population pressure on other Israelis to settle in the territories, which would exacerbate tensions among Palestinians and further complicate peace negotiations.

Moreover, Palestinians within Israel fear that their political status will now be further marginalized. Arab voters currently constitute about 12 percent of the Israeli electorate — a percentage which will decrease with the influx of Soviet Jewish voters. Arab workers, particularly in the Occupied Territories, are worried about being replaced by the newcomers. Public opinion surveys of Palestinians in Israel show that only 18 percent of the Arab respondents reported having any contacts with the Soviet newcomers compared with 50 percent of Israeli Jews responding to the survey. While 66 percent of Jews surveyed indicated that Soviet immigration would contribute to the Israeli economy, only 18 percent of Arabs expressed the same view. While 70 percent of Jews see Soviet immigration as vital to the Israeli state, only 6 percent of Palestinian Arabs do. [25] These differences reflect differences in national aspirations. While the Israeli Jews see the immigrants as offering hope for a stronger country and a more dynamic economy, the Palestinians see the immigrants as a threat — a threat to their political aspirations, their economic hopes and ultimately their access to land. Migration issues in Israel are central to the ongoing debate about the future of their society and the possibilities of a peace agreement that would meet both Israeli needs for security and Palestinian aspirations for justice.

* * *

For churches and NGOs, the challenges raised by refugee and migration questions in the Middle East are particularly sensitive. While the department on service to Palestinian refugees programme of the Middle East Council of Churches continues to provide services to a large number of Palestinian refugees, other uprooted groups also receive attention from its offices. Unlike other refugee situations, where moves to resolve the roots of the conflict have only developed relatively recently, advocacy and relief work in the Middle East have occurred simultaneously since the beginning of the refugee phenomenon. Efforts to advocate for a just solution to the Palestinian crisis have gone hand in hand with efforts to provide assistance to the refugees. And the issues raised by work with refugees in the Middle East are having an impact far beyond the region.

For example, in recognition of the growing need for Christians and Muslims to work together on questions of refugees and migrants, an international seminar on "Migration and Refugees: Christian and Muslim Perspectives and Practices" was held in Valletta, Malta, 22-24 April 1991. The seminar was convened by an interfaith planning group of international Christian and Islamic organizations, including the World Council of Churches, the International Catholic Migration Commission, the Islamic Call Society, the Islamic Call Foundation, the Lutheran World Federation and the World Moslem Congress. The seminar was an acknowledgment that concerns for migrants and refugees are major — and growing — preoccupations for both Christians and Muslims. The seminar called for the establishment of an international interfaith working group on refugees, migrants and internally displaced persons.

In order for the human needs and aspirations of Middle Eastern refugees to be addressed, the churches will have to do more not only in providing assistance and in convening international meetings, but also in working for reconciliation of divergent groups.

NOTES

[1] The literature on the Palestinians is extensive. For a general overview, see Elias Chacour, *Blood Brothers*, Old Tappan, NJ, Revell, 1984; Walid Khalidi, *Before Their Diaspora*, Washington, DC, Institute for Palestine Studies, 1984; Amos Oz, *In the Land of Israel*, Toronto, Collins, 1988; Edward Said, *The Question of Palestine*, New York, Random House, Vintage Books, 1980; Rosemary Sayigh, *Palestinians: From Peasants to Revolutionaries*, London, Zed Press, 1979; Ze'ev Schiff and Ehun Ya'ari, *Intifada*, New York, Simon & Schuster, 1990. For analysis of some of the theological issues, see Naim Ateek, *Justice and Only Justice: A Palestinian Theology of Liberation*, Maryknoll, NY, Orbis, 1979; Marc Ellis, *Towards a Jewish Theology of Liberation*, Maryknoll, NY, Orbis, 1989; Rosemary Radford Ruether and Herman Ruether, *The Wrath of Jonah*, San Francisco, Harper & Row, 1989. For analysis of church engagement with the Palestinian refugees, see the classic history by Michael Christopher King, *The Palestinians and the Churches, vol. 1: 1948-1956*, Geneva, WCC, 1981 and its sequel by Larry Eakin, *Enduring Witness: The Churches and the Palestinians, vol.2*, Geneva, WCC, 1986. For interviews with Palestinians and Israelis, see *Unified in Hope: Arabs and Jews Talk about Peace*, interviews by Carol J. Birkland, Geneva, WCC, 1987, and *Justice and the Intifada: Palestinians and Israelis Speak Out*, eds Kathy Bergen, David Neuhaus and Ghassan Rubeiz, Geneva, WCC, and New York, Friendship, 1991.

[2] Lex Takkenberg, "The Protection of Palestine Refugees in the Territories Occupied by Israel", in *International Journal of Refugee Law*, vol. 3, no. 3, July 1991, p.433.

[3] *Ibid.*, p.247.

[4] For example, see Yezid Sayigh, "The Politics of Palestinian Exile", in *Third World Quarterly*, vol. 9, no. 1, January 1987, pp.28-66, for a survey of the development of Palestinian political consciousness and organization for liberation.

[5] Kathy Glavanis, "Changing Perceptions and Constant Realities: Palestinian and Israeli Experiences of the Gulf War", in *The Gulf War and the New World Order*, eds Haim Bresheeth and Nira Yuval-Davis, London, Zed Books, 1992, p.124.

[6] Friedhelm Ernst, "Problems of UNRWA School Education and Vocational Training", in *Journal of Refugee Studies*, vol. 2, no. 1, 1989, p.92.

[7] *Ibid.*, p.93.

[8] Angela Williams, "UNRWA and the Occupied Territories", in *Journal of Refugee Studies*, vol. 2, no. 1, 1989, pp.156-162.

[9] Glavanis, *op. cit.*, p.118.

[10] *International Herald Tribune*, 20 February 1992.

[11] See King and Eakin, *op. cit.*, for a full account of these initiatives, and especially the work of the Middle East Council of Churches.

[12] Bill Frelick, "Troubled Waters in the Middle East, 1990-91", in *World Refugee Survey 1991*, Washington, DC, USCR, 1991, p.93.

[13] *Ibid.*, p.2 and Bill Frelick, "Gulf Relief Efforts Must Include Refugees in Iran", in *Christian Science Monitor*, 30 May 1991.

[14] Frelick, "Gulf Relief Efforts...", *op. cit.*, p.93.

[15] *International Herald Tribune*, 2 April 1992.

[16] Cited by Roger P. Winter, "Statement on Iraqi Refugees and Displaced People before the US House of Representatives, Committee on Foreign Affairs", Washington, DC, USCR, 23 April 1991, p.10.

[17] *Refugees*, UNHCR, no. 87, October 1991, pp.13-15.

[18] Majid Al-Haj, "The Attitudes of the Palestinian Arab Citizens in Israel Toward Soviet Jewish Immigration", in *International Journal of Refugee Law*, vol. 3, no. 2, 1991, p.249.

[19] Gregg A. Beyer, "The Evolving United States Response to Soviet Jewish Emigration", in *International Journal of Refugee Law*, vol. 3, no. 1, 1991, p.32.

[20] Roberta Cohen, "Israel's Problematic Absorption of Soviet Jews", in *International Journal of Refugee Law*, vol. 3, no. 1, 1991, p.62.

[21] Beyer, *op. cit.*, p.41.

[22] Cited by Beyer, *ibid.*, p.40.

[23] Cohen, *op. cit.*, pp.73-74.

[24] *Newsweek Magazine*, 18 November 1991.

[25] Al-Haj, *op. cit.*, pp.250-256.

10. Refugees, Migrants, Security and Culture in Europe

Democratization in Eastern Europe, the collapse of the Soviet Union and a new political momentum in the European Community have all fundamentally altered the pattern of European politics and society. In this context, migration and refugees have become hot political issues in all European countries. The pressure of the movements of people both accompanied and triggered the political changes in the former members of the Warsaw Pact. Demographic and migration pressures from the South are leading to questions about the role of Europe in the world. European governments talk of "uncontrolled migration" as a security threat and devise common policies to respond to the threat — just as a decade ago they co-ordinated their defence policies to respond to the Soviet threat. From Moscow to Madrid, politicians throughout Europe raise the spectre of potential hordes of migrants threatening political stability and national culture. Racism, anti-Semitism and xenophobia are increasing throughout Europe as scapegoats are sought for economic and political problems.

The debate on refugees and migrants raises fundamental questions for European societies. What is the place of multi-national, multi-cultural societies in the Europe of the future? How are minorities to be protected? What is to be the nature of European societies? How much immigration can be absorbed without undermining national identity? What is European responsibility to address the causes of population displacement — in the Soviet Union, the Maghreb, Yugoslavia, the Middle East and a hundred other places?

These questions are being raised in the context of both regional political change and dramatic increases in the number of new arrivals of migrants and asylum-seekers. But behind the concern with the actual number of new arrivals is the fear that many more people will come. This fear is expressed in a number of ways: in restrictionist governmental policies towards asylum-seekers, in politicians' campaigns against immigration, in popular expressions of anti-foreigner sentiments. In some cases the fear is expressed in foreign policies intended to prevent further population movements, as in Italy's economic assistance to Albania or Southern European governments' co-operation with North African governments.

The issues raised by discussion of refugees and migrants in Europe also raise questions about the interconnections between Europe and the rest of the world and about the viability of the international system for responding to uprooted people. This chapter presents an overview of some of these issues, beginning with the historical context.

The historical context

Historically Europe has been a continent of emigration. For the past 350 years, Europe has partially dealt with its problems of unemployment and transition to industrial economies as well as political repression through emigration. Younger sons in England were sent off to make their fortunes in the colonies, desperately poor Italians and Spaniards began new lives in the Western hemisphere, religious and ethnic minorities have fled repressive governments. Over the course of a hundred years, from the mid-1800s to the mid-1900s, over 50 million people left Europe for the Western hemisphere in the greatest recorded migratory flow of all time.

In the aftermath of the Russian revolution of 1917, some 2 million Russians left the country, emigrating largely to North and South America. The turmoil as a result of the first world war displaced millions in the Balkans and elsewhere. As seen in the chapter on the evolution of the global refugee regime, these population movements triggered a massive international response. The first High Commissioner for Refugees, the League of Nations, and later the United Nations all evolved an international humanitarian response based on the experiences of Europe.

After the second world war, the 30 million displaced people throughout Europe were viewed as an international problem — not just a European one. During the cold war, refugee issues were highly charged political East-West issues; with a few exceptions, the refugees from communism were not seen to be a particularly European issue, requiring a particularly European solution. Rather, most of the refugees were resettled outside the region. The refugees from Eastern Europe and the Soviet

Union were often well-educated political dissidents; those who settled in Europe, like those resettled in North America, Australia and New Zealand, contributed greatly to their new societies.

As a result of pressure from UNHCR and governments outside Europe, over the years European governments have accepted a small number of "quota refugees" — that is, individuals deemed by UNHCR to be refugees in need of resettlement. Thus South-east Asian refugees have been resettled throughout Europe, although in relatively small numbers. These quota refugees have generally received generous assistance from the governments in adapting to their new countries.

During the 1960s, European governments sought to meet their demands for labour by allowing for temporary immigration. Although the specific policies differed in the various Western European countries, most countries allowed for the temporary work migration of so-called "guest workers" who provided needed labour, and who had only provisional resident status in the countries. But even temporary immigration had a long-term consequence as migration routes became established and family members joined relatives working in Europe. By the early 1970s, there were about 10 million guest workers and about 2 million persons from former colonies who had been admitted to Western European countries. [1] But in the mid-1970s in the wake of the oil shocks, European countries began scaling back these programmes or eliminating them altogether. In 1973, for example, France received 100,000 foreign labourers. In 1989 the figure was a little more than 15,000. [2] Germany even chalked up high net emigration figures — mostly Turks returning home — before the wave of asylum-seekers from the south and later the opening of Eastern Europe and the reunification of Germany. By 1990, there were still some 10 million legal immigrants in Europe and many more illegal immigrants, primarily concentrated in Germany, France and Great Britain. Today, legal immigration to the European Community alone is estimated to be more than 400,000 per year. [3]

One of the largest groups of labour immigrants to Europe have been the Turks who have been migrating to West European countries for decades. More than two-thirds of the nearly 3 million Turks working outside their own country live in Germany where their remittances back to Turkey are an important source of foreign exchange. During the 1980s alone, they transferred some US$15 billion to Turkey. [4] But the guest-worker programmes in Germany that saw millions of Turks, Italians, Yugoslavians and Greeks imported to fill the labour shortages have been closed and there is little political momentum for their reinstatement.

When jobs were plentiful and the economy was booming, the presence of foreigners was tolerated and even welcomed. But with economic difficulties, rising unemployment and particularly the entry of thousands of asylum-seekers, reactions to foreigners — legal immigrants, clandestine workers, refugees and asylum-seekers — became more and more negative.

The countries of Eastern Europe also received considerable numbers of foreign workers, approximately 200-500,000 in 1990. Many of these came from socialist allies, especially from Vietnam and later Mozambique; emigration here was an issue to be negotiated between the governments involved. These individuals, as will be seen later, were also affected by the dramatic changes in Eastern Europe during the late 1980s.

The drama of the 1980s: North-South dimensions

> You risk being invaded tomorrow by multitudes of Africans who, pushed by misery, will land in waves in the countries of the North... You can pass all the immigration legislation you want, but you won't stop the tide. [5]

By the early 1980s, increasing numbers of asylum-seekers were arriving in Western Europe. Unlike in earlier periods, most came from third-world countries. Throughout the decade the numbers rose — from 70,000 asylum applications in Europe in 1983 to 442,000 in 1990. Britain saw increases from 2,000 in 1980 to 5,500 in 1988 to 25,000 in 1990 to 50,000 in 1991. [6] Table 1 on the following page presents the number of spontaneous arrivals of asylum-seekers in Europe and North America from 1987 to 1990.

As the number of asylum-seekers increased, the backlog of cases to be examined grew as well. Decisions about status determination sometimes took years — with the state paying the costs of assisting the asylum-seekers. The asylum systems in European countries were constructed to respond to a limited number of individual requests — not to thousands of applicants whose cases required systematic individualized investigation. For the individual asylum-seeker whose case dragged on for years, the legal limbo caused uncertainty and pain.

As the number of cases mounted, the percentage of successful asylum applications dwindled; by 1991, only about 8 percent of asylum applications were accepted. Most of those presenting applications did not meet the strict criterion of individual persecution; rather, most came from war-torn countries, such as Sri Lanka and Lebanon, or from countries with policies of ethnic discrimination such as Turkey, or from countries

TABLE 1:   SPONTANEOUS ASYLUM-SEEKERS
IN EUROPE AND NORTH AMERICA, 1987-1990

Host country	1987	1988	1989	1990
Austria	11,400	15,800	21,900	22,800
Belgium	6,000	5,100	8,100	12,950
Canada	25,950	40,000	21,750	36,550
Denmark	2,750	4,650	4,650	5,300
Finland	50	50	200	2,750
France	24,800	31,600	58,750	49,650
Germany (FRG)	57,400	103,100	121,300	193,050
Great Britain	5,150	5,250	15,550	25,250
Greece	6,950	8,400	3,000	6,200
Hungary	—	—	27,000	18,300
Italy	11,050	1,300	2,250	3,400
Netherlands	13,450	7,500	13,900	21,200
Norway	8,600	6,600	4,450	3,950
Portugal	450	350	150	100
Spain	2,500	3,300	2,850	6,850
Sweden	18,100	19,600	30,350	29,350
Switzerland	10,900	16,750	24,400	38,850
Turkey	6,800	56,950	3,650	2,950
USA	26,100	60,750	101,700	73,650
Total	**241,550**	**391,350**	**472,950**	**552,550**

Source: H. Barrabass, UNHCR, cited by Janina Wiktoria Dacyl Världens Flyktingar, Stockholm, Swedish Institute of International Affairs, 1992, p.17.

experiencing both political upheaval and desperate economic conditions, such as Somalia and Zaire. Although their applications for refugee status were rejected, governmental authorities were reluctant to deport these individuals back to their countries. And so various criteria were used to enable their temporary stay — such as humanitarian grounds, B-status, and exceptional leave to remain — until conditions in their countries of origin changed sufficiently to enable their return. For these individuals, the immediate fear of deportation was replaced by living in a sort of legal limbo with the uncertainties and vulnerabilities to exploitation that that entailed.

By the mid-1980s, European governments were protesting that the influx of asylum-seekers had to be stopped, that their administrative capacities were over-burdened, and that most of those arriving and applying for refugee status were economic migrants, not refugees. Indeed, the lack of routes for legal immigration has forced many would-be immigrants to seek entry via the political asylum route. In spite of the distinctions made in international law, the issues of asylum-seekers and migrants have become linked in the minds of the public and policy-makers alike. Twenty million immigrants — as much as 5 percent of the population — now call Western Europe home, including nearly 5 million North Africans and Turks on the continent and about 1.2 million South Asians in Britain. This has had far-reaching consequences on the political, economic and cultural lives of European citizens. In Germany, for example, there are now more than 1,000 mosques and throughout Europe questions are surfacing about the nature of European society and the relationship of immigrant groups to national culture.

On a political and economic level, the cost of caring for and processing these asylum-seekers has increased tenfold during the past seven years and is currently estimated at more than $6-8 billion a year.[7] In comparison, in 1991, the total UNHCR annual budget was less than $1 billion — which in itself was almost double its normal operational budget due to the Gulf emergency and to several costly repatriation initiatives. But this disparity in expenditures also heightened awareness of the different treatment of refugees and asylum-seekers in Europe and elsewhere in the world. Even 500,000 asylum-seekers a year is less than 3 percent of the world's total 17 million refugees. Yet the resources devoted to that 3 percent were more than five times greater than that spent by the UNHCR on the 97 percent of the world's refugees.

During the 1980s, then, European governments experienced dramatic increases in overall numbers of asylum applications, growing migration from the third world and increasing numbers from Eastern Europe. These factors combined to produce a fear that if something wasn't done Europe would be inundated with refugees and migrants.

European governments respond

Governments throughout Europe have responded to the increase in the number of asylum-seekers by making it more difficult for them to get asylum and by imposing so-called deterrence measures to make the prospects of coming to Europe less attractive to would-be immigrants. This has led to serious anomalies and distortions in the refugee system. People recognized as refugees and treated as refugees in first-asylum countries frequently find their cases rejected in Europe. "Those who are recognized as refugees in Western Europe have had their cases examined much more thoroughly than most of those who are recognized as refugees under UNHCR elsewhere in the world."[8] Different rules of the game apply for refugees — one in Europe and another in the UNHCR-system elsewhere in the world. In Europe the focus is on the individual and yet most of those forced to leave their countries do so because of generalized violence, not individualized persecution. By applying individualistic criteria to people fleeing widespread social conflict, individual applications may be legitimately and procedurally proper and yet endanger the lives of those the system was designed to protect. Church and human-rights groups, such as Amnesty International, have documented cases of rejected asylum-seekers who were deported from European countries after their claims were rejected to face imprisonment, harassment, torture and even death at the hands of the authorities back home.

There are, as might be expected, significant differences in the treatment of asylum-seekers in different European countries. Spain and Italy, for example, have traditionally been more tolerant of clandestine immigration; it is often tolerated — if not legalized — by authorities. But partially as a result of moves towards harmonizing European policies, governmental asylum policies are converging. When countries enact more stringent policies on admission of asylum-seekers, governments with more lenient policies may see an increase in arrivals — leading that government in turn to adopt more restrictionist policies. For example, in March and April of 1985 the Dutch government, faced with increasing arrivals of Sri Lankan Tamils, applied more restrictive criteria in the asylum process with the widely rumoured possibility of forced repatriation for those rejected cases. This situation resulted in the dispersal of the Tamils from the Netherlands, many of whom went to Great Britain in late April and early May 1985. The British government in turn imposed a visa requirement for Sri Lankan passport-holders (at 48 hours' notice) and the flow stopped — or was diverted to another friendly state to cope with.[9] This pattern was, in fact, repeated throughout continental Europe in the mid-1980s, leading to a consensus that policies with regard to asylum-seekers needed to be co-ordinated through negotiations between European governments.

Harmonization of European asylum policy

Policies towards immigrants and refugees are essentially national policies, and governments have been reluctant to give up their sovereignty in this area. As we have seen, individual European governments have taken measures to restrict the entry of asylum-seekers or potential asylum-seekers. And as the numbers of new arrivals on European borders increased in the 1980s, there were new efforts to develop these national policies in a broader European context. European co-ordination of policies was thus important to governments trying to develop rational asylum policies.

European co-ordination of asylum policies is occurring in many forums, including the Conference on Security and Co-operation in Europe (CSCE), the Council of Europe with its various steering committees and parliamentary assembly, the European Community institutions, inter-governmental forums such as the Trevi group and the Schengen Treaty, and ad-hoc consultations organized by UNHCR. [10]

These efforts to co-ordinate and harmonize European policies towards refugees, asylum-seekers and migrants raise many concerns for the churches and NGOs. There are fears that harmonization will mean in practice adopting the most restrictive procedures in use by member states as a benchmark for a common policy. In the past, asylum-seekers who had their applications for asylum rejected by a European government could try again with another European government; often they were successful in these subsequent efforts. But when policies become fully harmonized, a rejection by one European government will automatically rule out efforts to apply for asylum in another European country. The Schengen provision for setting up a common data base on asylum requests raises other fears. For example, a person seeking asylum will tell his or her story of persecution back home to an immigration official in a particular country. That story will be entered into a data base to which officials of all member governments will have access. Given the sensitive nature of some of the information presented, the fear is that safeguards will be inadequate to provide protection to the individual — particularly if his or her claim for asylum is rejected. Partly because of these concerns and the lobbying work done by human-rights activists, plans for setting up such a data base have been postponed until 1995.

These negotiations at the European level are also influencing national policies towards refugees and immigrants. To win membership in the Schengen group in 1990, Italy enacted a comprehensive immigration law that resulted in the expulsion of more than 6,000 illegal aliens and turned back more than 13,000 from its borders in the first four months of 1991. Although allowing 28,000 new Albanian arrivals to stay in March 1991, five months later Italy deported 17,000 Albanians without allowing any to enter the asylum process. The Italian government, which had changed its laws and procedures to conform with emerging European policies, found little support from other European governments in its difficulties. Vincenzo Scotti, Italy's interior minister, complained: "Italy has faced a difficult situation alone. Europe has left us to ourselves."[11]

Fortress Europe

> Across the continent, a curtain of red tape is descending to limit asylum sharply and to shut out foreigners who come looking for a better life... From Norway to Greece and from Germany to Spain, a wall is rising around Europe, perhaps the beginnings of a fortress that will seek to keep out today's economic refugees as desperately as the old iron curtain held back political refugees from the East.[12]

As governments sought to respond to the arrival of asylum-seekers and migrants through national legislation and co-operation with other European governments, popular sentiment was growing in support of more restrictive policies. At its extreme, right-wing nationalist movements opposing further immigration gained in visibility and strength. Demonstrations, violence against immigrant communities and political movements were evidence of growing public disquiet at the prospect of further immigration — even in countries which had prided themselves on their tolerance. National politicians used the issue of immigration to bolster their popular support. In France, which has 2 million residents of Arab-Muslim origin, Jean-Marie Le Pen's National Front built on anti-foreign sentiment and now wins about 16 percent in national polls. From Sweden to Switzerland, popular feeling against immigrants has been manifested in violence and small right-wing parties, and from Russia to France anti-Semitism has become more visible.

Behind these expressions of concern — from both right-wing political groupings and governmental leaders — is the fear that the very fabric of European societies is endangered by migration. "The rise of Islamic fundamentalism, Sikh militancy and other ethno-religious political movements has not only introduced a new element into Europe's emerging multicultural societies, but is also seen to present a security threat to governments."[13] And when governmental leaders look at demographic patterns and predict future migration trends, there is cause for concern.

Demographics and the movement of people

Today, in spite of its restrictionist measures, Europe accounts for the largest population of foreign workers in the world; the proportion of foreign-born in many European countries amounts to 10-15 percent, compared with only 6 percent in the US and 16 percent in Canada. Immigration now plays a more prominent role in Europe than in North America. The present annual influx of immigrants to European countries (700,000) actually outnumbers the total flows to North America.[14] Europe is changing; its societies and cultures are coming under inexorable pressure as a result of these migration pressures. And there is growing concern that these population movements may only be the harbinger of far greater South-North migration in the future. Indeed, analysis of the demographic and economic patterns of surrounding developing countries makes it clear that in future migration may well increase.

Jonas Widgren, the UNHCR official charged with co-ordinating consultations among European governments on asylum issues, analyzed some of these demographic trends. He found that if only 5 percent of Africa's future population growth in the next twenty years (estimated to be 550 million with a total African population of one billion) comes to Europe, that would add 25 million African immigrants in Europe.[15] He notes that this is not a far-fetched prospect, but rather a likely result of population growth and economic underdevelopment in Africa. Other nearby countries face similar demographic and economic pressure.

Some argue that in spite of recent tendencies, Europe will need foreign labour in the future. Europe now accounts for 6 percent of the world's population; in ten years that figure will decline to 3 percent, and 15 percent of Europe's population will soon be of retirement age.[16] Belgium and Austria already face population declines. Before reunification, West Germany's population was expected to shrink by nearly one-quarter over the next four decades. France's population would be nearing decline if not for the high birth rate of immigrant populations.

During the 1980s, particularly the late 1980s, these were the issues being raised in discussions of refugees and immigrants. Questions of asylum-seekers were seen in North-South terms. While some politicians stirred up fears of an invasion from poor countries in the South, others sought a response in European foreign policies to address the causes of the migration.

Churches and NGOs were active during this period. They lobbied and raised awareness about the human costs of the deterrence measures being devised by their governments. They protested deportations and offered a range of services for individual asylum-seekers. In the Netherlands, the Council of Churches of Groningen organized public campaigns on behalf of asylum-seekers and offered sanctuary to those whose claims had been rejected by the government. In Britain, the sanctuary movement acquired a multifaith dimension as faith communities co-operated in offering protection to families facing deportation. National church bodies developed position papers on refugee and asylum issues and pressed their governments to adopt more generous and open admission policies. But even while individual churches and national church organizations were taking these initiatives, there was a realization that many of the people in their congregations were supportive of efforts to restrict the entry of foreigners. The complexity of the European institutions engaged in discussions of refugee and asylum questions made it difficult for individual churches to know how to influence these processes.

In 1988 the Conference of European Churches and the World Council of Churches set up the European Churches Working Group on Asylum and Refugees to serve as a forum for understanding what was happening in the region and to co-ordinate church initiatives in advocacy and awareness-raising. The working group provided documentation and suggestions for advocacy. Working closely with groups such as the European Consultation on Refugees and Exiles in Europe which had developed considerable expertise on these issues, the churches' working group tried to react to the pressures.

In some cases, international co-operation between church bodies in Europe and elsewhere was used as an effective tool for countering the government's policies. For example, when the Canadian government was considering deporting asylum-seekers to Denmark, arguing that their claims could be safely pursued in that country, the Canadian churches used data collected by the Danish churches to show that Denmark was, in fact, not safe for all asylum-seekers. When the Swiss government deported asylum-seekers to an African country in the mid-1980s, the churches in that country were able to contact the deportees after their arrival back home.

Christenson and Kjaerum draw connections between the situation in Europe and the rest of the world. They note that during the 1970s and 1980s, few Afghans, Vietnamese or Mozambicans spontaneously arrived on Western borders. They could turn to more or less well-functioning international systems which protected them. Virtually none of the spontaneous applicants — Iranians, Iraqis, stateless Palestinians, Lebanese — who have sought asylum in Europe during the second half of the 1980s have been able to find protection anywhere else. So when European governments say they want more "quota refugees" rather than spontaneous asylum-seekers, it is a dangerous distinction "as long as no alternatives have been established for the refugee groups who come to this part of the world". [17] For example, the sudden influx of Somali asylum-seekers is the result of UNHCR budget cuts in the region; refugees had to move on to survive. "If the work of UNHCR and others in Ethiopia and elsewhere had been strengthened earlier, these refugees would not have been forced to seek further to the Nordic countries and elsewhere to find protection." [18]

While the 1980s transformed thinking about refugee issues in Europe from a "victims of communism" approach to a North-South issue, by the end of the decade, changes in the Eastern part of the continent were forcing still another change in the conceptual approach to the movement of people.

The drama of the 1990s: East-West dimensions

The well-known political changes in the Soviet Union and Eastern Europe in the late 1980s were dramatically shaped by the movement of people. Perestroika and glasnost in Moscow were accompanied by a surge in democratic movements throughout the Warsaw Pact countries — and by a surge in the movement of people from East to West. As in other global situations, the evidence suggests that when governments ease their repressive policies, people seize the opportunity to leave — even when objectively conditions are improving. That mass movement of people, in turn, became a powerful impetus for change. But even as old governments fell and new ones were consolidated, people continued to leave. The implementation of new economic policies in the East were painful as people experienced both a decline in their standards of living and the elimination of social safety nets. Many found the experience too painful and decided to seek opportunities in the West. The establishment of different, in some cases more democratic, regimes did not mean an end to conflict. On the contrary, in many cases, the establishment of democratic processes led to an escalation of old, long-latent conflicts which the fragile democratic institutions were unable to cope with. The resurgence of ethnic conflict in the republics of the former Soviet Union and of the former Yugoslavia led to a surge of people on the move. The movement of people throughout the region and their movement westward created new pressures on Western governments, which already felt beleaguered by the pressures of South-North migration.

Not since the 1940s and 1950s have so many people moved from East to West. Between the 1949 creation of the German Democratic Republic and the erection of the Berlin Wall in 1961, an estimated 3 to 3.5 million East Germans — about 20 percent of the population — fled to West

Germany. The 1956 Hungarian uprising and the 1968 Soviet invasion of Czechoslovakia both produced substantial numbers of refugee. But gradually, the East-West flow declined to a trickle as a result of more stringent policies of control by the governments of the East. Indeed, from the early 1970s to the first half of the 1980s, outflows from Warsaw Pact countries to the West involved no more than 100,000 annually. These refugees were seen as "victims of communism" and were allowed to settle in Western countries either through resettlement programmes in North America and Australia or through local integration in Western European countries.

But by the late 1980s, the pace of change in the East produced dramatically higher numbers of uprooted people. In 1989, a total of 1.3 million people left Eastern Europe and the USSR for the West, including 720,000 ethnic Germans, about 320,000 Bulgarian Turks (of whom half later returned to Bulgaria), 71,000 Soviet Jews and 80,000 asylum-seekers. In 1990, another 1.3 million people left the East as more than 200,000 Jews emigrated from the USSR, nearly 400,000 ethnic Germans poured into Germany and thousands of Romanians and others sought a better life.

The changes in former Eastern Europe have also produced dramatic increases in migration for economic purposes. In the last ten years, about one million Poles have left their country and chosen not to return.

A recent report indicates that unemployment could reach 14 million, or 21 percent of the working populations in Eastern Europe by 1994. [19] The burden of controlling East-West migration has shifted from governments of the East to governments of the West. An estimated 200-500,000 foreign workers, including Vietnamese, Cubans, Mozambicans, Cubans, Angolans and Ethiopians are serving out their contracts in the former USSR, former East Germany, Czechoslovakia and Bulgaria. Economic restructuring in those countries will eliminate most of their jobs; Western governments fear that they will ask for asylum instead of going home. [20] The German government now provides US$2,000 and a one-way air ticket home to the 25,000 remaining guest-workers in the former East Germany.

For Western European governments, the arrival of so many refugees and migrants — accompanied by fears that even more would arrive in the future — created many tensions and contradictions. For years, European and North American governments had been urging the governments of the Eastern bloc to relax travel restrictions on its citizens. Now, as travel restrictions were eased and political changes made it possible to leave,

Western governments were forced to consider how they would respond to the sudden influx. Ironically, the fact that repression was easing in the East — thus making it possible for people to get out — weakened their claims to asylum as victims of persecution. Western governments, including the United States, analyzed the situation in the East and concluded that people leaving certain countries such as Poland, Hungary and Bulgaria no longer qualified to be treated as refugees.

The special case of Germany

As we have seen, by the late 1980s — even before the fall of the Berlin wall — Germany was coming under increasing pressure from emigration from the East as well as the South. Already the European country with the highest number of asylum-seekers from the third world, the Federal Republic was adopting more restrictive policies towards asylum-seekers from the South. But the movement of ethnic Germans created a new situation. Germany has always had an open-door policy towards ethnic Germans seeking to live in Germany. Legally and politically, ethnic Germans are admitted to the country as citizens rather than as asylum-seekers. All that is required is an ethnic identification traceable to Germany — even if it dates back to the seventeenth century. As conditions in the East changed, increasing numbers of ethnic Germans migrated to Germany. The number of arriving ethnic Germans from the Soviet Union, for example, increased from 14,500 in 1987 to 45,500 in 1988. Ethnic Germans from Poland increased from 48,500 in 1987 to 140,000 in 1988. In 1989 an estimated 300,000 additional ethnic Germans arrived for settlement in Germany. [21]

The ethnic Germans arriving in the Federal Republic of Germany in the late 1980s found a very different legal situation from that confronting the 100,000 asylum-seekers. As ethnic Germans, they were immediately given German citizenship and were eligible for the same generous welfare and unemployment benefits enjoyed by all West German citizens. At the same time, they faced serious difficulties in finding jobs and housing. Unemployment rates were high, public housing led to resentment from Germans without housing and, in many cases, and there were serious language problems as the refugees do not speak German.

The pattern of increasing ethnic German migration was compounded by a steady rise in the number of East Germans, or *Übersiedler*, coming to the USSR. When the Hungarian government in 1989 lifted travel restrictions to Austria, East Germans began transiting through Hungary to the West. The numbers increased dramatically, eventually forcing the

East German government to open its borders. All together 3 percent of the population of East Germany left their country between July 1989 and 1990.

The German government was thus faced with the simultaneous pressure of increasing numbers of East German migrants, ethnic Germans from countries throughout the East, the highest number of third-world asylum-seekers in Europe and 1.5 million Turks. Most immediately this meant serious pressure on housing as asylum-seekers and migrants were crowded into German schools and shelters. The backlog of asylum cases mounted.

Moreover, there was concern about the potential migration of more ethnic Germans. There are at least 3 million ethnic Germans still living in the East who can qualify for citizenship under German law. Reports are that half a million people of German ancestry living in the Soviet Republics had applied to emigrate to Germany by mid-1992. "At the current growth rate," says Heinrich Vogel, director of the Federal Institute for East European and International Studies in Cologne, "Germany could digest 2 million ethnic Germans. It may not be popular politically, but it could be done."[22] There are about 2.5 million ethnic Germans in the former Soviet Union. The Russian government is trying to induce them to stay, by establishing an ethnic German region for them in the Volga area — a move supported politically and economically by the German government.

The mass movements of people to Germany have made the subject of immigration and asylum a central political issue. Many Germans are questioning the generosity of their policies and politicians are suggesting changes in the basic law of the country in order to restrict asylum. The fear of many, including the churches and NGOs, is that while the door will remain open for those able to show German ancestry, it will be closed for people seeking asylum from both the third world and other European countries.

While Germany has been the Western country most affected by migration and refugees from the East, the countries of the East have also suffered the consequences of both immigration and emigration.

Hungary

Traditionally, Hungary has been a country of emigration. Some 200,000 Hungarians left after the October 1956 uprising, about 40 percent of whom went to the US and Canada. With the movement towards democratization, refugee-like emigration came to an end in the

1989-90 period and most Western countries declared Hungary to be a safe country in terms of human rights. [23]

But in the turbulent years of the late 1980s, when change was sweeping across Eastern Europe, Hungary was forced to respond to a wave of refugees from Romania. In 1987-89, some 40,000 Romanians (over 90 percent of whom were of Hungarian-speaking origin) arrived on Hungary's borders in search of protection and assistance. The refugees claimed that they were forced to flee because of their government's efforts to physically resettle them, taking them out of their villages into "modern" settlements, and to suppress their culture. Given their shared ethnic heritage with Hungarians in Hungary, it was perhaps natural that they sought security in that country when conditions became more difficult. This flow of Romanians to Hungary marked the first significant East-East refugee flow and was perhaps the first sign that the traditional understanding of European refugee issues as East-West questions and later as South-North migration was an inadequate one. By and large, the refugees were well-received in Hungary. The ethnic and linguistic similarities between most of the refugees and the Hungarian population eased major problems of integration. By 1989, there were about 16,000 registered refugees, plus 5,000 asylum-seekers and another 15,000 who were officially unregistered having crossed the "green border" or having arrived as tourists and simply stayed. Initially, the refugees were cared for by the churches and the Red Cross. The Ecumenical Council of Hungary developed programmes to assist the refugees and the churches in the areas bordering Romania opened their doors to the refugees, providing them with food and clothing. This experience of working with refugees was a new one for the Hungarian churches who, unlike their Western counterparts, had few professionals working in the area.

It was also a new experience for the Hungarian government which struggled with the legal and political implications of developing policies in regard to the new arrivals. According to bilateral treaties with Romania, some unpublished, the refugees should have been returned. [24] But they weren't and in 1989 the government decided to adhere to the 1951 Geneva Convention on refugees and the 1967 protocol. This marked a turning point for Hungary, one which must have an impact throughout Europe. Nagy explains that the decision to adhere to the 1951 Convention was "not assumed after any thorough debate among the political actors in the Hungarian arena; rather, it was the consequence of an almost personal initiative of the then foreign minister. He shared the general, but erroneous, view that refugee law could provide the means to settle the politically very uncomfortable dispute with Romania, a military ally of Hungary, over those Romanian citizens, who refused to return to their home country and wanted to remain in Hungary." [25]

Hungary indicated its intention to sign the Convention in early 1989; later that year UNHCR opened an office in Budapest. For Hungary, there were clear benefits in being part of the international system for meeting the needs of the thousands of Romanian refugees in its territory. But adhering to the Convention also had obligations to other groups of people. In the summer of 1989, the Hungarian government allowed tourists from the GDR to transit the country in order to go to the FRG — a move which was to culminate in the fall of the Berlin wall.

Since then, Hungary has moved to play a more active role in international and regional affairs. In addition to being an observer at the UNHCR executive committee and IOM, the Hungarian government has attended the meetings of the intergovernmental consultations on asylum-seekers in Europe and North America and has been actively involved in migration-related work at the Council of Europe. [26]

But the Hungarian situation also points to some of the larger issues in Central Europe. Presently, Hungary does not recognize non-European asylum-seekers (although they can apply for status with UNHCR and be resettled outside the country.) The government argues that it does not have the economic means and that the Hungarian people are not yet ready to accept non-European refugees.

Moreover, there are more than 3 million ethnic Hungarians living elsewhere in Europe: 2 million in Romania, 250,000 in Ukraine, 800,000 in Slovakia and about 500,000 in Serbia, Croatia and Vojvodina. [27] The violence in the former Yugoslav republics has already produced a large refugee flow into Hungary which once again finds itself trying to cope with an influx of new arrivals. Regarding the presence of ethnic Hungarians outside of Hungary, the government's official policy is that it wants to improve the condition of Hungarians in other countries without encouraging immigration. Indeed, Hungary's present population is around 10 million; the prospects of an additional 20-30 percent of ethnic Hungarian immigrants would certainly change the economic and political conditions of the country.

Turkey

Unlike Hungary, Turkey was one of the original signatories to the 1951 Convention although it also maintains the geographic exclusion. Given its geographical position, Turkey is vulnerable to large-scale migration from troubled areas near its border. Over the last five years, over a million refugees have entered the country. Their treatment in Turkey, however, depends on whether they are considered Convention refugees, non-Convention refugees, or ethnic Turks.[28] Convention refugees in Turkey — as in Hungary — are those individuals who become refugees as a result of events in Europe; they are granted asylum by the Turkish government on the condition that they are resettled in third countries. These Convention refugees number only a few hundred per year and most are resettled by UNHCR and the International Catholic Migration Commission.

A far larger group are the non-Convention refugees most of whom come from the Middle East. Iranian refugees began to arrive in large numbers in the very early 1980s and are reported to number from 200,000 to a million. While they are not granted refugee status, and no official records exist, the government has treated them leniently, allowing them to stay as tourists. Kurdish refugees from Iraq and Iran have posed more serious difficulties for the Turkish government which for 35 years has waged campaigns against its own Kurdish population. As was seen in the last chapter, close to a million Iraqi Kurds massed on the Turkish-Iraqi border as a result of the Gulf war.

Given the present uncertainty in the former Soviet republics, it may be that Turkey will receive far larger numbers of displaced people from the region in the future.

A third major ethnic group has been the ethnic Turks. Turkish municipal law allows ethnic Turks to migrate to Turkey, so they are treated as immigrants rather than as refugees. In May 1989, ethnic Turks began arriving in Turkey from Bulgaria complaining of discrimination and the intent to eliminate their culture from Bulgarian society. The stories they told of persecution were greeted with deep concern in Turkey and an announcement by the Turkish government that it would accept all Bulgarians of Turkish origin who arrived on its borders. The situation quickly escalated with a major exodus of more than 300,000 ethnic Turks arriving in only a few months and fears that they would be joined by more of the 1.5-2 million ethnic Turks living in Bulgaria. In response to the emergency, Turkey's generous offer was replaced with a governmental announcement of visa requirements for Bulgarians. The difficult economic situation in Turkey and other problems have led about half of the 300,000 ethnic Turks to return to Bulgaria.

The prospects for larger numbers of refugees arriving in Turkey will be shaped in part by developments in the former Soviet Republics.

Indeed, the potential of mass migration from the former Soviet republics is creating fears and uncertainty throughout Western and Central Europe.

The former Soviet republics

No empire has ever collapsed without inducing large movements of people and the Soviet Union is hardly an exception... Europe's unwillingness to devise a joint approach — it could include standardized entry requirements, allocation of quotas and pooling of relief resources — greatly alarms the Eastern Europeans. They know their frontiers may become porous at any moment and they fear that the West may react by simply re-erecting the wall which divided the continent since 1945... Indeed the response to this mass migration could ultimately decide the borders of the continent. [29]

The break-up of the Soviet empire has already displaced hundreds of thousands of people. In early 1992, the Soviet statistical office estimated that there were 710,000 displaced people within the former Soviet Republics of whom 336,000 were in Armenia and Azerbaijan and about 200,000 in Russia. Unofficial estimates placed the numbers much higher — one or two million. [30] With each week, the situation in the former Soviet Republics is changing. Ethnic conflicts in Nagorno-Karabakh, between South Ossetia and Georgia, Moldova and the Ukraine are all leading to unknown — but undoubtedly large — numbers of displaced people. Russians living in other republics are returning to Russia or moving to other republics.

Conflicts between different nationalities within the former Soviet republics are a major reason for population displacement. The fear is that they will intensify and that far larger numbers of people will be displaced by discrimination and violence, or fears of violence. The potential for such migration is enormous. Presently there are 72 million people in the former USSR who are living outside their "titular units"; 25 million of these are Russians living outside of Russia. Perhaps the most politically sensitive group are those with no affiliation to any of the republics: 700,000 ethnic Hungarians, more than one million Poles, as well as significant numbers of sub-Carpathian Ukrainians, Romanians outside Moldova, Jews and Germans.

In addition to the ethnic tensions and conflicts are concerns about economic conditions in the republics. An estimated 30 million people are facing unemployment. The then-Soviet labour minister estimated that 2-3 million citizens of the republics would seek temporary jobs in the West because of economic upheaval; some Western observers put the number at 6 million and suggest that the migration may not be temporary. [31] Park reported that a recent survey showed that 50 percent of college graduates in the republics said they want to work abroad. He also reported that the US embassy in Moscow has received one million applications for emigration to the US.[32]

While future migration from the former Soviet republics will depend on the way in which the economy and the nationalities problems are resolved, the poor travel infrastructure, difficulties in converting rubles to foreign currency, visa requirements throughout Europe for citizens of the former Soviet republics and tightening border controls are all deterrents to such migration.

Discussion of the scale of potential migration from the former Soviet republics often turns into a consideration of alternative scenarios. What will happen in the Central Asian republics if Islamic republics are established? What if negotiations between Russia and Ukraine break down? What if the Russian troops in the Baltics don't return to Russia? While the uncertainties about the shape and direction of future migration make predictions impossible, governments throughout West and Central Europe are worried. "A mass exodus from the Soviet Union would, however, present major security problems for Central European states. Poland, Czechoslovakia and Hungary are going through major structural changes that leave them with little capacity to admit, house and feed large numbers of immigrants without undermining their own attempts at economic and political reform." It is unlikely that they could absorb large numbers of people and they will probably demand burden-sharing agreements with the West.[33] Some East European participants in a 1990 seminar on "the ramifications of Soviet emigration" expressed "concern that the West expected their countries to erect the new walls to keep the Soviets out. There was general agreement, nevertheless, as to the need for these new democracies to implement migration policies in co-operation with the West."[34]

Torn apart: the republics of Yugoslavia

Throughout 1991 and 1992, the world watched as Yugoslavia, a European country, disintegrated into civil war and ethnic conflict. By early 1993, almost 2 million former Yugoslavians had been displaced by the war, 250,000 of whom had sought protection outside the country — and the war continued, creating the largest flood of refugees in Europe since the second world war.

The roots of the conflict are many. Ethnically, Yugoslavia was the most heterogeneous of all European countries, composed entirely of "ethnic groups *all* of which are 'minorities'".[35] Differences in religion, language, and economic disparities partly parallelled these ethnic differences. The border of Yugoslavia had been an artificial creation — as was recognized from its inception. Under the regime of Marshal Tito, the country had been held together and external pressure helped to maintain a Yugoslavian cohesion. But with the passing of Tito in 1980 and the demise of Soviet influence a decade later, tensions and conflicts between different ethnic groups and religions emerged with unexpected viciousness. The desire of ethnic groups to establish independent states created problems because these groups were dispersed throughout the country. Thus Serbia stated its fears concerning the fate of Serbs living in Croatia and claimed to be acting to safeguard them when fighting with Croatia. Croatia, seen as the victim of Serbian aggression, is not a disinterested party in the conflict in Bosnia-Herzegovina. But while the ethnic differences and difficulties stemming from changes in the external environment can help explain why ethnic groups wanted to go their own separate ways, they don't explain why war erupted or why the war has been so violent. As Clements explained: "It is not just differences of language, culture and religion that bedevil the situation, but the issues of power and perceptions of domination and control among the ethnic groups and republics, infused with their very different understandings of their own and each others' histories."[36] And indeed the history of the region is a bloody one, particularly during the second world war when hundreds of thousands died, charging each other with collaboration with other powers. That history has been resurrected in the current conflict.

The bitter war between Croatia and Serbia and the even more violent conflict in Bosnia-Herzegovina raise fears about other parts of the former Yugoslavian republic. Albanians make up 85 percent of the population of Kosovo and there is speculation that an independence movement there might lead to union with Albania. The desire of Macedonians for independence brings up the question of Greece and fears of the Yugoslavian conflict being broadened into a larger conflict in the Balkans. These ethnic conflicts are reflected in religious differences, particularly between Serbian Orthodox and Croatian Catholics and Bosnian Muslims. "But essentially the problem appears to be that Catholicism and Orthodoxy, having for centuries been so closely bound up with the identity of specific and separate communities, will almost inevitably tend to act as the legitimators of the aspirations of their respective peoples, especially where it is felt that their liberty and rights are under threat."[37] However, demonstrations led by the Serbian Orthodox Church indicate a readiness for the church to distance itself from the policies of Serbian President Slobodan Milosevic.

The tragic war has killed thousands of people, possibly hundreds of thousands, and generated calls for international intervention. But none of the European institutions — from the European Community to the CSCE — could stop the escalation of the conflict, in spite of repeated efforts at negotiations. The United Nations imposed tough economic sanctions against Serbia, but few felt that they would result in the short term in an end to the war. As Sarajevo was besieged and under heavy attack, residents were reportedly bitter at the lack of international intervention, feeling that military intervention from abroad represented the only hope for the city's survival.[38] Yugoslavia represents one of the first test cases of the "new world order"; the new order has failed to provide alternative means of conflict-resolution in the country.

Yugoslavia has also been an exceedingly difficult area for the provision of humanitarian assistance. Operating within the borders of the former Yugoslavia, UNHCR has worked with both refugees and displaced people — indeed, in the current situation it is hard to distinguish between the two. The UN has established protected areas in parts of the countries but many of the displaced people come from places outside those protected areas.

The initial flood of refugees and displaced people were from Croatia. In August 1991, the International Committee of the Red Cross launched its first appeal for 90,000 displaced people; two months later the figure had jumped to 300,000. By mid-1992, the figure reached 500,000. Displaced Croatians moved to Croatian areas while displaced Serbs moved into Serbia. In early 1992, about two-thirds of those displaced within the borders of the former Yugoslavia were women. Most of the displaced people are cared for by relatives and other individuals and by voluntary organizations. But the pressures of growing numbers have led to plans to establish refugee camps. By December 1991, there were 45,000 Yugoslavs in Hungary, most of whom were unregistered and living with private families.[39] In Serbia, the government formulated plans to resettle displaced Serbs in homes abandoned by fleeing Croatians.

The status of refugees varied by host country. In Slovenia, for example, the government entered into an agreement with the Croatian forces that only people of a certain age and sex and from designated areas would be allowed to enter — to prevent men of military age from leaving. Should people leaving Serbia or Croatia because they oppose military service be granted refugee status? The nature of the war and the changing status of borders make it difficult to apply traditional concepts of refugee status. As Frelick asks: "Should Croatians seeking refuge in Slovenia be assisted by ICRC as displaced persons or by UNHCR as refugees?"[40] By mid-1992, UNHCR had signed agreements with Croatia, Slovenia, Austria and Hungary on the right of displaced people to return to their communities, but there are many questions about how and when the displaced can go back.

* * *

The pressures faced by European governments and societies are many: how to resolve conflicts in areas such as the former Yugoslavian republics, how to formulate foreign policies to enable people in the South to live in dignity and well-being, and how to respond to growing numbers of asylum-seekers appearing on their borders. The way in which European and North American governments respond to these questions will shape the entire international system for responding to uprooted people. Before considering some of these broader issues, however, we will take a brief look at the policies of other Western governments — the United States, Canada and Australia — to understand their role in shaping a new international order for uprooted people.

North America and Australia: different traditions, similar responses

Unlike European countries, the United States, Canada and Australia have traditionally seen themselves as countries of immigration and have prided themselves on their openness to victims of persecution and the development of multicultural societies. All three countries were settled by Europeans leaving their homelands for a variety of reasons, including political and religious persecution, poverty and as punishment for crimes committed back home. This sensitivity to immigration sets these countries apart from Europe; in all three countries refugee resettlement programmes were developed in the post-war period. However, like their European counterparts, the governments and NGOs of these three countries faced major challenges from asylum-seekers arriving on their borders in the mid-1990s.

The United States

As a nation of immigrants, the United States has always been particularly sensitive to immigration issues. US political culture has stressed the nation's traditional welcome to the persecuted and downtrodden of the world. But, as Keely points out, US concern with those seeking a new life has not been consistent over time.

> The United States has always been of two minds about new immigrants. On the one hand, the country has historically been a refuge, a place of new beginnings, accepting and even recruiting new settlers to build the nation and its economy. On the other hand, the theme of protectionism has found recurrent expression in apprehension over the capacity of the culture and economy to absorb newcomers, in the desire to limit labour market competition and assure minimal health standards and even in nativism and racist theories. The history of immigration policy is a dialectic of these two themes of acceptance and protection. [41]

Since 1945, more than 2 million foreigners have entered the US outside of regular immigration channels. They have gone by different names — refugees, displaced persons, parolees, etc. This figure includes more than 800,000 Cubans, 700,000 Indochinese and at least a half million Central and Eastern Europeans. [42] But refugee policy in the US was developed for more than altruistic reasons and served to reinforce American anti-communist foreign policies. Since the second world war, 95 percent of the people admitted as refugees to the United States came from countries with communist governments. [43]

Thus, before 1980, US refugee policy was explicitly designed to reflect foreign-policy objectives. By defining refugees solely as products of communist governments or Middle Eastern states, the US government ensured that its refugee admissions policies would directly support foreign policies based on a cold-war mentality. In 1980 the US congress passed a new refugee law which incorporated the definition of refugees as included in the UN Convention (which the US had ratified in 1968). This act eliminated the statutory preference for victims of communism and constructed an elaborate bureaucratic structure for processing and dealing with refugees. The annual limit on regular refugee admissions was raised from 17,400 to 50,000 and the act provided for that number to be changed after annual consultations with the congress. The act also provided for an explicit asylum provision in the immigration law that included a lengthy appeals process. The assumption, of course, was that very few asylum cases would be filed. As Leibowitz notes, by changing the definition of refugee, the 1980 refugee act created serious problems for future admissions policies. While the number of refugees who would be eligible for refugee status in the US was increased from about 3 million to 13 million (by eliminating the geographic restrictions), the act established clear numerical limits on responding to those refugees. "Congress had, consciously or unconsciously, created large numbers of claimants who could not be satisfied."[44]

A month after the refugee act of 1980 was passed, it was immediately challenged by the Cuban Mariel boatlift of April 1980 in which 150,000 Cubans migrated to the US in a mass exodus that overwhelmed the procedures established to cope with asylum-seekers. Within a few years the procedures were further pressured by the arrival of large numbers of Central American asylum-seekers, fleeing the violence of their countries.

Latin American immigration issues are particularly sensitive in the US, given the traditional problems caused by illegal immigration of Mexicans to the US, the growing social and political presence of Hispanics among the US population, and the politicization of immigration questions. When the violence in El Salvador and Guatemala was displacing hundreds of thousands of people and hundreds of thousands were making their way north, the US government largely ignored these movements in determining its refugee policy.

Central Americans were not welcomed by the US government for largely political reasons. They contradicted its foreign-policy objectives of support for the Salvadoran government of Napoleon Duarte and they were evidence that democracy in El Salvador was not working. While the US provided massive amounts of military aid to the Salvadoran government, hundreds of thousands of Salvadorans were turning up on its borders. President Ronald Reagan further used fear of the refugees as support for his policies in the region, referring to "a tidal wave of refugees swarming into our country" if the leftist movements in Central America were successful. And there were fears that granting asylum to the Central American claimants would lead to further flows. As one congressional staff member explained: "If we legalize the presence of the half million Salvadorans who are already here, how many more millions will come?"[45]

So the US government did not grant asylum to the Central American uprooted people and most of them were forced to live illegally on the margins of US cities. In 1984, only 3 of 761 Guatemalan applicants (less than 0.5 percent) and only 328 of 13,373 Salvadorans (less than 2.5 percent) were granted asylum. This contrasts sharply with the corresponding rates for Bulgarians (52 percent) Russians (51 percent) and Hungarians (28 percent).[46] Many Central Americans were apprehended, detained and subsequently deported. Estimates of the number of Salvadorans deported by the INS range from 500 to 1,000 per month.[47] Many more Salvadoran and Guatemalan refugees lived in fear that they would be sent back.

Western similarities

In many important respects the development of Canadian and Australian refugee policy followed different directions — as might be expected given the differences in their foreign policies. For Canada a major change occurred in 1973, in the aftermath of the violent overthrow of Salvador Allende and the exodus of Chileans.

> While the Canadian government initially moved slowly to establish a refugee admissions programme, pressure from members of parliament, organized labour, and a number of humanitarian organizations including the churches, ultimately resulted in Canada accepting approximately 7,000 refugees from Chile for permanent resettlement between 1974 and 1977. [48]

Australia, which had begun large-scale resettlement programmes for European refugees in the post-war period, became more responsive to Asian refugee situations and resettled a large number of Vietnamese refugees.

But in some respects, the orientation of the three governments was quite similar. All three saw themselves as countries for permanent resettlement and not merely temporary havens from which people could be repatriated after stability in their homeland was restored. In all three countries, national legislation was developed and large bureaucracies created to enable refugees to resettle permanently in their countries. In all three countries, the basic policy was that refugees would be selected by governmental officials "over there". Those refugees who met the criteria and who would adapt well to life in Western society would be supported and admitted to the country. It was to be a relatively neat and orderly process which would be both humane for the refugees and fit into the bureaucratic procedures. Those selected for resettlement, for example, would be given language training and cultural orientation before leaving the camps in the countries of first asylum.

In all three countries, community and church involvement was essential for the successful adaptation of the refugee. Through a variety of sponsorship programmes (some through specific congregational sponsors, others through broader "community sponsorship" plans), individual refugees would be welcomed to the country and would receive the necessary support to find employment and housing, to enrol children in school and to come to understand life in the new world. In all three countries, the churches played central roles in enabling refugees to begin new lives. In a world where much ecumenical refugee work is being handed over to specialized agencies, the local congregational involvement in refugee resettlement in these countries is striking.

In spite of the programmes developed and the rhetoric of being open, welcoming societies, there were always tensions between the governments on the one hand and the churches and NGOs on the other. Governments generally wanted to give priority to those refugees who would contribute to their societies: the educated, healthy and young. Churches and NGOs were more anxious that resettlement be used to assist those who were most vulnerable, including disabled, elderly, and those with protection problems. The Inter-Church Committee for Refugees (ICCR) in Canada had annual meetings with the government to express their views on regional allocations of refugee slots. Churches in Australia and the US engaged in a similar negotiating process.

But these resettlement policies came under strain with the arrival of large numbers of asylum-seekers in the mid-1980s. In Canada, for example, the number of asylum-seekers jumped from about 5,000 in 1984 to approximately 30,000 in 1988, straining the system and putting increased pressure on the Canadian government. The backlog of cases grew and in 1989 the government introduced new refugee determination procedures to speed up the process. But the government still faced a huge backlog of pending cases under the old system. For individual asylum-seekers, the pain of being in limbo for years while decisions were made about their refugee claims was often unbearable. In late 1990, the Inter-Church Committee submitted a report to the UN Human Rights Commission charging that this backlog constituted cruelty to asylum-seekers who had, in some cases, been waiting for years for a decision. A year later, the ICCR began a campaign to challenge the new refugee laws in the supreme court.

In spite of the problems with the Canadian refugee determination procedures, it still has the most favourable conditions for asylum-seekers in the Western world, with about two-thirds of asylum requests approved in the early 1990s (for comparison in the fiscal year 1990, the approval rate for asylum requests in the US was 14.7 percent). But the number of refugees resettled in Canada has decreased, with only 2,300 admitted in 1991.

As in Canada and some European countries, the Australian government also faced a backlog of pending cases. By December 1991, 23,000 people were waiting to have their cases settled, 72 pecent of whom were

Chinese. One of the Australian respones to the growing number of asylum-seekers — and even more dramatic fears that far larger numbers would arrive on its shores — was to change their laws so that people admitted as refugees would get only a four-year temporary residence rather than permanent status.

For the governments and the NGOs of Australia, Canada and the United States, the past decade has led to major changes in policies concerning refugees. Whereas in earlier times, most of the refugees coming to those countries did so through orderly processes of government-organized resettlement programmes, increasing numbers of asylum-seekers created confusion and pressures in the system. NGOs and churches which had worked with the governments in developing programmes to support resettled refugees now found themselves taking up the role of advocate for asylum-seekers. This implied not only taking a more visible role on refugee issues, but also taking a more confrontational stance towards their governments. These changes occurred among ecumenical agencies, but also took place on the local level as churches struggled to find new ways of protecting people threatened with deportation. Local church organizations developed public education programmes to inform asylum-seekers and illegal immigrants of their rights. In some cases, local church congregations declared themselves public sanctuaries for refugees who were not recognized by their governments. In the United States, for example, by the mid-1980s, some 400 congregations and other community groups had declared sanctuary for Central American refugees in defiance of their government's policy. In Canada, churches and NGOs formed an organization known as Vigil to monitor the fate of those rejected as refugees by the Canadian authorities. Increasingly churches and NGOs began to work with their counterparts in other countries. Thus, several consultations were held between Canadian and US ecumenical agencies to plan ways of working together, particularly for cases where Central Americans facing deportation in the US could be supported in their efforts to receive asylum in Canada. And as the governments of all three countries began to work more closely with European governments in developing policies for asylum-seekers, churches and NGOs sought to strengthen their ties with their European counterparts.

While there are many differences between the situations facing NGOs and churches in Europe, North America and Australia, there is a growing and shared realization that decisions made about refugees and asylum by Western governments would have an impact far beyond the borders of their countries. The erosion of the international system for refugee protection and assistance is most apparent in the policies of Western governments. In this regard the actions of Western NGOs and churches to challenge those policies are steps to influence the nature of the evolving international response to uprooted people. We turn in the final chapter to a consideration of some of the alternative ways for NGOs and churches to play a greater role in the international debate which is now taking place about the future international system.

NOTES

1 Gil Loescher, "Mass Migration as a Global Security Problem", in *World Refugee Survey 1991*, Washington, DC, US Committee for Refugees, 1992, p.12.
2 *Time Magazine*, 26 August 1991, p.22.
3 *Christian Science Monitor*, 8-15 August 1991, p.16.
4 Jonas Widgren, "South-North Migration and its Political and Humanitarian Implications for Europe", paper presented at the international conference "Refugees in the World: The European Community's Response", The Hague, December 1989, p.12.
5 Interview of Senegalese President Abdon Diouf by *Le Figaro*, cited by *Christian Science Monitor*, 9-15 August 1991, p.13.
6 Loescher, *op. cit.*, p.12; *Time Magazine*, *op. cit.*, p.21.
7 Loescher, *ibid.*, p.12. Refugee Policy Group, "The Ramifications of Soviet Emigration", summary of a meeting held 8-10 December 1990 of the North American-European Dialogue on Politics and Migration, Washington, DC, Refugee Policy Group, 1990.
8 Arne Piel Christenson and Morton Kjaerum, "Myths and Reality in the Refugee Debate", Danish Refugee Council, mimeo, 25 November 1990, p.2.
9 Roy McDowall, "Co-ordination of Refugee Policy in Europe", pp.179-186 in *Refugees and International Relations*, eds Gil Loescher and Laila Monahan, Oxford, Oxford University Press, 1989, p.182.
10 For further information on these mechanisms, see Keith Jenkins and Jan Niessen, "Moving the European Institutions", and José Leite, "The CSCE, the European House and Priorities for the Churches", both in "Refugees and Asylum Seekers in a Common European House", *Refugees*, WCC, August 1991. "A Churches Guide to the European Institutions", Brussels, Ecumenical Centre. Antonio Cruz, *An Insight into Schengen, Trevi and Other European Intergovernmental Bodies*, Churches Committee for Migrants in Europe Briefing Papers, no. 1, 1990. European Consultation on Refugees and Exiles, *Refugee Policy in a Unifying Europe*, report of a seminar held in Zeist, Netherlands, April 1989, London, ECRE. *Fortress Europe: The Meaning of 1992*, ed. P. Gordon, London, Runnymede Trust, 1990. Amnesty International, "Europe: Harmonization of Asylum Policy", briefing paper, EUR/01/90, London, Amnesty International, November 1990. See also Gil Loescher, "Refugee Movements and International Security", *Adelphi Papers*, no. 268, London, International Institute for Strategic Studies, 1992.
11 Cited in *Time Magazine*, *op. cit.*
12 *Ibid.*
13 Gil Loescher, "The Single European Market and the European Community's Asylum Policy", paper presented at the international conference on "Refugees in the World: The European Community's Response", The Hague, 7-8 December 1989, p.11.

[14] Widgren, *op. cit.*, p.6.

[15] *Ibid.*, p.9.

[16] *Ibid.*, p.12.

[17] Christenson and Kjaerum, *op. cit.*

[18] *Ibid.*, p.7.

[19] Loescher, "Mass Migration", *op. cit.*, p.10.

[20] *Ibid.*

[21] Elizabeth Ferris, "New Winds in Europe", in *Refugees*, WCC, September 1989, no.104.

[22] *Time Magazine*, *op. cit.*, p.18.

[23] Gaza Tessenyi, "The Development of Immigration and Refugee Policy in a New Host Country: The Case of Hungary", pp.109-128, in *The New Refugee-Hosting Countries: Call for Experiment-Space for Innovation*, Netherlands, SIM special issue no. 11, 1991, p.111.

[24] Boldizsar Nagy, "Before or After the Wave? Thoughts on the Adequacy of the Hungarian Refugee Law", in *International Journal of Refugee Law*, vol. 3, no. 3, July 1991, pp.531.

[25] *Ibid.*, p.531.

[26] Tessenyi, *op. cit.*, p.127.

[27] Figures from *ibid.*, p.119, and *The Economist*, 13 October 1990.

[28] See, for example, Kemal Kirisci, "The Legal Status of Asylum Seekers in Turkey: Problems and Prospects", in *International Journal of Refugee Law*, vol. 3, no. 3, July 1991, pp.510-528.

[29] Jonathan Egal, "A Hungry Army Ready to March West", in *Guardian Weekly*, 9 December 1990.

[30] Andreas Park, "Change and Migration in the Post Soviet Republics", paper presented at the International Refugee Advisory Panel meeting at Oxford University, 3 January 1992.

[31] Susan Forbes Martin, "Soviet Migration a Ticking Bomb", in *Chicago Tribune*, 5 November 1990. See also Gil Loescher, *Refugee Movements and International Security*, Adelphi Papers no. 268, London, International Institute for Strategic Studies, summer 1992.

[32] Park, *op. cit.*

[33] Loescher, "Mass Migration", *op. cit.*, pp.7-14.

[34] Refugee Policy Group, "The Ramifications of Soviet Emigration", summary of meeting held 8-10 December 1990 of the North American-European Dialogue on Politics and Migration. Washington, DC, Refugee Policy Group, 1990, p.5.

[35] Keith Clements, "Yugoslavia: A Briefing Paper for the Churches", London, British Council of Churches, 1991.

[36] *Ibid.*, p.9.

[37] *Ibid.*, p.10.

[38] *International Herald Tribune*, 20 June 1992.

[39] Bill Frelick, *Yugoslavia Torn Asunder: Lessons for Protecting Refugees from Civil War*, Washington, DC, US Committee for Refugees, 1992, pp.2-11.

[40] *Ibid.*, p.24.

[41] Charles B. Keely, *US Immigration: A Policy Analysis*, New York, Population Council, 1979, p.8.

[42] Gil Loescher and John A. Scanlan, *Calculated Kindness: Refugees and America's Half-Open Door, 1945-Present*, New York, Free Press, 1986, p.209. This book is the most comprehensive of the many studies of US policy towards refugees. For additional

information on US policy, see Loescher and Scanlan, *Human Rights, Power Politics, and the International Refugee Regime: The Case of US Treatment of Caribbean Basin Refugees*, Princeton University Centre for International Studies, World Order Studies Occasional Paper Series, no. 14, Princeton, NJ, 1985. Also Loescher and Scanlan eds, *The Global Refugee Problem: US and World Response*, special issue of *The Annals of the American Academy of Political and Social Science*, no. 467, May 1983. Naomi Flink Zucker and Norman I. Zucker, *The Guarded Gate: The Dilemma of Contemporary American Refugee Policy*, New York, Harcourt, Brace Jovanovich, 1987.

[43] Loescher and Scanlan, *Calculated Kindness, op. cit.*, p.215.

[44] Arnold H. Leibowitz, "The Refugee Act of 1980: Problems and Congressional Concerns", in *The Annals of the American Academy of Political and Social Science*, no. 467, May 1983, p.167.

[45] Frances X. Cline, "Reagan Says Salvadoran Foes Would Bring US Refugees", in *New York Times*, 23 June 1983. Quote from congressional staffer from personal interview, 1984.

[46] Loescher and Scanlan, *Calculated Kindness, op. cit.*, p.215.

[47] Elizabeth Ferris, *The Central American Refugees*, New York, Praeger, 1987.

[48] Gerald E. Dirks, "Canada's Policy towards the Refugee Phenomenon in Central America", paper presented at the 1983 meeting of the International Studies Association, p.6.

11. *Alternatives to the Present System of Refugee Assistance and Protection*

In the preceding chapters, we have seen that the international system for responding to uprooted people is in crisis. On every continent, new pressures are emerging which are chipping away at the system. And the signs are that the international system for responding to uprooted people will come under more — not less — stress in the future.

Future trends

1. The new process of state-formation in the republics of the former Soviet Union, the upsurge in ethnic tension and conflicts in some countries of the former Eastern bloc and growing economic difficulties, coupled with increased freedom for people from those areas to travel, make it likely that there will be higher numbers — perhaps far higher numbers — of migrants travelling from East to West.

While the attention of Western Europe and the US is focused on potential East-West mass movements, the process of state formation and the ethnic conflicts are intensifying in countries of the South. As Adelman warns, the ethnic conflicts which we have seen in the former Eastern bloc are

> only the beginning. The implosion of India, of Indonesia, of Nigeria — the largest country in Africa — has yet to occur, though each has had or is experiencing degrees of rebellion against central state authority. The rebellions of ethnic groups such as the Sikhs or of the Ibos in these countries were not akin to the secessionist southern states of the United States, forced to reunite to forge the common American nation. For India, Indonesia and Nigeria are not nations forged by states. Rather, each consists of nations that existed prior to the construction of the state. [1]

This process of state-formation, of developing political structures which incorporate more than one nation, has historically been a violent process which uprooted people. In sum, political and social change in the East and in the South uproots people and will continue to uproot people in the near future.

2. Moreover, there is some reason to believe that governments will see the departure or even the expulsion of certain minority groups as useful to policies of national consolidation and to ridding the country of potential dissidents. [2]

3. Given the fact that economic problems in the countries of the South are increasing, that democratic regimes are notoriously difficult to consolidate in periods of economic scarcity (particularly when imposed from above à la IMF), it is likely that more people will try to migrate for both political and economic reasons from South to North. The connection between economic difficulties and political repression is not, of course, an automatic one, but the record suggests that there is a definite relationship. [3] Implementing structural adjustment policies, with their concomitant requirements of reducing public spending, increasing unemployment, reducing imports, and declining subsistence agriculture, are not popular policies in the most stable of democracies. The pressure to use military force to quell dissent for their implementation is substantial. But people who flee — either because of the direct economic consequences of such policies or the repression that frequently accompanies them — will find less welcoming policies in Southern host countries which are under the same economic pressures as the countries of origin.

4. Simply looking at population trends over the next decade, where countries of the South are expected to increase their populations far faster than their governments or economies can provide for them, makes it obvious that South-North migration will increase. [4] The lack of legal immigration channels will probably mean more use/abuse of the asylum procedure. At the same time, the foreign remittances of migrant workers will continue to be an important foreign exchange source for the countries of origin.

5. While peace agreements will be implemented in some countries, and some refugees will return, repatriation will not be an automatic or an easy process. In some cases, such as that of Central Americans living in the US, many of the refugees will continue to stay on, even if political change occurs back home, for economic reasons. In other cases, such as Cambodia and Eritrea, most of the refugees in neighbouring countries will return and try to rebuild their lives. But peace in those countries, as in

Angola and Mozambique, will be fragile and violence could easily break out again, leading to new flows of refugees. Moreover, the repatriation of refugees — particularly when coupled with the reconstruction of the areas to which they are returning — is expensive and requires substantial political will from the international community. The difficulties in raising funds for the Cambodian peace-keeping and repatriation project suggest that funds may not be forthcoming for such future initiatives, particularly in countries of less concern to Western governments.

6. In spite of the end of the cold war and despite talk of a "new world order", the arms trade will continue — and perhaps even intensify as arms dealers seek new markets for their products so widely advertised in the Gulf war. In fact, as the US and other Western countries cut back their military spending, the arms merchants will come under increasing pressure to market their wares elsewhere.

7. There are some indications that the US may play a less active role in international politics as a result of mounting domestic political concerns and a presidential election campaign which has focused largely on domestic issues. This, of course, has both negative and positive implications — positive in the sense of possibly leading to less US intervention in other countries, negative in the prospect of declining funds for foreign aid and foreign humanitarian concerns in the absence of an "enemy". But it may be that the lesson of the Gulf war for the US government was that new enemies need to be found in strong third-world countries[5] in order to justify continued high domestic spending and the maintenance of a military establishment whose reason for existence has come into question. Most obviously in the United States, but also in other Western countries, there is a need to develop a new rationale for support for refugees. In the past, such support was often explicitly or implicitly couched in cold-war terms, as necessary to prevent destabilization or help victims of communism or support freedom-fighters. Without that cold war overlay, there is a need to build a new base of support for humanitarian issues.

All of these trends suggest not only that there will be more refugees and more migrants in the future, but that there will be more inter-regional migration in the coming years.

8. The trends also suggest that issues related to the reception of refugees and migrants will become more politically sensitive — or politically explosive in some cases. We have already seen evidence of increasing racism and xenophobia in Europe and the United States; such pressures are unlikely to dissipate in the absence of more far-sighted leadership and economic growth. Although the negative reaction to

foreigners may also lead to the growth of more progressive sectors and more vocal demonstrations against racism, the tendency will grow for politicians and others to blame foreigners for a whole range of problems, from unemployment to crime to loss of cultural identity.

9. Questions of cultural identity and about what the concept of "nation" means in this day and age will become burning political issues in all regions. The emergence of new nation-states to reflect those cultural values — as well as political and historical ones — may not only affect migration patterns, but will also determine how refugees and migrants will be treated.

10. Finally, the increased visibility of the United Nations in the aftermath of the Gulf war and its willingness to take initiatives to resolve conflicts in Cambodia and the republics of former Yugoslavia lead many to conclude that the time is propitious for transforming the UN into a real force for peace and conflict-resolution in the world. But critics, particularly from the South, are suspicious of giving the UN greater authority and interventionist powers as long as it remains under the domination of powerful Western governments.[6]

* * *

These trends mean that NGOs and churches working with refugees will face greater challenges in the future. It won't be enough for NGOs to work to improve the quality and level of their services or to try to raise more money for refugee work. Such efforts will be overshadowed by the arrival of more groups of refugees, asylum-seekers and migrants and by more hostile reactions from host populations. NGOs, as we have seen, are minor actors in the international refugee game. The rules of the game are largely determined by governments. Unless NGOs and churches play a role in shaping those rules — in determining how refugees and other uprooted people will be treated by the governments that receive them — they will remain marginal to the international system in responding to uprooted people. The movement of NGOs and churches towards more active advocacy roles, as outlined in chapter 3, is an indication of both a recognition and a willingness to do more to address the root causes of refugee flows and to participate in shaping the rules of the game for responding to them. But unless such NGO initiatives can be co-ordinated and addressed to governments and UN agencies as well as to their like-minded constituents, these advocacy efforts are unlikely to transform the system.

The main priority for NGOs is to address the causes which force people to leave their homes and communities. In this respect, resolving ethnic conflicts, promoting non-violent means of resolving conflicts and supporting peace processes after agreements have been signed stand out as particularly important areas for NGO action. Transforming the international system for responding to uprooted people must be seen in this larger context.

The present international system for responding to uprooted people is seriously flawed and there are many contending proposals to change it. These proposals are based on different understandings of the nature of the problems. Some governments see the problem in terms of too many refugees arriving on their borders and thus view the solution in terms of developing more effective ways of preventing their entry. Some human rights groups see the problem the other way around — in terms of the fact that individuals who need protection are not receiving it. Still others see the problem as evidence of the declining effectiveness of UNHCR or the inadequacy of the 1951 Convention definition of refugees or the breakdown of the international consensus on shared responsibility for refugees. And still others point to the fact that in spite of commitment, good will and much talk, the international community has been unable to address the causes which uproot people from their homes. All of these criticisms are describing facets of a common reality — that is, the international system for refugee assistance and protection is falling apart or, in more academic terms, undergoing a transformation the direction of which is unknown.

The combination of the present crisis in the international refugee system and increasing optimism (at least in some quarters) about the potential role of regional and international organizations to shape a "new world order" makes this an important time to consider alternatives to the present system of refugee protection and assistance. NGOs have played an important role in pointing out the shortcomings of the present system and in advocating more humane policies at the national level. But this is the time for NGOs to make a more concerted effort to advocate changes in the international system. It isn't enough for churches and NGOs to denounce injustices in UNHCR's policies or governmental treatment of specific groups of asylum-seekers. Rather, if NGOs and churches are to play a role in shaping the emerging international system for responding to uprooted people, they need to advocate specific alternatives to existing policies.

Alternatives: criteria

In the sections that follow, five groups of alternative policies are considered:
— substantive reform of the international system, and particularly the United Nations ("towards a new world order?");
— reforms in the operational humanitarian work of the United Nations ("towards a new humanitarian order?");
— reforms of international law, particularly the 1951 United Nations Convention relating to the status of refugees ("towards a new convention?");
— regional initiatives ("towards a world of regions?")
— changing national policies ("towards better refugee and immigration policies?").

These alternatives are by no means mutually exclusive; on the contrary, they can be mutually reinforcing. For example, strengthening regional mechanisms for conflict-resolution can help build up confidence and competence for United Nations action in similar directions. Improving national policies for responding to refugees can serve as models not only for other governments but also for emerging regional standards. The reform of UN humanitarian agencies could be a step in the direction of a more rational and comprehensive system of international organization, which could be a step towards some kind of world government. Similarly, while prospects for radical reform of the international system seem far-fetched, discussion of such prospects — and their relative advantages and disadvantages — could be an important input into discussions about reform of other structures.

It is thus quite possible for NGOs and churches to advocate, at the same time, more humane policies on the national level, regional mechanisms for upholding asylum-seekers' rights, and a new international humanitarian structure. In fact, their efforts on any one level will be more credible and more effective when combined with advocacy at other levels.

In evaluating the following alternatives, various criteria can be used. In particular, I suggest the following:

• An alternative system for international protection of and assistance for refugees should be *humane*. It must meet the needs of those uprooted from their communities through no fault of their own, uphold their dignity and enable them to play an active role in deciding upon their future.

• It should also be *feasible* in either the short or long term. NGOs need to offer credible alternatives which meet governments' security needs as well as refugees' needs for protection and assistance. To advocate that governments abandon national sovereignty or that they open their borders to all arrivals is not a realistic alternative in the short term. To advocate that wars cease or that economic disparities be overcome through a sudden change of heart on the part of the rich is equally unrealistic. NGOs and churches have a long history of calling for a more just world and identifying the causes of injustice. While it is important that they maintain this prophetic role and constantly keep these goals in mind, it is also essential that they engage in the political process. Otherwise they run the risk of being marginalized from that process, of being seen as naive do-gooders, while governments continue to shape the rules of the game — rules which affect people's lives. While some of the proposals discussed below may seem too radical and thus not feasible, long-term thinking can provide a credible alternative as long as the interim steps are spelled out. World government seems hopelessly utopian, and yet one can imagine a long-term process in which decision-making on certain issues is gradually transferred to a supranational authority.

• It should *build* on the best of past experiences. Alternative proposals shouldn't start from scratch, but rather build on previous practices. For example, much can be done through human-rights law, as well as humanitarian law, to construct alternative models. Similarly, NGOs and governments alike have developed some very creative ways of responding to extraordinarily difficult situations — precedents which can serve as a basis for future mechanisms for intervention. By building on past experiences, alternatives become more credible as a policy option.

• An alternative international refugee system should address *causes* as well as human consequences. Any future international system for refugees should include provisions for resolving conflicts before they uproot people and for resolving conflicts to enable them to return.

• Finally, an international system should identify the *steps to be taken*. An alternative should include a strategic action plan which spells out how the objective can be achieved and who can take responsibility for moving forward in this area. Just as groups working to reform the international financial institutions are concentrating on a five-step action plan, so too those advocating a change in the international system of refugee protection should be constantly aware of how a particular alternative can be implemented. It isn't enough, for example, to call for a new convention on refugees without thinking through what a new convention would entail — and the potential obstacles to such an action.

This, then, is one set of criteria which can be used to evaluate the efficacity of the following alternatives. How humane is the alternative for meeting the needs of refugees? How feasible is the alternative? How would it resolve conflicts? How does it build on past experiences and what steps does it identify for further action? Each alternative is also discussed in terms of its implications for national sovereignty, for host countries, for internally displaced people, for UNHCR, and for churches and NGOs.

Substantive UN reform: towards a new world order?
From 1981 to 1986 a UN group of governmental experts examined the root causes of mass population displacements.

> If mass displacements are to be averted [the report suggests] states must respect the UN Charter, use peaceful means to resolve disputes, refrain from pursuing policies which create displaced people, and co-operate in efforts to prevent future refugee flows. The various organs and agencies of the UN should improve their co-ordination and make fuller use of their respective mandates to tackle situations and problems which could give rise to mass displacements.[7]

This is an inherently sensible policy on which most governments, NGOs, churches, UN agencies and refugees would probably agree. Unfortunately the group of experts did not come up with specific suggestions on how to implement these somewhat general policy recommendations.

In today's post-cold war period, post-Gulf war climate, there is renewed interest in building a new world order which would better meet the needs of the world's people. Some peace researchers, for example, are looking again at the possibilities of abolishing war as a social institution and considering some of the more radical proposals for global restructuring which seemed impossible during the cold-war period.[8] Among the many ideas circulating, some of the most comprehensive — and most politically feasible — focus on reforming the United Nations and other institutions in order to meet the goals of their original founders.

The movement to create a world government or, failing that, to develop international instruments which would be able to resolve conflicts non-violently, has a long history. The creation of the League of Nations and then the United Nations were efforts to provide a machinery for the peaceful resolution of conflicts. Over the years a number of specific methods and techniques were developed (mediation, peace-keeping forces, negotiation, arbitration, sanctions, etc.). And there are many cases where such measures have prevented the outbreak of war or brought about an end to ongoing conflicts.[9] Although governments continue to resort to war — often in spite of UN resolutions and earnest efforts by the UN Secretary-General — alternative UN instruments do exist to prevent the use of military force. But UN action to prevent wars has been limited by the fact that it is governments which start international wars and it is governments on whom the United Nations depends in its roles of peace-making and peace-keeping. The problem with UN instruments is mainly one of governments who prefer to use military means rather than multilateral efforts to resolve conflicts with other states.

> There is no lack of ideas as to what should be done...The problem is instead to make greater use of the existing machinery for the peaceful settlement of disputes. It is unrealistic to expect all international disputes to be submitted to such machinery. The use of the machinery assumes a rational frame of mind by the parties and the very fact that a conflict is in the offing suggests that emotions are replacing rationality.[10]

Advocates of UN reform suggest a number of changes that could be made to strengthen both the UN's peace-making machinery and its actual use by conflicting parties. There is a good deal of discussion over the enhanced use of the Security Council (possibly with a changed membership), the use of peace-keeping forces, the possibilities of a peace dividend and ways of making the UN more democratic. Among specific suggestions are changing the structures of decision-making, more frequent meetings of the Security Council, and strengthening the mandate of the Secretary-General.[11] The intent of such suggestions for a reform of the UN's peace-keeping machinery is to enable the international community to take actions before a conflict reaches the stage where violence is used. If international pressure were effectively mobilized to deter aggressors, resort to war would become less likely. If alternative means of pressure — such as economic sanctions — were applied by the international community in defence of weaker states, future aggression by more powerful states could be deterred. The logic here is irrefutable, but the reality — that political power continues to be concentrated in a limited number of countries — makes it difficult to apply even more effective international machinery in cases where a major power is opposed to it.

All of these reform efforts are necessarily long-term projects which will require the political commitment of governmental leaders. Issues of UN reform are rarely discussed by those concerned with the plight of refugees and displaced people. But if the causes which uproot people and the wars which cause suffering are to be addressed, such reforms are essential. In this context, work with refugees provides a human dimension to discussions of international structures. For churches and NGOs concerned with refugees, the possibility of shaping a new international order in which conflicts are resolved through non-violent means is an important challenge. The discussion of these issues also raises serious ethical questions, about the shape of a new world order and about the dreams and hopes of people living on this planet. Even if the proposals are not politically feasible — at least not in the short run — they deserve attention because of the questions they raise.

The proposals themselves vary greatly, and we cannot undertake here any detailed study of their relative strengths and advantages. In general, however, we can say that they offer the potential of creating a more humane world by focusing on the causes which uproot people. By doing so, they will respond to the needs of internally displaced people as well as refugees. Virtually all of the proposals have their roots in earlier efforts to reform the United Nations and thus build on a reservoir of knowledge and at least some political interest. In terms of their political feasibility, the proposals are long-term initiatives. To varying degrees, the proposals for reform challenge the practice of national sovereignty in that they seek to limit the ability of governments to pursue military options for resolving conflicts. The energy needed to develop a political consensus around the various proposals is substantial and there is considerable debate among NGOs about whether the best strategy is to improve the implementation and performance of existing agreements and structures or to concentrate on the whole-scale reform measures under way.

An action plan for churches and NGOs seeking to influence the debate on UN reform would include: studying the various proposals and their potential impact on the conflicts which uproot people and monitoring their progress; working at the national level to influence governmental policy on specific proposals; linking up with peace groups and organizations seeking to influence the direction of UN reforms; and becoming active in community discussions to build public awareness about the issues and the questions they raise.

Wars kill, maim and uproot people. Although UN reform seems far removed from the day-to-day work with refugees, the United Nations remains the only institution to take steps which can reduce the incidence and duration of wars. Moreover, as will be seen later, in recent years the UN's effectiveness in resolving conflicts and decreasing tensions has grown. These regional initiatives need to be supported as well as efforts to strengthen the UN's global structures and processes which would reduce the threat of war, human-rights violations and economic injustice which are the major causes of population displacement.

At the same time that these proposals are being developed to reform the whole United Nations system, other proposals focus on the possibilities of developing a new international humanitarian order.

Reforming the operational humanitarian work of the United Nations: towards a new humanitarian order?

Among the suggestions for reforming the United Nations system is the call for greater co-ordination of UN agencies' response to humanitarian emergencies.[12] These ideas have been echoed by some UNHCR staff and by NGOs concerned with providing humanitarian access to victims of civil war and other violence.[13]

As Minear points out, humanitarian issues and questions of reform of the UN system for responding to humanitarian emergencies have a long history. The General Assembly passed resolutions on humanitarian issues in 1985, 1988 and 1991. In 1988, Secretary-General Javier Pérez de Cuellar was asked to consult with all parties on "enhancing the effectiveness of international mechanisms". In November 1991, the Secretary-General issued a number of recommendations which included:

— the appointment of a high-level official with a UN system-wide co-ordination mandate to work during emergencies for needs assessment, monitoring, resource-mobilization, information-provision and trouble-shooting;

— creation of an emergency revolving fund of US$50 million through a one-time assessment on members;

— improvement of existing early-warning systems and of the disaster prevention and preparedness capacities of governments, especially in disaster-prone areas; and

— strengthening of staff employed by or available to the United Nations, including provisions for seconding specialized assistance teams from governments.

A UN working group studied these recommendations and adopted some of them. In particular the designation of Jan Eliasson as Under Secretary-General for Humanitarian Affairs with responsibility for co-ordinating international responses to emergency situations is one step towards increasing the organization's ability to respond to situations of great human need.

The calls for a new international humanitarian order focus around three key issues. First, there is a widely-recognized need for better co-ordination and streamlining of UN operations. The role and mandates of UN agencies such as UNDRO (UN Disaster Relief Organization), UNHCR, UNDP (UN Development Programme), WFP (World Food Programme), WHO (World Health Organization), FAO (Food and Agriculture Organization), and UNICEF (UN Children's Fund) are often unclear in emergency situations. In particular, proposals have been made either to strengthen or eliminate UNDRO, to name lead agencies for particular disaster situations, or to determine a priori UN agency responsibilities for specific types of situations. A related concern revolves around the way that funds are mobilized to respond to emergency operations — which has been a serious problem for many UNHCR operations and those of other agencies.

A second issue to be addressed in a new international humanitarian order concerns access to people affected by natural and man-made disasters. The experiences with cross-border relief operations and provisions for safe passage are evidence that such access can be secured at times (even in the absence of a new international humanitarian order). But they also point to the difficulties of providing assistance during conflicts and the need for better means of ensuring such access on a more secure basis. The whole question of humanitarian intervention has become a hot political issue in the aftermath of the Gulf war, with many third-world governments raising fears that their sovereignty will be violated by international intervention justified on the grounds of humanitarian need.[14] Certainly such fears will have to be addressed if the question of access is to be addressed by a new international humanitarian order. At the same time, the experiences of Iraq also raised expectations that the UN would intervene in other conflict situations, such as the war in Bosnia-Herzegovina. The inability of the UN — or any international body — to develop an appropriate and timely means of intervention in the case of the former Yugoslav republics is a sign of the difficulties the international community faces in responding to humanitarian need in the midst of war.

The question of access also brings up another set of issues revolving around the possibilities of using military force, either UN peace-keeping forces or national military units charged by the UN to provide safety for those distributing humanitarian assistance.[15] These issues have been brought to the fore in the aftermath of UN-sanctioned intervention in Somalia.

A third issue concerns the link between measures to assist victims of disasters, including refugees, and UN mechanisms to resolve the conflicts. The lack of such a linkage has meant that disaster relief can allow hostilities to be pursued more single-mindedly.

> One of the weaknesses of the current UN system is that it does not routinely pair disaster interventions with political efforts to resolve conflicts. For every Operation Salam, in which UN efforts to provide humanitarian assistance were linked with efforts to resolve the conflict through negotiations, there are several aid initiatives in places such as Ethiopia and Mozambique where the diplomatic track is conspicuous in its absence. [16]

This linkage, discussed in more detail in the following section on early warning, will be an important element in efforts to reform the UN system on international humanitarian response to disaster situations.

Finally, a new international humanitarian order would have to recognize that the UN is not the only actor in the system and that governments and NGOs play important roles which, if not co-ordinated, can be at cross-purposes with one another. NGOs providing emergency assistance in zones of conflict face difficult ethical decisions with far-reaching political consequences. For example, Jennie Borden of Christian Aid recently pointed out the difficulties of deciding to undertake relief work in the areas of Mozambique under RENAMO control. Estimates in mid-1992 are that half a million people living in those areas will starve if relief assistance is not provided on a large scale. And yet the provision of such assistance would strengthen the position of RENAMO and thus possibly prolong the war. [17]

Given the amount of energy that would be required to build the political consensus necessary to address all these issues, questions have been raised about the wisdom of devoting so much energy to creating a new system when existing mechanisms and principles have not been fully implemented. Former UN Secretary-General Javier Pérez de Cuellar expressed his preference that attention be devoted to the distillation and wider dissemination of existing universal humanitarian principles. Similarly, some NGOs have expressed the view that "a new convention on safe passage and related issues would be undesirable at the present time when governments, particularly those in developing countries, to which such a convention would most apply, are so anxious to defend their national sovereignty against outside intervention". [18] However, changes are already under way as evidenced in the appointment of a UN Under Secretary-General for Humanitarian Affairs.

While proposals to reform the United Nations as a whole raise questions about national sovereignty, these issues are intensified in the debates over an international humanitarian order. In the case of general UN reform, the sovereignty of all governments would be reduced as the UN takes on responsibilities formerly assumed by individual states. For third-world governments, this offers the prospect of somewhat reduced interventionist efforts by Northern countries (although that would depend, of course, on the nature of the reforms). But in the case of a new international humanitarian order, the fear is that national sovereignty would be *selectively* eroded and that in practice third-world countries would be most affected. National sovereignty is the last protection of weak states in the international system; any erosion of that sovereignty opens the door to abuse.[19] This question of the impact of such reforms on national sovereignty is the greatest obstacle to the possibilities of developing a new international humanitarian order.

This alternative would provide for more humane treatment of refugees and especially of displaced people by providing for more effective means of rendering international assistance. Although the obstacle of national sovereignty is a major one, these proposals are probably more politically feasible in the medium-term than proposals to reform the whole UN system. The proposals build on a substantial body of humanitarian law and a growing number of cases where assistance has been rendered in very difficult situations — a factor which makes such an alternative more politically feasible. Depending on the way in which linkage was drawn between humanitarian assistance and conflict-resolution, this alternative could also be an important step in addressing the causes which displace people.

In developing a concrete plan of action for promoting the alternative of a new international humanitarian order, the steps are largely the same as those involved in advocating UN reform: studying and monitoring the various proposals, influencing national governmental positions on the proposals, and raising public awareness. However, given the fact that NGOs and churches have concrete field experience in working with displaced people, they could be expected to play a more active role in developing the proposals themselves. The experiences of church-related agencies in mounting cross-border operations in the Horn of Africa and elsewhere are particularly relevant in these discussions. In this respect, NGO initiatives, as for example the new "Humanitarianism and War" project, offer important forums for the development of proposals and of criteria by which existing proposals can be evaluated.

Both UN reform and proposals for a new international humanitarian order will have important effects on international law and practice. But in both of these cases, refugees and other uprooted people will be but one group of beneficiaries. A third alternative also seeks to change international law, but with a more specific focus on refugees.

Changing international law: towards a new UN convention on refugees?

As has been earlier discussed, it has been recognized for some time that the definition of refugee as enshrined in the 1951 UN Convention relating to the status of refugees (and its 1967 Protocol which removed the geographical restriction of the Convention) is seriously limited. [20] Although UNHCR operates on the basis of the definition as included in the 1951 Convention, its activities have been expanded over the years to include those who have been displaced by their countries because of "severe internal upheavals or armed conflicts" as well as those who are internally displaced in some cases, such as Sri Lanka and Iraq.

In spite of these efforts to expand the definition of refugee in particular regional contexts and to expand the mandate, in practice, for the UNHCR, the 1951 Convention definition remains the basis of international law relating to refugees. This definition is based on individual persecution, and was developed at a particular historical moment to meet the needs of the Western powerful countries. The definition doesn't correspond to the reality of most of the world's uprooted who are fleeing not individualized persecution but generalized violence. One alternative would be to change international law, to develop a new convention and a new definition of refugees which more accurately reflects current international reality. In fact the door is being opened to address some of these concerns. In August 1991, UNHCR's working group on solutions and protection — a group composed of governmental representatives — recommended that "the question of a possible application on a global basis of a refugee definition to persons not protected by the 1951 Convention/1967 Protocol or by regional instruments could be considered further". [21]

Beyer outlines four options in working on the definition:
1) leave the Convention definition alone and narrow the operational involvement of UNHCR to people fitting the classic refugee definition;
2) apply the existing definition to include other groups in similar situations (which is, of course, the present trend);

3) officially expand the definition to include those "persons of concern" to UNHCR who were previously included on an ad-hoc basis; or
4) develop an international consensus on a series of additional categories of people deserving humanitarian concern.

Specifically Beyer proposes the inclusion of the following categories: Convention refugees, victims of civil strife (internally and externally displaced), conscientious objectors, self-exiles, victims of natural disasters and migrants (both legal and illegal). Recognizing that these groups have different needs for protection and assistance, he has produced a matrix specifying particular ways in which the needs of each of the groups could be met. For example, people who are internally displaced because of natural disasters might not need international legal protection while those externally displaced because of civil strife would need only temporary refuge rather than temporary or durable asylum.

As Beyer notes:

> The problem with the fourth option is the argument that additional categories bring additional complexity, not clarity, and that such a system of categories may be abused during its application by governments, to the detriment of *bona fide* Convention refugees who need the full range of refugee rights and protection. [22]

The main obstacle to even opening the debate on refugee definitions, it must be recognized from the beginning, is the fear that Western governments would use the opportunity of a new convention to press for a more restrictive, rather than a more inclusive, definition of refugee. Given the fact that it is still the Western industrialized countries which have the political power to shape such a convention — and the economic power to back up their political dispositions — the opposition of the Western powers would preclude adoption and ratification of such a new convention. [23] Thus, in order to be a feasible alternative, efforts towards a new definition must address the economic, cultural and security concerns of Western governments as well as the needs of those uprooted by violence.

But if it were possible for a new convention to be drafted, circulated and eventually adopted by the international community, what should such a convention look like? It should:

— recognize that people are uprooted for many reasons and provide for the means to address the needs of people who are displaced within their national borders as well as those who leave their country;

— be solution-oriented, that is, provide in its framework a concern with solutions, particularly with return, from the very beginning;
— include measures to prevent mass exodus;
— overcome some of the inadequacies of the present definition, for example the regional disparities in refugee determination; and
— establish agencies or concrete means of co-operation between existing agencies which work together to address the causes and minister to the victims.

All of this implies much more active involvement of the countries of origin in the process. The present convention, as Coles points out, makes little effort to include the countries of origin in the process; rather, by focusing on persecution by the countries of origin, the 1951 Convention almost ensures their lack of involvement in resolving the problem. This means that the countries of origin assume little responsibility either in terms of resolving the conflicts which uproot people or in establishing conditions which would allow them to return. As Coles notes, the present Convention was developed to serve the specific foreign-policy interests of Western powers and permanent settlement and permanent refugee status were viewed as the most convenient way of resolving the problem of refugees from communism. [24] But most of the world's refugees today do not fall into this category and permanent settlement outside the country is not a feasible or a desirable alternative. Thus, more needs to be done to recognize a temporary solution while working to address the causes which impede the return of people to their communities and countries of origin.

Specifically, such a convention could start with the definition included in the Cartagena Declaration, expanding it to include internally displaced people. This definition would overcome some of the shortcomings of the 1951 Convention. In order to involve the countries of origin in the process, some recognition should be given that there may be many reasons for such conditions provoking flight, and that it is the responsibility of the international community to work with the governments of the country of origin to rectify the problems. The expanded definition would have little chance of adoption unless accompanied by a clearer statement on the obligations of states to address the needs of uprooted people. Specifically, such a statement of obligations could include the responsibility of host countries, with the support of the international community, to work towards conditions enabling their return and towards the establishment of peace and justice. For host governments, a range of options could be explored — from temporary safe haven to asylum to immigration where appropriate. The range of options could be further refined by differentiating between the scale, type and location of displacement. For example, a sudden mass influx into a first-asylum country as a result of widespread violence (as in Mozambique or Guatemala or Cambodia) could lead to a particular response by the international community, including temporary legal status in the host country, international assistance, and at the same time the triggering of a range of mechanisms to address the causes of the violence. While this seems quite utopian in 1992, in fact these provisions have been suggested not only by NGOs but also by UN bodies.[25]

Such a system would thus include an early-warning system, which would not only warn about impending refugee movements, but would trigger a series of political actions to be taken by the UN Secretary-General or perhaps regional bodies so that mechanisms would be instituted from the beginning to provide a solution.

There are many advantages in undertaking measures to reform the Convention:

— National sovereignty is maintained. Governments would remain the principal actors in the system.

— It builds on the present Convention and the past seven decades of efforts to address the needs of uprooted people through international law. Elements from previous efforts to develop a convention on territorial asylum, the UN report on mass exoduses, and the whole body of human rights and humanitarian law could all be used in developing the language of a new convention which would be more politically acceptable than starting from scratch — and which would go a long way towards meeting the needs of groups presently not covered by the Convention.

— It would codify the responsibilities of states more clearly, including the countries of origin, and could provide a range of options.

— It would increase the ability of UNHCR to take actions to prevent refugee movements or to allow refugees to return home.

— If adopted after an extensive public education campaign, the new convention would provide the basis for more generalized acceptance of refugees and migrants in the host societies and perhaps lead to a recognition of the benefits of multi-cultural societies. Similarly, if the rights and obligations were carefully spelled out, it could reduce the public perception in the West that refugees and migrants are a threat. Similarly, by involving all countries, it could reduce perceptions that some countries are paying a heavier price than others.

The principal disadvantage is that it does not seem feasible right now for such a convention to be drafted and accepted. Governments' fears that a new expanded convention would increase their obligations could be expressed in a convention that further restricts the definition to an even narrower group of people and limits the obligations of states in the process of examining and determining refugee status.

Another disadvantage is that this is, like all of the options discussed here, a long-term strategy. The process of drafting and adopting an international convention would probably take close to a decade. The process of implementation would undoubtedly take longer. Urgent pressing needs of refugees and the necessity to develop means of conflict-resolution which would prevent the uprooting now going on, would seem to take precedence over this long-term legal reform. It may well be that in the decade in which these legal efforts take place, the objective conditions will change and new needs will be created or become obvious. For example, it might be that in the coming decade, environmental causes of population displacement might become much more important, making any new convention obsolete before it's even finished. [26] On the other hand, it is hard to imagine what the world would look like for refugees if the 1951 Convention remains the principal international instrument for responding to the needs of displaced people in the year 2001.

If this means is to be pursued, a logical strategy would be for a draft convention to be discussed and debated, perhaps by an NGO with experience in both refugee and human-rights issues. [27] A draft convention could be circulated among governments and UN personnel, and changes made. This could be accompanied by a widespread public education campaign on the causes of uprooting, on possible remedies, and on tracing the interconnections between causes and victims.

This discussion has focused primarily on changing the definition of refugee in international law, but there are alternative ways of using international law to create a new structure for refugee protection as well as a new definition of refugee. Hathaway notes that it is unrealistic to advocate a broader notion of refugeehood without simultaneously addressing the structure of the protection regime and he develops an alternative model based largely on human-rights law. The system he proposes is more radical than most current proposals in that it would include an international supervisory body with far greater power than the present UNHCR, and protection would be conceived as an interim responsibility pending the return of refugees to their homes. His model illustrates the importance of thinking creatively about alternative models and of looking beyond traditional humanitarian law in devising alternatives to the present system. [28]

While some feel that this emphasis on reforming international law offers the best options for restructuring the international system for refugees, it is also possible that an easier alternative would be to work on the regional levels.

Regional solutions: towards a world of regions?

In recent years there have been efforts to look at the situation of refugees and displaced people within an overall regional context. In Africa, there has been a steady expansion of such efforts, including the conference on the situation of refugees in Africa (Arusha, May 1979); the international conference on assistance to refugees in Africa, ICARA I (Geneva, April 1981) and ICARA II (Geneva, July 1984); the international conference on the plight of refugees, returnees and displaced persons in Southern Africa, SARRED (Oslo, 1988). The international conference on Central American refugees, CIREFCA (Guatemala, May 1989), and the 1979 and 1989 international meetings on Indochinese refugees are other regional efforts to develop consistent approaches to refugees and other displaced people within a framework of efforts to address the causes of such displacement. Thus CIREFCA made important links between the process of peace negotiations and the return of refugees. Similarly the ICARA conferences sought to relate the plight of displaced people to questions of the region's economic development. [29]

While these initiatives represented efforts to deal with problems on a regional basis, they all included a significant role for the international community although the nature of the international-regional collaboration differed from region to region. In the case of Indochinese refugees, South-east Asian nations agreed to continue to provide temporary first asylum to new Indochinese arrivals in return for the guarantee by the international community that the refugees would be resettled outside the region. [30] In the case of Central America, the international community was to support projects to ensure the safe return and rehabilitation of communities destroyed by the decade of violence. Similarly in Africa, the international community was to provide financial assistance to enable the refugees to be cared for in the region.

Much has been written about the initiatives in Europe to co-ordinate refugee policy. [31] The efforts of European governments to negotiate common policies towards asylum-seekers have taken place in different forums and been widely discussed. The Schengen agreement, signed in

1990 by the governments of France, Germany, Belgium, Netherlands, Luxembourg and Italy, in particular, seems to be a harbinger of common policies within the European Community. As many observers have noted, the trend is towards common policies designed to restrict the application of refugee law to would-be asylum-seekers and to deter the arrival of such asylum-seekers by means of common visa policies, airline sanctions, etc.

In the case of Europe, the churches and NGOs have taken a leading position in offering prescriptions for improving the treatment of asylum-seekers. The 1987 and 1988 publications of the European Consultation on Refugees and Exiles[32] are efforts by the NGO community to shape the course of governmental debate on these policies. In the 1992 CSCE follow-up meeting, NGOs and particularly the Quaker representative played a major role in drafting resolutions on refugees and in lobbying for their adoption. In other regions, the process of developing alternatives has not been as extensive. Thus in the CIREFCA meeting, international and local NGOs actively participated, and played important roles in lobbying on particular issues, but their role was largely one of *reacting* to government proposals rather than developing alternatives. Similarly in the SARRED process, NGOs were rather marginal to the decisions being made by the official delegates to the meeting. In both cases, this may reflect the fact that many NGOs are involved in somewhat tense relationships with governments and are more accustomed to playing a role of denouncing government policies than of advocating specific alternatives.

Depending on how the regional efforts to co-ordinate refugee and asylum policies emerge, they could either play a role in developing universal standards and thus be a positive development for the emergence of a new international system of refugee assistance and protection, or they could serve to reinforce disparities between regions.

In addition to these efforts to develop regional policies towards refugees and asylum-seekers, regional co-operation/integration mechanisms offer considerable hope for effective conflict-resolution at the regional level, and thus may serve to address the root causes which displace people. The regional mechanisms take different forms, including co-ordinated foreign policies (e.g. European foreign policies in some instances) or regional conflict-resolution mechanisms (such as the Organization of American States in Haiti) or more ad-hoc regional measures (as in the ECOWAS intervention in Liberia). The mechanisms vary tremendously in effectiveness; but it must be recognized that they are relatively new in nature and that a certain period of trial and error is needed. But in general the regional agreements can serve as means of moving towards more universal mechanisms, growing acceptance of such forms of international intervention, and as confidence-building measures. They also offer the possibility of redressing regional inequalities, stimulating economic growth (though redistribution may be more difficult), overcoming North-South disparities, etc. Such initiatives offer the possibility of more effective monitoring of compliance with peace agreements and upholding of human rights by countries in the region (e.g. Vietnam, Cambodia). If they were to grow and expand in scope and effectiveness, they could also include work with internally displaced in terms of resolving conflicts, and providing regional pressure for international access.

Such regional mechanisms would assume different forms in different regions. Perhaps one of the strongest effects of the current changes in the international system is the impetus given to regional developments. Certainly the most viable alternative to a unipolar world is the strengthening of the European Community which presently is a stronger economic power than the United States but has not been as effective in translating that power into united, effective and independent foreign policies. In reaction to the example of the European Community and also out of fears of a unipolar world, governments in all regions are considering afresh regional integration schemes and various co-operative endeavours. Thus in West Africa, there are some seventy intergovernmental co-operation agreements — many of which have been inactive for years, but which now are being reconsidered. Japan's efforts to build an economic community with Asian countries and Latin American efforts to revitalize regional forums are but two examples of the increasingly common perception that in order to survive in this world, one needs regional allies to counter the military power of the United States and the economic power of the European Community. The future international order may well be a world of regional blocs rather than an enhanced global co-operative mechanism.

But this too puts the third world at a disadvantage. Given the realities of existing patterns of trade and financial flows, it has historically been extremely difficult for third-world governments to devote the necessary resources to develop viable independent regional organizations. The fact is that nations in a particular region, whether the Andean countries of South America or the East African nations or the member countries of the Association of South-east Asian Nations (ASEAN), rarely have complementary economies. Rather, they are more used to competing with each other for the sale of primary products to countries of the North and often have perceived that their stable futures are more dependent on close relations with a dominant industrial country than with each other. But the current pressures may be more successful in encouraging regional integration than previous endeavours.

Thus regional initiatives offer two sorts of possibilities for restructuring the international system of refugee protection and assistance. On the one hand, they offer the possibilities of reduced conflicts within regions and the emergence of new mechanisms of conflict-resolution. On the other hand, they offer the possibility of developing regional collective approaches to refugees, migrants and asylum-seekers. These two approaches are both being implemented at the present time and hence it is politically feasible to try to shape their outcome.

That is, two parallel initiatives need to be taken by those seeking to use regional mechanisms as a way of reforming the international system. On the one hand, efforts need to be made to ensure that the co-ordinated policies towards refugees, asylum-seekers, internally displaced people and migrants are humane and provide the necessary human rights guarantees. On the other hand, efforts must also be made to strengthen these as ways of addressing root causes — either through co-ordinated foreign and human-rights policies or through encouragement of regional conflict-resolution mechanisms.

The advantages of working on the regional level are many. Since the conflicts occur within regions and the effects are most keenly felt there, it makes political sense to concentrate efforts on influencing regional processes. Changes made at the regional level could influence international norms — as in the case of the international impact of the refugee definitions developed by the Organization of African Unity and the Cartagena Declaration. It is probably easier to develop a comprehensive approach to refugee and peace issues within a particular region and to gain the necessary acceptance by governments than to work with the much more diverse international community.

The option of working through regional mechanisms is also a feasible one. Regional initiatives are already under way and there are opportunities to shape the development of alternative policies. Such initiatives could build on present work being done in the European Community, in Central America, in Africa, in Asia and elsewhere. One of the problems in pursuing this line, however, is that there is rarely a mechanism for representation of refugee voices in the chambers where decisions are made. NGO access to decision-making forums is also limited although, in many cases, NGOs are in close contact with their respective government representatives.

The disadvantages of a regional approach stem from the global nature of forced migration; a regional approach could be developed, for example, to meet the needs of refugees and displaced people in Sri Lanka and India (though one looks in vain for creative regional initiatives to actually resolve the conflict), but given the fact that many Sri Lankan refugees are seeking asylum in Western countries, such an approach would of necessity be limited. It is also important to recognize that even in the post-cold war era, foreign intervention plays a major role in the continuation of conflicts. It is also possible that regional initiative would reinforce the present regional disparities — where individuals are given protection and assistance in one region and denied them if they move to another.

Practical steps to influence regional policies include:
— determining the regional bodies in which decisions are being made (which is not always an easy task!) and identifying the principal actors in the regional process;
— lobbying to see that issues of refugees and displaced people are dealt with in regional peace initiatives;
— seeking means of strengthening regional conflict-resolution mechanisms;
— lobbying at the national level for governments to pursue policies at the regional level which both address the causes of uprooting and provide for humane treatment for refugees; and
— urging inter-regional co-operation and multilateral action to prevent regional blocs from playing a divisive role in the international community.

Since regional policies depend on the support and will of their member governments, efforts to influence the shape of regional agreements will of necessity involve efforts to change national policies.

National policies: towards better refugee and immigration policies?

It is on the national level that most NGO and church efforts to change policies towards uprooted people have taken place. This reflects the fact that governments remain the principal actors in the international system of refugee protection and assistance.

In terms of national policies towards asylum-seekers, most NGOs have devoted substantial energy to trying to influence their government to be more open and accepting of applicants, to develop policies which respect the dignity of the asylum-seekers, and to prevent deportations and family separations. While some of these efforts have been successful, there are limits to the role of NGOs in this area. As Loescher states:

In the current political climate, it is not sufficient for UNHCR, the churches and the voluntary agencies to denounce government policies regarding asylum-seekers and to argue for expansive new notions of who is entitled to refugee status. If governments are to be persuaded to develop their policies in a humane direction, it is more important to put forward a realistic strategy which responds to their desire to restore orderly mechanisms and burden-sharing arrangements to asylum procedures. Most states are clearly prepared to accept shared responsibility and involvement for uprooted populations who are unable to return home safely because of threat of persecution or political violence. But it is extremely unlikely that in the near future states will be willing to host streams of migrants who flee a variety of less advantageous economic and social conditions in their home countries. [33]

In other words, lobbying for more open admissions policies must be combined with efforts to reform or restructure the international or regional mechanisms to deal with the same problem.

Certainly the perception in Europe is that if a government adopts policies which are more open and more humane towards asylum-seekers than those of its neighbours, it will receive more requests and more arrivals on its borders. And indeed that has been the case; one has only to examine the pattern of national asylum-policy reform in Europe to trace the arrivals of more asylum-seekers to those countries which moved to restrict entry later.

At the same time, it can be argued that deterrence policies don't work. There are many cases where governments have adopted increasingly restrictive policies, but the response has been higher numbers of arrivals. This has been the case in Great Britain and Switzerland in the late 1980s/early 1990s, and it has also been true in Hong Kong where even the prospect of forced repatriation to Vietnam did not deter new arrivals.

In order for NGOs to be more effective in lobbying for more open admissions policies on the national level, they need to have a clear idea of why and how such increases should take place. It is usually not effective to argue that all arrivals from countries where there is war should be admitted as refugees — a prospect that fills most immigration officials with terror. Which groups have a special claim for admission — and why? While NGOs can often argue credibly and effectively for admission of particular individuals, it is more difficult to advocate more open policies unless there is a clear understanding of who and why and how many should be admitted.

There has been considerable debate within the international NGO community about the feasibility of temporary safe haven as meeting the protection needs of some displaced people. NGOs in the United States have argued that temporary safe haven (or, in US terms, extended voluntary departure) is an appropriate mechanism to provide temporary protection to certain groups who are in danger if returned to their countries of origin. Thus in the US, this policy was implemented in the case of Salvadorans, Nicaraguans and assorted other groups. In Europe, the reaction has been much more cautious. Although various forms of such safe havens presently exist and are extensively used ("B" status, tolerated immigrants, exceptional leave to remain, etc.), there is fear that if such practices become codified into law, the principle of asylum will be undermined. [34] If governments have a relatively easy option of temporary asylum, they will be more likely to use it and those who need permanent protection will be denied it.

In terms of national policies to address the causes of forced migration, churches and NGOs (although usually a different set of NGOs) have devoted substantial energy to issues such as sanctions in the case of South Africa, pressure for restoration of diplomatic relations with Vietnam, and opposition to US military intervention in Central America.

More generally, advocacy on the national level has focused on human rights, development assistance and, to a lesser degree, initiatives to bring about the peaceful resolution of conflicts and reform of global economic structures. Human-rights violations and internal conflicts are perhaps the major cause of population displacement. Human-rights groups have come a long way during the past decade in monitoring the human-rights situation in various countries, in developing effective ways of responding to patterns of human-rights violations, in lobbying governments, in using the UN system, in developing and expanding the international human rights machinery, and in increasing public awareness about human rights. Much more needs to be done, and is being done, in this area. In comparison with most policy issues, the area of human rights is one where churches and NGOs have played a pathbreaking role, sometimes at great personal risk. [35] Their presence in countries where human rights are being violated is an obvious asset, but also their use of the media and skilful use of research has made them an effective voice in lobbying at the national level. Increasingly too, we see that regional mechanisms are beginning to implement human rights-based policies which have the potential of magnifying the impact of such efforts.

Less progress has been made, certainly from the NGO side, at looking at the ways of stopping wars and building peace. There are some creative examples of course where NGOs and intergovernmental organizations have played positive roles in resolving conflicts — the monitoring of elections, for example, or the stationing of UN peace-keeping forces or other international observers in tense situations. But perhaps more could be done to develop mechanisms for resolving conflicts *before* they result in massive displacements of people. Churches and NGOs could play a role in advocating with their governments to support peace initiatives in concrete situations — for example, to de-escalate tensions between Russia and Georgia over the South Ossetians or to station international human-rights observers in Guatemala or to press for sanctions in situations of conflict, such as Burma. NGOs and churches can play a more activist role in devising realistic solutions to ongoing conflicts and in lobbying their governments to support such initiatives. For example, the presence of UN peace-keeping forces or NGO volunteers on borders where violence is likely has been used in some cases, and could be extended in the future.

Increased development assistance has been advocated by NGOs and some governments as a way of forestalling movements of people. At times perhaps there has been more than a touch of self-interest in such initiatives; in Albania, for example, the argument was frequently and openly made that aid was needed to prevent Albanians from coming to Europe. But drawing direct connections between development assistance and refugees is difficult on three levels. First, we don't know that development assistance, particularly development assistance alone, has any impact at all on refugees fleeing violence, human-rights violations and internal conflicts. We don't even know if such assistance has any impact on the movement of economic migrants; and indeed it may be that increased development aid in a third-world country would result, at least initially, in an increase of people leaving that country to look for better working conditions (as proportionally more migrants to industrialized countries come from middle-income rather than low-income countries). [36] So it is difficult to argue for increased development assistance as a way of resolving the causes which uproot people.

A second question has to do with the structural nature of economic problems. Providing more development assistance when the international economic structures are siphoning funds from poor to rich nations is not an adequate response. If one of the conditions exacerbating conflicts is the international financial system, then what is required is the overhauling of that system, not increased foreign aid. Thus, NGOs wishing to address the root causes of refugee movements by changing economic conditions would do well to link up with those NGOs working on issues of international debt and seeking to reform the international financial order.

A third problem in looking at foreign aid as a way of reducing displacement of people has to do with the structures of governments — and, indeed, of NGOs. Decisions about development assistance are made, in most governments, by ministries different from those dealing with immigration and refugee issues. The issues, criteria and priorities for these different ministries may differ, making it difficult to advocate for more assistance. [37] Within the NGO community, there are few NGOs with expertise in development, human rights, refugees and international financial structures. It is always easier to work with people and organizations working in the same area and it has been notoriously difficult for refugee-serving NGOs to see the common bonds, much less work together on specific campaigns, with NGOs working in other fields. For example, the International Council of Voluntary Agencies has two principal working groups — one on development issues and the other on refugees. Although their meetings are held on consecutive days, differences in participation in the meetings are striking.

Nonetheless, it may be that development assistance by developed countries has a role to play in reducing refugee flows — and certainly in enabling refugees to stay in their region (if not in their country) of origin.

> Providing development assistance to solve problems which generate refugee movements could help to avert new flows of asylum-seekers coming to Europe, enlarge the possibility of local integration in host countries and enable others to return voluntarily to their home countries. Clear co-ordination at the national and European level between the ministries responsible for asylum policy and those responsible for development assistance will be necessary in order to make the required funds available for the implementation of this new approach to refugee problems. [38]

In particular, development assistance is crucial in the reconstruction of countries seeking to establish peace after years of war. Such assistance may facilitate the voluntary repatriation of refugees.

Initiatives on the national level thus should include efforts to influence the government's policy regarding refugees and asylum-seekers arriving on their borders, towards development assistance, foreign policy and human-rights policy, and towards regional and international organizations. There have been some successes on the part of NGOs in co-ordinating their lobbying initiatives in order to bring about change in UNHCR policies. But most of these successes have been on specific cases (e.g. refugee women, refugee children) which were relatively non-controversial. NGOs have been much less successful in developing such efforts on the broader issues of reform of the international system itself.

Working on the national level has certain clear advantages. It affirms national sovereignty and is directed towards the actors who are presently most responsible both for policies which uproot people and those which deal with them once they have been uprooted. It builds on a long history of NGO involvement and on their natural strengths within particular national contexts.

The disadvantages of solely pursuing a national strategy stem from the international nature of refugee movements. One Western government alone probably cannot bring about an end to the violence in Mozambique or Peru; co-ordinated efforts have a greater chance of success. Similarly one government's policies towards a particular group of asylum-seekers may negatively influence the policies of another government — and do nothing to resolve the causes of the violence.

Advocacy on the national level is an important component of efforts by NGOs and others to influence policy decisions which affect refugees and other displaced people. However, their impact is greater when combined with an understanding of the various alternatives being discussed at the regional and international levels — alternatives which have the potential to fundamentally restructure the international system of refugee protection and assistance. None of the alternatives discussed here meets all of the needs for a new refugee system and many of them probably have little chance of being adopted by the international community. Given the amount of energy required to enact some of the proposals, NGOs may well decide to put their energies into strengthening existing instruments and to improving implementation of present structures and mechanisms. The future international refugee system may emerge not from a major international conference or a new convention, but from many small incremental steps which together will reshape the system. But in order to play a role in the development of whatever international system that will emerge, more serious work is needed on the alternatives to the present system.

An action plan for the churches

The churches are involved in advocacy and mechanisms have already been created which are serving as a basis for co-ordination of lobbying actions. Moreover, individual churches are taking initiatives in many different settings and on many different issues. What is lacking, however, is a coherent plan for formulating alternatives to the present system and working for their adoption.

An action plan for the churches could be developed through consultation between church partners from all regions to plan a co-ordinated advocacy effort. Such a consultation could agree on priorities for action, and develop a plan by which church groups in different regions could develop policy positions and advocate their adoption in different forums. Such a consultation could agree, for example, that priority be placed on strengthening regional efforts to resolve conflicts before large numbers of people are uprooted. European and North American partners could agree to work within the CSCE process and assign responsibilities to particular church groups for monitoring developments and for advocating particular measures with parliamentarians in their capitals. African church partners could agree not only to advocate with their governments for humane treatment of refugees but also to support the African human-rights centre and to strengthen ad-hoc peace initiatives. In Asia, churches in some countries have been very active in addressing human-rights issues, but have not usually drawn the connections with refugees and displaced people.

The formulation of a co-ordinated church advocacy programme could also agree on priorities for advocacy on the international level. The churches were quite successful in urging the UN Human Rights Commission to take up the issue of internally displaced people and in raising international awareness about the issue. But perhaps the time has come for the churches not only to raise awareness about a particular problem but to suggest and advocate solutions. Through a process of consultation with church partners in all regions, specific elements of an international response to internally displaced people could be identified and a draft resolution circulated through national church partners to governments. The experiences of many church advocates in lobbying for specific proposals in intergovernmental forums suggest that governments would welcome such proposals.

There are many areas where the churches could play a positive — rather than a reactive — role in shaping a new international system for uprooted people. Initiatives could be taken, for example, in developing a church position on reform of the UN, on building a consensus on issues such as the right of access to relief for victims of armed conflict, on revising the definition of refugees.

Developing such a church strategy would not necessarily involve more financial or staff resources. The expertise in these issues already exists within church networks. The commitment to working together is a major asset which has only begun to be tapped. Individual churches and church agencies have already taken some important steps, but what is needed is for those individual steps to be strengthened with the active support of the international church community. For example, Dutch Interchurch Aid has drafted and is circulating an NGO protocol on humanitarian assistance. This is an important step but one which would be strengthened in content by the input of church partners from all regions; moreover, its impact would be far greater with the support of churches working with other NGOs in their own countries.

Throughout this book I have referred to "churches and NGOs" as actors and potential actors in the international system. Churches do not operate in a vacuum. Sometimes their close connections with each other — based on common Christian commitment and sometimes on transfers of resources — make them less open to reaching out to other people of good will in their communities. But there are thousands of NGOs with expertise and resources which are eager to work more closely with the churches. These groups are not just resources to be used by the churches in pursuing their own agendas. They are allies in the struggle for a more just world. As such the churches have a role to play in strengthening the role and witness of the vast non-governmental community. In some cases, secular and religious NGOs have worked out complementary relationships which build on the relative strengths of both groups. For example, the World Council of Churches and Amnesty International developed a close working relationship in which Amnesty International's research on situations where the lives of refugees and asylum-seekers were endangered could be shared with church partners for their action. In some cases, the churches were unable to respond, in other cases they used the information to approach their governments through non-official channels. In still other cases, the churches had already responded to a particular emergency before the Amnesty alert was received in Geneva. These types of operational relationships need to be strengthened — not just on the international level, but also at the national and regional levels.

* * *

There is much that needs to be done in reforming — or transforming — the global system for responding to the growing number of the world's uprooted people. This chapter has indicated a number of areas where NGOs and churches can direct their efforts. But changing structures and procedures also involve changing values and perceptions. The international system was based on the consensus that it was the responsibility of the international community to protect and assist those forced to flee their countries through no fault of their own. That consensus, as we have seen, has broken down, and now we see governments competing with each other to keep asylum-seekers out. Any new international system will have to be based on a new consensus — a consensus that includes shared responsibility in preventing the violence that uproots people and that sees uprooted people in terms of the search for peace and justice. In their efforts to reform structures and influence policies, NGOs and churches have the potential to define the parametres of that consensus. It is by engaging in both the big issues of international politics and direct personal involvement with uprooted human beings that NGOs and churches can help lay the foundations for a new international order for uprooted people.

NOTES

[1] Howard Adelman, "Ethnicity and Refugees," in *World Refugee Survey 1992*, Washington, DC, US Committee for Refugees, 1992, pp.6-7.
[2] See for example, Myron Weiner, "Security, Stability and International Migration", mimeo, 1991.
[3] See Elizabeth Ferris and Lynne Jones, "International Debt and Refugees", in *Refugees*, WCC, no. 100e, February 1989.
[4] See, for example, Jonas Widgren, "South-North Migration and its Political and Humanitarian Implications for Europe", paper presented at the international conference "Refugees in the World: The European Community's Response", The Hague, December 1989.
[5] See for example Michael Klare, *The New Pax Americana: US Interventionism in the Post-Cold War Era*, Uppsala, Life & Peace Institute research report, 1992.
[6] See for example, contributions by Erskine Childers, Chandra Muzzafar, Alejandro Bendaña and Clement John in *The Challenge to Intervene: A New Role for the United Nations?*, ed. Elizabeth G. Ferris, Uppsala, Life & Peace Institute, 1992.
[7] Reported in *Refugees: Dynamics of Displacement*, report for the Independent Commission on International Humanitarian Issues, London, Zed Books, 1986, p.136.
[8] See for example, John Mueller, "The Obsolescence of Major War", in *Bulletin of Peace Proposals*, vol. 21, no. 3, September 1990, pp.321-329. Arthur H. Westing, "Toward Eliminating War as an Instrument of Foreign Policy", in *Bulletin of Peace Proposals*, vol. 21, no. 2, March 1990, pp.29-35. Also see the forthcoming report by the Life & Peace Institute, *Overcoming the Institution of War*. For a rejoinder to these views, see Akhtar Majeed, "Has the War System Really Become Obsolete?", in *Bulletin of Peace Proposals*, vol. 22, no. 4, 1991, pp.419-425.
[9] See, for example, the description of cases in A. LeRoy Bennett, *International Organizations*, 2nd ed., Englewood Cliffs, NJ, Prentice-Hall, 1980.

[10] Keith Suter, *Alternatives to War,* Sydney, Women's International League for Peace and Freedom, 1986, p.126.

[11] See, for example, recent work by the International Peace Bureau, as reported in the *Geneva Monitor*, Geneva; also see the publications of the Campaign for a More Democratic United Nations. Also *Peaceful Resolution of Conflicts: NGOs in the International System*, ed. Olle Dahlen, Uppsala, Life & Peace Institute, 1988. Richard A. Falk, Samuel S. Kim and Saul H. Mendlovitz, *The United Nations and a Just World Order*, Boulder, CO, Westview Press, 1991. Paul F. Diehl and Chetan Kumar, "Mutual Benefits from International Intervention: New Roles for United Nations Peace-keeping Forces", in *Bulletin of Peace Proposals,* vol. 22, no. 4, 1991, pp.369-376.

[12] See, for example, Brian Urquhart and Erskine Childers, *A World in Need of Leadership: Tomorrow's United Nations*, Motala, Sweden, Dag Hammarskjöld Foundation, 1990.

[13] See for example, statement by Michel Moussalli, Swiss Institute, 1991. For the NGO perspective, I rely heavily on the work of Larry Minear, including Larry Minear et al., *Humanitarianism under Siege*, Trenton, NJ, Red Sea Press, 1990. And particularly his articles in *Humanitarianism and War: Learning the Lessons from Recent Armed Conflicts*, eds Larry Minear, Thomas G. Weiss and Kurt M. Campbell, Providence, RI, Thomas J. Watson Jr Institute for International Studies, Occasional Paper no. 8, 1991.

[14] See for example, *The Challenge to Intervene: A New Role for the United Nations?, op. cit.*

[15] See Leon Gordenker and Thomas G. Weiss eds, *Soldiers, Peacekeepers and Disasters*, London, Macmillan, 1991.

[16] Larry Minear, "Testimony to House Select Committee on Hunger", US Congress, 29 July 1991, reprinted in *Humanitarianism and War, op. cit.*, p.41.

[17] Jennie Borden, remarks made at the seminar "The Challenge to Intervene: A New Role for the United Nations?", organized by the Life & Peace Institute, Sigtuna, Sweden, May 1992.

[18] Cited by Minear, *Humanitarianism and War, op. cit.*, p.21.

[19] See contributions, for example, in *The Challenge to Intervene, op. cit.*

[20] The Convention defines as refugees those who are outside their country of origin and who are unable or unwilling to return home due to persecution or a well-founded fear of persecution for reasons of race, religion, nationality, membership of a particular social group or political opinion.

[21] Report of the working group on solutions and protection to the 42nd Session of the Executive Committee of the High Commissioner's Programme, EC/SCP/64, 12 August 1991.

[22] Gregg A. Beyer, *Improving International Response to Humanitarian Situations*, Washington, DC, Refugee Policy Group, December 1989.

[23] This is perhaps unfortunate, given the fact that most of the world's refugees are in third-world countries. But a failure to recognize the interests of the presently powerful countries would almost certainly doom efforts to draft a new refugee convention. One has only to look at the ill-fated efforts at a new convention on territorial asylum to see the importance of such efforts being accompanied by intensive lobbying and consultation with governments.

[24] Gervase Coles, "Approaching the Refugee Problem Today", in *Refugees and International Relations*, eds Gil Loescher and Laila Monahan, Oxford, Oxford University Press, 1989.

[25] In 1981 the Special Rapporteur to the Human Rights Commission in a study on mass exoduses came up with the suggestion for an early warning system which would provide

the UN Secretary-General with regular information on situations where a mass exodus might be in the making. The Secretary-General "might at an early stage initiate discussions with the governments most closely concerned with the volatile situation as well as appropriate regional organizations". An executive designated by the Secretary-General would bring the situation to the attention of parties which are in a position to take preventive action, e.g. member states, appropriate UN organs, etc. For further information on this see the report of the Special Rapporteur or the summary in *Refugees: Dynamics of Displacement*, report for the Independent Commission on International Humanitarian Issues, London, Zed Books, 1986.

26 See Jodi Jacobsen, "Environmental Refugees — A Yardstick of Habitability", in *Worldwatch Paper*, no. 88, Washington, DC, Worldwatch Institute, 1988.

27 For example the Lawyers Committee on Human Rights, the Refugee Policy Group, the European Consultation on Refugees and Exiles or the US Committee for Refugees. Alternatively one of the recognized legal experts on refugee/human-rights law could be hired as a consultant to review existing international agreements (as well as the previously unsuccessful efforts) and to draft a new convention as a basis for discussion. While such a draft would obviously go through many versions, it would serve as a basis for discussion of what has become a virtually taboo subject.

28 James C. Hathaway, "Reconceiving Refugee Law as Human Rights Protection", in *Journal of Refugee Studies*, vol. 4, no. 2, 1991, pp.113-131.

29 Although for a variety of reasons the ICARA processes did not result in the transfer of funds which had been hoped for.

30 Gervase Coles presents a compelling argument that the arrival of the boat people and the international community's response marked a turning point in the development of the international refugee system. Specifically he argued that the South-east Asian states "played both sides of the coin: on the one hand, they called the Vietnamese illegal immigrants and detained them as such; and, on the other, they facilitated their resettlement in the West by allowing them to be called refugees who had been granted first asylum — but only on the strict understanding that their resettlement elsewhere would ensue speedily". He goes on to say that "[t]he African countries successfully exploited this development by means of an accusation of double standard in order to finally obtain the large sums of money for refugees in Africa that the West had not made available in the past. Shortly afterwards Latin American countries followed suit." Coles, "Approaching the Refugee Problem Today", *op. cit.*, pp.380-381.

31 But see various publications by the European Consultation on Refugees and Exiles, "The Law of Asylum and Refugees", The Council of Europe, Parliamentary Assembly, *Report on the Right to Territorial Asylum*, Strasbourg, Council of Europe, Legal Affairs Committee, Doc. 5930, 23 August 1988. Gilbert Jaeger, "Study on Irregular Movements of Asylum/Seekers and Refugees", in Gary Rubin, *The Asylum Challenge to Western Nations*, Washington, DC, US Committee for Refugees, 1984. Also see Gil Loescher, "The European Community and Refugees", in report of the international conference, *Refugees in the World: The European Community's Response*, The Hague, December 1989, SIM special no. 10.

32 ECRE, *A Refugee Policy for Europe*, October 1987, and ECRE, *Towards Harmonization of Refugee Policies in Europe? A Contribution to the Discussion*, October 1988 (both published in London by ECRE). These two documents represent efforts by European NGOs to offer feasible alternatives to governments seeking to implement new asylum policies and to work within the framework of co-ordinated European policies. Although they have not been adopted in toto by the European governments (and indeed portions of

the suggested alternatives have been outright rejected), they have served a very useful function in raising issues and shaping the parameter of the debate. Together with some of ECRE's other initiatives (such as its study on practices of airline sanctions), these represent efforts by the NGO community not only to criticize governmental policies but to shape the discussion of the alternatives.

[33] Loescher, "The European Community and Refugees", *op. cit.*, pp.135.

[34] For further discussion of these arguments, see Dennis Gallagher, Susan Forbes Martin and Patricia Weiss-Fagen, "Temporary Safe Haven: The Need for North American-European Responses", in *Refugees and International Relations*, Oxford, Oxford University Press, 1989.

[35] See, for example, Laurie S. Wiseberg, "Protecting Human Rights Activists and NGOs: What More Can be Done?", *Human Rights Quarterly*, vol. 13, 1991, pp.525-544.

[36] Jacques Cuenod, "European Community Assistance to Regions with Large Numbers of Refugees", in report of the international conference, *Refugees in the World: The European Community's Response*, *op. cit.*, p.157.

[37] *Ibid.*, pp.175-176.

[38] Loescher, "The European Community and Refugees", *op. cit.*, p.135.

Abbreviations

AACC	All Africa Conference of Churches
AIDS	acquired immune deficiency syndrome
ANC	African National Congress
CEAR	Comisión especial de atención a repatriados (Special Commission on Assistance to Repatriates) (Guatemala)
CGDK	Coalition Government of Democratic Kampuchea
CIDA	Canadian International Development Agency
CIMADE	Comité inter-mouvements auprès des évacués (Inter-Movement Committee for Evacuees) (France)
CIREFCA	International Conference on Central American Refugees (1989)
CPA	Comprehensive Plan of Action (Vietnam)
CRS	Catholic Relief Services
CSCE	Conference on Security and Co-operation in Europe
CWS	Church World Service (USA)
ECOERSA	Ecumenical Co-ordination Office for Emergencies and Rehabilitation in East and Southern Africa
ECOMOG	ECOWAS Monitoring Group (West Africa)
ECOWAS	Economic Community of West African States
ECRE	European Consultation on Refugees and Exiles
FAO	Food and Agriculture Organization (of the UN)
FMLN	Frente Farabundo Martí de Liberación (El Salvador)
FRELIMO	Frente de Libertação do Moçambique (Front for the Liberation of Mozambique)
FRG	Federal Republic of Germany
GDR	German Democratic Republic

ICARA	International Conference on Assistance to Refugees in Africa
ICCB	International Catholic Child Bureau
ICCR	Inter-Church Committee for Refugees (Canada)
ICEM	Intergovernmental Committee for European Migration
ICM	Intergovernmental Committee for Migration
ICRC	International Committee of the Red Cross
ICVA	International Council of Voluntary Agencies
IDB	International Development Bank
IGCR	Intergovernmental Committee on Refugees
ILO	International Labour Organization
IMF	International Monetary Fund
INPFL	Interim National Patriotic Forces of Liberia
INS	Immigration and Naturalization Service (USA)
IOM	International Organization for Migration
IPKF	Indian Peace Keeping Force
IRO	International Refugee Organization
LWF	Lutheran World Federation
MNR	Movement of National Resistance (i.e. RENAMO) (Mozambique)
MPLA	(Movimento Popular de Libertação de Angola (People's Movement for the Liberation of Angola)
NCCCUSA	National Council of the Churches of Christ in the USA
NGOs	non-governmental organizations
NPFL	National Patriotic Forces of Liberia
OAU	Organization of African Unity
ODP	Orderly Departure Programme (Vietnam)
OEOA	Office for Emergency Operations in Africa (UN)
ORC	Open Relief Centres (Sri Lanka)
PAC	Pan-Africanist Congress
PVOs	private voluntary organizations
RENAMO	Resistencia Nacional do Moçambique (National Resistance of Mozambique)
SADCC	South African Development Co-ordination Conference
SPLA	Sudan People's Liberation Army
SWAPO	South West Africa People's Organization
ULIMO	United Liberation Movement for Democracy in Liberia
UNBRO	United Nations Border Relief Operation (Thailand/Cambodia)

	United Nations Development Programme
?O	United Nations Disaster Response Organization
?SCO	United Nations Educational, Scientific and Cultural Organization
.HCR	United Nations High Commissioner for Refugees
.NICEF	United Nations Children's Fund
JNITA	National Union for the Total Independence of Angola
UNKRA	United Nations Korean Reconstruction Agency
UNRPR	United Nations Relief for Palestine Refugees
UNRRA	United Nations Relief and Reconstruction Agency
UNRWA	United Nations Relief and Works Agency for Palestine Refugees in the Near East
USCR	US Committee for Refugees
USSR	Union of Soviet Socialist Republics
WCC	World Council of Churches
WFP	World Food Programme (of the UN)
WHO	World Health Organization
WOLA	Washington Office on Latin America (USA)